JOSEPH PULITZER

AND THE

NEW YORK WORLD

JOSEPH PULITZER

AND THE

NEW YORK WORLD

BY

GEORGE JUERGENS

PRINCETON, NEW JERSEY

PRINCETON UNIVERSITY PRESS

1966

TO MY MOTHER AND FATHER

PREFACE

This book describes how, almost overnight, Joseph Pulitzer converted the *New York World* from a moribund sheet into one of the most prosperous and influential dailies of its time. The intention is not to provide a biography of the publisher or a history of the newspaper, but to understand how and why he accomplished what he did during the critical early years when the metamorphosis occurred. The emphasis is upon journalistic techniques, and the meanings and subtleties behind those techniques.

Such a theme, in itself, is of great importance, for the *World* was no ordinary paper and the period under consideration no ordinary period. Between 1883 and 1885 Pulitzer competed for circulation against some of the most entrenched and prestigious journals in the country. He succeeded so well that by the end of the period he had increased the *World*'s audience tenfold, and had made it the most widely read daily in the Western Hemisphere. From that point, for the next decade and a half, the *World* constantly added to its circulation, and each addition represented a new high-water mark in American journalism. It is worth examining how a newspaper that sold 15,000 copies daily in 1883 reached the eminence of almost 1,500,000 copies daily in 1898.

But the theme has broader relevance, for the techniques that worked for Pulitzer did not long remain his property alone. Other publishers tried to duplicate his record by imitating his methods, and although none succeeded (until the arrival of William Randolph Hearst in 1895), in the attempt the face of American journalism was irrevocably altered. The period 1883 to 1885 is pivotal in the history of the *World*, but also in the history of the national press. It was a turning point because during that period Pulitzer introduced many of the techniques other papers later borrowed, some of them guardedly and almost against their will, others wholeheartedly. Although years would pass before the transition was complete, before the innovations of one decade became the conventions of another, the enormity of Pulitzer's accomplishment was clear as soon as people by the tens of thousands endorsed the radical journalism he offered. When that happened, the rest of the press could no longer debate whether or not to follow his leadership. A great newspaper was born between 1883 and 1885, but more important, the first modern newspaper.

Inevitably, much is lost by approaching the *World* in this way. There is no mention of the part the paper played in fostering a war between the United States and Spain in 1898, nor of its successful crusade between 1905 and 1907 against insurance corruption in New York State, nor even of the color and excitement it inspired in 1889 by sending Nellie Bly around the world in seventy-two days to beat the record Jules Verne conceived for Phineas Fogg. The justification for a treatment which ignores such milestones in journalistic history is simply that their origins go back earlier, to the period immediately following 1883, when modern sensationalism was born.

To be sure, there were precedents for what Pulitzer accomplished. His strategy of attracting a large audience by concentrating on stories of timeless appeal—sex, crime, tragedy—had been tried long before. Pulitzer variously referred to the method as "modern journalism," "western-style journalism," or "journalism for the masses," but it is more accurate to put him in context and say that he refined and brought up-to-date the techniques of sensationalism pioneered by James Gordon Bennett, Sr. and Benjamin H. Day, and later carried forward by such modern practitioners of the art as William Randolph Hearst and Joseph Medill Patterson.

Bennett and Day before, as surely as Hearst and Patterson after, understood that the goal of sensational journalism is to catch the interest, even to titillate, the vast body of men and women who for one reason or another are unconcerned with happenings in government, business, or the arts. The press has followed a fairly consistent formula since the 1830s in appealing to those people. The first rule is that a different standard must apply in determining what articles will be printed. Sensational newspapers expanded the meaning of the human interest story to report what had hitherto been regarded as private, the gossip and scandal about individuals, and discovered a rich source of news in crime and everyday tragedy. A corollary of the same point, they began to pay as much attention to personalities as to local or national events, to the extent that some of the less inhibited journalists even took to personalizing themselves. James Gordon Bennett shocked his colleagues in 1840, but delighted the *Herald* audience, by devoting lead space to the announcement of his engagement, including an effusive and lengthy declaration of love for his intended bride.

The second rule follows directly from the first. Sensational newspapers have their own idea of the relative importance of different stories. They can usually be counted on to evict matters of statecraft from the front page if a provocative item of scandal is available to take its place. Some years ago, when the teenage daughter of a famous film actress shot and killed her mother's lover, the *New York Daily News* and the *New York Times* each devoted about the same inches of copy to the tragedy. The difference between the two papers is that what appeared with large headlines and abundant pictures on the front page of the *Daily News* was modestly relegated to a back page in the *Times*.

Finally, the form requires a unique prose style. The argument applies with different force to different papers, but in general the language in a sensational newspaper, unlike a conservative paper, tends to be slangy, colloquial, personal. In such a way does the sensational journal express its identity with the masses of people who patronize it.

But if all of this has been true since the days of Bennett and Day, in what sense was Pulitzer a revolutionary? More specifically, in what sense did the rise of the *World* represent a watershed between an old journalism and a new? The answer is twofold, partly a matter of Pulitzer's innovations, and partly a matter of his refinements on a traditional craft.

The argument about innovations is best made by comparing a pre-Pulitzer with a post-Pulitzer newspaper. Were one to scan through the *World* prior to 1883, or through any of the other famous or obscure dailies prior to that year (including the *Herald* and the *Sun*), it would become apparent that they have certain important traits in common. The first thing to strike the eye would be the unrelieved greyness of their pages. Not only did the pre-Pulitzer publisher favor a small-sized type (as did Pulitzer himself for many years), he knew nothing about enlivening his format with multi-column headlines or, most important, pictures and illustrations. The technical problems involved in using illustration as an adjunct to the printed word had already been surmounted—a stray illustration appeared in the *Sun* as early as 1833, and in 1873 a Canadian firm of engravers founded the *New York Daily Graphic* as a paper devoted to illustrations rather than news—but as yet nobody regarded pictures as other than an occasional novelty. The same could no longer be said after the four-column cut of the Brooklyn Bridge that appeared on the front page of the *World* on May 22, 1883. Pulitzer had taken the first step in changing the appearance of his own paper, and ultimately all papers.

Some of his innovations which contributed to the same result —the use of ears on the masthead of the front page, for example —were trivial but widely imitated. Others, like the headlines that spanned several columns, or a whole page, came after the period between 1883 and 1885. When the *World* introduced them, however, they were adopted by every other newspaper, and a revolution in typography was carried forward. Beginning in 1883, and for a decade and a half following, Pulitzer in ways major and minor led the profession in fashioning a new style for the dowdy American newspaper.

The period from 1883 to 1885 marks a watershed between the old journalism and the new in still other respects. Pulitzer borrowed ideas of sensationalism that were not original with him, and brought them up-to-date to fit a modern America of cities and factories. Publishers of the pre-Pulitzer era may have realized the appeal of human interest material, but they had neither the resources nor the techniques to meet the demand in a way common after 1883. Pulitzer and the men who succeeded him were simply more adept at a traditional craft. Far from depending on police court news, with the sameness and uncertainty attaching to it, they could take from the wire services scandal and sensation from every state and many lands. They could use the resources accumulating from vast circulations to mount stunts that seemed sometimes to dwarf the events of real life. Bennett and Day had nothing to match a Nellie Bly racing around the globe against a fictional rival, or a Henry Stanley searching for and finding a Dr. Livingstone in "darkest" Africa. Indeed, in the days before celebrities had surrendered their right to privacy, and before the press had refined the art of invading that privacy with probing, persistent questions, they had not even available the tool of interviewing, so rich a source of private and public news. Pulitzer enjoyed all sorts of advantages in publishing a popular journal. His greatness is that he taught himself and his successors how to use them.

Some of his contributions in modernizing the techniques of sensationalism entailed changes of considerable substance. It was Pulitzer who responded to the needs and desires of a modern city population by providing a daily sports page, no small concession to men who had little opportunity to play games themselves. It was Pulitzer who bowed to women's rising status by running material specially tailored to their interests. It was Pulitzer who used frivolous pictures, poetry, short stories, and the like, to make the newspaper a medium to entertain as well as inform. Each of these responses, unknown or conceived in only a rudimentary way prior to 1883, became the journalistic conventions of a later decade. They, too, measure the difference between the pre- and post-Pulitzer press, and the scope of the revolution that the immigrant publisher inspired.

Finally, and again in response to pressures from without, Pulitzer added an element to his variety of journalism which no newspaper has ever since been quite able to ignore. His role, he thought, was to speak for as well as to the masses of people who patronized the *World*. He decided at the outset that their need would be the *World*'s cause. There is nothing prior to 1883 to match its crusades on behalf of immigrants, workingmen, tenement dwellers, middle-income taxpayers, and so on. This was militant journalism of a new intensity, not concerned solely with Star Route frauds and Tweed Rings (although the latter-day equivalents were not neglected), but also with the conditions that bore down directly upon thousands of anonymous men and women in their daily lives. Pulitzer conferred a dignity of sorts on popular journalism, a raison d'être beyond profits and losses, that ultimately influenced all newspapers, and that is still reflected in the lip service the press renders to its role as servant of the people.

It will be argued in the chapters to follow that the *World*'s uniqueness rested in part on this constant and conscious appeal to the most vulnerable members of the society. The paper prepared articles with their interests specifically in mind, and as has been mentioned, took their side on a wide variety of political and social issues. Its unprecedented success, measured by a circulation several times higher than any previously known, and a rate of profit that quickly earned a fortune for its owner, is explained by several factors, but none more important than its ability to win the confidence of a group that until Pulitzer's time had never really been reached.

There are certain problems with this thesis that should be anticipated at the outset. The most obvious one, and also the most damaging, is the failure to buttress it with final statistical verification. The case calls for a table of numbers showing that a considerable proportion of the *World*'s daily press run was delivered to newsstands in immigrant or working-class neighborhoods. Unfortunately, such records, proving or disproving the argument, are not available. Of course it is altogether possible that even if they did exist, they would show only that the bulk of each day's copies were sold at newsstands adjacent to the elevated stations where all classes mingled on their way to work.

The admitted failure to provide one sort of proof should not be interpreted as a further admission that the thesis is cut out of whole cloth, a happy inspiration with neither evidence nor logic to sustain it. The historian makes do with the data available to him, and in this instance there is a considerable body to work with. At worst, the case rests on evidence second only to numbers in reliability. It accepts the *World*'s own evaluation of its readership, and shows that the paper used that evaluation in determining what would and would not appear in print.

The emphasis throughout is upon Pulitzer's part in leading the revolution, a decision that poses its own problem. Any metropolitan newspaper is a product of many minds working together. It is senseless to imply that the *World*, like a novel or a poem, was simply an expression of one man's genius. Pulitzer had help, and the origin of many of the most imaginative innovations is doubtless lost in the noise and tension of a newspaper office working to meet a printing deadline. But in a more important sense we can equate the publisher and his property, because it was his imagination which was most fertile, and his presence which dominated the paper. Joseph Pulitzer was first of all a newspaperman, which meant that he composed copy, and worried about makeup, and most important of all, understood the meaning of news. If all of the ideas conceived between 1883 and 1885 did not originate with him, certainly he passed on them, and they were realized in print because they measured up to what, in his phrase, "a modern newspaper should be."

Several readers have pointed out that Pulitzer's *St. Louis Post-Dispatch* differed fundamentally from the *World* during the period under consideration. Its social bias was middle class rather than lower class, and in politics it preached Mugwump reform rather than up-dated Democratic reform. Does this not suggest, they wonder, that the alleged appeal in New York City to a lower class audience was largely mythical, and that Pulitzer did no more than object, as any other Mugwump would, to the obvious political and economic inequities of the time? I think not. The publisher attempted a unique feat when he set up shop in the east. He wanted nothing less than to achieve for the *World* the greatest circulation in the nation's history. He needed that circulation if he was to have a podium from which his liberal principles could be heard, and to obtain it he had to win the confidence, as well as to excite the interest, of the masses of people. One man owned the two papers, but the two papers were not twins. They differed in style, in influence, in readership, and to a notable extent, in principle. Just as we learn little about the *Post-Dispatch* from reading the *World*, we learn little about the *World* from reading the *Post-Dispatch*.

This is not to deny, as will become apparent in later chapters, that the *World*'s prescription for reform was often cautious, conservative, or to twist a word, "Mugwumpean." Nor is it to claim that a reading of the *World* is enough by itself to define Pulitzer's personal convictions. Any man's thought is shrouded in inconsistencies, sometimes even in contradictions, and undoubtedly the best understanding of Pulitzer will finally include material from both papers. But it is the *World* we are analyzing, not the man, and to discover that he was capable of different policies elsewhere should not distract us from our primary focus.

It would be wrong to take the thesis here defended and stretch it too far. Many of the features that appealed to a working-class audience—pictures, lurid accounts of crime and violence, the very air of irreverence—were bound to appeal to others as well. The newspaper must have found its way into many different types of homes as its circulation mushroomed. It would be absurd to suggest that *only* people of small means and limited prospect were included in a readership that within a few months soared over 100,000. Just as many of the readers of the *New York Daily News* today are not unsophisticated, many of the readers of the *New York World* during the 1880s were not oppressed. In order to make a case, primary emphasis has been put on what has previously been neglected. If as a result, obvious points have sometimes been left unelaborated, it is enough justification to say that they are thereby no less obvious.

The most common remark heard from those who read the book in manuscript form concerned my sparing use of the Pulitzer Papers. Would it not have been better, they asked, to have made greater use of his letters and memoranda in defending the various arguments, rather than to rely so heavily on editorials and features in the *New York World*? The question is pertinent, and requires a careful answer. The first thing to understand is that the Papers become a storehouse of material only after 1890, when blindness and ill health forced Pulitzer to surrender active control of his journals. He never lost interest in the *World*, and thereafter dispatched an almost daily barrage of memoranda to Park Row, instructing the staff how the paper should be edited. Nothing approaching such riches exists prior to 1890. After all, the reason commonly cited for Pulitzer's final nervous collapse is that he wracked his frail system at the beginning to put the *World* on its feet. He did not have time or occasion to keep a log setting forth his philosophy of journalism. He was there himself, doing rather than theorizing.

Why not, in that case, make greater use of the Papers for the later period? To a certain extent they have been used, but with extreme caution. The *World* of the 1890s was a much more sedate, conservative, dignified journal than its younger self of the previous decade. It is only barely a metaphor to say that the newspaper was well into its life cycle by then, and had noticeably matured. (The yellow press phase at the end of the century, when Pulitzer competed with Hearst for circulation by helping to stir up a war with Spain, was an aberration, a result of special circumstances, and should be treated as such.) Pulitzer's later memoranda are fascinating, but for present purposes are as likely to mislead as to inform. They have been cited when they corroborate judgments derived from the paper itself during the 1880s. It would be an abuse of historical method to rely on them more.

One of the pitfalls involved in writing history is that a spirit of objective inquiry can easily be transformed into partisanship. It is difficult to live with a man for two or three years, to spend late nights and long weekends in his company, without knowing him too well and becoming his champion. Over the months his warts disappear and only the warmth of familiarity remains. I have tried to avoid that snare in evaluating Joseph Pulitzer's contribution to American journalism. Whether or not the attempt has been successful, it is some comfort that the decision reached in this book is shared by his fellow professionals. In a special feature for its fiftieth anniversary issue on July 21, 1934, *Editor & Publisher* polled newspapermen throughout the nation to discover who they considered to be the greatest American editor of all time. They agreed decisively, some twenty years after his death, that the honor belonged to Joseph Pulitzer. If they were right, hopefully much of the reason why is contained in the following chapters.

I owe a deep debt to several men for their generous and unstinting help in reading through the manuscript and making constructive suggestions. They have repeatedly saved me from error, inconsistency, and clumsiness of language. Of course the inadequacies which remain are entirely my own. My thanks go to Professor David Roberts of Dartmouth College, Professor Louis Starr of the Columbia University School of Journalism, and Professor Julian Rammelkamp of Albion College for their careful, wise, incisive criticisms. The staff of Baker Library at Dartmouth College provided help at every turn. Mr. Roy Grisham of the Princeton University Press was the unsung hero who edited the manuscript and in the process pointed out to me numerous inaccuracies. The book was written as a doctoral dissertation under the supervision of Professor Richard Hofstadter of Columbia University. My debt to him is immense, and only in part because he demanded of me as much as I could give. So is my debt to Professor Robert Cross of Columbia University. He proposed the subject in the first instance, commented on it through its various raw stages, and freely offered to me his friendship and advice when I needed both.

They have been the generous ones, but there are others to whom I owe still more. I am grateful to my parents and sister for caring about scholarship from the beginning, and helping every step of the way. Above all, I am grateful to my wife, not least for years of putting up with the sudden and, I fear, often odd enthusiasms of an apprentice historian.

GEORGE JUERGENS

Amherst, Massachusetts
August 1966

CONTENTS

JOSEPH PULITZER

AND THE

NEW YORK WORLD

CHAPTER ONE

PULITZER COMES TO

NEW YORK

On the morning of May 9th, 1883, a carriage eased out of Manhattan's downtown traffic and stopped outside the Western Union Building at 195 Broadway. The passenger who emerged—a tall, slim man, six feet two inches in height, with jet black hair and full, reddish-brown beard—quickly crossed the sidewalk and entered the building. His name was Joseph Pulitzer, and he was on his way to the offices of Jay Gould to complete a transaction giving him control of the *New York World*. He brought with him the first installment on an agreed price of $346,000, which represented what Gould had paid for the newspaper four years before, plus the losses he had incurred during his proprietorship.[1]

Pulitzer was almost completely unknown in New York City, having lived most of his life since immigrating to America in St. Louis. The likelihood is that none of the bystanders who saw him enter the building paid particular attention. They might have, however, if they had looked at him more closely. He was not handsome, but something about the set of his mouth, his long forehead and sloping nose, and particularly his piercing blue eyes, which peered out at the world through thick lenses, set him apart. In 1909 John Singer Sargent attempted to capture the special quality of that face by portraying it as half-Mephistophelean and half-saintly. The imagery was apt, for Pulitzer's intense manner and long, tapering fingers constantly in movement, as well as his striking features, gave the impression of a

---

[1] According to Allen Churchill, who is not an altogether reliable source, Pulitzer handed over $100,000 as a first installment. See Allen Churchill, *Park Row* (New York, 1958), p. 9. Whatever the amount, it was drawn out of the profits of the *St. Louis Post-Dispatch*. Later installments came directly out of the *World*'s own profits.

— 3 —

man whose soul was inhabited by demons or angels. Theodore Dreiser, not entirely a friendly critic, suspected the former possibility. He described the publisher as "undoubtedly semi-neurasthenic, a disease-demonized soul, who could scarely control himself in anything, a man who was fighting an almost insane battle with life itself, trying to be omnipotent and what not else, and never to die."[2]

Whether Dreiser judged wisely, the man who arrived at the Western Union Building that May morning was no ordinary visitor, and he was engaged on no ordinary errand. It is not too much to say that the moment Joseph Pulitzer entered Jay Gould's office, and deposited his check on the financier's desk, marked the start of a revolution in journalism that eventually worked its influence upon every metropolitan and rural paper published in the United States. A great newspaper, what observers recognized in retrospect as the first modern newspaper, was born that moment.

The *New York World* looked back on a short but already checkered career by the time it came into Pulitzer's possession. It had been established in 1860 by Alexander Cummings, a Philadelphia journalist, as a one-cent daily edited along religious lines. Cummings filled the front page with church notices, devoted the editorials to messages of uplift, and rigorously excluded such material as liquor or theatrical advertisements which might tend to sully the minds of readers. Although he tried to make a go of it by raising the *World*'s price to two cents on November 24, 1860, and the next year absorbing the *Courier and Enquirer*, heavy losses forced him to surrender the paper. Its stock passed into the hands of a syndicate of Democratic financiers and politicians, headed by August Belmont and including Fernando Wood, then Mayor of New York City. The group installed Manton Marble, who himself held some stock, as managing editor, and under his leadership the *World* prospered briefly as a Democratic organ during the mid- and late 1860s.[3]

[2] Theodore Dreiser, *A Book About Myself* (New York, 1922), p. 470.

[3] It achieved a certain notoriety during the Civil War when it printed a bogus Presidential proclamation calling for a draft of 400,000 men. The forgery had been circulated by Joseph Howard, city editor of the *Brooklyn Eagle*, who hoped that the publication of his hoax would enable him to make

Marble continued to purchase stock until he acquired outright control in 1869, but by that time the paper's initial burst of prosperity had about spent itself. Discouraged by the vigorous competition of the *New York Sun,* and by Democratic defeats in the last few Presidential elections, Marble sold the *World* in 1876 to a syndicate headed by Thomas Scott, the railroad magnate.

The newspaper continued to lose circulation despite the brilliant editorial direction of William Henry Hurlbert, a stickler for the niceties of language and grammar. Scott decided in 1879 that he could no longer afford the luxury of publishing a red ink journal, and he included the *World* property as part of a sale of stock to Jay Gould. According to Gould's account of the transaction:

> I never intended to have the paper and got it more by accident than by design—almost against my desire. The way of it was this: In the summer of 1878 or 1879 I met Mr. Tom Scott, of the Pennsylvania Railroad in Switzerland, in Berne. Mr. Scott was very much depressed and broken up—financially, physically, and mentally. I felt a profound sympathy for him. He asked me as a favor to take his Texas Pacific Railroad off his hands and I concluded to do so. In arranging the details Mr. Scott appealed to me to include the *World* in the transaction. He owned it absolutely. I cared nothing about it but finally yielded.[4]

Most authorities agree that the price Gould exacted from Pulitzer was much too high.[5] By 1883 the *New York World* had

---

a quick profit on the stock market. (Ironically, Howard joined the *World* staff in later years to work under Pulitzer.) Most of the press sought verification before running the item, but the *New York World* and the *Journal of Commerce,* as well as the *New Orleans Picayune,* neglected that first axiom of journalism, and were penalized accordingly. The *World* offices were occupied by troops under the command of General John A. Dix, Provost Marshal for New York, and for three days—May 19, 20, and 21, 1864—publication of the paper was suspended.

[4] Quoted in Don C. Seitz, *Joseph Pulitzer, His Life & Letters* (New York, 1924), p. 126.

[5] See *ibid.*, p. 131; James Wyman Barrett, *Joseph Pulitzer and His World* (New York, 1941), p. 60; Frank Luther Mott, *American Journalism* (New York, 1941), p. 434.

a circulation of only about 11,000 daily and 15,000 on Sundays. A proportionate drop in advertising lineage meant that the paper lost about $40,000 annually.[6] In drawing up the articles of sale, moreover, Gould carefully excluded his most valuable asset. The contract specified that he would retain ownership of the three-story World Building he had erected at Nos. 31-32 Park Row, transferring title only to the newspaper's plant, equipment and good will. There is some reason to be skeptical about the value of those assets. Gould's name and the *World*'s reputation as a sick man of journalism did not leave much in the way of good will, while a fire which razed the World Building on January 31, 1882, had destroyed a valuable stock of unused Bullock presses stored in the basement.[7]

Whether Pulitzer decided on the spur of the moment to purchase the property at Gould's price, as his biographers maintain, or the transaction resulted from several years of trying to break into the New York newspaper field, the young man who had arrived in the United States as an immigrant less than twenty years before, and who had behind him barely four years experience as proprietor of the *St. Louis Post-Dispatch*, found himself at the age of thirty-six suddenly in competition with the leading figures in American journalism[8]

[6] The estimate of Gould's losses appears in several sources: Seitz, *Joseph Pulitzer*, p. 127; Barrett, *Pulitzer and His World*, p. 59; Mott, *American Journalism*, p. 434; *et al.*

[7] Walt McDougall, speaking admittedly from the bias of a Republican upbringing, tried to convey just how little good will the old *World* enjoyed. "It is almost impossible now," he wrote in 1925, "to make clear the bitter disfavor and scorn in which the *World* of Jay Gould and Manton Marble was held by persons of refinement and Republican principles at that time. Its copperhead record, its vulgar, coarse methods and Tammany principles had long since reduced it to the condition of a pariah, a slinking mangy outcast prowling in the gutters. Of this public disesteem Pulitzer and Cockerill were scarcely aware—or at all events, they disregarded it—when they acquired what was considered by the Park Row fraternity to be the largest white elephant in captivity." Walt McDougall, "Old Days on *The World*," *The American Mercury*, IV (January 1925), 21.

[8] Pulitzer also spent several months during 1871-73 as part owner of a German daily, published in St. Louis, called the *Westliche Post*. He soon discovered that there was not enough excitement in catering to the special interests of immigrants scattered throughout the midwest, and sold his share at a profit to the founders of the paper, Carl Schurz and Emil Preetorius. See Seitz, *Joseph Pulitzer*, p. 114; and Willard Grosvenor Bleyer, *Main Currents in the History of American Journalism* (New York, 1927), p. 325, for a description

The major metropolitan dailies were concentrated at that time along the southeast slope of City Hall Park, on a street called Park Row. The location had been picked before the days of telephones and rapid communications, when newspapers had to settle as near as possible to the sources of their stories. Politicians were available for interviewing just across the street in City Hall; high finance enacted its daily drama a few blocks to the south on Wall Street; and endless miles of slums pressed in on all sides, a rich source of crime news and sensation.

In fact, Park Row was two streets, roughly bisected by Printing House Square. New York's major dailies occupied the southern half, not more than one good city block long, while the foreign language press clustered in the less famous northern half, extending to the present entrance to the Brooklyn Bridge. The New York Tribune Building, erected in 1875 at a cost of $1,000,000, remained for some time the most famous in the neighborhood, even, many would have said, in the city. Rising nine stories, and capped by a thin clock tower which reached up 285 feet, it stood directly off Printing House Square, facing City Hall, and marked the northern limit of America's Fleet Street. James Gordon Bennett's white marble Herald Building occupied the southern outpost, at Ann Street. The *World, Sun, Times,* and all the other permanent and transitory contributors to New York's competitive press nestled between them.[9]

Pulitzer's competitors included four morning dailies of national repute, and several others of varying reputation. The *New York Herald*, established by James Gordon Bennett on

of Pulitzer hearing of the *World*'s availability while in New York waiting to sail on a European vacation, and deciding on the spur of the moment to purchase the paper. We know also, however, that Pulitzer had tried for some time to break into New York journalism, notably in 1875 when he negotiated unsuccessfully for the purchase of *Belletristische Journal*, a German-language weekly. The following year he had even casually discussed with Marble the possibility of buying into the *World*. When he finally did so, he not only fulfilled an old ambition, but acquired a newspaper with an established name and, even more important, an Associated Press franchise.

[9] The arrangement lasted until 1890, when Joseph Pulitzer completed the *World*'s triumph by dedicating a new home for it at the northern corner of Park Row. The building towered an unprecedented sixteen stories, and culminated in a huge golden dome. Unkind rivals likened it to a brass-headed tack, but most people were impressed, if for no other reason than at 310 feet it was the tallest structure in the city.

— 7 —

May 6, 1835, as a sensational penny journal, and now owned and directed in absentia by James Gordon Bennett, Jr., dominated the morning field. Other newspapers boasted of larger circulations, but none matched the *Herald* in advertising lineage, prestige, and, what is the final measure, profits. By the 1880s, the sensational antics of Bennett Senior had been toned down long since, and at three cents a copy (the issues generally ran to ten or twelve pages) the respectable element in the city found the *Herald* a reliable as well as colorful source for news and opinion.

The *New York Sun* bore the personal imprint of Charles Anderson Dana, a throwback to the days when giants dominated metropolitan journalism.[10] Benjamin H. Day founded the newspaper on September 3, 1833, as the first of the penny journals, but long before the Civil War it had started to go downhill. Dana's take-over in 1868 restored wit and vivacity to the pages of the *Sun*. Restricting himself to four pages per issue—he believed in newspapers for reading rather than browsing—he remade the *Sun* into a model of condensation and sprightly prose.[11] It enjoyed for a while the largest circulation of any paper in the United States, selling well over 100,000 copies daily, at two cents a copy.

Henry J. Raymond, backed by George Jones and Edward B. Wesley, established the *New York Daily Times* on September 18, 1851. Despite temporary triumphs along the way, notably its exposé of the Tweed Ring during 1870-1871, and its important role in uncovering the Star Route fraud in 1881, the newspaper had to wait until the turn of the century to win its reputation as the great grey eminence of journalism. Jones had taken a firm grip on the paper, however, after Raymond died in 1869, and at four cents a copy, it offered at the time of Pulitzer's arrival eight pages daily of sober, solid reporting for people themselves sober and solid.

Horace Greeley published the first edition of the *New York Tribune* on April 10, 1841, and dominated it until his death in

[10] Many of the great names in the profession had passed away during the previous decade. Henry Raymond died in 1869, Horace Greeley and Bennett Senior in 1872, Samuel Bowles of the *Springfield Republican* in 1877, and William Cullen Bryant of the *New York Evening Post* in 1878.

[11] The *Sun* expanded to eight pages in 1887.

1872, only weeks after his disastrous campaign for the Presidency. Under Whitelaw Reid, who succeeded him, the paper grew increasingly conservative, developing by the 1880s into an eight-page organ of Republicanism, dedicated to protectionism and allied with high finance, and sold for four cents to families who preferred the highest orthodoxy in both politics and religion.

The other entries in New York's morning field were a mixed lot. Albert Pulitzer arrived in the city one year before his brother to establish the *New York Morning Journal*, a one cent daily which enjoyed considerable popularity among workingmen until 1894, when it raised its price.[12] *Truth*, a penny journal edited by C. A. Byrnes, never found its audience, and died almost unnoticed in 1884. Cyrus W. Field organized the two-cent *Mail and Express* out of two moribund papers in 1882, but his reputation weighed as heavily against him as Gould's, and he soon sold out. The *Star*, which also sold for two cents, continued to appear until 1891, but by the 1880s was already an undisguised organ of Tammany Hall, and as such had only limited appeal.

[12] Albert and Joseph Pulitzer did not get on well together, and there is evidence that their rivalry as newspaper proprietors was the cause of considerable bitterness. Thus, Albert tried to dissuade his older brother from buying into the *World*, while Joseph, in turn, hired some of his best men by repeated raids on the *Morning Journal* staff. Authorities disagree as to whether Joseph Pulitzer provided financial backing for Albert when he established the *Morning Journal* in 1882. Don Seitz speaks of Joseph's contributing a small amount to Albert's working capital of $25,000, even though he had little faith in the practicability of penny journalism. *The Journalist*, a trade periodical, alleged that Pulitzer "watched with concealed anger the establishment of the *Morning Journal*, and refused point-blank to put one dollar in it, predicted its early ruin, ran down the men Albert employed on the paper and in various ways did what he could to discourage his brother from going on any further." (See Seitz, *Joseph Pulitzer*, p. 113; *The Journalist*, July 12, 1884, p. 4.) The trade periodical also accused Pulitzer of competing for news with his brother in devious and underhanded ways. "Here is a case in point to show how Jo acts toward the editor of the *Morning Journal*," it reported. "On Thursday, the *World* contained half a column of a clipping about the forthcoming divorce of Mrs. Langtry and her subsequent marriage to Frederick Gebhardt. Jo Pulitzer credited the article, which was a fairly sensational one, to the *Chicago Tribune*, whereas, as a matter of fact, it appeared originally in the *Journal* of last Tuesday. Jo wanted the story all along, but he would not credit it to the *Journal*, so he waits long enough to give the necessary time, and credits the article to the *Tribune*, in which Jo knew perfectly well that it did not originally appear. He could not bag the story entire, and he cribbed it in an underhand way." (*The Journalist*, October 18, 1884, p. 2.) However Joseph Pulitzer behaved, Albert lived to derive some satisfaction for slights real and imagined when he saw his newspaper become the property of William Randolph Hearst.

For all its variety and prestige, contemporaries found much to criticize in the New York press. *The Journalist* argued, for example, that the very success of the great dailies had bred timidity and dullness into them:

> No more conspicuous evidence of the fact exists than the *New York Herald*, with which the elder Bennett started to fight the whole world. On that principle he made his fortune. But when it was made he toned down to conservatism. For many years the *Herald* has ceased to be outspoken on any subject. . . . There is a list of two hundred and fifty or three hundred people at the *Herald* office who must never be spoken of disparagingly, no matter what happens. These are personal and business friends of Mr. Bennett. . . .
>
> Here is Mr. Dana, in the sere and yellow leaf of manhood, with a son whom he wants to see well started in life before he himself passes away. And so he becomes conservative, easy and inoffensive in spite of his natural tendencies. . . . The sharp, personal, incisive and sometimes abusive *Sun* of twelve, yes even seven years ago, exists no longer. . . .
>
> Like Paul Dana, Whitelaw Reid has society aspirations which clog the wheels of his presses so that they turn out not a virile, strong, decided sheet as the paper used to be under Horace Greeley, but a molasses and water style of journalism that reads like the compositions written by pupils from an academy of young ladies.[13]

As for the other newspapers, if success did not emasculate them, something else did.

> The *Star* is a . . . case in point. . . . Everything is judged from through the limited vision of John Kelly, who cares nothing for journalism and everything for politics, so it becomes the personal organ of a gang of Hibernian ward heelers who have personal and petty axes to grind.
>
> The *Mail and Express* is the property of Mr. Cyrus W. Field. This means of course that, while on general matters it may be a good newspaper, it is crippled by

[13] *The Journalist*, May 17, 1884, p. 1. Paul Dana was the son of Charles Dana, the publisher of the *Sun*.

a financial connection, the counterpart of which at one time brought the *World* and the *Tribune* to the verge of ruin.[14]

Pulitzer must certainly have been alive to such criticisms, and anxious to exploit them. "A little gumshoeing had sufficed to show him," one of the publisher's close associates is quoted as having said, "that all New York needed to set its monetary glands flowing was a daily dose of tingling sensations. Such sensations were as plentiful as mushrooms, but were being trampled underfoot unnoticed by the editors of the sedate old-fogey newspapers, who thought a bit of snappy personal repartee on the editorial page was a humdinger and that pictures were degrading, if not actually improper."[15] He could not help but be aware also that the Democratic Party was poorly represented by New York's press. The *Herald* and *Sun* called themselves independent, which in the *Herald*'s case meant fairly predictable support of Republican candidates for national office, and in the *Sun*'s, such aberrations as half-hearted support in 1880 of Winfield Scott Hancock ("a good man, weighing two hundred and forty pounds"), and the upcoming editorial backing of Benjamin Butler in 1884. The only avowed Democratic newspapers in the morning field were Gould's *World* and the *Star*, which contributed little to the party because of its lack of prestige.

Before he could arrest the *World*'s decline, and make it an effective organ of Democracy, Pulitzer first had to erase the memory of the newspaper's previous ownership. He firmly rejected Gould's proposal that some of the previous editorial staff be retained, and that his son, George, be allowed to keep a small bloc of shares in the newspaper.[16] According to Colonel John A. Cockerill, Pulitzer's respected managing editor, the negotiations "were two or three times broken off solely because Mr. Gould hesitated about giving up all his interest in the paper. He wanted Mr. Hurlburt to stay. Then he wanted his son George to take

[14] *Ibid.*, The last sentence refers to Gould's ownership of the *New York World* from 1879 to 1883, as well as to the fact that Gould helped Whitelaw Reid to purchase stock control of the *New York Tribune* in 1873, an alliance which plagued Reid for years after.

[15] Quoted in Allen Churchill, *Park Row*, p. 6.

[16] See John L. Heaton, *The Story of a Page* (New York, 1913), pp. 10-11; also Seitz, *Joseph Pulitzer*, p. 131.

— 11 —

hold of the business department. But none of these things suited Mr. Pulitzer, who knew he must have it all or nothing. And it was not until Mr. Gould so arranged that he could get out entirely that they came to terms."[17]

Pulitzer arranged a front page interview with Gould within days of assuming control to make the change of ownership still more emphatic. "Mr. Gould," the reporter asked, "what do you think of the new *World*?" "I like it first-rate. I think it will be a great success. All that I'm afraid of is that it will be a little too bright, and pitch into me. . . . It is wonderfully improved in its news and general appearance, but its new editorial tone is not to my liking. I am afraid it might become dangerous."[18]

If the approach was not subtle, neither was the avidity with which Pulitzer's enemies kept rumors afloat. *The Journalist*, a trade periodical established by Leander Richardson and C. A. Byrnes about a year after Pulitzer arrived in New York City, worked hardest to link the names of the despised financier and the immigrant editor. Richardson had at one time written the "Town Listener" department for the *World*, but he had a falling out with Pulitzer and devoted himself for many months to attacking his adversary's growing reputation.[19] One way was to cast

[17] *The Journalist*, April 19, 1884, p. 4.
[18] *New York World*, May 13, 1883, p. 1.
[19] Richardson worked almost a year under Pulitzer before resigning to take over *The Journalist*. A short item which appeared in the *World* in May 1884 might explain the hostility he felt towards the immigrant publisher. "Mr. Leander Richardson," it reported, "has ceased to write The Town Listener department in the *World*. It was a sort of man-about-town gossip column which was popular, but it has been abandoned for the present by reason of the difficulty which the *World* is experiencing with its presses, which has necessitated the giving up of the extra supplement on Sundays." *New York World*, May 10, 1884, p. 6. While it is true that the newspaper was having considerable problems with the Hoe presses it had recently installed, this seems rather a feeble excuse for dropping a popular column, particularly when new columns and features were constantly being added. Richardson maintained a tenuous connection with the *World* for several weeks thereafter, sending back reports on the party conventions in Chicago to his old paper, as well as to the *Boston Herald* and the *St. Louis Post-Dispatch*, but he had already formed a partnership with C. A. Byrne to establish *The Journalist*, and had launched on the vendetta against Pulitzer. The pair sold their interests to W. G. MacLaughlin in February 1885, at which time Richardson revealed proudly that he was responsible for the dozens of unsigned articles castigating the owner of the *World*. "I presume everybody who read *The Journalist* in its early days know what my sentiments are regarding Mr. Pulitzer," he wrote in a public letter to MacLaughlin. "The only enmity [*The Journalist*] purposely fostered

Joseph Pulitzer, shortly before he left St. Louis to purchase the *New York World*. He had only recently cultivated the beard that in later years became almost a trademark. (Courtesy New York Historical Society)

John Cockerill, Pulitzer's trusted lieutenant on the *Post-Dispatch* and later the *World*. From a woodcut made in 1884, when their collaboration in New York City had just gotten underway. (Courtesy New York Historical Society)

A view of Park Row, dominated at the northern corner by the brass-domed World Building that was dedicated in 1890. The sixteen-story structure—towering 310 feet—was the tallest in the city at the time, and a striking symbol of Pulitzer's achievement in dominating New York journalism in the span of a few years. All of the other great dailies, as did the *World* prior to 1890, had their offices in the two blocks extending south to Ann Street. (Courtesy New York Historical Society)

Several gentlemen of the press pass the time in a room across the street from Manhattan's downtown police headquarters while waiting for news to break. The station provided a staple source of material for newspapers during the 1880s. It had the added advantage, in the days before telephoning had become commonplace, of proximity to Park Row. As is apparent here, journalism was still largely a male profession. (Jacob Riis Collection. Courtesy Museum of the City of New York)

The last edition of the *World* under Jay Gould's ownership. Note the sedate appearance of the page, the sober masthead, the sameness of the headlines, the use of the left-hand column for summarizing the news rather than reporting it, and the trivial nature of the story in the right-hand column. (Courtesy New York Public Library)

The *World* as it looked two weeks later. The old masthead and column of news summary is gone. A horse race occupies the place previously filled with dog show news. Most important, with this issue illustration becomes a part of daily journalism. (Courtesy New York Public Library)

The most famous of the *World*'s front page cartoons, which helped to swing the 1884 election to Grover Cleveland, was this one, depicting James Blaine's attendance at a banquet in New York City, tendered him by the nation's foremost millionaires. His image as a man of the people was badly sullied. (Courtesy New York Public Library)

The "Pig Market," perhaps the most colorful of the downtown shopping districts. It was so named because it provided the Jewish immigrants in the vicinity of Hester Street with everything but pork. The market offered some of the clearest evidence that New York City had become an amalgam of sub-cultures, with only the barest contact between them. (Courtesy New York Historical Society)

A family from eastern Europe arrives in New York City. Much of the reason for the *World*'s unprecedented rise in circulation was that it took the lead in pleading the cause of immigrants like these, and through such devices as illustration encouraged them to become newspaper readers. (Lewis W. Hine Memorial Collection)

The foyer of the William Astor mansion at Fifth Avenue and 65th Street, representing a style of life beyond the imagination of all but a privileged few. (Courtesy New York Historical Society)

The street scenes in wealthy neighborhoods were unique in their own way, as evidenced by this view of Fifth Avenue and 52nd Street, with the twin mansions of Mrs. W. H. Vanderbilt and her daughter in the foreground. (Courtesy New York Historical Society)

A Bohemian cigar-maker and his family, victims of the sweatshop system. They have converted their home into a factory, and enlisted the labor of even the youngest children in order to subsist. (Jacob Riis Collection. Courtesy Museum of the City of New York)

Traffic flows heavily up Broadway, looking north from Chambers Street, during an era when the city won recognition as the foremost metropolis of the New World. (Courtesy New York Historical Society)

An English immigrant coal hauler and his family pose in their one-room flat, mutely testifying to the extremes of wealth and poverty in New York City at the time. (Jacob Riis Collection. Courtesy Museum of the City of New York)

No immigrant group fared worse during the 1880s than Italians, such as this one making his home in a shanty beneath the manure heaps on the bank of the East River. (Jacob Riis Collection. Courtesy Museum of the City of New York)

doubt on the ownership of the new *World*. "The interesting puzzle has been propounded again during the past week," he wrote in April of 1884, "whether Jay Gould still possesses an interest in the *World* newspaper. Now and then an ear-mark comes out which makes men jump to this conclusion: notably, of late, the attack on Vanderbilt the day after Gould returned from his yachting. . . . There is no doubt that all that was wanted to make the *World* successful was smart management and the destruction of the popular notion that Gould had a controlling interest in it. . . . Nothing is more important to its prosperity than a continuance of that impression. . . . But whether or not [Pulitzer] is a partner of the little man is open to suspicion."[20] Colonel Cockerill's strong statement, that "Mr. Gould does not own one penny's worth of the *World*," plus the evident hostility towards Gould in the *World*'s editorial pages, soon put the rumor to rest, but not until another one replaced it.[21] "Would anybody like to know who are the owners of the *New York World*?" Richardson asked some months later. "If they would, let me gently whisper the names of a syndicate including Jewseph Pulitzer, August Belmont and Roscoe Conkling. Thus, gentle reader, do we find the reason why the *World*, a Democratic paper, so persistently booms Roscoe Conkling, a Republican politician, for the post of United States Senator from New York."[22]

Not even the friendliest critics easily denied that unknown partners held an interest in the paper. W. G. MacLaughlin, who succeeded Richardson as publisher of *The Journalist* in February 1885, frankly admired Pulitzer's newspaper genius, but admitted that the old question still perplexed him. Referring to the *World*'s financial statement for the year 1884, he pointed out that "the report is signed by 'Joseph Pulitzer, President, Joseph Pulitzer and Melville C. Day,' 'a majority of the Trustees.'

---

was the Pulitzer affair, and I am not concerned as to who knows that this was my personal racket." *The Journalist*, March 14, 1885, p. 3.

[20] *The Journalist*, April 7, 1884, p. 7.

[21] Cockerill's statement appeared in an interview denying Richardson's allegation. See *The Journalist*, April 19, 1884, p. 4.

[22] *The Journalist*, November 29, 1884, p. 5.

This looks as though the *World* is published by a company."[23]

Pulitzer and his lieutenants could issue denials as quickly as the rumors appeared, but the only way to dispel them finally would be by what they made of the paper. The new owner wasted no time in announcing his independence. Badgered by E. C. Hancock to issue some statement on the change (Hancock had come over from the *Morning Journal* to serve as Pulitzer's first managing editor), Pulitzer quickly scribbled the following for the lead press run of the new *World*.

> The entire *World* newspaper property has been purchased by the undersigned, and will, from this day on, be under different management—different in men, measures and methods—different in purpose, policy and principle—different in objects and interests—different in sympathies and convictions—different in head and heart.
>
> Performance is better than promise. Exuberant assurances are cheap. I make none. I simply refer the public to the new *World* itself, which henceforth shall be the daily evidence of its own growing improvement, with forty-eight daily witnesses in its forty-eight columns.[24]

He followed within the week with a ten-point list of new *World* doctrines that could not have pleased many financiers.

1. Tax luxuries.
2. Tax inheritances.
3. Tax large incomes.
4. Tax monopolies.
5. Tax the privileged corporations.
6. A tariff for revenue.
7. Reform the civil service.
9. Punish corrupt office-holders.
10. Punish employers who coerce their employees in elections.[25]

The fact that all of the items on the list, save that referring to the tariff, were soon realized, is perhaps less significant than Pulitzer's consistency in supporting them.[26] For all the wealth

[23] *The Journalist*, March 21, 1885, p. 5.
[24] *World*, May 11, 1883, p. 4.   [25] *World*, May 17, 1883, p. 4.
[26] Indeed, the editor himself cooled somewhat over the years on the idea of a tariff for revenue only.

and influence which came to him, Pulitzer was no less a reformer during the Progressive heyday of the early 1900s than he had been twenty years before. He recognized early that success could seduce the best of intentions, and he carefully shielded himself from its temptations. An editorial which appeared months after he purchased the newspaper revealed his awareness of the pressures on a crusading journalist.

> A newspaper conductor with an income of a quarter or half a million a year or more, with yachts, town houses and country houses to keep up, with an intimate circle of millionaire friends to entertain and be entertained by—above all, with a surplus income which must be invested and which naturally goes into bonds and stocks and other securities of corporations and monopolies—which side would he be apt to drift into? Is he likely to be eager and zealous and earnest in resisting the encroachments of monopoly and the money power, in defending the rights of the common people?
>
> . . . But there is one [paper in this city] not controlled nor in any way swayed or influenced by the side of capital. . . . That is the *World*.[27]

The large role that editorial integrity played in the success of the *World* will be examined in later chapters, but it raises another item in the Pulitzer philosophy which merits mention now. Although most men of intellect and serious temperament deplored the space given in the *World* to stories of sex and violence, they were mistaken if they made judgments on that basis about Pulitzer's personal tastes. Alleyne Ireland has written of the

[27] *World*, September 9, 1883, p. 4. Don Seitz, who served many years as Business Manager of the *World*, recalled a dramatic instance when the publisher acted on those principles. "Mr. Pulitzer had himself a fear of the influence of his growing wealth upon his views and their consequent reflection in the paper. In 1907 he sent for Frank I. Cobb, his chief editorial writer. It was during the tremors that preceded the 'Roosevelt' panic. The editor was addressed in this wise: 'Boy, I am, as you probably know, a large owner of stocks. Some of them are bound to be affected by public actions. I am not sure of myself when I see my interests in danger. I might give way some day to such a feeling and send you an order that would mean a change in the paper's policy. I want you to make me a promise. If I ever do such a thing swear you will ignore my wishes.'" Of course Cobb never had to act on the instructions. Don C. Seitz, "The Portrait of an Editor," *Atlantic Monthly*, CXXXIV (September 1924), 299.

difficulties experienced by a battery of secretaries in keeping his wide-ranging mind occupied during the years of his blindness, while the publisher himself admitted in an interview that his own favorite newspaper was Edwin Godkin's *New York Evening Post*, the journal of the intelligentsia.[28] Why then did he not make the *World* more like the *Evening Post*? "Because," he told an interviewer, "I want to talk to a nation, not to a select committee."[29]

Mass circulation was as much a part of the *World* creed as liberal ideology, and the reason for the one derived from the other. It wasn't simply that the political independent desired his audience, but that the audience gave him financial strength to maintain his independence. "If a newspaper is to be of real service to the public," Pulitzer commented to Alleyne Ireland just before his death, "it must have a big circulation, first because its news and its comments must reach the largest possible number of people, second, because circulation means advertising, and advertising means money, and money means independence."[30]

[28] For a description of how Pulitzer's secretaries labored to satisfy his curiosity, see Alleyne Ireland, *Joseph Pulitzer, Reminiscences of a Secretary* (New York, 1914), especially pp. 45-64, 79-85, and 118-26. We have further evidence of the publisher's personal standards in a memorandum cabled to the *World* office at the time of Edwin Godkin's death. "Mr. William H. Merrill," Pulitzer instructed, "must write an editorial, a tribute to Godkin's ability, all the more so because the man never failed in fifteen years to abuse the *World*, and no doubt hates me. I think the profession has lost the ablest mind since the death of Greeley." Cable dated November 10, 1899, *Joseph Pulitzer Papers*, Manuscript Division, Library of Congress.

[29] James Creelman, "Joseph Pulitzer—Master Journalist," *Pearson's Magazine*, XXI (March 1909), 246. See also his cabled instructions some years earlier to a member of the *World* editorial board. "Nothing is worth printing, . . ." Pulitzer declared, "that is not sure to be read by the masses, the many, not the few." This philosophy applied to back-page material as well as to the major news on page one. In a letter to George Cary Eggleston, the novelist, asking him to write a Sunday column on books and literary matters, Pulitzer specified that the column should be "not too academic and technically literary that appeals only to the few but something, rather, understandable to the instincts of the largest number." The cable is dated November 1, 1899; the letter August 19, 1898. *Pulitzer Papers*, Library of Congress.

[30] Ireland, *Joseph Pulitzer*, pp. 115-16. In so reasoning, the publisher evidently overlooked the fact that advertising revenue could itself restrict a newspaper's independence. He was right in recognizing a trend which became more pronounced with each succeeding decade. The amount of total revenue derived by newspaper publishers from advertising rose from 44.0 percent in 1879, to 49.6 in 1889, to 56.7 in 1904, to 70.9 in 1929. (Cited in Alfred McClung Lee,

The fact that he wished to publish a newspaper for the millions rather than the thousands meant that it would be a sensational paper, tapping hitherto untapped audiences, and appealing to a lowest denominator in taste and literacy. Even the gentlest people, as the *World* exuberantly pointed out, found spiciness hard to resist. "Matthew Arnold tells the Chicago reporters that our newspapers contain too much about the woman who married the skeleton and the woman who turned out to be a man and all that sort of thing, you know, with racy head-lines. Still he says he laughs at the racy way in which these sensational and trivial things are written about. Like everybody else, Matthew buys and reads the newspapers that are racy."[31]

Understanding with remarkable clarity what he wished to accomplish in New York City, Pulitzer's next problem was to assemble the staff to carry it off. The point is often missed, largely because only a few journalists in the 1880s rated by-lines above their copy, but within a few years Pulitzer had risen to the challenge in a way that deeply affected all of Park Row. He not only found his staff, but made the *New York World* the fashionable paper on which to work.

E. C. Hancock impressed almost immediately upon the publisher his unfitness to be Managing Editor. A call went out to St. Louis, and within a week Colonel John Cockerill left the *Post-Dispatch* to take Hancock's place. It was the best of many fine appointments. Cockerill acted as Pulitzer's lieutenant more than subordinate, his "long head and quick judgment acting as a balance wheel" against the ideas constantly tumbling from Pulitzer's head.[32] He demonstrated his usefulness on more than

---

The Daily Newspaper in America [New York, 1937], p. 172.) He did not foresee, however, what went with such figures, that advertisers would often be able to determine policy for the journals they subsidized. The *New York Times* admitted in 1886 that it had accepted $1,200 from the Bell Telephone Company for printing ostensibly as news a company handout, while in recent years the press has shown an interesting reluctance to report on the relationship between death on the highways and badly engineered automobiles. (The *Times* episode is mentioned in Lee, *Daily Newspaper in America*, p. 321.) Of course not all newspapers are equally susceptible to pressures from advertisers, and the prosperous papers are almost immune, but Pulitzer's faith in the liberating quality of such revenue seems to have been too sweeping.

[31] *World*, January 25, 1884, p. 4.

[32] The phrase, and appraisal, are from *The Journalist*, November 14, 1885,

one occasion by keeping the *World*'s momentum going even during the publisher's absences.

Pulitzer subscribed to the principle that two men occupying the same slot compelled both to their competitive best. Cockerill's turn came in March of 1885, when the *Journalist* announced that Ballard Smith had been hired away from the *New York Herald* to join the *World*.[33] Although the one took the title of Editor-in-Charge, and the other Managing Editor, insiders were hard-pressed to distinguish their functions. According to James Wyman Barrett, who served as last City Editor of the *World* before its sale to the Scripps-Howard chain, "whatever distinction existed in JP's mind was not apparent to the editors or the staff. However, this was only the beginning of a long series of conflicts and duplications of effort. As nearly as we understand the Pulitzer theory, the idea was to arouse competition, not di-

---

p. 1. Cockerill verified the judgment in an interview the following year. "Of all the departments on the *New York World*, and all the writers in charge of the specialties, there are just two persons authorized with unlimited license to discriminate what shall go in and what shall be left out. These two persons are Joseph Pulitzer and John A. Cockerill." He added, however, that "this authority is mine only in the absence of Mr. P." (*The Journalist*, January 30, 1886, p. 5.) I have relied heavily upon *The Journalist* in discussing the merits of Pulitzer's staff. Obviously this poses risks, since a trade periodical is apt to be uncritically complimentary in evaluating the practitioners of the trade, and since flattery might as easily be inspired by personal friendship as by professional judgment. It seems to me, however, that the advantages in citing the periodical outweigh the risks. *The Journalist* is the only source we have in which professionals of that time were exposed to criticism by fellow professionals. It appeared regularly from 1884 to 1895, and again from 1897 to 1907, when it was absorbed by *Editor & Publisher*. During the period under review, it provided the only running commentary on affairs in Park Row. A second consideration is that *The Journalist*, as with any trade periodical, was more likely to distort the record by what it left unsaid than by what it revealed. Newspapermen—or doctors, lawyers, academics—who are singled out for praise in their professional publications probably merit the praise. The publications only cease to be useful when we look to them for criticism of those who have not measured up; in such cases they are often silent. Finally, and most important, *The Journalist*'s pronouncements on the *World* staff seem worth quoting by their very tone. When a man is identified as the best in his field, or the staff as a whole is cited as the most respected in the country, the statements cannot be dismissed as back-scratching of the sort which will be repeated in subsequent issues for other men and other newspapers. There must be some significance in the fact that *The Journalist* reserved most of those accolades for the *World* and its employees.

[33] *The Journalist*, March 21, 1885, p. 5.

rected toward the undoing of each other, but competition in doing most for the paper."[34]

Other observers were far less complacent about the Pulitzer system. Theodore Dreiser, who contributed articles to the *World* for a short time during the mid-1890s, remembered a city room which seethed with tension and distrust. Each man regarded the man next to him as the one who might deprive him of a job. Dreiser blamed the publisher's "vital, aggressive, restless, working mood, and his vaulting ambition to be all that there was to be of journalistic force in America . . . [for] making a veritable hell of his paper and the lives of those who worked for him. . . .

> [The reporters] had a kind of nervous, resentful terror in their eyes as have animals when they are tortured. All were either scribbling busily or hurrying in or out. Every man was for himself. If you had asked a man a question, as I ventured to do while sitting here, not knowing anything of how things were done here, he looked at you as though you were a fool, or as though you were trying to take something away from him or cause him trouble of some kind. In the main they bustled by or went on with their work without troubling to pay the slightest attention to you. I had never encountered anything like it before. . . .[35]

[34] Barrett, *Joseph Pulitzer*, p. 98. Competition for primacy between Cockerill, Smith, and George W. Turner, who joined the organization two years after Smith as Business Manager, persuaded Pulitzer that it was time for a house-cleaning. To placate Cockerill, Smith was exiled to Brooklyn in 1890 to take charge of the *World* edition published in that city. The following year, rather than accede to their demands for stock interest in the newspaper, Pulitzer discharged Turner and ordered Cockerill to St. Louis to resume management of the *Post-Dispatch*. Cockerill declined the assignment, and resigned to become editor of the *New York Commercial Advertiser*.

[35] Dreiser, *op.cit.*, pp. 469-70. Most of the men who were exposed to the system agreed with Dreiser. Don Seitz said that "it never worked; either hopeless deadlocks followed or the men divided their domain and lived peacefully." (Seitz, "Portrait of an Editor," *Atlantic Monthly*, p. 296.) Walt McDougall was even more severe, terming the plan "as unproductive as it was mean and clumsy. It produced in time a reign of suspicion and hatred, a maelstrom of office politics that drove at least two editors to drink, one to suicide and another into banking." He went further, and cited a personal example to show that Pulitzer purposely tried to foster antagonisms between the staff. Over the years Arthur Brisbane and McDougall had developed a dislike for each other which at times brought them close to physical combat. The publisher did his best to encourage the feud, and in the simplest possible way. "Whenever Brisbane wrote letters to J. P. aspersing my usefulness to the paper," McDougall

— 19 —

And yet even this stern critic admitted that the result was some-how exhilarating. He concluded the catalogue of despair by noting that the atmosphere "was immense, just the same—terrific."

John B. McGuffin came from St. Louis at the same time as Cockerill to take charge of the *World's* business department, a position he held until his death a few years later. Although con-temporaries rated him as one of the most competent men in his field, accident more than reputation determined that he would not undergo the same competitive trial as Cockerill. In May of 1884, William Henry, who had served Bennett as Business Manager of the *New York Herald* for sixteen years, accepted an invitation to handle advertising for the *World*. His acquisition at that juncture represented a boon for Pulitzer, since Henry's ex-tensive acquaintance among New York merchants meant that he could bring with him a sizable number of accounts. Within a year, the two men had a falling-out which, to Pulitzer's discredit, became public gossip. An announcement appeared just below the masthead of the *World* on Friday, February 20th, 1885, and for several days thereafter, that "Mr. William Henry is not author-ized to make contracts for the *World*."[36] Although a certain amount of confusion surrounds the episode, its beginnings prob-ably go back several weeks. Pulitzer had been infuriated the previous December to learn of a gentleman's agreement con-cluded between Henry and James A. Hearn & Son, a famous department store on 14th Street, giving that establishment a sub-stantial reduction on advertising rates. He immediately repudi-ated the agreement in a sharply worded letter to Hearn.

> As Mr. Henry has probably told you verbally, the understanding or conversation, which you are pleased to call a contract, between him and a representative of your firm was wholly unknown to me, totally un-authorized by me, and absolutely unprecedented in the history of any paper that I ever had anything to do with. Mr. Henry had no more right or authority to

---

wrote, "the Chief would promptly send them on to me, thus keeping my hot blood in circulation." McDougall, "Old Days on *The World*," *The American Mercury*, p. 24.

[36] *World*, February 20, 1885, p. 4.

— 20 —

enter into an understanding of that character than he has to commit forgery or burglary. I consider it as the greatest offense ever committed by an employee of mine.

It will probably cost him his place in addition to the cost of advertising charged to him personally.[37]

Two considerations influenced this highly irate response. In part, Pulitzer's ethical sense must have been offended, for the publisher who made a career of castigating railroad owners and monopolists who trafficked in rebates could hardly countenance similar policy in his own shop. Florence White, a Managing Editor of the *St. Louis Post-Dispatch* and later the *New York World*, points out that when an instance of favoritism was discovered in St. Louis, Pulitzer ordered an immediate audit of the books, and had checks to the amount of several thousand dollars mailed to the advertisers who had been injured.[38] His fear that other clients might get wind of the arrangement, and demand similar favors, must also have been a factor. At least Hearn tried to reassure the publisher on this point by writing back to say that Henry had stressed that he must be discreet, and promising that he would be.[39]

The incident provides a convincing reason for the falling-out between Pulitzer and Henry, but it does not explain why two months passed before the notice appeared under the masthead of the *World*. *The Journalist*'s interpretation, which followed within a week of the announcement, adds a further, and perhaps final, dimension to the story. It reported that Pulitzer decided to

[37] Letter dated December 26, 1884. *Pulitzer Papers*, Columbia University Libraries.

[38] Florence D. White, as told to Charles Edmundson, "Pulitzer Vignette by an Associate," Special Supplement Commemorating the 100th Anniversary of Joseph Pulitzer, *St. Louis Post-Dispatch*, April 6, 1947, p. 5.

[39] *Pulitzer Papers*, Columbia University Libraries. Of course, as a pragmatic businessman, Pulitzer tailored his advertising rates to what the traffic would bear, and as we see in the rivalry with Bennett, did not hesitate to undercut the opposition. "We must walk before we can run, . . ." he once remarked to his business manager. "The start is more important and difficult than the following." Pulitzer did not object to low rates, but to discriminatory rates. Perhaps a personality quirk also influenced the publisher's reaction. According to Walt McDougall, he was "oppressed by a dread of dishonesty among his employees, and suspected or detected commissions taken by his buying agents drove him to extremes of passionate indignation." McDougall, "Old Days on *The World*," *American Mercury*, IV, 23.

replace Henry because he felt that the advertising superintendent had not sufficiently considered the *World*'s rising circulation in negotiating recent contracts.[40] This explanation is hardly satisfying, since the paper was purposely charging low rates to win advertisers from the *Herald*, and since it takes no account of the Hearn episode. The article also alleged, however, that Pulitzer lost interest in Henry as it became clear that he had exhausted the list of old customers that he could steer to the *World*. When that happened, his $5,000 salary became a liability. According to *The Journalist*, Henry responded to the suggestion that he accept another position on the paper by pointing out that he had a signed agreement which guaranteed his tenure so long as he properly attended to the duties of the office. The announcement brought their disagreement to public view, and although Pulitzer withdrew it a few days later, Henry never again enjoyed his employer's confidence.

Probably the best known of the *World* staffmen was Andrew C. Wheeler, who wrote dramatic criticism under the nom de plume, Nym Crinkle. Along with Sporting Editor H. G. Crickmore, he was the only member of the old *World* to survive the change of regime, and at a salary variously estimated from $50 to $80 weekly, as opposed to the norm of $20 to $25, was one of the best paid of Pulitzer's employees. Few contemporaries denied his preeminence among critics of the theatre. "Wheeler is undoubtedly the ablest man writing criticisms for the more important New York dailies," *The Journalist* declared in 1884. "He has a flow of unique language which is extremely entertaining, and he possesses a power of analysis which is quite unusual."[41] On other occasions *The Journalist* praised Wheeler as "the ablest analytic critic of the drama in America. A man of varied gifts, brilliant aspirations and ingenious mind."[42] He "has certainly attained eminence in his particular line."[43]

---

[40] *The Journalist*, March 7, 1885, p. 1. In evaluating the validity of the account, it is worth remembering that Richardson and Byrnes had already sold out their interest in the magazine, and that far from carrying on a vendetta against Pulitzer, the new management was generally sympathetic.

[41] *The Journalist*, May 24, 1884, p. 1.

[42] *The Journalist*, May 9, 1885, p. 5.

[43] *The Journalist*, January 23, 1886, p. 4.

His presence in the World Building was not an unmixed blessing, however, for with a facile pen went an even more facile set of ethics. The same periodical which saw so much to commend admitted that "his reputation for impartiality has always fallen far below his conceded merit as a man of letters. . . . A. C. Wheeler has a mind of crystal on a backbone of gelatine."[44] Although the critic fell in and out of scrapes, notably one in 1886 when he allegedly tried to pressure Belle Urquhart into paying him 25 percent of her salary in return for favorable notices, his admitted talent outweighed a shady reputation, and he lent invaluable tone to a newspaper long on enterprise but still short on stylistic grace.[45]

Other *World* men, anonymous to the public, enjoyed the highest reputation within their profession. John W. McDonnell, still a young man in the 1880s, exploited his contacts among politicians high and low to become Pulitzer's personal advisor on party matters. According to *The Journalist*, "there isn't a politician from the Battery to the Bronx River of high or low degree that Johnny is not acquainted with. . . . He is a terse writer and can solve a political problem as fast as men who have grown grey in the business. There is one comfort this bright young journalist has, viz.: that he need not, unless he feels like it, run much after the news of the day, for he has hundreds of followers who keep him posted as faithfully as a ticker announces the transactions on Wall Street."[46] McDonnell's rise was rapid. Starting as a

[44] *The Journalist*, May 9, 1885, p. 5.

[45] See *The Journalist*, October 11, 1884, p. 6, for an early attack on Wheeler's ethics, in which he was accused of forming a partnership with Jerome Eddy, the press agent, to see that the right people got favorable notices at a price. The periodical's comment on the Urquhart affair elicited a vigorous reply from Cockerill. "So far as our employees are concerned, . . ." he said, "if you, or anybody else, will produce any tangible evidence of any dishonesty practiced upon the public, or any individual, through the columns of the *New York World*, then I will discharge such person immediately, regardless of his professional work. But I am not supposed to be governed either by rumor or assertion. Take, for instance, the case of Wheeler. You positively refuse to furnish any evidence against him, on the ground that your open statement, warning him of the danger he was drifting to, was punishment enough for him, and that there is no disposition to do him any harm. What can I do but wait for evidence?" *The Journalist*, January 30, 1886, p. 5. Without impugning Cockerill's sincerity, it is difficult to believe that he would have been equally unwilling to act upon rumors surrounding a lesser member of the staff.

[46] *The Journalist*, March 14, 1885, p. 2.

— 23 —

correspondent at City Hall, he traveled to Chicago to report both major party conventions, covered state affairs in Albany until Cleveland's inauguration, and then followed the Governor to Washington to serve as second in command of the *World* bureau under Theron C. Crawford.

Crawford had the reputation on Park Row of being one of the more polished practitioners of his craft. His expert management of the *World* force at the Republican convention in June of 1884 earned him accolades from *The Journalist*.[47]

> Crawford is a man of exceedingly great ability. He seems to know everybody in political circles, and he is about the coolest headed man in the newspaper crowd. He is quick to seize the pith of any proposition, and he knows the value of news down to a dot. . . . He has systematized the work in his bureau here admirably. He keeps young McDonnell busy covering the delegates who are centered at the Grand Pacific, and employs Lang in doing the same service at the Palmer House. Meanwhile he moves about among the more prominent men himself, and after writing his own dispatch, edits the copy of the two younger men. In that way the *World* does not repeat itself, and pays for the transport of no useless matter.[48]

The list could go on. David Sutton, the City Editor, managed a stable of veteran reporters and bright newcomers. They included fat and jolly Jacques Dreyfus, who had spent years developing his contacts on the police court beat. "He has been around different courts for quite a while," the trade periodical pointed out, "which gives him many advantages, for he knows nearly all the headquarters detectives, and very frequently through this intimacy gets a rattling good story in advance."[49] Two more oldtimers, Douglas Levine and Phillip Ripley, wrote most of the famous editorials on page four, while Charles Southerland and G. B. Harvey managed the *World*'s Brooklyn and Jersey City editions, respectively. Contemporaries described S. S. Pratt as small and unaggressive, but his habit of "narrowly investigating the smal-

---

[47] Pulitzer personally managed the *World* staff at the Democratic convention a couple of weeks later in Chicago.
[48] *The Journalist*, June 14, 1884, p. 2.
[49] *The Journalist*, April 25, 1885, p. 1.

lest point" made him a reliable source of news from the financial district.[50] H. G. Crickmore, himself an authority on horse racing, headed a particularly strong array of sportswriters, including Peter J. Donohue, one of the most respected men in the field. The bright newcomers on the staff included Frederick A. Duneka, later to serve as the *World's* correspondent in London, Fred Shipman, whose father also worked on the paper, Yorriel Goddard and R. L. Hanson, both hired away from the *Herald*, and Nicholas Biddle.

The news gatherers were supported by an equally prominent crew of feature writers and illustrators. M. M. Tyner handled literary reviews, and a young graduate of Princeton, James B. Townsend, delivered the *World's* judgments on art. "He has a wide artistic acquaintance, is newsy, understands his subject, and is sensational enough to please his present employers, . . ." *The Journalist* said of Townsend. "His criticisms are valued . . . by the artists; whether from the influence the *World* now wields or their own merits, it is hard to say."[51] The illustrations, of which there will be much to say later, were the work of Walt McDougall and Valerian Gribayedoff.

It was an expert staff, and as its reputation grew, became always better. *The Journalist* commented in 1885 that "it is approaching something of a craze now in the newspaper circles of the metropolis to get on the *World*.

> Every few days one or another of those who had been regarded as fixtures on the other great dailies is heard of as filling a corner in the busy workshop where the all-embracing, ever-booming *World* is sent out with a rattle and a rush each morning. The staff now is one of the largest and strongest in the country, and in many of its members possesses the best attainable talent.[52]

Pulitzer wanted the finest journalists in America, and he was willing to pay to get them. "I employ the best available talent," his Managing Editor remarked to an interviewer, "and make, of course, the best bargain I can, usually paying, however, the

---

[50] *The Journalist*, March 28, 1885, p. 1.
[51] *The Journalist*, September 12, 1885, p. 6.
[52] *The Journalist*, November 14, 1885, p. 1.

— 25 —

highest prices paid anywhere for similar service."[53] Even those who preferred to work free-lance, selling stories to the highest bidder, soon discovered that the *World* offered their most likely market.

> The prices paid equal those of any paper in New York. There is no arbitrary price per column. For an exclusive piece of important news which is wanted exclusively the *World* is probably the best of all the city newspapers to go to now. The *Herald* plan is to refuse all such items and hold the man responsible in whose department it is. This is why the *Herald* is so often beaten.[54]

Striving for excellence, "with always room for one who can bring good news grist to its greedy maw," the *World* did as much as any newspaper to encourage young men of promise seeking to make their way in journalism.[55] Pulitzer received a letter in December of 1884 from one such youngster, asking how to go about getting his first position. His reply appeared on the editorial page.

> So far as we know, the *World* is the only newspaper in New York that holds out encouragement to developing young men. We are always on the lookout for bright reporters, correspondents, editors, poets, artists, &c. We are always willing to give an ambitious young man a trial. You can send us a bit of your manuscript, Mr. O'Brien, and if you are capable of evolving bright thoughts, or if your work bears the slightest trace of genius, we want you. We are thinking of opening a Lyceum or school for the development of reporters, but our plans are not yet perfected.[56]

Of course the last sentence was prophetic, and says something about Pulitzer's philosophy. The man who endowed the Columbia School of Journalism, and who later established a separate fund for prizes bearing his name to be awarded annually in various categories of newsgathering, regarded journalism as a profession, demanding all the preparation, and deserving all the

[53] *The Journalist*, January 30, 1886, p. 5.
[54] *The Journalist*, June 28, 1884, p. 2.
[55] The passage is from *The Journalist*, November 14, 1885, p. 2.
[56] *World*, December 7, 1884, p. 4.

respect, of other professions.[57] He sought out and hired the best men not simply because they would benefit the *World*, but because they brought honor to their calling. In later years such men included Arthur Brisbane, Frank Irving Cobb and Herbert Bayard Swope as editors; David Graham Phillips, Claude Bowers, Charles Michelson, Walter Lippmann, Heywood Broun, Laurence Stallings, Maxwell Anderson, Franklin P. Adams, John Heaton, Allan Nevins, and James Cain as reporters and editorial associates; James Gibbon Huneker, Deems Taylor, and Alexander Woollcott as music and drama critics; and William Nye and Irvin S. Cobb writing humor. The list makes its own point.

Despite all that has been said about Pulitzer's drive, the new *World* did not radically depart from the old in makeup and typography. It remained for several years an eight-page daily, each page originally divided into six columns of the standard 13½ ems pica width. The headlines were set in Roman condensed capitals, somewhat smaller and lighter than those used previously, with two hanging indentations under the display heads. The paper put out larger Sunday editions after the change in ownership, and went from six columns per page to seven during the week, but its appearance remained about the same.

The headlines offer perhaps the best example of the *World*'s conservative typography during most of the 1880s. Rather than using streamer heads running across several columns to report items of special interest, the editors simply added several more indented subheads to the single column display headline at the top.[58] Thus, when the *World* issued an Extra in March 1884 to report a riot in Cincinnati, the accumulated headlines occupied a good part of column one.[59]

[57] William Inglis recounts an anecdote that illustrates Pulitzer's thoughts about a career in journalism. The publisher asked a young man on his staff how he had developed his powerful arm muscles, and was told that they were the result of daily exercise. He exercised, the young man continued, to maintain his good health, which he considered a valuable asset in his business. " 'In your profession,' J. P. corrected. 'Don't think I am criticizing, my dear boy. I am not critical, but journalism is a profession—the profession.' " William Inglis, "An Intimate View of Joseph Pulitzer," *Harper's Weekly*, LV (November 11, 1911), 7.

[58] The first double column head appeared in the *World* in 1889.

[59] *World*, March 30, 1884, p. 1.

A NIGHT OF TERROR.

CINCINNATI IN THE HANDS
OF A MOB.

THE BATTLE RENEWED.

ARMED WITH DYNAMITE THE MOB RETURNS
AND FIRES THE COURT HOUSE.

BERNER RE-ARRESTED.

THE MILITIA AGAIN FIRE ON THE
MADDENED RIOTERS.

BLOODY MIDNIGHT WORK.

ARMORY HALL ON FIRE - COL. HUNT'S HOTEL
THREATENED - A REIGN OF TERROR.

The effect did not strikingly contrast with that of other papers in the morning field.

To leave it at that, however, is to underestimate the considerable technical skills Pulitzer called upon in editing his paper. In order to create new journalism out of the old he first had to be accomplished in the fundamentals of newspaper work: makeup, headlining, news gathering. The lessons he learned in St. Louis were indispensable for leading a revolution in New York City.

Of course Pulitzer made changes in the *World*'s appearance, and they were almost always for the better. On his very first day in the office he altered the masthead, which read "THE NEW YORK WORLD," to what it had been originally, "THE WORLD," with a vignette of two globes, surmounted by a hand-printing press from which rays of light issued, between the words.[60] He also consigned to the hellbox Hurlbert's pet "Five Minutes With the News of the Day," which took up half of column one.

His most enduring innovation, one which other papers borrowed and still retain, came a few weeks later. He filled the blank space created at the top of the page by the shorter masthead with circular, and later, square ears.[61] Although they are

[60] The original masthead also included the slogan, "Its field, The World."
[61] The first edition with ears appeared on Sunday, June 10, 1883. They came and went for the next two weeks, but returned for good on June 25. The switch from round to square ears occurred on August 16, 1883.

typically used now for capsule weather reports and the like (or in the *New York Times'* case, for "All the News That's Fit to Print"), Pulitzer conceived them as ideally situated for self-advertisement. "Only 8-page Newspaper in the United States sold for 2 cents," the original caption read, later going to such slogans (which themselves say a good deal about the *World*'s image of itself) as "Spicy, Pithy, Pictorial," "Bright, Newsy, and Entertaining," "Good Stories, Bright Sketches, Fresh Gossip." Still later, with the triumph of illustration, the ears became places for humorous little cartoons depicting the *World*'s rising circulation, or its effectiveness as an advertising medium.[62]

Pulitzer demonstrated his newspaper genius still more clearly with his radical concept of the proper slot for a lead story. Editors had traditionally run their major stories in the first column on page one, and their second leads in the last column, on the logical assumption that the eyes of the reader went from left to right. The owner of the *World* suspected, however, that the opposite applied when people glanced quickly at a newspaper; he decided to experiment by reversing the positions for lead story and second lead. The description of the ceremonies opening the Brooklyn Bridge, a story which the *World* had heralded for the previous two weeks, appeared in the last column on page one, while the first column carried a routine item off the wires on the Czar's forthcoming coronation.[63] Pulitzer did not commit himself to the experiment all at once, but over the months a large share of the *World*'s major reports appeared in what the modern press now recognizes as the lead story slot.

His effort to catch the eye of the reader was also responsible for the first use of linecut illustration. "They call me the father of illustrated journalism," he remarked to a visiting group of newspapermen.

> What folly! I never thought of any such thing. I had a small paper which had been dead for years, and I was trying in every way I could think of to build up its circulation. I wanted to put into each issue something that would arouse curiosity and make people want to buy the paper.

[62] The first cartoons appeared on Saturday, February 14, 1885.
[63] *World*, May 25, 1883.

What could I use for bait? A picture, of course. . . .
On page one, in a position that would make the
World stand out as the paper lay folded on the newsstand. . . . There was a talented Russian artist in New
York with a real genius for making portraits—Valerian Gribayedoff. I sent for him. Could he, with a
photograph for model, draw a portrait so that it
could be printed in the *World*?

He could. Next day and every day thereafter, we
showed in the upper right-hand section of our first
page the picture of a statesman, a blushing bride, a
fugitive absconder, or a murderer on occasion—whoever was most prominent in the day's doings. Circulation grew by the thousands.[64]

The publisher anticipated modern practice not only by using
pictures, but by running them on the top half of the page so that
they would be visible to passersby as the newspaper lay folded
over on the newsstand. He was a modern in many respects, not
least in recognizing that packaging helps to sell a product.

Pulitzer also had decided notions on how a paper should be
edited. His first principle he shared with all other good journalists. "You do not know," he told his secretary, "what it costs me
to try and keep the *World* up to a high standard of accuracy—
the money, the time, the thought, the praise, the blame, the
constant watchfulness. . . ."

It is not enough to refrain from publishing fake news,
it is not enough to take ordinary care to avoid the
mistakes which arise from the ignorance, the careless-
ness, the stupidity of one or more of the many men
who handle the news before it gets into print; you
have got to do much more than that; you have got to

[64] Quoted in Barrett, *Joseph Pulitzer*, pp. 81-82. William Inglis reports the
same conversation in "An Intimate View of Joseph Pulitzer," *Harper's Weekly*,
p. 7, although the words he puts in the publisher's mouth are somewhat different. In both versions Pulitzer derided the notion that he saw the potentials
of illustrated journalism at the very outset. What he did not mention, however,
is that once he stumbled across the technique, he quickly mastered its possibilities and uses. Walt McDougall put him among the few editorial writers
who could think pictorially. Looking back on a career of illustrating for newspapers and magazines, he noted that "it is very remarkable how rarely in all
those years was a really serviceable cartoon suggested to me by any editor
save Pulitzer or Cockerill." Walt McDougall, "Pictures in the Papers," *The
American Mercury*, VI (September 1925), 71.

make everyone connected with the paper—your editors, your reporters, your correspondents, your re-write men, your proof-readers—believe that accuracy is to a newspaper what virtue is to a woman.

When you go to New York ask any of the men in the dome to show you my instructions to them, my letters written from day to day, my cables; and you will see that accuracy, accuracy, accuracy, is the first, the most urgent, the most constant demand I have made on them.[65]

Theodore Dreiser touched on this consuming passion for accuracy in his account of how he first secured a position on the newspaper. After spending days trying to work up courage, he finally brushed past the guards in the lobby of the World Building and entered the main city room to ask for a job. The pursuing horde had almost overtaken him when a young man, whose name he later learned was Arthur Brisbane, came forward and, on hearing of the situation, offered to speak on his behalf to the city editor. Dreiser took the opportunity, as he waited nervously for an answer, to survey his surroundings. He found himself in a large room, fully fifty feet wide and a hundred deep, crammed from front to rear with desks and writing tables. The only decoration in it, testifying to Pulitzer's obsession, were cards pasted on the walls at regular intervals exhorting the staff to: "Accuracy, Accuracy, Accuracy! Who? What? Where? When? How? The Facts—The Color—The Facts!"[66]

Barely less important than getting the facts right was the constant effort to see that every edition of the *World* contained a unique blend of colorful reporting and crusading zeal. Pulitzer's

---

[65] Quoted in Ireland, *Joseph Pulitzer*, p. 110. Ireland says of Pulitzer's speech, "I give it in considerable detail, because it was the longest speech he ever addressed to me, because he subsequently made me write it out from memory and then read it to him, and because it was one of the few occasions during my intercourse with him on which I was persuaded beyond a doubt that he spoke with perfect frankness, without allowing his words to be influenced by outside consideration." (p. 113)

[66] Dreiser, *Book About Myself*, pp. 465-67. The same moral was repeated insistently in the memoranda which descended upon the *World* office after 1890. On January 5, 1900, for example, he had this to say: "The story 'How Standard Oil Manages a Bank' is exaggerated, sensational, & objectionable because inaccurate in one single point, although excellent otherwise. . . . Accuracy! Accuracy!! Accuracy!!!" *Pulitzer Papers*, Library of Congress.

letters to the *World* office during the years of his blindness, when he roamed the globe seeking repose, suggest how relentlessly he stressed the formula. "Concentrate your brain upon these objectives," he wrote on July 30, 1910, to Charles M. Lincoln, his Managing Editor:

> 1st. What is original, distinctive, dramatic, romantic, thrilling, unique, curious, quaint, humorous, odd, apt to be talked about, without shocking good taste or lowering the general tone, good tone, and above all without impairing the confidence of the people in the truth of the stories or the character of the paper for reliability and scrupulous cleanness.
>
> 2nd. What is the one distinctive feature, fight, crusade, public service or big exclusive? No paper can be great, in my opinion, if it depends simply upon the hand-to-mouth idea, news coming in anyhow. One big distinctive feature every day at least. One striking feature each issue should contain, prepared before, not left to chance.
>
> 3rd. Generally speaking, always remember the difference between a paper made for the million, for the masses, and a paper made for the classes. In using the word masses I do not exclude anybody. I should make a paper that the judges of the Supreme Court of the United States would read with enjoyment, everybody, but I would not make a paper that only the judges of the Supreme Court and their class can read.[67]

None of his editors shared Pulitzer's sure touch for news value. A typical letter, on October 14, 1910, shows him rebuking Lincoln for mishandling a story with obvious dramatic impact.

> Apropos of the destruction by explosion of the *Los Angeles Times*, what is the matter with twenty people killed? The story is put on the thirteenth page of the Main News section. I wonder it was not put on the eighty-seventh page. Has there been any story like this for years? Did it not happen on Saturday morn-

[67] Quoted in Seitz, *Joseph Pulitzer*, pp. 416-17. See also his memorandum to the editors on November 28, 1905: "I want the news, gentlemen, to balance, counteract and antidote. If I make a deuce of a fight on the editorial page . . . I do not want the news columns to go off also." *Pulitzer Papers*, Library of Congress.

ing? That would be four o'clock New York time. Kindly explain. It was worth front page position, more than that it was a dreadful story. The P-D printed it Saturday afternoon and a hundred times better. Whose fault? Whose judgment?[68]

Successful application of the formula involved much more than recognizing a newsworthy item when it fell into the editor's lap. The greater challenge was to go out and find the news, and then to write it up interestingly.

Pulitzer had decided opinions about interviewing, that most obvious way of manufacturing news.[69] He urged his reporters to

[68] Quoted in Seitz, *Joseph Pulitzer*, pp. 418-19. See also the memorandum written on September 16, 1899, to Bradford Merrill, one of his editors, chastizing him for failing to judge the news value of another major story. "In regard to the Vanderbilt death: If the death of the richest man in America is worth only a single column head, there was not an item in the paper of that day worth more than an agate paragraph." (*Pulitzer Papers*, Library of Congress.) Pulitzer's interest in the paper never flagged, and the restlessness he felt at not being on hand to manage it himself is apparent in hundreds of the memoranda he addressed to the editors. His already taut nerves could not have been soothed by the realization that nobody could manage the *World* as capably as he. Often the communications sounded a note of despair, as this one written on March 26, 1899: "Apros pos Sunday page. Amazing stupidity. Page has been dreadful last week. One idea monotonous. Monopoly, trust, corruption. I forbid emphatically that sort of dulness [sic] and politics on the Sunday pages. I forbid more than one article on national politics any day. . . . I forbid editorials to exceed . . . [a] single column. This is the way you drive me to distraction." (*Pulitzer Papers*, Library of Congress.) Taken in their entirety. the messages comprise a wonderful primer in the art of journalism. Pulitzer would sometimes complain that "It is difficult to direct a game by telegraph, from a distance, without seeing the gamesters' faces or hearing their voices," but his criticisms were almost always sound, and sometimes brilliantly so. (The quoted passage is from a letter to Seitz, dated September 23, 1899, *Pulitzer Papers*, Library of Congress.) So great is the temptation to discover Pulitzer's ideas from his own writings that a note of caution must be introduced. As pointed out in the Preface, newspapers go through life cycles, and as they get older they tend to mature and become more moderate. The *World* of the 1890s, save for the unreal period of the Spanish-American War, had already toned down considerably from the bumptious *World* of the early 1880s. As a result, the Pulitzer memoranda, most of which date to the 1890s and early 1900s, are not entirely relevant to this essay. (None appeared more frequently, for example, than those delivering the "strongest injunction" against sensationalism.) They are useful when they corroborate what has been discovered in the *World* itself between 1883 and 1885, but in no other way. They deal, after all, with a different era, and in many senses, a different newspaper.

[69] The journalistic device of formal questions and answers was of fairly recent origin. Although it is difficult to set a precise date, many authorities take Horace Greeley's interview with Brigham Young at Salt Lake City in 1859 as the first of its kind. See, for instance, Alfred Lee, *Daily Newspaper in America*, p. 616.

be the most aggressive in the city, to go anywhere and ask anything if it meant getting a story. Indeed, as an editorial on January 25, 1884, made clear, the *World* rather took pride in its impertinence.

> The insolence and impertinence of the reporters for the *World*, when approaching such men as Jay Gould, fill the refined and esteemed heart of the delicate editor of the *Commercial Advertiser* with a sorrow that is almost as mellow as a paw-paw poultice. We have observed at times a disposition on the part of our reporters to be obtrusive and unrelenting in their efforts to acquire information, but the majority of them are young and inexperienced, and we cannot muster up the nerve to reprove them. Besides, this is a rushing, busy world, and we do not always have the time to look after the deportment of our reporters. We are thinking seriously, however, of having dress suits made for all of them.[70]

As a result it printed more than its share of exclusives. T. C. Crawford scored a particular triumph with an interview that appeared in the *World* on March 22, 1884, in which General Ulysses S. Grant announced his support of John Logan for the Republican Presidential nomination—causing a sensation in political circles, since no other newspaper shared it. It is "one of the most striking pieces of work recently seen in New York journalism," the trade periodical declared at the time.[71] The *World* could scarcely contain its glee. "The interesting interview with Gen. Grant published in yesterday's [edition] is a valuable contribution to the political history of the hour," an editorial proclaimed. "Gen. Grant, although peculiarly reticent and averse to interviews, speaks freely and deliberately to our reporter and

[70] *World*, January 25, 1884, p. 4. The *World's* attitude was more radical than it might seem. Public figures in the 1880s still assumed that they had a right to privacy, and the inquisitive newsman was regarded as not much different than anybody else who asked prying questions. *Puck* satirized the ubiquitous journalist in a page of cartoons in March 1877, and of course the zeal of the press in reporting President Cleveland's marriage and honeymoon in 1886 caused something of a national scandal. The President lashed out at "certain newspapers which violate every instinct of American manliness, and in ghoulish glee desecrate every sacred relation of private life." Quoted in Mott, *American Journalism*, p. 511.

[71] *The Journalist*, May 31, 1884, p. 2.

chooses the *World* as the medium through which to talk to the public."[72] Other beats included a conversation with Jay Gould in which the magnate diagnosed conditions on Wall Street;[73] with General Gordon's brother in London just prior to the fall of Khartoum, in which Sir Henry William Gordon expressed full confidence as to his brother's safety;[74] and with Queen Victoria in the churchyard at Crathie. "He is as audacious as the rest of his nation," the Queen was reported to have remarked as the *World* man approached her.[75]

Writing up the interview posed as many problems as getting it. Reporters were constantly urged to come away with personal details on their subjects. "Please impress on the men who write our interviews with prominent men," Pulitzer wrote to Lincoln, "the importance of giving a striking, vivid pen sketch of the subject: also a vivid picture of the domestic environment, his wife, his children, his animal pets, etc. Those are the things that will bring him more clearly home to the average reader than would his most imposing thoughts, purposes or statements."[76] Nor did it end there, for inexact description was hardly better than no description at all.

> Apropos of the sketch of Stimson in the paper of Sunday, October 2d, what is ordinary height? Would it not have been just as easy to have said "The man is five feet six, or seven, or eight?" Just ask any number of men, "What is ordinary height?" and see whether you can get two men to agree.
>
> Again, "A sizeable nose!" Who edited that copy? Who was the reporter? Who was the editor in charge? Is this the result of over twenty-seven years of teaching the importance of personal description on special occasions like this? I want to know every man who had anything to do with this description. . . . I really do hope that if I have any influence, this story of a "sizeable nose" and "ordinary height" will be pasted up as a warning example.[77]

[72] *World*, March 23, 1884, p. 12.

[73] *World*, January 17, 1884, p. 1. This was the interview which inspired the *Commercial Advertiser* to object to the aggressiveness of *World* reporters.

[74] *World*, April 11, 1884, p. 1.   [75] *World*, June 17, 1883, p. 1.

[76] Quoted in Seitz, *Pulitzer, Life and Letters*, p. 422.

[77] *Ibid.*, pp. 418-19. The extract is part of the same letter to Lincoln cited above.

In insisting upon the minutiae of description, a practice continued by the mass circulation news magazines of today, the publisher further justified his reputation as a founder of modern journalism.[78]

Ironically, for all this emphasis on putting out a lively publication, Pulitzer's greatest weakness, and thereby the greatest weakness of the *World*, lay in his inability to find a prose style to match his vitality and imagination. The newspaper tried to be earnest, and succeeded admirably, but earnestness is not necessarily the handmaiden of literary style. Pulitzer must have recognized as much, for he responded petulantly whenever the point came up. "It may interest Mr. Savage . . . to know," he replied to one critic, "that the *World* does not attribute a particle of its great success to its knowledge of grammar. Its syntax is entirely satisfactory to itself and a large number of American citizens who manage to get along tolerably well without pedantry, hyper-criticism or snobbish affectation of grammatical knowledge."[79] Charles Dana's jibes were no better received. He spoke of the *New York Sun* as "a professed purist . . . which for years has tried to bully New York newspapers and the public generally into the use of its own peculiar and uncertain English."[80]

The *World*'s heavy-handedness was most apparent in its ill-advised stabs at humor. Its delight with plays on words resulted in such gems as: "Cyrus H. McCormick invented a great reaper, but the Reaper whose name is Death cut him down, and now he is no mower."[81] Or: "A paper has been started in Memphis bearing the primitive title of Adam. Of course it is issued in the Eve-ning, and it is also Adam poor newspaper."[82]

---

[78] Pulitzer's blindness, dating to 1890, more than likely exaggerated his demand for exact description. See Ireland, *Joseph Pulitzer*, pp. 180-84, for an account of how he made his secretaries describe men and women to him down to the smallest detail. "Describing people to J. P. was by no means an easy task. It was no use saying that a man had a medium-sized nose, that he was of average height, and that his hair was rather dark. Everything had to be given in feet and inches and in definite colors. You had to exercise your utmost powers to describe the exact cast of the features, the peculiar texture and growth of the hair, the expression of the eyes, and every little trick of gait or gesture." (p. 181) William Inglis comments on the same trait in "An Intimate View of Joseph Pulitzer," p. 7.

[79] *World*, December 4, 1884, p. 4.

[80] *World*, January 22, 1885. p. 4.   [81] *World*, May 16, 1884, p. 4.

[82] *World*, March 11, 1885, p. 4. To be sure, styles of humor change, and the

Clumsy prose also influenced the writing of straight news stories. The concept of a lead sentence had not yet fully evolved, with the result that *World* men tended to plod manfully through all their material before coming to any essential point. In reporting a speech, for instance, the story would typically unravel in chronological order: the arrival of the audience (with a full list of who attended), the arrival of the guest, the speeches of introduction, and finally, the main speech of the evening. Only the headline conceded to the reader any clue as to whether the story merited his attention. The point is classically illustrated by the *World*'s treatment of what was certainly one of the most important stories during the first three years of Pulitzer's proprietorship. On October 30, 1884, after a long and bitter Presidential campaign in which the editor had staked his reputation, and which so far boded catastrophe because of the probable defection to Blaine of thousands of normally Democratic voters among New York's Irish community, providence interceded in the form of a pompous Protestant cleric with a penchant for alliteration. The Reverend Dr. Burchard's description of the Democratic Party in the presence of Blaine as one of "Rum, Romanism, and Rebellion," which the exhausted candidate allowed to pass without protest, gave the *World* an opportunity to win back at least enough of those disenchanted Irish voters. It alertly seized on the phrase, and emblazoned it prominently in the headline reporting the reception.

HIS BLACK WEDNESDAY

MR. BLAINE RECEIVES THE BENEFIT OF
CLERGY AT HIS HOTEL

Dr. Burchard's Reference to "Rum, Romanism
and Rebellion"

---

puns of the 1880s seem unfunny now partly because they are terribly dated. Certainly the lines Hurlbert inserted in the old *World* were no better: "A new trade paper named the Corset announces in its prospectus that it has come to stay." Or: "A Pittsburgh girl, who had refused a good looking telegraph repair man three times within six months, gave as a reason that he was too much of a wanderer. That he wandered from pole to pole, from one clime to another, and if he did come home he'd be insulate that the neighbors would be sure to talk." *World*, May 10, 1883, p. 4.

But the fact that this was a break of unparalleled importance, something to be emphasized in every issue until Election Day, did not have any bearing on how the story was reported. The *World* proceeded in its stately, gracious way, content to make its points all in good time. The report began:

> James G. Blaine arose about 9 o'clock yesterday morning. He breakfasted in company with Mrs. Blaine, Miss Margaret and Messrs. Emmons and Walker Blaine. Shortly after 10 o'clock a delegation of pastors, representing churches in New York, Brooklyn and other cities in the vicinity, gathered in Parlor F. Word was sent to Mr. Blaine that his presence was desired in the grand salon, and before Mr. Blaine made his appearance several hundred pastors of churches and divinity students were assembled. Mr. Blaine was attired in a plain black Prince Albert suit. Upon his left hand he wore a glove of brown kid. The mate was carried in his hand. He appeared exceedingly haggard, giving unmistakable evidence that the recent forty days of hippodroming had told severely upon his health. He was introduced to the clergy by the Rev. Dr. King, and the Rev. Dr. Burchard, the chairman of the delegation, delivered an address of welcome. He said: ". . .

What followed were several inches of copy summarizing Burchard's remarks, and then the pregnant phrase:

> We are Republicans, and don't propose to leave our party and identify with the party whose antecedents have been Rum, Romanism and Rebellion. We are loyal to our flag, we are loyal to you.

Immediately the account moved on, devoting two-thirds of a column to reporting Blaine's reply, and another one-third to listing the names of those present at the reception.[83]

[83] *World*, October 30, 1884, p. 2. In fairness, by the next decade Pulitzer realized the importance of a good lead paragraph, and tried to educate his staff to the same awareness. As he wrote to one of the editors on September 16, 1899: "Every great story should be prefaced by a summary—please distinguish from an introduction—and when a story is jumped from the first to some other page, it is especially necessary to bring the climax—the explosion—to the front of the story, so it will not disappear from the first page entirely, as is now almost always done, and be lost somewhere on the inside." *Pulitzer Papers*, Library of Congress.

In part, this is just to say that the *World* followed a nineteenth-century style in reporting the news. The modern sense of news writing, where all the pertinent facts are found in the first sentence or paragraph of the story, is mainly a concession to the people who absorb what they can while being jostled and jarred in crowded commuter cars. Although that group had already come into being by the 1880s, the press had not yet adjusted to it. The conventions of a more relaxed age still ruled journalism, with the result that stories were written to entertain the reader, something like magazine articles today, rather than to be instant dispensers of news. And yet to leave it at that is to exonerate the *World* too easily. It did not require a cub reporter's obsession with the principle of the "five w's" to realize that Burchard's maladroitness had introduced an important new element into the campaign. The newspaper dissipated what it recognized in headline by burying the "Rum, Romanism and Rebellion" remark in a sea of grey type. Journalistic convention in the 1880s was not completely oblivious to the principle that the important news must be highlighted in the story, as even the *World* demonstrated the following week when it reported Cleveland's election in a lead sentence and used the rest of the column for details.

If the *World*'s weaknesses in the way of clumsy prose and chronological reporting affected its coverage of political or diplomatic events, in other areas the newspaper excelled. Its style was well suited for sentiment, and there are worse ways to proceed with a human interest story than chronologically when the object is to entertain. Pulitzer's newspaper came into its own when it dealt with ordinary people in trouble, and when the smartness of the cynical metropolitan reporter was no longer appropriate. Its effectiveness as an organ of popular journalism will be the theme of the following chapters.

A similar dichotomy between Pulitzer's faltering sense of language on the one hand, and his evident genius as a journalist on the other, comes out in many of the headlines which the newspaper ran. For instance, the *World* took excessive delight in alliteration. Headlines such as the following clogged its pages for months: BACHELOR BANG'S BRIDAL;[84] TERRIBLE TIME IN TROY;[85] JIM-JAMES IN THE JURY;[86] BEN BREWSTER'S BAD BABY;[87] FACT, FANCY, FUSS, FUN AND PHILOSOPHY FOR THE FAIR SEX;[88] MANGLED BY MONGRELS;[89] BOREAS ON A BIG BENDER.[90] The criticism must be qualified again, however, by the fact that alliteration in headlines was a convention of the time. Helen Ogden Mahin points out that the technique was first used prominently between 1866 and 1870 in that most respectable journal, the *New York Times*, and that it became something of a commonplace during the next two decades, often with unfortunate results.[91] She cites as an example the *Chicago Times'* use of BROOKLYN'S BAKE on December 7, 1876, to announce a fire in a Brooklyn theatre that claimed the lives of 350 persons.[92] Moreover, whatever his other weaknesses, Pulitzer had a genius for exciting public interest, a genius which the *World* headlines often reflected. He was not easily satisfied, complaining later in life to Don Seitz, his city editor at the time, that the "heads must have more attention if they are to strike the eye, to hold the attention."[93]

To achieve this end the *World* sometimes resorted to the dubious practice of puffing minor items out of proportion. In a full column account of the previous day's business in Congress,

[84] *World*, June 5, 1883, p. 1. The story reported the marriage of tragedian Frank Bang to Alice Singer, daughter of the inventor.

[85] *World*, June 12, 1883, p. 1. An account of a labor dispute in upstate New York.

[86] *World*, June 14, 1883, p. 1. A report about a juror in the Star Route case who had a sudden seizure in the courtroom, presumably because he was cut off from liquor.

[87] *World*, January 28, 1884, p. 1. Occupying lead space, this story seems to have been filler material on a dull day. It describes how the infant son of Attorney General Benjamin Brewster, who was taken along with the Presidential party when Arthur traveled to New York to dedicate the Brooklyn Bridge, misbehaved on the journey.

[88] *World*, March 9, 1884, p. 13. It was a column of miscellany for women.

[89] *World*, December 14, 1884, p. 9. It introduced an account of how half-starved dogs mauled a Brooklyn youngster.

[90] *World*, February 12, 1885, p. 3. Perhaps the most far-fetched of all, the headline announced a conventional story about bad weather in the New York City area the day before.

[91] Helen Ogden Mahin, *The Development and Significance of the Newspaper Headline* (Ann Arbor, 1924), p. 101.

[92] *Ibid.*, p. 101n.

[93] The conversation is quoted in Seitz, *Joseph Pulitzer*, p. 28.

filled with resolutions on postmen's holidays and debate on proposed new judgeships, an announcement appeared halfway down the column that "The House bill making appropriation for the support of the Military Academy, with an amendment providing that hereafter any cadet dismissed for hazing should not be eligible to reappointment, was taken up and passed." That is the full report, but the column received as its headline:

HAZERS CUT OFF FROM HOPE.

THE SENATE PLACES A FLAMING SWORD AT THE PORTALS OF WEST POINT.[94]

A much more typical technique was to ask a question in the headline, usually one the newspaper could not answer.

WHO MURDERED MRS. BUSH?[95]

WHICH ONE DOES SHE LOVE?[96]

DID HE MURDER HIS WIFE?[97]

The *World's* headlines crackled with excitement and indignation. To describe a political opponent we get:

BUTLER'S PUBLIC RECORD.

THE POLITICAL PECKSNIFF'S TEN YEARS IN CONGRESS.[98]

Let the story be a scandal, or a crime of violence, and the staff became almost inspired. Two brothers argue in a Newark boardinghouse, one shoots the other, and the grief-stricken mother clasps the dead son's body to her breast. The *World* eschewed such obvious headlines as YOUTH KILLS BROTHER, or A TALE OF CAIN AND ABEL, and instead seized the reader's attention with: BLOOD ON A MOTHER'S LIPS.[99] Patricians might decry such journalism as tasteless, but Pulitzer could point to a steadily rising circulation to prove its effectiveness.

In short, the man John Singer Sargent depicted as half-devil

[94] *World*, March 5, 1884, p. 2.
[95] *World*, May 6, 1884, p. 1.
[96] *World*, September 6, 1884, p. 7.
[97] *World*, September 11, 1884, p. 5.
[98] *World*, August 9, 1884, p. 1.
[99] *World*, December 24, 1883, p. 1.

and half-saint arrived in New York City already skilled in the basic arts of popular journalism. It would take him two years to bring his gifts to bear in rejuvenating the *World*, but when he was finished he had done more than breathe life into a newspaper about to die. His real significance is that he introduced revolutionary concepts to the profession, and by his success pointed the way for others to follow. We trace in the chapters to follow the first triumphs of one who acted as midwife to the modern newspaper.

CHAPTER TWO

SENSATIONALISM

There is a tendency in genteel circles to assume that a great newspaper is necessarily one which soberly, and at length, dissects every item of intelligence gleaned the previous day from the four corners of the earth. The assumption carries with it a corollary that the so-called "popular" newspapers, because they strive for circulation and try to entertain as much as inform, are not only inferior in intellectual content, but in skill and purpose as well. These assumptions help to explain why Joseph Pulitzer's reputation as the foremost purveyor of sensationalism is often misunderstood, and his contribution as a journalist underestimated.

In fact, to comment upon Pulitzer's successful use of sensationalism in the pages of the *New York World* is really to comment upon two kinds of achievement, each of them of considerable importance. Obviously, he was uniquely skilled in the various technical arts involved in gathering and disseminating the news. The challenges which must be met in putting out a successful popular newspaper are no less, and in some senses greater, than those posed by serious journalism. An editor of a serious paper has the advantage, after all, of knowing what his subject matter will be, and when inspiration fails, of knowing that exhaustive coverage of the news is generally an adequate substitute for intelligent coverage. Joseph Pulitzer was not so fortunate, because what he could not say well he had best not say at all. The following pages will discuss the high order of artistry involved in each day discovering and preparing the precise ingredients which would please the popular palate. It meant that Pulitzer had to have a "nose for news," recognizing the appropriate stories when they appeared, and, when they did not appear, creating them. It meant making fine judgments about the stories that had no place in a mass circulation journal, and not least important, knowing how to present the right ones, and how to embellish them so that their potential was not lost on the reader.

Pulitzer's success in these areas is noteworthy, but is not enough by itself to explain his reputation. Taste was as important to him as virtuosity, for however well edited his paper might be, if it offended public morality it could not hope to win the approval of the public. His second great achievement was that he entertained the public, and even titillated it, without crossing the invisible line that separates good taste from bad taste. He managed to discourse upon the subjects of universal interest—and in some cases they were interesting because they were provocative —while remaining true to the morality of the time. The proper measure of the magnitude of his feat is in the list of newspaper owners who hoped to emulate Pulitzer's success by emulating his methods, only to come to grief.

To be sure, historical circumstance played a part in creating the Pulitzer legend. Other men before him had made their fortunes by publishing cheap, sensational newspapers for the masses. The form goes back at least to September 3, 1833, when Benjamin H. Day founded the *New York Sun* as a one-cent daily of wide appeal for its flippant coverage of police court news. James Gordon Bennett entered the field on May 6, 1835, with the one-cent *New York Herald*, a saucy amalgam of sex, crime, scandal, and gossip. The respectable element in the city, including many of Bennett's competitors, tried to wage a moral war to drive him out of business, but every lapse of taste added to his following. By 1850 the *Herald* had built a circulation of 30,000, and straddled the New York newspaper world like a colossus.

Nor was Pulitzer the only editor to practice sensationalism during the years when he remade the *World* from a moribund sheet into the most widely discussed paper in the United States. Several of his contemporaries competed with him on his own terms. Bennett Junior had not so forgotten his father's example that he allowed the *Herald* to ignore stories of obvious human interest appeal, while Dana's *Sun* shuddered for every *World* story that escaped its attention.[1]

[1] Robert Park credited all of them with a role in the birth of modern journalism. "The men who may be said to have made the modern newspaper—James

Why, then, is sensationalism associated with the name of Joseph Pulitzer more than that of his predecessors? Part of the answer is that the *World* of 1898, using black headlines and jingoistic, irresponsible reporting to compete with Hearst's *Journal* for circulation, is confused with the *World* of 1883. To do so is to misunderstand what Pulitzer meant by sensationalism, and what he achieved by using it. The brief period when he played Hearst's game was an aberration, one which Pulitzer always regretted. As early as 1899 he scolded an editor for duplicating past mistakes by making too much of a bigamy case then in the news. The treatment, he complained, "distinctly tends to lower the tone of the paper and to revive the idea of sensationalism, the giving of the foremost place and extraordinary headlines to what is after all, a salacious story and not an important or serious matter. . . . Although the wisdom of placing such stories in the most important column is a question, there is no question about the four column headline being bad."[2]

There are better reasons for singling out the *World*'s use of sensationalism. Most important is the fact that Pulitzer arrived in

---

Gordon Bennett, Charles A. Dana, Joseph Pulitzer, and William Randolph Hearst—are the men who discovered the kind of paper that men and women would read and had the courage to publish it." Robert E. Park, "The Natural History of the Newspaper," reprinted in Robert E. Park, Ernest W. Burgess, and Roderick D. McKenzie, *The City* (Chicago, 1925), p. 80.

[2] Letter of December 5, 1899. *Pulitzer Papers*, Library of Congress. This is not meant to deny the considerable respect Pulitzer had for Hearst's newspaper genius. He addressed himself to that subject in a letter written to Don Seitz on December 23, 1897. "I personally think Geranium [the *World*'s code word for the *Morning Journal*] a wonderfully able and attractive and popular paper," he wrote, "perhaps the ablest in the one vital sense, of managing to be talked about; of attracting attention, of constantly furnishing something which will compel people wherever they meet, whether in the drawing room or in the poor house, elevated car or dinner table, to talk about something in that paper." (*Pulitzer Papers*, Library of Congress.) Even the code provides a clue, because Pulitzer often displayed a pixie-like sense of humor in choosing the symbols. He used a popular garden flower to designate the *Journal*, and called himself "Andes," which as Seitz waggishly noted, represented only the second highest altitude on the earth's surface. (Seitz, "Portrait of an Editor," p. 296.) On the other hand, the *Herald* was "Geologist" (hardly the word to suggest a lively, brisk newspaper), Theodore Roosevelt "Glutinous," and of course William Howard Taft "Rotund." The point is not that Pulitzer held Hearst and the *Journal* in low esteem—he could hardly afford to—but that the sort of sensationalism practiced by the *Journal* was not what he wished for his own paper.

New York City at a time when vast social changes offered opportunities previously unknown to a journalist intent on addressing a
mass audience. It was a time, for example, when immigrants
poured into the city by the tens of thousands annually, each one
potentially what he had not previously been: a regular purchaser
of a daily newspaper. For most of them the newspaper habit was
something to be learned, much as they had learned to speak
falteringly in a strange tongue and to satisfy their hunger with
strange foods. An article in *Russkoye Slovo*, a Russian-language
periodical, reported shortly after the turn of the century that of
312 subscribers polled, only 16 had regularly read newspapers in
Russia. Many times that number acquired the habit of buying
English-language newspapers in America on a more or less
regular basis.[3] The change came partly because of great pressure
on the newcomers to assimilate and conform, and partly because
even an imperfect system of universal education had the effect
of raising literacy throughout the United States. While one out
of five Americans in 1870 could not read or write his own language, that number had been reduced by half thirty years later.[4]
Illiteracy among white residents in New York State dropped
from 11.5 percent in 1870, to 9.4 in 1880, to 7.7 in 1890.[5]

But the problem is more complicated, since the literacy of the
immigrant was not the literacy of the established and native
gentry uptown. Many of the participants in the *Russkoye Slovo*
poll, for example, reported that they could barely read one English word in five, and that still they purchased English-language
dailies just to scan the headlines. The headlines "are easy to
understand, and you know all the news," explained one of those
who answered the questionnaire.[6] They needed a special sort of
journalism (as did the poor, semi-literate workingmen who

[3] Mark Villchur, article in *Russkoye Slovo* (June 10, 1919); quoted in
Robert E. Park, *The Immigrant Press and Its Control* (New York, 1922), pp.
7-9. Park remarked in another article that "how to bring the immigrant and
his descendants into the circle of newspaper readers has been one of the problems of modern journalism." Robert Park, "The Natural History of the Newspaper," *op.cit.*, p. 81.

[4] *Historical Statistics of the United States* (U.S. Government Printing Office,
Washington, D.C., 1957), Series H 407-11, p. 214.

[5] Archie E. Palmer, *The New York Public School* (New York, 1905), ap-
pendix.

[6] Quoted in Park, *The Immigrant Press*, p. 8.

shared their problems) before they could be introduced into the ranks of newspaper readers, and that need led to the rise of sensationalism. Papers like the *World*, aware of the uncertain literacy of the new readers, splashed abundant pictures and bold headlines across each page, and urged upon their reporters the virtues of simple vocabulary and uncomplicated sentence structure. Aware, too, that a very real class structure in America prevented immigrants from acquiring the sophistication and polish associated with cities, they concentrated on stories of time-less interest: sex, violence, crime, tragedy, farce. And aware, finally, of the special needs and prejudices of the newcomers, they carefully avoided what the untutored might consider in-tellectual "airs," and maintained—a point that applies to Hearst's *New York Journal* and Patterson's *New York Daily News* as much as to Pulitzer's *World*—at least a pretense of liberality.

Other aspects of the developing social and technological revo-lution contributed to the same result. Rapid transit (symbolic of a general heightening tempo of urban life) had a profound im-pact upon the profession by determining that men would read their papers while traveling to and fro in crowded, noisy cars, rather than in the comfort of their homes. Newspapers responded by printing shorter, livelier stories, and condensing the im-portant news into a lead paragraph so that it could be grasped instantly, without ploughing through columns of grey matter. They turned to blacker headlines, larger type, more pictures, less demanding subjects. Almost without exception (modern tabloids are only an extreme example), they reduced the size of the page to make the newspaper easier to handle in tight quarters. "We, as a people, read largely in the horse cars, the elevated railroads and the omnibuses," *The Journalist* declared in 1887 when the *Evening Post* joined the rest of the major dailies in New York City by abandoning its blanket format. "We do not want a paper which requires a whole conveyance in which to turn its pages."[7]

[7] *The Journalist*, November 5, 1887, p. 4. The same motivation explained an experiment on January 1, 1901, when Alfred Harmsworth, publisher of the tabloid *London Mirror*, brought out an edition of the *World* in half-sheet size. "I ask America for an impartial verdict on this 20th century newspaper," he declared, but Pulitzer was among those who failed to see its potential, and the

The new style of urban life encouraged the growth of a sensational press in still another respect. Men who purchased their papers each morning at a station newsstand were more likely than subscribers to be influenced by a front page either startling, or shocking, or bright. They had to be persuaded to buy six mornings in the week, and six mornings in the week the readers of a rival newspaper could be won away. Editors competed to catch the eyes of readers in the split second it took to make a decision. "The front page would probably never have evolved from the first page," Helen Hughes points out, "were it not for the fact that purchase by annual subscription was largely replaced by single sales made by newsboys on the street to passersby."[8] The change forced editors to regard themselves as something more than purveyors of news. Arthur Brisbane justified the banner headlines in the *New York Journal* by likening them to the displays department stores set up in their windows. "Perhaps headlines do take up too much space," he wrote some years later. "The display windows of the big stores take up too much space also. But in a busy nation the first necessity is to attract attention. The big store window, wasting space, and the big type, apparently wasting space, are necessary features of quick development."[9]

The rise of an entertainment industry in cities—from nickelodeons to vaudeville shows to professional sporting events—also played a part by forcing the press to compete for the time and money each family allocated for diversion. The result was sports pages in the 1880s, comic strips in the 1890s, and by the 1920s, crossword puzzles. Most obvious of all, sensationalism flourished

---

World reverted to standard size on January 2. Cited in Alfred M. Lee, *The Daily Newspaper in America* (New York, 1937), p. 274.

[8] Helen MacGill Hughes, *News and the Human Interest Story* (Chicago, 1940), p. 31. Pulitzer recognized the same wisdom when he instructed his staff to make sure that the paper contained every day an article or feature that would steal attention away from its rivals. "The *World*," he wrote in a memorandum dating probably to 1899 or 1900, "should print not only all the news worth printing, but should have, daily, some striking development or feature in the news line that will lift it away from its competitors and make it talked about. 'Did you see that in the *World*?' should be asked every day and something should be designed to cause this." *Pulitzer Papers*, Library of Congress.

[9] Quoted in John K. Winkler, *William Randolph Hearst: An American Phenomenon* (New York, 1928), p. 119.

in the 1880s because newspapers shared in the technological revolution affecting all branches of commerce and industry. It would be idle to speak of the influences behind illustrated journalism, for instance, if the facilities for illustration did not exist, just as the phrase "mass circulation daily" is meaningless without high-speed presses to turn out hundreds of thousands of copies of a newspaper within hours. The seeds of sensationalism are found as much in the new mechanical wonders of the late nineteenth century as in social movements: in such inventions as the telephone and typewriter; in press folders that could cut, paste, fold, count, and deliver twenty-four page papers at the speed they were printed; in the Hoe Company's web feed quadruple press, capable of printing 24,000 sixteen-page papers per hour; in Ottmar Mergenthaler's Linotype machine, which relieved printers of the costly and tedious process of setting type by hand; and not least, in improved techniques of illustration, from woodcuts to zincographs to halftone photo-engraving.

Joseph Pulitzer did not originate sensationalism, and he certainly was not responsible for the social and economic changes which enabled sensationalism to flourish in the 1880s and 1890s. But he played a crucial role in the history of American journalism simply by being present at the time their influence was felt, and responding quickly and imaginatively to the opportunities they offered. The *World*'s attempts to attract a wider audience, and its experiments with new editorial techniques, are significant precisely because they occurred at such a time, and met with such success, as to make it the first of the modern, mass circulation dailies.

This is not to suggest that the ultimate responses all came within the first two or three years of Pulitzer's ownership. It has been noted, for example, that neither streamer headlines nor lead-sentence story construction appeared in the *World* until the 1890s. History is not usually so tidy that a single date can be assigned to a complex social phenomenon. But the list of Pulitzer's innovations is impressive, and it measures his leadership in adapting journalism to the needs of a new age.

The second of his achievements follows directly from the first. No newspaper before had ever attained such a massive circulation, a feat all the more remarkable in light of its low initial base. On May 6, 1883, the last Sunday under the old ownership, the *New York World* sold 15,770 copies; two years later on Sunday, May 10,1885, it sold 153,213 copies.[10] A tenfold rise in circulation within two years had never been seen before. Other papers later borrowed Pulitzer's methods to match his record, but in doing so they were only disciples to the teacher.

Finally, Pulitzer used sensationalism to achieve something more than a cheap reputation. The splash on page one attracted readers, but the editorials on page four educated them, uplifted them, crusaded for them. Alleyne Ireland, Pulitzer's urbane private secretary, admitted as much when, in the course of criticizing the paper, he described his ideal as "a combination of the *World*'s editorial page with the *Evening Post*'s news and make-up."[11] Pulitzer himself believed, or so he maintained, that page four contributed as much to the *World*'s circulation as page one. "The *World* attributes [its] success," he wrote, "not only to its news and conceded ability but to its principles and convictions."[12]

[10] The figures given throughout for the *World*'s circulation are derived from the newspaper itself. This poses something of a problem, since daily papers commonly overstated their circulations, and since for at least half of the period under consideration the *World* did not accept unsold copies back from dealers. (For a long while, the *Sun* was the only New York newspaper that did.) I have decided to use the *World*'s figures, rather than those in *N.W. Ayer & Son's Annual*—which are somewhat lower—for two reasons. First, every figure cited was sworn to before a notary public by either Pulitzer, McGuffin, Henry, or some other *World* official; second, the *World*'s continued difficulties with its presses during the period that it did not accept back unsold copies meant that most dealers were supplied with less, rather than more, copies than they could handle. The *World*'s bitterest enemy, Leander Richardson, admitted that it had been handicapped by this problem. "The trouble is," he wrote, "that newsdealers coming down for the paper at the same time they get the other morning dailies, are obliged, in order to reach their stands in time to open for the early morning trade, to either go without any *Worlds* whatsoever, or to accept a short supply. The end of this naturally is that they soon sell out, and that not two-thirds of the inquiries for *Worlds* are satisfied." (*The Journalist*, May 24, 1884, p. 6.) It seems probable, in short, that the newspaper's own account of its growth provides a more accurate gauge than *Ayer's Annual*.

[11] Ireland, *Joseph Pulitzer* (New York, 1914), p. 109.

[12] *World*, December 7, 1883, p. 4. The publisher insisted upon having a crusade prominently featured in every issue of the paper. "It is Mr. Pulitzer's wish," one of the editors reported after an interview with him, "to have constantly on hand and waged vigorously a campaign, crusade or battle directed on proper lines; this is a fixed principle. Subjects of wide interest should be

What, then, did this controversial sensationalism consist of, and what techniques did Pulitzer use to raise the paper to unparalleled heights of popularity? A partial answer comes by contrasting the last edition of the old *World* with the first edition of the new. On May 10, 1883, Mr. Hurlbert devoted major attention to two stories. Since he reserved column one for his "Five Minutes With the News of the Day," we look to column two for the lead item, in this case a report that Mayor Edson had submitted to the Board of Aldermen a list of nominations for city positions. The story was headlined: NEW COMMISSIONS. Column six announced the winners in various categories in the dog show at Madison Square Garden (the names of the winners took up over 80 percent of the column), and reported in headlines the ELECTION OF AN EXECUTIVE COMMITTEE OF THE AMERICAN COCKER SPANIEL CLUB. The only other item of interest on the front page has survived as an example of maladroit journalism. Hurlbert's treatment of the forthcoming celebrations to dedicate the Brooklyn Bridge—a story Pulitzer was to make uniquely his own—demonstrates that determined dullness would have its way with almost any material. According to the lead paragraph:

> It is the intention of the Brooklyn Common Council to have a big celebration over the opening of the East River Bridge. Alderman Dimon, Chairman of the Committee of Arrangements, requests that communications may be sent to him by military, social, religious, benevolent, protective and other societies and all persons and firms willing to take part in the celebration. Various trades and business firms are expected to join in the parade.[13]

It is only appropriate that the report failed to mention the date of the celebrations, or the fact that President Arthur and his cabinet, as well as several Eastern Governors, were due to attend.

Although the new *World*'s first issue could hardly be more stodgy, few were prepared for the enormity of the change. Pulitzer seized on a fire in New Jersey, which took six lives and

---

taken always." Undated, unsigned memorandum, about 1900. *Pulitzer Papers*, Library of Congress.

[13] *World*, May 10, 1883, p. 1.

destroyed 100,000 barrels of crude oil, for his lead story in column one, headlining it THE DEADLY LIGHTNING.[14] For column three he resurrected an item which Hurlbert had previously buried on a back page with a stickful of type,[15] and dispatched a reporter to White Plains to describe the last hours of a condemned killer. The story amateurishly failed to mention what crime Angelo Cornetti had committed, but even the most jaded readers must have been enthralled by the account of his stubborn claim of innocence, his rattling of the cell door, his refusal to see a priest, and his demeanor during the reading of the death warrant.[16] Column four personalized the workings of high finance by reporting that James R. Keene had suffered a loss in selling to Jay Gould a painting by Rosa Bonheur, entitled "Cattle Going to a Fair."[17] The newspaper correctly deduced from the transaction that Keene was on the verge of bankruptcy. As a companion piece to the Cornetti story, Pulitzer devoted column five to a wire report on the execution in Pittsburgh of Ward McConkey, who paid the penalty for killing George McGuire in the aptly named Pennsylvania hamlet, "Dead Man's Hollow." The headline exploited the story with: WARD M'CONKEY HANGED. SHOUTING FROM UNDER THE BLACK CAP THAT HIS EXECUTIONERS ARE MURDERERS. To round out the page, column six carried a largely unsubstantiated report on rebel terrorism in Haiti, alleging that 400 persons had already been killed or wounded by the use of dynamite.

The emphasis on crime and tragedy was not in itself a unique way of attracting readers. The *World*'s triumph is that it did it so well, resurrecting buried items or ranging far from New York City to find the desired material. Pulitzer, like Day and Bennett before him, meant his front page to be startling and eye-

[14] Since newspapers had not yet devised the technique of jumping stories to back pages, the New Jersey report filled all of column one and about half of column two.

[15] A stickful consists of two and one-quarter inches of 8-point type, or a little less than 150 words.

[16] The oversight was corrected in the following day's account of his execution. Cornetti had slashed the throat of a fellow inmate while already in prison for beating his wife to death in a drunken brawl.

[17] According to the report, Keene purchased the painting for $24,000 and disposed of it for $16,000.

catching. He also had an instinctive sense of which stories would arouse public curiosity. The Cornetti report, for example, immediately became a conversation piece in New York City, his execution the next day a standard item for front page coverage, and in the *World*, a subject for editorial comment.[18]

Some items have such obvious human interest appeal that there is no credit in exploiting them. They are so obtrusive in their own right that even the most sober newspapers must give them prominent attention. General Gordon's death at Khartoum, after months of anxious concern on the part of the whole Western World, represented one such story.[19] It contained all the ingredients of high drama—bravery, treachery, suspense—played out against an exotic setting. The *World* inevitably milked the story for all it was worth, if only to compete with the rest of the metropolitan press. Its initial account of Gordon's death, on February 6, 1885, filled three entire columns on the front page, and two columns on the second page.[20] Not even Cleveland's election three months before inspired bolder or deeper headlines. On February 11, with the receipt of further information over the wires, the *World* duplicated its earlier effort, devoting three more complete columns on the front page to a description of Gordon's every move in the hours before he died.

Charles Delmonico's death under very different circumstances provides another example of a story with built-in appeal. The heir to the catering fortune had disappeared from home, and for days the press built suspense by speculating where he might be. When his frozen body was discovered in the ice and mud of a

[18] *World*, May 12, 1883, p. 4.

[19] It is an axiom of journalism that a story which takes several days, or weeks, to reach a climax is more exciting, and sells more newspapers, than one which can be reported in a single issue. Helen Hughes points out that not the least important aspect of the Lindbergh kidnapping story, a classic of sensationalism, was that the matter hung in the balance for seventy-two days. (Hughes, *News and the Human Interest Story*, p. 62.) Certainly Pulitzer appreciated the value of building suspense. He complained to his staff in an undated memorandum (probably 1899) that "the great lack both in the Sunday and Daily Editions is a continuing and great mystery, a great romance, or a great cumulative exposure, feature, crusade story of any sort deeper and deepening which can go on from day to day with sustained interest (not merely one day flies)." *Pulitzer Papers*, Library of Congress.

[20] The fall of Khartoum, and Gordon's death, actually occurred on January 27, but over a week passed before the Western world received the news.

railroad gully in Orange, New Jersey, evidently the final resting place after hours of wandering, every paper emblazoned the news across its front page. Again the story was a natural, not only because it involved a noted figure, but because death came after a period of suspense, and under mysterious circumstances.[21]

Such situations were rare, and because of their intrinsic interest, not a proper measure of sensationalism. The *World*'s strength lay in playing up material ignored by the other papers, or at best dismissed in a brief paragraph. It demanded a sure touch, for to puff up something trivial, and often not even local, could lead to a loss of both reputation and circulation (a newspaper must have one or the other) if the story failed to elicit interest.

The *World*'s instinct seldom failed. In January 1884, for instance, it spotted a minor incident that occurred in the Shenandoah Valley in Virginia and blew it up to lead story proportions. A thirty-eight-year-old woman announced that she had mistaken her sex all those years, and now—as a man—was engaged to be married.[22] The newspaper's exclusive account aroused such interest that it printed an elaborate follow-up on the second day. The article described Mr. John Calhoun (nee Elizabeth Rebecca) Payne's appearance in, and difficulties with, male attire, and carried the arch headline: HOW SHE GOT HER BOOTS ON.[23]

Another example of the *World*'s printing what the other papers missed, and transforming it into front page news, occurred some weeks later when one of Pulitzer's reporters got wind of an argument between two members of the exclusive Union Club. For all his dedication to the principle of workingmen's democracy, Pulitzer realized that the poor are eternally fascinated by the activities of the rich. An example of leisured gentlemen acting in ungentlemanly fashion offered rare possibilities for development. The incident was certainly insignificant—Mr. James Boggs

[21] *World*, January 15, 1884, p. 1. It might be noted that in the cases of both Gordon and Delmonico the *World* reversed usual procedure, as described in Chapter One, and printed the lead news on the righthand side of the page.

[22] *World*, January 26, 1884, p. 1.

[23] *World*, January 27, 1884, p. 5. One reason why the follow-up appeared on an inside page is that January 27 fell on a Sunday, a day when the *World* usually filled its inside pages with human interest material.

— 54 —

Livingston went up to Mr. Frederick Gebhardt and said: "You are a coward and a liar."—but the *World* kept it on the front page for days, until the other papers themselves relented. WILL THERE BE A DUEL? it asked in headline, and punctuated the question with line drawings of the principals going about their daily activities.[24] The duel never took place, but for two or three more days the hungry public had been satisfied.

When the newspaper ran short of news items for sensational treatment, it filled the void by conjuring up equivalent feature material. Its resourcefulness in this respect was most apparent in the Sunday editions. Over the months the articles that appeared on the Sabbath included:

1. An account of recent examples of human sacrifice among fanatical religious sects in the United States.[25]

2. A long treatise on weapons used to commit murder in recent years, including a nail, a coffin lid, a red-hot horseshoe, an umbrella, a matchbox, a window brush, and a tea kettle.[26]

3. A description of the careers of two Vienna cutthroats who had specialized in courting lonely women and then murdering them. It bore the headline: SATAN AMONG THE SERVANT GIRLS IN THE CAPITAL OF AUSTRIA.[27]

4. Another overseas item, with the self-explanatory headline: HOW MURDERERS ARE EXECUTED IN THE REALM OF FRANZ JOSEF.[28]

5. A description of life in the death house at Sing Sing, and of some of the criminals "who have crossed the bridge of sighs."[29]

6. A "thrilling narrative" from the past, of cannibalism at sea, in which shipwrecked British sailors cut the jugular vein of the weakest in their number, the cabin boy, and lived off his flesh.[30]

7. A seasonal item on Christmas in the State Penitentiary, describing "how some of the prominent inmates enjoyed the holiday."[31]

[24] See the *World*, March 27, 1884, p. 1; and March 29, 1884, p. 1, for examples of the newspaper's coverage of the story. The drawings and headline appeared in the latter issue.

[25] *World*, May 13, 1883, p. 9. [26] *World*, June 10, 1883, p. 10.

[27] *World*, April 13, 1884, p. 10. [28] *World*, May 11, 1884, p. 11.

[29] *World*, July 6, 1884, p. 12.

[30] *World*, September 28, 1884, p. 12.

[31] *World*, December 26, 1884, p. 5.

This ability to discover offbeat ways of publicizing gore was particularly important during the 1880s, as Sunday editions grew in size. Prior to that time, and to a certain extent after, moralists had bitterly resisted Sunday papers as a violation of the Sabbath. William Cullen Bryant's statement in the *Evening Post* in 1832, on hearing that one would begin publication in the city, was echoed by similar statements half a century later. "We should be well pleased," he wrote, "if the experiment were to end in showing the persons who have undertaken the matter that there is too much moral sense in our community to allow such a speculation proving profitable."[32] In 1866, the New York Sabbath Committee predicted what results would follow were the menace not soon contained:

> A Sunday paper, filled with secular news and advertisements, becomes a dangerous rival of the pulpit and the Sabbath school; unfits the mind for devotion; undermines the regard for Sunday as a day of sacred rest; is apt to lead, step by step, to more flagrant forms of Sabbath-breaking; swells the current of worldliness already so fearfully strong and debasing; helps to demoralize the public mind on important questions of duty, and encourages scepticism and unbelief.[33]

The hopes of those who would have the Sabbath kept free for worship and meditation ran afoul of deeper forces which could not be reversed. Industrialization brought men into factories and workshops for up to sixteen hours a day, six days a week, and made it all the more necessary for them to have the seventh day for recreation. Four terrible years of Civil War had accustomed newspapers to publishing special editions on Sundays, reporting the outcome of battles upon which the fate of the Union might depend. Most important, the hundreds of thousands of immigrants who arrived in New York City during the decades immediately preceding and following the Civil War did not share American tradition about the inviolability of the Sabbath. They, more than other groups, demanded diversion on the one day of

[32] Quoted in Alfred M. Lee, *Daily Newspaper in America*, pp. 379-80.
[33] A. M. Lee, p. 395.

rest, and they looked to the Sunday newspaper as an obvious agent to provide it.

The impact of these influences is easily measured. In 1842, about one New Yorker in twenty-six purchased a Sunday weekly or Bennett's *Sunday Herald*, as opposed to one in 6.5 who purchased a daily paper. Eight years later, after almost a decade of Irish immigration, one in 8.8 bought a newspaper on the Sabbath. By 1889, six years after Pulitzer introduced a new style of journalism to the city, and after three more decades of industrialism and immigration, the proportion had risen to one in 2.2. More people that year purchased newspapers on Sundays than during the week.[34]

The popularity of Sunday newspapers meant that they attracted advertising, and developed into the bulky packages of the modern era. Publishers welcomed the trend because it offered a new source of income for them, but they soon learned that it also confronted them with a new challenge. In order to maintain a parity between editorial and advertising copy, they either had to print more news each year, or when that became unrewarding, to pad the extra pages with feature articles that would appeal to the men and women who bought their papers.

Pulitzer's resourcefulness in this respect set him apart as much as anything else from the run of popular journalists. The Sunday *World's* growth from eight, to twelve, twenty-four, and finally forty-eight pages, seemed only to spur him on to greater inventiveness.[35] He used the Sunday edition as a laboratory to test ideas that finally proved to be applicable throughout the week. Sensationalism, illustration, sports, special features for women, all were prominently displayed, and the techniques for handling them refined, in the paper published on the one day of the week that men and women could read at their leisure.[36] Robert Park

[34] The figures are cited in A. M. Lee, p. 83.

[35] The *World's* Sunday edition on May 7, 1893, mushroomed to 100 pages in honor of the tenth anniversary of Pulitzer's ownership.

[36] Pulitzer's sense of what was suitable led him to address a warning editorial to a Cincinnati newspaper which proposed to adorn its Sunday edition with essays contributed by serious authors. "A Cincinnati newspaper," the editorial declared, "proposed to take what it erroneously calls an 'advance step in journalism' by publishing in its Sunday issue matter written by Agassiz, Tyndall, Huxley, Hugo, Gladstone, Whittier, Tennyson, Tupper and other great scien-

summed it up when he declared of the *World* that "it was in the Sunday [edition] that the methods of yellow journalism were first completely worked out."[37]

After deciding what stories should go into the paper, there still remained the problem of presenting them in an effective way. The first consideration was the type of words to be used. As a sensational journal, the *World* found much of its audience among men and women of little education and scant literacy. It could hope to inspire them with prose of literary merit or dramatic impact, but that was a secondary concern. Much more important, the language had to be clear and simple enough for ordinary people to understand. "The first object of any word in any article at any time must be perfect clarity," Pulitzer instructed his writers. ("I hate all rare, unusual, non-understandable words. Avoid the vanity of foreign words or phrases or unfamiliar terms. Editorials must be written for the people, not for the few." Simplicity was as important as clarity.) "What is the use of writing above the heads of readers?" the publisher asked. "Go over that testimony, analyze it, summarize it, condense it, so that a child can understand it. . . . Begin with the beginning."[38]

Of course there is no reason why simple writing cannot be colorful, absorbing, and effective in what it tries to accomplish. Chapter One touched on the weakness of the *World*'s prose, but made the point that those very weaknesses often were turned to advantage in handling sensational or human interest material.

---

tists, dramatists, philosophers, poets, statesmen and generals, living and dead, the whole to be presented, two pages at a time, in the . . . form characteristic of the *North American Review* and similar publications. . . . If it is intended to furnish 'serious' reading for Sunday, the scheme will be successful in limiting the circulation of the proposed Sunday issue to an extremely and constantly diminishing circle of readers. Our esteemed contemporary would do better to model its paper on the bright, sparkling, varied, amusing and attractive pages of the *World*'s Sunday issue—alive with articles of contemporary interest. People who want essays or poems on the Pyramids or the War of 1812 buy other papers." *World*, December 26, 1884, p. 4.

[37] Robert E. Park, "The Natural History of the Newspaper," reprinted in Robert E. Park, Ernest W. Burgess, and Roderick D. McKenzie, *The City* (Chicago, 1925), p. 95

[38] Quoted in Irving Dilliard, "How J. P. Ran a Newspaper—and His Staff of Editors," in Special Supplement Commemorating the 100th Anniversary of Joseph Pulitzer, *St. Louis Post-Dispatch*, April 6, 1947, p. 9.

A leisurely, plodding style and undisguised "earnestness" of intent, often so unfortunate when compared to the clever, brittle prose of the *Sun*, enabled the *World* to indulge effectively in sentiment and wide-eyed horror when it reported the various catastrophes of ordinary life.[39] Its account of a New Jersey girl who lost her life to an abortionist offers a fair case in point. It began:

> Nestled in one of the loveliest little valleys of Burlington County, six miles from this city, lies the pretty hamlet of Cookstown. Thirty cottages, two little vine-twined churches, a grist-mill and a hotel constitute the built-up portion of the village, while 200 quiet and peaceable people inhabit them. Twice a day the shriek of the locomotive arouses the villagers from their slumbers, the Pemberton and Hightstown Railroad Company having risked a depletion of its treasury by erecting a little clapboard structure to shelter temporarily from the storm the one or two travellers who daily board or step from the train. To-day this little hamlet has been horrified and thrown into the most intense excitement by the exposure of a crime which has caused the death of a beautiful girl, the arrest of her lover for complicity and the disappearance of a physician, who performed an operation which brought the girl to an untimely grave.
>
> Ida Grant, eighteen years old, was until Sunday the favorite daughter of Levi Grant, proprietor of the Grant Hotel, the only public hostelry in the village, and the resort on Saturday nights of the farmers and farmers' sons for miles about. Just across the street stands the old-fashioned residence of Lorenzo Woodward, the village miller. Miller Woodward has an eighteen-year-old son named Frank. He is a splendid-

[39] Such a style's appeal rested on its resemblance to the prose familiar to men and women of limited education. As Robert Park points out, "the yellow press grew up in an attempt to capture for the newspaper a public whose only literature was the family story paper or the cheap novel. The problem was to write the news in such a way that it would appeal to the fundamental passions." (Robert E. Park, "The Natural History of the Newspaper," reprinted in *The City*, pp. 94-95.) Pulitzer himself believed that the human interest story, with all that it implied, was particularly suited for a newspaper addressing a mass audience. As he wrote in a memorandum dating probably to 1899 or 1900, "Human interest stories as a rule are far better for a paper of wide circulation like the *World* than politics or other news which may be designated as class." *Pulitzer Papers*, Library of Congress.

looking lad, tall, erect and his head is adorned with golden curls, which are the admiration and envy not only of the village maidens but of his fellows. Ten years ago Ida Grant and Frank Woodward attended the little village school together. Each morning the gallant little fellow called at Ida's home and proudly carried by her side her books and lunch basket to the little box of a seat of learning, just under the hill. As time drew on, Ida developed into a very beautiful girl. No eyes were so bewitching, no complexion was so fair, no teeth so pearly and no lips so tempting in all the village. Her boy lover, too, as he developed into manhood excited the envy of his companions by the constant attentions to the landlord's pretty daughter. . . .[40]

The article goes on at the same leisurely pace—almost like a short story—to describe the developing love affair between Ida and Frank; the announcement to the village that they were to be married; their mysterious ride into the country together; Ida's sudden illness and death the day following; the grief of her family and friends; the nagging suspicions of the family which resulted in having her body exhumed; and finally, the coroner's discovery, and Frank's confession, that she had died of a mishandled abortion. Like many other *World* stories about lads with golden curls and lasses with bewitching eyes, it threatens constantly to collapse into utter sentimentalism, but somehow never quite does. At least an increasing proportion of New Yorkers in the 1880s found themselves fascinated by the tragedies that befell the Franks and Idas in their midst.

Part of the reason for the *World*'s success in handling such material is that it did not go out of its way to be a sophisticated or worldly-wise paper. While a veteran reporter who prided himself on having seen it all before might have regarded the tragedy in a New Jersey hamlet as little more than an exercise in sobstory journalism, the *World* man capitalized on his innocence, and fresh vision, to convey a sense of horror equivalent to what the average man would have felt, and to notice the details the average man would have noticed. The topflight journalist who

[40] *World*, June 29, 1884, p. 1.

has lost his capacity for shock must be much more wary. His professionalism is an advantage in writing straight news stories which require that the facts be set down accurately and succinctly, and which benefit from background knowledge on the reporter's part, but it does not necessarily equip him for compelling tears when he has none himself.[41] Lincoln Steffens recognized the problem when he moved from the *New York Evening Post* to accept a managerial position with the *New York Commercial Advertiser*. In his autobiography he recalled warning the staff that jaded minds could not produce the articles which the *Commercial Advertiser* wanted to run:

> When a reporter no longer saw red at a fire, when he was so used to police news that a murder was not a human tragedy but only a crime, he could not write police news for us. We preferred the fresh starting eyes to the informed mind and the blunted pencil. To express this, if not to enforce it, I used to warn my staff that whenever a reporter became a good all-around newspaper man, he would be fired.[42]

Having found the story, and written it up in a style pleasing to the mass mind of the 1880s, there still remained the challenge of adding those final embellishments which confirmed the newspaper as a superior purveyor of sensation. Without a doubt, the most important embellishment was illustration, an art at which the *World* excelled, and which played so important a part in its success as to be material for a separate chapter. One aspect of newspaper line illustration, however, deserves mention here.

Pulitzer discovered early that when the public became interested in a murder, its curiosity and appetite for detail was almost insatiable. It seemed almost as if 100,000 *World* readers would assign themselves to the case as police investigators, and demand to know the position of each piece of furniture, the condition of

[41] This is not meant to minimize the very high degree of skill that went into writing articles about the Franks and Idas. In many ways the "sob story" is the most difficult of all journalistic forms. A good reporter quickly learns that he cannot fabricate such material. His job is to tell the facts and leave the weeping to the reader. But before he can accomplish even that subtle mission, he must feel himself the emotions he hopes others will feel. A journalist too conscious of his worldly wisdom is apt to lack the sensitivity required.

[42] Lincoln Steffens, *Autobiography* (New York, 1931), pp. 314-15.

the body, and so on. Other newspaper proprietors had noticed the same thing and, depending on the sort of journal they published, had tried to satisfy the morbid craving by printing as detailed descriptions as space allowed. Of course Pulitzer demanded equally thorough accounts from his own reporters, but within months of acquiring the *World* he outdid his competitors by printing simple drawings, sometimes no wider than a single column, to show at a glance the physical layout of the murder scene. For example, in the fall of 1883 a New York clergyman named Kemlo slashed his wife to death and then cut his own throat before leaping from a fourth-floor window. The goriness of the deed, together with the perpetrator's profession, made it a natural for front page coverage. The *World* rounded out its report with a drawing of the apartment in which the crime occurred, including the following sanguinary details for special notation:

A - Door stained with blood.
B - Window stained with blood from which Kemlo leaped.
C - Bed covered with blood.
D - Table set and covered with blood.
E - Chair in which Mrs. Kemlo sat.
F - Sink in which the knife was found.
G - Pool of blood.[43]

Similar diagrams were used to locate the position of the bodies in a double murder committed by a tramp on Long Island, and in a rape-murder committed by a tramp in New Jersey.[44]

These exercises in "X marks the spot" journalism immediately captured the fancy of the newspaper reading public. They added an important graphic dimension to the *World*'s reporting of crime and tragedy, which was reflected almost weekly in a steady climb in circulation.

Provocative, gruesome, coy—but never dull—headlines provided still another embellishment. All of the enterprise and skill that experienced journalists could muster would go for nothing unless the banners over their stories persuaded readers to pay attention. However the *World* erred, it was never on the side of overly modest display.

[43] *World*, September 19, 1883, p. 1.
[44] *World*, November 19, 1883, p. 1; November 26, 1883, p. 1.

The newspaper appreciated the electric quality of certain words, and used them freely, not so much to convey a message as to stir the emotions. A good example is the word "blood." On May 30th, 1883, just days after the Brooklyn Bridge had been dedicated, a particularly large Memorial Day crowd took advantage of the balmy Sunday weather to visit the newest civic wonder spanning the East River. Panic broke out among the dense throng jammed onto the pedestrian causeway, and before it subsided, eleven people had been trampled to death. The *World* headlined its report: BAPTIZED IN BLOOD.[45] It used almost the same phrase later in the year to describe quite a different tragedy. During the christening party for an infant child, several of the guests who had imbibed too freely got into a violent argument. A free-for-all resulted, which ended with the child's father lying mortally wounded. The *World* headlined its report: A BAPTISM OF BLOOD.[46]

Other words had almost equal emotive power. When the newspaper reported the arraignment in Tombs Court of a man charged with sexually molesting a young girl, it described him in headline as A FIEND IN HUMAN FORM.[47] Sometimes a formula served as well as a single word. The suggestion of a mother slaying her child, properly conveyed, had obvious emotional impact. On three different occasions within a year, the *World* used identical headlines, A MOTHER'S AWFUL CRIME, to announce such tragedies, varying the formula on the fourth occasion with A MOTHER'S FEARFUL DEED.[48]

Techniques other than the emotive word or formula also helped to lend color to stories which might themselves be rather dull. The question headline, as has already been noted, was one such technique. In June 1883, for instance, on a day lacking in much

[45] *World*, May 31, 1883, p. 1.

[46] *World*, November 27, 1883, p. 8. According to a profile of William Randolph Hearst, which appeared in *Esquire* in 1936, Pulitzer's rival was, at least in this respect, much more restrained. He would not allow his copyreaders to use the words "blood" or "murder" in a headline. Robert B. Sullivan, "An Unidentified Man," *Esquire* (April 1936), p. 126; cited in Hughes, *News and the Human Interest Story*, p. 37.

[47] *World* October 30, 1883, p. 5.

[48] The identical headlines appeared in the *World* on May 18, 1883, p. 1; March 17, 1884, p. 1; and May 31, 1884, p. 1. The variation appeared on May 6, 1885, p. 2.

hard news, the *World* seized its readers' attention with a front page headline asking, WAS IT PEPPERMINT MARY?[49] The question by itself meant nothing, but few could resist finding out what Peppermint Mary might have done. The article concerned a jewelry establishment in Newark which had painted its upstairs windows white and nailed down the sashes, to prevent its female employees from flirting with passersby. Peppermint Mary's name appeared only in the last paragraph of the story, as a possible instigator of the trouble. Could it be, the *World* wondered, that Mary's good fortune as the only married employee on the floor had persuaded the other girls to flirt so that they, too, could find husbands? Clearly, the *World* had played a devious game, taking advantage of a colorful nickname to promise more than it could offer. But at the same time, the headline added spice to an otherwise drab front page.

A related trick was to whet the reader's interest by taking an emotion-laden quotation out of context. In the fall of 1883, a young mother who had been abandoned by her husband, and who had appealed in vain for charity assistance, attempted to drown herself and her children in the East River. (Such cases were not uncommon in New York City during the 1880s, when the extremes of poverty and opulence existed within blocks of each other.[50]) The *World* converted it from just another back page item on human misery to a sensational lead story with the headline, LET ME DIE! LET ME DIE!—words Mrs. Liebuchner sobbed as they dragged her out of the river.[51]

Similarly, the newspaper often emblazoned in headline the goriest details from the article below. The explicitness of its heads surpassed anything to be found in modern journalism. It announced Cornetti's execution, for instance, with:

[49] *World*, June 9, 1883, p. 1.

[50] As a matter of fact, the *World* had run an almost identical story on its front page the previous spring. See A MERCIFUL MURDERESS, *World*, May 28, 1883, p. 1. The newspaper suffered severe embarrassment on that occasion. After drumming up sympathy for the woman, and in an editorial contrasting her condition with that of the perfumed pets on Fifth Avenue, it developed that she was a chronic alcoholic, crazed not by lack of money but lack of drink. For the editorial, see the *World*, May 30, 1883, p. 4; for the embarrassing revelation, June 3, 1883, p. 1.

[51] *World*, September 9, 1883, p. 1.

SCREAMING FOR MERCY.

HOW THE CRAVEN CORNETTI MOUNTED THE SCAFFOLD.

Gagged and Pinioned by the Guards and
Dragged Resisting to a Prayer-
less Doom.[52]

The newspaper exercised even less restraint in reporting an execution several months later.

BUNGLED BY THE HANGMAN.

ALEXANDER JEFFERSON, THE NEGRO, SLOWLY TORTURED TO DEATH.

He Struggled While His Body Swings, Tears the
Black Cap from His Face, and Stretched Out
His Arms Pleadingly to the People—Sheriff
Stegman Faints in the Prison.[53]

An account of a particularly gruesome crime included the following particulars.

PIERCED HIS WIFE'S EYES.

JOHN M'CARRON BLINDS A HELPLESS WOMAN WITH A SHOEMAKER'S AWL.

He Accuses Her of Flirting and After Dragging
Her Around the Room by Her Hair Deliber-
ately Destroys Her Sight, so that She May
Never Again Boast of Her Beauty—The Brute
Locked Up and the Woman Blind for Life.[54]

[52] *World*, May 12, 1883, p. 1. Public sensitivity about capital punishment was not much of a factor at that time, with the result that newspapers often used descriptive phrases which would be impossible in the twentieth century. The *Chicago Times*, for example, announced a hanging in 1875 with the headline: JERKED TO JESUS. (Cited in Frank L. Mott, *American Journalism* [New York, 1941], p. 467.) Alfred Lee argues that the Civil War made Americans more impervious to human suffering, and hence contributed to the rise of sensationalism. A. M. Lee, *Daily Newspaper in America*, p. 618.

[53] *World*, August 2, 1884, p. 5. The headline might have been used as argument by an opponent of capital punishment, but such was certainly not Pulitzer's intention. He made clear on several occasions that he believed the only thing to do with murderers, rapists, and the like, was to execute them. For his thoughts on the need for capital punishment, see the *World*, July 2, 1884, p. 4; February 4, 1885, p. 4; and February 11, 1885, p. 4.

[54] *World*, November 29, 1884, p. 1.

The *World* prided itself on its comprehensive news coverage, but a respect for the rules of sensationalism determined that some items would not receive front-page attention. Publishing a successful journal for the masses entailed not only knowing which stories to feature, and how to do so, but which to run modestly on an inside page. Politics, for instance, had little popular appeal, unless an election was involved and the gyrations of the candidates could be regarded as part of a great sporting event. What applied to domestic politics applied still more to foreign affairs. Pulitzer constantly cautioned his editors against letting their attention wander to faraway places. "Concentrate your brain on local, immediate features, . . ." he instructed Charles Lincoln by letter in 1910. "Let Panama go to the devil and all far-away, speculative conjectures. Concentrate on the six or seven million people in Greater New York and its easily accessible region."[55]

Pulitzer personally could hardly be labelled a provincial, but experience had taught him that the curiosity of his readers was bounded approximately by Coney Island on the one side and the Hudson River on the other. He elaborated on the point in an editorial lecture to two of his competitors: "The *Herald* makes a great show of special cable news, and the *Tribune* is largely devoted to letters which deal with European affairs, but we doubt whether either of these journals would suffer in circulation if they curtailed their foreign departments and gave more space to home news."[56]

Of course immigrants were interested in news from the "old country," and a dispatch from overseas might sometimes contain a spicy bit of gossip. The point, then, was not to indiscriminately play down every item of foreign intelligence, but to use discretion in deciding which items would have wide appeal. Pulitzer

[55] Letter from Pulitzer to Charles Lincoln, dated November 11, 1910. Quoted in Seitz, *Joseph Pulitzer*, p. 420.

[56] *World*, May 14, 1884, p. 4. Horace Greeley offered similar advice some years before in a letter to a friend who was about to start a newspaper. "Begin with a clear conception that the subject of deepest interest to an average human being is himself," the publisher of the *New York Tribune* wrote; "next to that, he is most concerned about his neighbors. Asia and the Tongo Islands stand a long way after these in his regard." Quoted in Robert E. Park, "The Natural History of the Newspaper," reprinted in Robert E. Park, *et al.*, *The City*, p. 84.

demonstrated how it was done by contrasting the editorial policies of the *World* and the *Herald*.

> With all its vast foreign bureaus and its cable facilities the *Herald* shows as poor judgement in gleaning European news as it does in picking up—or rather gliding by—home news. The *World's* Cable Letter fairly glistens every day with matters of contemporaneous human interest. For instance, while the *Herald* was looking after the Servian [sic] Skuptchina yesterday we had the interesting news about the Marquis of Lorne's scheme for the political pacification of Ireland, and while the *Herald* was keeping its cable eye on the Hovas of Madagascar the other day the *World* was showing up the divorce suit of Lord Colin Campbell. It will be observed that whether at home or abroad the *World* manages to catch in its net the kind of news that the American people take an interest in.[57]

He defined the facility more succinctly the next day, when he asserted that "our cable man is imbued with American instincts."[58]

The concept of what is important news in a sensational paper, and what is not, can be seen best by comparing a random sampling of headlines in the *World* and the *New York Times*. Take for example, the articles each newspaper ran in its right-hand column on page one during one week in March of 1884:

THE *WORLD*	THE *TIMES*
Tuesday, March 4	
A CHILD FLAYED ALIVE.	GENERAL TELEGRAPHIC NEWS.
A BRUTAL NEGRO WHIPS HIS NEPHEW TO DEATH IN SOUTH CAROLINA.	COLORED MEN AS REPORTERS.
	INDIGNATION IN JOURNALISTIC CIRCLES IN PHILADELPHIA.
Inhuman Gloating Over the Little Fellow's Suffering —"Ki, Yi! How de Pieces Do Come!"—Blacks and Whites Trying To Lynch the Monster	

[57] *World*, April 2, 1884, p. 4. The "Skuptchina" referred to was the national assembly of Serbia.
[58] *World*, April 3, 1884, p. 4.

THE *WORLD*   THE *TIMES*

Wednesday, March 5

A QUINTUPLE TRAGEDY.   IN AND OUT OF CONGRESS.

AN ENTIRE FAMILY   REPRESENTATIVE POTTER'S
ANNIHILATED   REFUNDING BILL.
BY ITS MURDEROUS HEAD.

Not a Living Witness Left to   Treasury Officials Examining
Tell the Tale of Blood—   and Criticising Its Provisions—
"You Had Better Go to the   Some of Their Objections.
House: I Have Played the
Devil Up There!"—
Jealousy or Insanity.

Thursday, March 6

ASSASSINATION FORETOLD.   IN THE GOVERNOR'S HANDS.

A SENSATIONAL STORY   THE ANTI-CONFIRMATION BILL
RELATED BY EX-POSTMASTER-   PASSED BY THE SENATE.
GENERAL JAMES

Lawyer Cook Explains How He   Its Opponents Threaten to
Came to Warn Garfield and   Elect John Kelly Mayor of
Why He Did It - Did Guiteau   New York City - Proceedings
Have Accomplices? - Why Was   in the Assembly.
No Attempt Ever Made to Find
Out?

Friday, March 7

STRANGLED BY ROBBERS.   H.B. PAYNE FOR PRESIDENT.

A WEALTHY STOCK-RAISER   THE OHIO MACHINE HARD AT
MURDERED FOR HIS MONEY.   WORK IN HIS INTEREST.

Tell-Tale Marks That   The Diplomatic Answer Which
Betrayed the Crime - A   the Senator-Elect Gives His
Handkerchief that May   Friends When Asked About His
Lead to the Conviction of   Candidacy.
the Thugs - Two Men Arrested
for the Murder.

Saturday, March 8

DIED A DESPERADO'S DEATH.   GENERAL TELEGRAPH NEWS.

THE OUTLAW RANDE HANGS   A PAYMASTER'S OFFICE
HIMSELF TO THE DOOR OF   ROBBED.
HIS CELL.

Mortified at the Failure of   The Work of a Thief in a
His Attempt to Kill His Keeper Railroad Office in Chicago.
- Planning to Get Free by
Pleading Insanity - His Numerous
Crimes - Arranging to Die
Comfortably.

THE *WORLD*	THE *TIMES*

Sunday, March 9

OUR MILITIA "BOSSES."	WHISKEY MEN DEFEATED.
MEN OF IRON WHO COMMAND THE NATIONAL GUARD.	A MOTION TO CONSIDER THE BONDED PERIOD BILL LOST.
HANDSOME HANNIBALS AND NATTY YOUNG NAPOLEONS.	Admitting that the Measure is Gone Beyond Recovery, But Determined To Have a Decided Vote on It.
THE FUTURE MARSHALS OF THE ARMIES OF THE REPUBLIC.	

Monday, March 10

A LADY GAGGED IN A FLAT.	GENERAL TELEGRAPH NEWS.
DRAGGED FROM HER BED AND ROBBED BY A BURLY NEGRO.	CONNECTICUT TAFIFF REFORMERS.
He is Captured in a Servant's Room - Miss Maggie Harvey, the Victim, in Imminent Danger of Death - Her Terrible Experience in the Night.	Starting a Movement to Make Their Convictions Felt and Effective.

The *New York World* and *New York Times* clearly had different concepts of the important news of the day.

And yet to leave it at that is to disregard the important moral element in sensationalism. Pulitzer never denied that the major reason for printing accounts of sex and scandal is that they sell newspapers, nor did the logic embarrass him. Replying to a minister who had attacked the "low moral tone" of the press, charging that "newspapers are made to sell," Pulitzer cheerfully conceded the commercial instinct of men like himself, and found it not too different from the instinct of artists, scholars, and indeed, ministers. "Of course newspapers are 'made to sell,'" he wrote, "and in that respect they resemble the highest work of art and intellect as well as the sermons preached in pulpits."[59] Journalists who restricted themselves to polite accounts of the doings of polite people soon discovered that they addressed a shrinking audience.

But the editor pleaded still other reasons for publicizing scandal when it occurred. He argued that the responsibility of the

[59] *World*, May 6, 1884, p. 4.

— 69 —

press to report the news, fully and accurately, took precedence over the qualms of a few sensitive readers.

> A few days ago we received a letter from a subscriber expressing the opinion that the daily journals are as objectionable as the weekly story papers because they record so many crimes, give detailed accounts of murders and executions and publish other matter of a sensational character. He made the request that the *World* would exclude all such subjects from its columns.
>
> This complaint of the "low moral tone of the press" is common but very unjust. A newspaper relates the events of the day. It does not manufacture its record of corruptions and crimes, but tells of them as they occur. If it failed to do so it would be an unfaithful chronicler. . . .
>
> The daily journal is like the mirror—it reflects that which is before it. . . . Let those who are startled by it blame the people who are before the mirror, and not the mirror, which only reflects their features and actions.[60]

Pulitzer considered the point important, and repeated it on several occasions. "The *World* most assuredly does not seek to make a specialty of crime," he insisted some months later, "and it regrets that there is so much wickedness in the land that must be mentioned in the newspapers. The *World* is a newspaper."[61]

He liked to believe, moreover, that the sensational press played a role equal to that of the so-called moral agencies in leading men from the paths of unrighteousness. When The Reverend Wilbur F. Crafts, pastor of the First Union Presbyterian Church, preached against the example of Sunday newspapers, the paper challenged him on his own terms:

> With all due deference to the good Pastor Crafts, we must be permitted to say that the newspaper, whether printed on Sunday or on week days, is a great aid to the preservation of peace and order. Sinners do not shrink from vice, but they are awfully afraid of exposure in the newspapers. No pulpit orator can

[60] *World*, April 13, 1884, p. 4.
[61] *World*, December 27, 1884, p. 4.

— 70 —

reach the evil-doer like a Sunday newspaper with a quarter of a million of readers.[62]

A woman subscriber who objected to the *World's* extensive coverage of a "professional beauty's" love life was mollified in much the same way.

If there is a professional beauty before the public (there are, in fact, a good many) who is defying

[62] *World*, May 27, 1884, p. 4. Pulitzer's argument is debatable, but all sorts of evidence points to its sincerity. He really believed that the moral and didactic function of sensationalism was at least as important as its role in selling newspapers. Earlier in the chapter a list of articles was offered to show his resourcefulness in finding sensational subjects when they did not appear of themselves. The list shows something else as well. Many of the articles, like the one cataloguing the variety of weapons used to commit murder over the years, or describing recent examples of human sacrifice by religious fanatics, were fact-laden in a way that precisely suited Pulitzer's analytical, and sometimes pedantic, mind. Others, describing how Austria–Hungary executed its murderers, or life in the death house at Sing Sing, presumably delivered a moral about the folly of committing capital crimes. The publisher's determination to see deeper values in the chronicles of crime and gore is apparent in the memoranda he addressed to the staff after 1890. On October 2, 1902, for example, he cabled Don Seitz from Bar Harbor, Maine, and urged that the paper prepare a feature story on the current outbreak of murders in New York City. The treatment he proposed was revealing. "I believe a man of good sense and good taste," Pulitzer wrote, "could take those 31 Murderers in the tombs and make a wonderfully interesting story without shocking our better nature by making it appear that the paper is indulging in a deliberate sensational criminal display. Even the most serious man least disposed to read a murder story under flaring flaming headlines is bound to become interested in the psychological or moral view of the question. . . . I think it would make a striking feature if you . . . get some man or men of intellect who have studied criminology to analyze the causes and make a comparison between the number of such crimes in New York and in other great cities such as London, Paris, Berlin. Do not make it a police gazette story, but one every serious man would read." He was equally high-minded in a memorandum to Charles Lincoln several years later, again suggesting New York City's high murder rate as an interesting subject for feature treatment. "Apropos of enclosed clipping from the *London Times* showing that there were 185 homicides in New York during 1910," he wrote, "this would make a good magazine feature if properly worked up. Pick out the most interesting cases. What were these homicides? Who committed them? What was the motive? Give a table of motives, of social rank, of age, of nationality, etc. [Note his obsession with facts for their own sake.] But give the facts more reliably, more strikingly than would the magazines. This is one of those big stories that the monthly magazines would print. But don't print it from the standpoint of mere sensationalism, but rather from the moral point of view. It should be a thoughtful article with a great moral to it." (Memorandum dated February 2, 1911; quoted in Seitz, *Joseph Pulitzer*, pp. 423-24.) The repeated injunctions to use murder, abortion, and the like, as material for moralizing may or may not have constituted a sort of self-deception on Pulitzer's part, but they certainly testify to his conviction that a sensational newspaper could serve high social goals.

— 71 —

morality and good taste by her conduct, Virtue ought to rejoice that the press acts like an argus-eyed conscience, and nothing extenuates and sets down nothing in malice. It thus prevents immorality from becoming general by preventing it from becoming hidden. The very indignation of our fair correspondent is a healthy sign. But how could she ever have experienced this wholesome emotion of outraged propriety if the newspapers had not pointed out to her the cause?

There is an old-fashioned notion—and our correspondent may have imbibed it—that vice and misconduct should never be recognized. That is a valetudinarian squeamishness that does not belong to an age of newspapers. There is nothing that wrongdoing so much desires as to be let alone. But it never has been since the printing press got fairly in motion.[63]

Pulitzer repeated the argument years later in conversation with Alleyne Ireland. "There is not a crime," he insisted, "there is not a dodge, there is not a trick, there is not a swindle, there is not a vice which does not live by secrecy. Get these things out in the open, describe them, attack them, ridicule them in the press, and sooner or later public opinion will sweep them away."[64]

Such arguments, insistently repeated, in part reflected Pulitzer's sensitivity to charges that the editorial practices of papers like the *World* contributed to juvenile delinquency and a rising crime rate. Although his faith in the importance of publishing all the news never wavered, he seemed at times to concede that sensationalism might have a malicious influence. "It is possible that crime is stimulated by the publication of criminal intelligence. It is also possible that there are weak-minded people who insist on breaking into penitentiaries simply because penitentiaries have a peculiar fascination for them. This is not an argument in favor of the abolition of penitentiaries."[65] Usually Pulitzer did not even

[63] *World*, July 17, 1883, p. 4. Although the lady did not specify which story she objected to, the reference is probably to Lily Langtry's cross-country romance with a society fop, an epic the *World* covered with some care. It should be pointed out in fairness, however, that even Pulitzer finally tired of serving as Miss Langtry's argus-eyed conscience. He cabled his business manager many years later: "If there is anything in next Sunday's magazine about that Langtry woman kill it at once." Cable from Pulitzer to Seitz, January 26, 1903, *Pulitzer Papers*, Library of Congress.

[64] Alleyne Ireland, *Joseph Pulitzer*, p. 115.

[65] *World*, December 27, 1884, p. 4.

concede that much. His more typical response was to argue that since the press—unlike pulp magazines—did not glorify the wrongdoer, it could not be held responsible for the wrongdoer's behavior. "The attempt of a few narrow purists to charge upon the daily press some share of the responsibility for this lamentable condition of things is a futile one. The daily press publishes vice, no doubt, but it does not idealize or palliate it. It publishes also the inevitable consequences of vice."[66]

In so arguing, Pulitzer did not mean to suggest that the *World* should be above all restraints; that any story immune from prosecution for libel properly belonged in a family newspaper. Like other reputable journalists, he obeyed what he understood to be the dictates of good taste. On one occasion he publicly rebuked the *New York Tribune* for printing on its front page a report of how a six-year-old girl was sexually molested by two boys only slightly older than herself. "The same matter in the *World* office," he pointed out, "was pitched into the waste-basket."[67] Godkin's *Evening Post* (to use the conventional symbol of sobriety) and Pulitzer's *World* did not disagree about the relevancy of good taste, but only about what it meant. Pulitzer, of course, argued for much the broader definition.

> Now about this matter of sensationalism; a newspaper should be scrupulously accurate, it should be clean, it should avoid everything salacious or suggestive, everything that could offend the good taste or lower the moral tone of its readers; but within these limits it is the duty of a newspaper to print the news. When I speak of good taste and of good moral tone, I do not mean the kind of good taste which is offended by every reference to the unpleasant things of life, I do not mean the kind of morality which refuses to recognize the existence of immorality . . . what I mean is the kind of good taste which demands that frankness should be linked with decency, the kind of moral tone which is braced and not relaxed when it is brought face to face with vice.[68]

[66] *World*, March 26, 1884, p. 4.
[67] *World*, November 4, 1883, p. 4.
[68] The statement was made in a conversation between Pulitzer and Ireland. Quoted in Ireland, *Joseph Pulitzer*, pp. 113-14.

The challenge lay in discovering when "frankness" is consistent with "decency," and on that issue the opposing schools could barely communicate. On December 17, 1883, the *New York Evening Post* reprinted a group of headlines from the *World* edition of November 29 to make a point about the salaciousness of its upstart competitor. Pulitzer carefully examined the evidence, and confessed to being confused. "We have studied the collection carefully," he wrote. "The heads seem to cover all the news obtainable in the country of that day. There is nothing particularly shocking about them. They can be read by persons in a normal condition, we think, without producing a tremor of the vertebral muscles."[69]

The fact that Pulitzer and Godkin could not agree about the suitability of the headlines is really less significant than their implied agreement on more basic questions. Both journalists believed that the press had a responsibility to serve the public. Pulitzer met that responsibility through the *World*'s editorials and crusades, but also, he insisted, by running sensational articles exposing criminals and culprits to punishment for their misdeeds. (The important question is not whether his faith in the deterrent value of sensationalism was justified, but whether it was sincere. And there is no reason not to take him at his word.) Both also believed that the first imperative in reporting the news was to maintain a constant "high moral tone." The fact that the *World* intended to lead the nation in circulation made it the last paper to consider every scandal and crime fair game for exploitation. It occupied the enviable ground where self-interest and principle converge, for only by tailoring its coverage to what society tolerated could society be made to listen.

The clearest evidence of the paper's respect for decorum is seen in its fussy attitude toward sex. The *World* shared most of the prejudices of the Victorian age, and just as a people who insisted on separating male and female authors on the bookshelf could sentence ten-year-old pickpockets to death, so the journal which graphically described a culprit's agony as he dangled from the gallows considered sex something best approached

[69] *World*, December 18, 1883, p. 4.

gingerly, if at all. It honored the ethic of the time by being more than a bit prudish.

Pulitzer's editorial blast at the *Tribune* for giving a "prominent place on its first page to a shocking story about an outrageous assault on a little six-year-old girl committed by two wicked boys" can be viewed as contrived criticism in an age of intensely competitive journalism. But there is too much supporting evidence of the newspaper's adherence to a nineteenth century gentleman's code to doubt that it placed sex and violence in separate categories. In the spring of 1884, for example, a scandal reminiscent of that involving Livingston and Gebhardt again rocked the Union Club. Mr. Joseph Loubat brought suit, demanding that his membership in the club be restored. He had been expelled three years previously after a quarrel with Henry Turnbull in which he had disparagingly mentioned a lady's name.[70] The *World* faithfully reported the court hearings on its front page, but at the same time called attention to the self-censorship it imposed upon itself along with the rest of the press.

> A great deal is said about the "license" and "sensationalism" of the press. . . . But it is a creditable and a gratifying fact that during the discussion of this club scandal and its trial before the courts not a single newspaper has mentioned the name of the lady entangled in the affair, or described the odious remark made by Loubat which caused his expulsion or the character of the indecent acts for which Mr. Turnbull is an outcast from decent society. . . .
>
> The fullest information on all points has long been in possession of all newspapers and newspaper men. Yet with great delicacy the name of the lady, the words of Loubat and the offense of Turnbull have been uniformly suppressed, although doubtless thousands of readers have been looking anxiously for their publication. . . .
>
> Will the hypercritical censors of the press make a note of this?[71]

[70] The court ruled against Loubat, holding that a private club must be allowed to govern itself. See the *World*, September 27, 1884, p. 5.

[71] *World*, April 27, 1884, p. 4. A querulous memorandum Pulitzer dispatched to the *World* office on November 28, 1905, is instructive in this respect. "I cannot make Van [C. M. Van Hamn, a *World* editor] understand that when

The same strict morality encouraged the newspaper, which otherwise had mixed feelings about comstockery, to support the voices raised against décolleté fashion at the opera house. Several mothers wrote to Pulitzer protesting the abundant display of feminine charms among the smart set, and thanking him for his crusade against such immodesty.

> As a mother and one who is solicitous for the welfare of her sons I am disposed to thank you for calling attention in your paper to the semi-nudity of some of the ladies who attend the opera and sit conspicuously in the boxes. One night last week I saw a modest miss of nineteen in one of the boxes belonging to a prominent millionaire, whose arms were entirely bare and whose back and front were so thoroughly exposed that I wondered how she kept her dress on. . . . I am not afraid that my sons will be demoralized by the cold and insensible pictures that Anthony Comstock is so much exercised about; but I shudder when I think of the temptations that are placed before them in fashionable society.[72]

The editor took several opportunities to concur with those sentiments, and was only prevented from making them the subject of a full-scale crusade by the receipt of last-minute fashion news from London.

> Just as the *World* is preparing to reopen its batteries upon low-necked dresses at the Opera, news arrives from England to the effect that low bodices are now considered in bad form. . . . This, we presume, puts an end to the awful exhibition in the fashionable boxes of New York Opera-houses.[73]

The *World*'s rage at the tactics of the Republican National Committee during the Cleveland–Blaine contest of 1884 becomes now more explicable. The revelation that Grover Cleveland had

---

I say more people are interested in a love story or romance such things can be done decently, properly, clearly and with a sense of balance and proportion *without* [his emphasis] stopping over and *without* [his emphasis] making the first page a page of crime altogether disgusting." *Pulitzer Papers*, Library of Congress.

[72] *World*, December 23, 1883, p. 4.
[73] *World*, December 29, 1883, p. 4.

carried on with Maria Halpin during his younger days in Buffalo, and probably sired a child by her, would in any case have inspired the strongest editorial counterattack in order to minimize the damage. What really infuriated the *World*, however—as it made clear after the election had been won—was that in publicizing the story the Republican Committee had violated the unwritten dictates of the gentleman's code. It caused smut unfit for decent eyes to be smuggled into millions of American homes. Consider the tone of the newspaper's stern indictment:

> Now that the campaign is closed and the result is on record, it remains to speak and to speak emphatically to and of the Republican journals that dragged the sewers to find filth to fling at Grover Cleveland. They have not harmed him. But the infinite harm done to hitherto pure households throughout the length and breadth of the country is incalculable. These filth flingers have even prostituted the public mails to their prurient purposes. They have sent into homes, and glaringly displayed the dirtiest documents —have thrust into the very faces of females and spread before the young of both sexes filth that they knew to be as false as it was feculent. They have made it possible for young men to familiarly speak to young women of matters that heretofore would have driven the bloom from, or brought the blush to the maiden's cheek. They have done more in the short campaign to debauch and defile the country than all the disseminators of obscene literature have been able to accomplish in the past half century. And what have they got for it? Nothing but the contempt of the clean, wholesome, virtuous and, thank Heaven! yet predominating element of the American people. And they will be held to an accountability of it.[74]

Hardly the statement of a journal which would, as a policy, print whatever scandal a police reporter in the great metropolis might come across!

To be sure, the *World*'s outrage in this instance is not altogether convincing. As the foremost spokesman in New York City for the Democratic cause, with the responsibility for defending

[74] *World*, November 7, 1884, p. 4.

Cleveland against charges of immorality, and as a sensational newspaper adept at interesting masses of men in the issues of a political campaign, the *World* made its own significant contribution to the mudslinging which went on in 1884. But it was rarely forthright in peddling scandal about Blaine, and to the great annoyance of Republicans, kept insisting upon its high motives.

The most notable examples of innuendo and rumor-mongering occur in its treatment of the gossip concerning Blaine's marriage. As early as July 8th, more than a month before the *Indianapolis Sentinel* reported as fact that Blaine had married his wife under duress when she was six months pregnant, the *World* commented obliquely on the rumors in the course of defending Cleveland against similar charges. "The opponents of Cleveland at Chicago are telling stories about the Governor's early days in Buffalo which reflect upon his chastity," an editorial declared. "They are probably the same kind of fellows who talk about Blaine and his schoolteaching days in Kentucky, which were marked by an excess of animal vitality."[75] Two weeks later, with the publication in a Buffalo newspaper of the Maria Halpin story, the *World* again made reference to Blaine's past. "There is a story in circulation concerning a record made by him 'in youth's hot blood'—a story which the *World* will never under any circumstances print —which may find its way into the channels of public gossip, if this lowest type of campaign tactics is to be adopted by the Blaine organs."[76] For a while thereafter it contented itself with teasing allusions to the scandal. In mid-August, for example, the newspaper published a letter from a subscriber pleading for information about "the story of J. G. Blaine and his female pupil, tar-and-feather business and shotgun affair," and highmindedly refused to comply. "No matter how much nor how disgracefully the Republicans should lie about the Democratic candidate, we have determined not to touch any of the Blaine scandals at our disposal."[77] Coy comments on gaps in Blaine's biography served the same purpose. "A reader of the *World* at White Plains writes

[75] *World*, July 8, 1884, p. 4.
[76] *World*, July 23, 1884, p. 4.
[77] *World*, August 12, 1884, p. 4.

to ask us if we can give him the date of Major James G. Blaine's marriage. We cannot. None of the biographies of Major Blaine that we have seen contain this piece of information."[78]

The wraps came off the story when the *Indianapolis Sentinel* reported that Blaine had seduced his future wife while teaching school in Kentucky, that he refused to marry her even after her pregnancy became apparent, and that he had to be tracked down to Pittsburgh and there forced into the ceremony. A son was born three months later. Blaine responded by suing the *Sentinel* for libel, a blunder which enabled the *World* to report every detail of the case in a series of front page reports, professing unhappiness all the while that it should become grist for public gossip.[79] "We deeply regret that the campaign has fallen to this debased level. We have used our best efforts to prevent it by the suppression of all personal charges. . . . We make war on a candidate's public record, not on his private relations. . . . With Mr. Blaine as a private citizen and his family history, good or bad, we would rather have nothing to do."[80] However unpleasant the responsibility, the hitherto unknown phenomenon of a Presidential candidate suing a newspaper in the course of his campaign warranted that all the facts be reported. The *World* supplemented its news articles with frequent editorials, before and after Election Day, challenging Blaine to exonerate himself.[81]

Pulitzer's enemies bitterly resented the deviousness of his attacks on Blaine. The first intimation in July of a "story in circulation" about the Republican candidate brought a spirited reply from Leander Richardson. "I should like to point out to Jewseph Pulitzer," he wrote, "that the man who casts nameless slurs at another is a thousand times dirtier a coward than he who boldly makes public his charges and places himself in a position to be punished under the law, if what he tells is shown to be

[78] *World*, August 27, 1884, p. 4.
[79] See, for example, the *World*, August 15, 1884, p. 1; September 5, 1884, p. 1; September 20, 1884, p. 1, and September 25, 1884, p. 9.
[80] *World*, August 15, 1884, p. 4.
[81] See, for example, the *World*, September 19, 1884, p. 4; September 25, 1884, p. 4; December 9, 1884, p. 4; December 17, 1884, p. 4; December 18, 1884, p. 4; and December 19, 1884, p. 4.

false."[82] He returned to the subject the following month, by which time Blaine's suit was receiving prominent coverage on the front pages of the *World*. "As a matter of fact," Richardson noted in *The Journalist*, "The *World* has from the first occupied a contemptible position toward Mr. Blaine.

> It has made no direct charge against him, but it has, on the other hand, steadily and persistently intimated that it knew something so supremely damning that if it chose to give the story words Mr. Blaine would be be forever lost. Everybody knew, of course, that the *World* referred to the statements subsequently printed with many embellishments by the *Indianapolis Sentinel*. As soon as the paper last mentioned had taken the responsibility of the publication, the *World* lost no time in giving the story the most prominent place it could in the first column of its first page. Clearly, then, it was no feeling of chivalry, no high-minded sentiment which had up to that time prevented the editor of the *World* from publishing the vile calumny against Mr. and Mrs. Blaine—a slander rendered cowardly by its assault upon the good name of a woman, and infamous by its reflections upon the standing of her children.[83]

Richardson summarized these judgments in the issue after Election Day, when he remarked that "the vileness of the *World*'s conduct throughout has been simply shocking."[84]

It is difficult to avoid the impression that Pulitzer protested his innocence too much. When the *Tribune* charged in August that the *World* had "spent months in circulating the foulest slanders against Mr. Blaine's personal character," he responded ingenuously by challenging the newspaper to produce "from the *World*'s columns a single slander against Mr. Blaine's 'personal' character."[85] The following month he insisted, with more justification, that the Republican candidate had largely himself to blame for the unfortunate publicity. "We should not even have alluded to the Blaine scandal if it had not been forced upon

[82] *The Journalist*, July 26, 1884, p. 5.
[83] *The Journalist*, August 23, 1884, p. 4.
[84] *The Journalist*, November 8, 1884, p. 4.
[85] *World*, August 21, 1884, p. 4.

us, as a newspaper, by Mr. Blaine's first fierce appeal to the courts. . . . If he had left the scandal unnoticed, it would have died in its birth."[86] Two days after the votes had been counted still another editorial appeared justifying the newspaper's coverage of the campaign. "In the conduct of the canvass," it declared, "we took truth and reason as our guide and avoided personalities, scandals and appeals to passion. . . . Despite great provocation, we refused to cast filth for filth. If we suppressed truth in any instance it was to the advantage of the Republican candidate and in the interest of decency."[87]

These repeated statements of innocence suggest a conscience not altogether at ease with itself. The *World* waged a hard and spirited campaign, and as a sensational newspaper in a year when personalities weighed heavier than issues, it inevitably was guilty of some of the mudslinging it so bitterly resented from others. But to charge, as *The Journalist* did, that the *World* trafficked in innuendo rather than slander because of moral cowardice is to miss an important point. It printed only veiled allusions to the scandal prior to the full report in the *Indianapolis Sentinel* and the suit by Blaine, precisely because it honored the social convention of the time. The gossip about Blaine was too rich to ignore, but a Victorian sensibility prevented the newspaper from openly exploiting it. The *World*, after all, belabored Blaine with cruel and slashing attacks, many of them personal and palpably grounds for suit, during the same period that it skirted the shotgun marriage issue. Leander Richardson missed the mark in charging that "Pulitzer did not originally publish the slander simply because he was afraid to. . . . The only consideration which guides this fellow in the control of his precious paper is to keep out of the reach of criminal prosecution."[88] Its sense of propriety, not timidity, inhibited the newspaper.

The *World* demonstrated repeatedly during the campaign its lack of concern about libel suits (a daring several times tested in court), just so long as it did not have to breach the nineteenth

[86] *World*, September 23, 1884, p. 4.
[87] *World*, November 6, 1884, p. 4.
[88] *The Journalist*, August 23, 1884, p. 4.

— 81 —

century ethic on sexual reticence.[89] An article in August about Neil Gillespie Blaine, the candidate's older brother, alleged that in 1859 he had forfeited bail and fled from St. Louis to escape trial for forgery. "I was told two or three years ago that he was in Georgia in the penitentiary there; but this may not be true . . . ," a neighborhood gossip who had known the Blaines told the *World* reporter who interviewed her. "Neil Blaine was the black sheep of the family. He was always up to some meanness or other. . . . I suppose he has gone to the dogs his own way."[90] The following month brought a different example of low-blow journalism. BLAINE A VERY SICK MAN. A PROMINENT PHYSICIAN SAYS HE HAS BRIGHT'S DISEASE, a headline reported. The story opened with a statement from a Democratic-minded physician that "if elected to the Presidency James G. Blaine may not live through his term of office."[91] In two weeks at Bar Harbor observing the candidate from afar, the physician had noticed pallor, puffed eyelids, loss of breath, and general weakness. Objections from Republican organs that the *World* had breached journalistic ethics brought the rejoinder that "they perhaps forget the vast amount of fun they have been having for years at the expense of Mr. Tilden."[92] A mysterious case of vandalism at the height of the campaign provoked an even cruder charge. Unknown culprits defaced the tombstone over the grave of the Blaine's dead son by chiseling out the last figure of the child's birth date. WAS BLAINE HIMSELF THE 'INFAMOUS PERPETRATOR OF THE DEED?' the *World* asked in headline. WHO HAD A MOTIVE TO MUTILATE THE TOMBSTONE OF BLAINE'S FIRST CHILD?[93] An

[89] The *World* was sued for libel, and taken to court, on twenty-one occasions between June 1883 and December 1885. Joseph Pulitzer wrote to the law office of Roscoe Conkling on December 19, 1885, proposing a lump payment of $10,000 for legal services in handling that litigation. (*Pulitzer Papers*, Columbia University Libraries.) It is worth noting that Walt McDougall commented on Pulitzer's dread of libel suits. "He was so obsessed by the fear, . . ." the cartoonist wrote, "that he nightly read almost every paragraph in the paper. This practice eventually cost him his sight." (Walt McDougall, "Old Days on the *World*," *The American Mercury*, IV (January 1925), 23.) McDougall's medical diagnosis is facile, and his allegation of timidity contrary to the evidence of what the *World* did dare print.

[90] *World*, August 17, 1884, p. 3.

[91] *World*, September 24, 1884, p. 5.

[92] *World*, September 28, 1884, p. 4.

[93] *World*, October 17, 1884, p. 5.

attack on Governor Cleveland in Albany by an ex-convict whose
application for pardon had been rejected inspired another question: DID REPUBLICAN POLITICIANS HOPE TO FIND IN HIM A
SECOND GUITEAU? The newspaper detected sinister connotations
in the incident. "The Governor attached no political significance
to the assault," its Albany correspondent wrote, "but information from various quarters leads me to think he may be mistaken. It certainly looks very much as if the local Republican
politicians, made desperate by their waning chances, are inclined
to adopt and realize the 'campaign of assassination.' "[94] Clearly,
Pulitzer did not let the laws on libel deter him from pitching into
Blaine and his party with abandon.

But if the only restraint the *World* accepted was on sexual
matters, how does one account for the many stories on its front
page which found a place there because they dwelt on sex? The
answer is that the headlines usually implied more than the stories
contained, and that stripped of false implication, they seldom
included anything to offend the strictest Victorian mentality. Indeed, they often reflected that mentality.

Consider five of the headlines typically included in histories of
journalism to illustrate the *World*'s use of sensationalism, and the
stories that went with them.

1. WHILE THE HUSBANDS WERE AWAY. The report concerned
two women in Chicago, wives of traveling salesmen, who
while walking down the street with a friend of their husbands'
were apprehended by a policeman for smoking, and otherwise
"conducting themselves without much regard to propriety."[95]

2. A BRIDE BUT NOT A WIFE. The article described how a
barber on Centre Street won his bride's hand on the understanding that he would deposit $300 in his future father-in-law's
bank account. An argument developed after the marriage ceremony when he reneged on the promise. The father walked out,
and took his daughter with him.[96]

3. ALL FOR A WOMAN'S LOVE. The promising headline led into
an account of how a Kansas City newspaper editor shot a the-

[94] *World* October 21, 1884, p. 1.
[95] *World* May 17, 1883, p. 1.
[96] *World* May 18, 1883, p. 5.

— 83 —

atrical manager because they both loved the same woman. The wound was not fatal.[97]

4. A PREACHER'S PERFIDY. Another out-of-town item, this one reported what happened when a Scranton minister suggested to his lady friend that she take him as a lover without worrying about the formality of marriage. (Therein lay his perfidy.) "Horrified, shocked, frightened, she repelled him indignantly and threatened to inform her friends if he dared to repeat his words."[98]

5. LITTLE LOTTA'S LOVERS. "Little Lotta" was the nickname of Miss Charlotte Crabtree, the actress, and the story concerned the fact that she had been engaged several times without making it to the altar.[99]

The evidence is overwhelming that the *World* did not achieve its great circulation by defying contemporary convention, but by going only so far as convention allowed.[100]

Furthermore, although social custom dictated far less restraints when dealing with violence, even here on occasion the *World* lectured to other newspapers on when good taste demanded a halt. During the summer of 1884 the country was

[97] *World*, June 10, 1883, p. 1.

[98] *World*, June 11, 1883, p. 1.

[99] *World*, June 19, 1883, p. 5. Happily, the *World* was able to report on July 4, in a front-page story, that Little Lotta had finally gotten married.

[100] The same attitude is seen in a memorandum Pulitzer addressed to Don Seitz on Ocotber 2, 1902. Pulitzer had been reading reports in the German press about an abortion ring uncovered in Dresden, and suggested that the *World* might wish to pick up the story. What is notable, however, is his demand that the utmost care be taken in handling such material. "If you will . . . pledge yourself," he began, "to be conscientiously careful in printing the story with utmost delicacy and cleanness I will . . . allow publication of one of the most terribly shocking stories I have ever heard of. It will certainly make a sensation, but you must put it in such form as not to create the idea that it is printed as a sensation but for its human interest, as a study of modern morals and German character. It is a case at Dresden in which some 40 women have been tried for abortion or infanticide. . . . Instructions are that no matter how interesting any point may be it must not be published in an indelicate or offensive form." He concluded with instructions about what sort of words might be used. "Nearly anything can be said if only the right words are chosen although these are often difficult to find. The word abortion must be avoided, 'Criminal Operation' is better." (*Pulitzer Papers*, Library of Congress.) Although the memorandum dates almost twenty years after the period under consideration, and applies to a newspaper considerably more sedate than the *World* of 1883 to 1885, it reflects a morality which remained fairly constant throughout Pulitzer's career.

horrified to discover that the survivors of an ill-fated American expedition to the Arctic had sustained life by eating their dead comrades. Every newspaper in the nation (with the *New York Times* taking the lead in uncovering the story) gave banner treatment to the accumulating evidence of cannibalism in the Far North. The *World* devoted three entire front-page columns to the first report, and another front-page column to the next day's follow-up.[101] Still it was Pulitzer who first suggested to his colleagues that the time had come to let the horror pass from public consciousness.

> The casket containing the remains of Whistler, one of the Greely party, has been opened and the evidences of cannibalism obtained. . . . What good does all this do? The whole country is convinced that the poor wretches constituting the Greely party were compelled to eat each other in order to subsist, and there is no further need of breaking open tombs. It is not proposed to prosecute the survivors, and no sensible people condemn the cannibalism under the circumstances. We have had enough of these sickening revelations to make Arctic exploration rather unpopular for some years. So let the matter drop.[102]

This is not to suggest that the *World* was a newspaper of delicate sensibility, but simply that its sensationalism consisted more of reporting what the other papers ignored than of exploiting a common story until sheer detail made it an offense against public morality and journalistic judgment.

It is only negative praise to say the *World* followed contemporary dictates of good taste. A sensational journal is also capable of rising about its commercial base to provide some of the most inspired news writing. The human interest story, which is at the heart of the form, becomes at its best more than a device to please the masses and takes on many of the characteristics of literature. Robert Park noted that "it is possible . . . to select certain particularly picturesque or romantic incidents and treat them symbolically, for their human interest rather than their

---

[101] *World*, August 15, 1884, p. 1, for the first report; and August 16, 1884, p. 1, for the sequel.
[102] *World*, August 20, 1884, p. 4.

— 85 —

individual and personal significance. In this way news ceases to be wholly personal and assumes the form of art. It ceases to be the record of the doings of individual men and women and becomes an impersonal account of manners and life."[103] We have an example in the account referred to previously of Ida Grant's death at the hands of an abortionist. Her tragedy is a sob story, but it is also a universal statement about suffering and grief in obscure places.[104] The *World* occasionally approached this ultimate dimension in its articles, if only because it considered the Ida Grants important.

Moreover, the *World*'s heavy reliance on accounts of crime and violence was at least partially determined by its commitment to crusade in a vice-ridden city. The next decade would see a committee of the State Senate uncover evidence of widespread collusion between New York City's police department and underworld.[105] It was often difficult in such a situation to distinguish between stories intended to stimulate circulation, and those that agitated for reform. For example, the newspaper printed a series of articles between the fall of 1884 and spring of 1885 describing instances in which policemen had indiscriminately used their clubs on innocent victims.[106] Although every one of the

---

[103] Robert E. Park, "The Natural History of the Newspaper," reprinted in Robert E. Park *et al.*, *The City* (Chicago, 1925), p. 84.

[104] Helen M. Hughes has provided the best analysis of what the human interest story involves, and what it can become. She writes persuasively about the universal meaning of ordinary events. "A story is said to be expressive when it outlives the moment when it is news. This means expressive of the familiar facts of human nature. To present the news in this, its most interesting and understandable aspect, is to subordinate its unique and sensational elements and to translate them into the common and the familiar; to make it a new variation on an old theme. For then the reader is able to appreciate it as the reporter has done.

"When, however, a unique event is reduced to commoner terms, its denotation grows. Other instances and associations are brought to bear on it; it grows 'adequate as a means of conveying the fulness of feeling' and it becomes a symbol for a type of experience. When the reporter sees it as another instance of human helplessness, of destiny, or of fate, and the reader reflects: Life is like that! both have gone beyond the immediate news. Its meaning is fuller; indeed, literature uses language for its symbolic value." Hughes, *News and the Human Interest Story*, p. 101.

[105] See M. R. Werner, *Tammany Hall* (Garden City, N.Y., 1931), pp. 356-420, for a summary of the Lexow Committee report of 1895, which revealed the extent of police corruption in the city controlled by Richard Croker.

[106] See, for example, the *World*, September 8, 1884, p. 1; November 17, 1884, p. 1 (a McDougall cartoon); or January 26, 1885, p. 8.

articles qualified as sensationalism, they culminated in an editorial statement against police brutality.[107] An even more extensive series of reports—of citizens robbed in broad daylight on the street, of brothels and gambling dens operating without police interference—satisfied the appetite of the public for scandal while laying the basis for a spirited attack on police maladministration.[108] The series—and issue—came to a head in the person of "Marm" Mandelbaum, notoriously the most active receiver of stolen property in the city, who while under indictment and free on bail, was allowed to elude police surveillance and flee to Canada. "No man possessed of his senses can for a moment believe that the notorious woman Mandelbaum could have carried on her business in this city for twenty years without the connivance of the police," the *World* declared editorially.[109] It drew together the evidence laid out in many previous stories, and incidentally avoided a suit for libel, by quoting an unnamed "prominent official" who charged that "the detective office is one of the most corrupt branches of the public service. It is thoroughly rotten. . . . They accept bribes and wink at open violations of the law. They are blackmailers and the people whom they select for their victims cannot very well but submit to their extortionate demands. They accumulate fortunes and become owners of real estate while they receive no larger salaries than a poorly paid reporter."[110]

The most striking example of how sensationalism could be used to crusade for a principle occurred in April of 1885, when a sixteen-year-old girl named Maggie Morris accused an off-duty policeman of luring her to the basement of a dance hall on East

[107] *World*, February 11, 1885, p. 4.

[108] For reports and comments on police inefficiency, see the *World*, December 11, 1884, p. 1; December 12, 1884, p. 4; December 13, 1884, p. 4. For articles on gambling and vice dens which the police left unmolested, see September 17, 1884, p. 1; September 18, 1884, p. 1; September 19, 1884, p. 8; October 20, 1884, p. 1; October 25, 1884, p. 1; January 14, 1885, p. 7; January 21, 1885, p. 1; January 22, 1885, p. 4.

[109] *World*, July 28, 1884, p. 4. Mrs. Mandelbaum was first arrested on July 23, 1884, and arraigned on July 25. Her arrest resulted in a public dispute between the District Attorney's office, which out of distrust for the police had hired Pinkertons to make the initial arrest, and Inspector Byrnes' Detective Bureau. Mandelbaum's flight came to light on December 4, when she failed to appear as scheduled in court.

[110] *World*, July 30, 1884, p. 8.

Broadway, and there raping her. The *World* used all the standard devices of sensationalism in covering the story, including a headline the first day which read FOR GOD'S SAKE KILL ME!—words the girl had sobbed as she reported the crime.[111] Yet this story was different; for while Maggie Morris waited in a cell for her charges to be heard, Police Sergeant Crowley, the accused, walked the streets on bail, openly boasting that his friends in high places would protect him. The *World* immediately responded to the challenge, and whether motivated more by a love of justice or love of circulation, made the girl's cause its own. It offered to put up bail for her; it raised money for her widowed mother; most important, it declared in a series of front page articles and editorials extending for several weeks that it would not allow political influence to impede the workings of justice. "The ruffian Crowley who assaulted poor Maggie Morris boasts of influence with the politicians," an editorial declared expansively when Crowley's inability to raise a newly imposed bail of $15,000 put him behind bars. "Although all the other journals were tame or completely silent, the *World* appealed for justice, and the whole city was aroused. We do not doubt that but for the *World*'s determined attitude Sergt. Crowley's influence could have stood him in good stead."[112] The newspaper intensified the campaign as the date for the trial approached, warning that it would "watch this prosecution narrowly."[113] Its vigilance was rewarded in mid-May, when a jury found Crowley guilty as charged, and he was sentenced to seventeen and a half years at hard labor in Sing Sing. At that moment the *World* could boast that its sensationalism had functioned for the public good. "When the assault was committed . . . the *World*, almost alone, insisted day after day that the case was one which should not only awaken the chivalric resentment of every man, but should be sharply and sternly dealt with. Now that Crowley passes out of

[111] *World*, April 22, 1885, p. 8.

[112] *World*, May 7, 1885, p. 4. To follow the *World*'s developing interest in the case, see April 29, 1885, p. 1; April 30, 1885, pp. 1, 4; May 1, 1885, pp. 1, 4; May 2, 1885, pp. 1, 4; May 3, 1885, p. 2; May 5, 1885, p. 8; May 6, 1885, p. 8; May 7, 1885, p. 4; May 10, 1885, p. 19; May 13, 1885, p. 1; May 16, 1885, pp. 1, 4; May 19, 1885, pp. 4, 5.

[113] *World*, May 2, 1885, p. 4.

public sight, perhaps forever, the *World* may be pardoned for saying that from the first it treated this case without sentimentalism and solely in the interest of a worthy body of public defenders no less than in the interest of the public itself."[114]

Finally, although the *World* itself admitted that it meant the front page to be so colorful that thousands upon thousands would become regular readers, and hence subject to conversion or enlightenment by the editorials on page four, the newspaper could—when occasion demanded—use that front page as an adjunct to the editorials within. The list of lead stories for the days immediately preceding November 4, 1884, when the nation went to the polls to elect Grover Cleveland, contrasts strikingly with an earlier list of *World* stories.[115]

Thursday, October 30

MAMMON'S HOMAGE.

BLAINE HOBNOBBING WITH THE MIGHTY MONEY KINGS.

THE BANQUET IN HIS HONOR AT DELMONICO'S LAST NIGHT.

MILLIONAIRES AND MONOPOLISTS SEAL THEIR ALLEGIANCE.

A LIST OF MEN GATHERED BY CYRUS FIELD AND JAY GOULD.

LUCULLUS ENJOYS HIMSELF WHILE THE COUNTRY SORROWS.

Friday, October 31

VAST REPUBLICAN FRAUD.

TEN THOUSAND "COLONISTS" REGISTERED IN THIS CITY ALONE.

Col. John J. Freeman, the Negro
Politician, and Several of his
Aides, Arrested - Warrants Issued
for the Capture of Others -
Pinkerton's Detectives at Work
in Every District.

[114] *World*, May 19, 1885, p. 4.
[115] In each case the headlines appeared in the lead story slot on p. 1.

Saturday, November 1

BURNING OF THE MAASDAM.

THE MIRACULOUS ESCAPE OF THE 185 PERSONS ON BOARD.

Landing of the Fortunate Passengers -
After a Night of Terror, Passed in
Attempting to Quench the Flames, the
Ship is Abandoned - Picked Up by the
Rhein.

Sunday, November 2

A REVOLUTION

SUSPENDING BUSINESS TO GREET CLEVELAND.

50,000 SOLID MEN MARCH- ING UP BROADWAY.

A SPLENDID ARRAY OF BUSINESS MEN'S CLUBS.

BANNERS, CHEERS, SONGS AND MARCHING CRIES FOR REFORM.

A PROCESSION OF VOTERS FIVE MILES IN LENGTH.

EVERY MOTTO AND EVERY VOICE A PROTEST AGAINST BLAINEISM.

Monday, November 3

DOING MURDER IN ARMOR.

LOUISIANA REPUBLICANS ARMED FOR A FIGHT AND GUARDED BY CORSELETS.

Attempted Intimidation of Democratic
Colored Voters Leads to the Bloody
New Iberia Riot - Eighteen Bodies
Collected to Date - One at Least
Dead of Fright - Kellogg Ruffians in
Louisiana Fire Upon Democrats.

Tuesday, November 4

GOVERNOR CLEVELAND AT HOME.

HE QUIETLY RETURNS TO BUFFALO TO DEPOSIT HIS VOTE.

Awaiting With Calm Confidence the
Verdict of the American People -
His Old Friends and Neighbors Grasp
Him by the Hand - How He Will Vote.

All of the stories save one bore on the *World*'s crusade to elect Cleveland, and the single exception was of such importance that every newspaper carried it as a first lead.

Pulitzer's most thoughtful statement on the uses of sensationalism came early in 1885, in commenting on the death of the *New York Extra*, and *Truth*. Such an occasion is always a grim one for newspapermen, a time for soul-searching and analysis. The fact that the journals in question had little to recommend them was of secondary importance. In soberly considering the reasons for their failure, Pulitzer blamed above all their misunderstanding of what sensationalism implied. A newspaper could not survive, he insisted, if it underestimated the intelligence of the populace and appealed only to base and vulgar instincts. The lifeblood of the press was its commitment to noble causes. It might use colorful devices to persuade the masses of men to read, but if it ever regarded the color as more important than the commitment, it had ceased to justify its existence. Pulitzer's statement is worth quoting at length.

> Two daily newspapers have just gone out of existence. . . . Is not the cause of their failure to be traced to the fact that neither of them represented any principle or definite purpose with which all decent people are in sympathy? That they appealed to the low and vulgar rather than the better instincts of man? That the one was given over to vile sensationalism and personalities,[116] and the other necessarily confined to the consideration of mere factional or personal interests, which excluded the higher aims and purposes of true journalism?[117]

[116] Pulitzer was referring to the *Extra*, and probably had in mind the newspaper's scandal-mongering treatment of the rumors concerning Grover Cleveland and Maria Halpin.

[117] *Truth* had been little more than a house organ for organized labor.

The time has gone by when a newspaper can be made permanently great and prosperous in this city on sensationalism or as a personal organ. . . .

At the outset of its new career the *World* expressed the conviction that the success of a journal must depend on its character; that an earnest, vigorous advocacy of the public welfare, a sincere devotion to the cause of good government and public virtue and a fearless and unceasing warfare against all fraud, sham, dishonest and false pretense would alone secure the approval and support of the masses. The history of New York journalism within the last two years vindicates our theory and our practice. . . .

In this country it is the highest evidence of the improved taste, the general intelligence and virtue of the people that personal organs and claptrap, sensational journalism no longer can live, and that to be a great and permanent success a modern newspaper must have honest convictions for its guide and the public good for its aim.[118]

The words bring us full circle. Sensational journalism as practiced by Pulitzer, if not the fare for cultivated and mature minds, served an important function in introducing thousands of men to the daily newspaper habit. It demanded a skill as impressive as any within the profession, and while offering color and excitement, was also careful to honor the mores of the time. The too-easy condemnation of the form, among Pulitzer's contemporaries as well as modern men, might well be reconsidered in light of the considerable good that it accomplished in making the daily newspaper a nearly universal habit.

[118] *World*, January 13, 1885, p. 4.

CHAPTER THREE

ILLUSTRATION

Illustration first appeared in newspapers two and a half centuries before Joseph Pulitzer acquired the *New York World*. On December 20th, 1638, the *Weekly News* in England printed a full page engraving of the Isle of Saint Michael to enliven its account of a calamitous volcanic upheaval there.[1] The process crossed the Atlantic on January 26, 1707, when the *Boston News–Letter* ran a woodcut of the new flag adopted for the United Kingdom of England and Scotland. On May 9, 1754, Benjamin Franklin demonstrated to the country the power of newspaper illustration by printing in the *Pennsylvania Gazette* a one-column woodcut of a snake divided into eight parts, with the caption, "Join, or Die." Its clear moral hastened the day when thirteen quarreling neighbors would unite as one nation.

Illustration has also been an important component of sensationalism almost since the form was born. The *New York Herald* under James Gordon Bennett used woodcuts in its first year of existence to supplement an account of a terrible fire which raged through the city's business district. A two-column cut showed the charred ruins of the Merchants' Exchange, and another mapped out the area of conflagration.[2] By 1873 techniques had improved enough for a Canadian firm of engravers to establish the *New York Daily Graphic*, the first of the so-called picture newspapers.[3]

[1] Mason Jackson, *The Pictorial Press: Its Origin and Progress* (London, 1885), pp. 42-43.

[2] The cuts appeared in the issue of December 21, 1835. The *New York Sun* experimented with the device even earlier. On September 14, 1833, it ran a two-column cut (a wood engraving made by hand) of "Herschel's Forty-Feet Telescope." (Cited by Alfred McClung Lee, *The Daily Newspaper in America* [New York, 1937], p. 129.) The illustration was part of a great journalistic hoax. Day's newspaper invented the telescope and the amphibious moon-man "of a spherical form" seen through it to thrill the country for a few days and add thousands to its circulation.

[3] The *Daily Graphic* used photo-engraved line illustrations from its inception, and in 1880 became the first newspaper to use the halftone process. S. H.

The question then arises why the *World* from its first years under Pulitzer was associated with the further development of the art. As with the broader subject of sensationalism itself, the contribution consisted more of carrying an existing form forward then of inventing a new form. Somewhat timidly at first, but with ever more assurance, Pulitzer and his staff came to see in illustration a great, unexploited medium of communication, and elevated it from an occasional novelty to an important tool in reporting the news.

The *World*, as already noted, took for its audience the great mass of men, not only "judges of the Supreme Court" but workingmen and immigrants—literates, semi-literates, and sometimes even illiterates. For the latter all the clichés about the greater descriptive power of pictures over words became particularly relevant. "We are very proud of our pictures," Pulitzer replied to a subscriber who objected to their use. "We observe that the populace appreciate them, and that there is always an extra demand for the *World* when it is illuminated, so to speak. A great many people in the world require to be educated through the eye, as it were. . . . We shall continue our illustrations."[4]

Pulitzer printed pictures for the same reason that he printed sensation: to stimulate circulation. It took a practical lesson, however, to convince him that he had hit on the key. According to *The Journalist*,

> When Joseph Pulitzer went to Europe he was a little undecided about the woodcuts. He left orders to gradually get rid of them, as he thought it tended to lower the dignity of the paper, and he was not satisfied that the cuts helped it in its circulation. After Pulitzer was on the Atlantic, Col. Cockerill began to carry out the express wishes of its editor and proprietor. He found, however, that the circulation of the paper went with the cuts, and, like the good news-

---

Horgan, who developed the process for the *Daily Graphic*, went on to become art director of the *New York Herald*, and later the *New York Tribune*. Because of his talents, Reid's newspaper printed the first halftone off a stereotype web-fed press on January 21, 1897.

[4] *New York World*, February 21, 1884, p. 4.

paper general that he was, he instantly changed his tactics. He put in more cuts than ever, and the circulation rose like a thermometer on a hot day, until it reached over 230,000 on the day of Grant's funeral. This ought to be conclusive as to the influence of woodcuts on the circulation of a newspaper.[5]

Ever the moralist, Pulitzer liked to make the case that his pictures, aside from selling newspapers, served a high social purpose. He justified lurid accounts of crime and violence by arguing that they taught potential offenders to respect, or at least fear, the law. The illustrations which accompanied those articles helped law enforcement officers to track down such knaves as ignored the *World*'s preachments. The first triumph occurred in the summer of 1884, when a Montreal detective arrested John Eno, a New York stockbroker under indictment for fraud, on the the strength of a *World* portrait.[6] Pulitzer was hardly the man to take refuge in modest reticence:

> Detective Farey, of Montreal, who captured Eno at Quebec, says that his attention was first attracted to the decamping ex-banker by recognizing him as the counterpart of the picture published in the *New York World*. This is a decided triumph for our artist. Some of our jealous contemporaries have affected great contempt for our efforts in the line of cut-work. The Montreal incident attests to the value of our illustrations, and demonstrates that while we are educating the masses with our pictures we are at the same time lending a helping hand to Justice. Our portrait of Eno was an achievement that we feel proud of. We shall continue the good work.[7]

Later in the year the opportunity for self-congratulations gloriously recurred. Authorities in Hamilton, Ontario, used a *World* portrait to recognize and apprehend "Marm" Mandelbaum, the notorious New York fence who had broken bail to flee the country. MARM MANDELBAUM ARRESTED, the newspaper trumpeted in a front page headline. TAKEN IN CANADA THROUGH

[5] *The Journalist*, August 22, 1885, p. 5.

[6] The episode is reminiscent of Boss Tweed's arrest by Spanish officials, who recognized him from an old Thomas Nast cartoon.

[7] *World*, June 1, 1884, p. 4.

— 95 —

"THE WORLD'S" PORTRAIT OF HER.[8] The warm glow of accomplishment was still reflected in the newspaper's headlines at the time of her arraignment two days later. MRS. MANDELBAUM'S QUERY. SHE DESIRES TO KNOW WHO DREW HER PICTURE FOR "THE WORLD."[9] Lest any of its competitors missed the message, the *World* carefully repeated it in separate editorials:

> While some of our esteemed, aesthetic contemporaries assume to censure the frequent illustrations in the *World* as sensational, we have the satisfaction of knowing that they are serviceable as well. Our perfect portrait of Eno led to his recognition and arrest in Montreal. The *World's* beautiful picture of "Marm" Mandelbaum brought about her arrest in Hamilton, Ont., . . . Thus, while we are contributing our share toward the advancement of American art and are educating as well as amusing our numerous readers, we are subserving the cause of public justice by presenting faithful portraits which enable the officers of the law, here and abroad, to arrest criminals.[10]

Of course any newspaper would have preened itself on scoring an equivalent triumph.[11] But there is something more in the *World's* tone, a sense of vindication needed and received, as if a newspaper which meant to be earnest and reforming could not base its editorial policies solely on the desire for circulation.

The *World's* achievement consisted in using illustration not only as a marvel to be admired for its own sake, as in the case of

[8] *World*, December 9, 1884, p. 1.

[9] *World*, December 11, 1884, p. 5.

[10] *Ibid.*, p. 4; see also editorial on December 9, 1884, p. 4.

[11] Just as the *World's* competitors, and enemies, would try to make light of the incident. Leander Richardson, who dipped his pen in vitriol every time he commented on Pulitzer for *The Journalist*, thought the display brazenly unjustified. "The *World* has certainly got the champion nerve. The editor of that paper now has the assurance to affirm that the arrest of John C. Eno and Mother Mandelbaum and her precious party of Canadian tourists were affected through the likenesses of these distinguished personages which had appeared in the columns of the paper mentioned. . . . Mother Mandelbaum has been known by sight to every well-ordered detective in America for twenty years. As for Eno, he was arrested through descriptions furnished to the Canadian police, who acted in his case with a good deal of skill. Some of the likenesses printed in the *World* are by no means bad, but it is an exhibition of vanity altogether too childish to be seriously considered which prompts the editor to make such breaks concerning his paper as that to which I have alluded." *The Journalist*, December 13, 1884, p. 4.

the *Daily Graphic*, nor as an occasional fillip for an otherwise dull page, as in the case of the *Herald*, but rather as a major tool in the art of reporting the news. It printed far more pictures than any other journal had ever dreamed of printing, but more important, it printed them for a purpose, to enhance accompanying news stories or editorial comments. Although the Sunday *World*, as shall be seen, considered a portrait of a pretty girl or dashing soldier its own justification, in the daily edition illustration ceased to be a toy and became an adjunct to the written word.

The achievement is all the more remarkable when one considers the laborious steps involved in running a picture off high-speed presses. Artists would transfer their initial sketches into pen and ink drawings, using thick, coarse lines so that the presses did not have to be continually stopped to eliminate ink smears. The drawings were next sent downstairs to be photographed on zinc. Engravers set to work immediately on the zinc cuts, painfully etching in by hand with acid the space between the lines. As soon as the job had been completed, a messenger rushed the cuts to the pressroom where they were put on blocks, and in later years stereotyped with the rest of the page and prepared for printing. Each step required skill and extreme care, but the work had to be done under the pressure of a deadline to have the cuts ready for the early morning pressrun.[12]

[12] See *The Journalist*, December 26, 1885, pp. 4-5, for a description of the *World* staff at work illustrating yesterday's sensation in today's newspaper. "I was chatting with McDougall, of the *World*, on Thursday, November 19th. . . . News was brought of the falling of a building in Bethune Street. McDougall and his assistant, Folsom, sprang to their feet, and . . . started for the scene of the accident. It was then five o'clock, and the pictures were to be in the paper the next morning. . . . Almost by feeling, McDougall sketched the scene with a blue pencil, while Folsom darted in another direction. Twice McDougall had to go to the street lamp to judge of the correctness of his sketch. . . . After taking a few notes we hurried back to the World Building, where we found Folsom already busy at work.

"With increasing interest I watched the pictures growing beneath their fingers. . . . At 7:45 the first double column sketch was finished. The drawing was made about ten inches wide, and with an amount of detail and shading that surprised me. This was despatched to the photo-engraver. A photograph is taken from the ink drawing upon zinc, and the spaces between the lines etched deeply with acid. This process occupies two hours at least, and after being looked over by an engraver, the block is sent to the press-room, a perfect fac-simile of the original sketch. It is then stereotyped with the rest of the type in the page, bent in the form of a half circle, and goes into the press,

During the early years, the *World*'s illustrations came from the pens of two artists, both of whom achieved fame working for Pulitzer. Valerian Gribayedoff, a Russian emigré with a particular knack for portraiture, arrived first. He had already started to make a reputation in the city when Pulitzer sent for him, and invited him to join the *World* staff as an artist-in-residence, his responsibility to contribute regular portraits of New Yorkers famous and unknown. Although magazines and specialized journals, like the *New York Daily Graphic*, had employed men in similar capacities for some time, Gribayedoff was possibly the first staff artist to be hired by a conventional daily newspaper.

Walt McDougall, a young man of cherubic appearance and vast good humor, had done free-lance work for *Puck* and the *Daily Graphic* when he decided one day in 1884 to submit a rejected cartoon at the *World* office. "The idea of offering a political cartoon to a daily paper," he wrote, "seemed so utterly absurd that I thrust the cardboard roll into the hand of the elevator boy . . . and stammered, 'Give that to the editor and tell him he can have it if he wants it.' "[13] Pulitzer and Cockerill so appreciated the drawing that they ran it across the top of the front page. They did not realize that its size could be reduced, and since it measured exactly five columns across, that is the way it appeared. The young man who arrived at Park Row the next morning to collect his fee was offered a steady job at $50 a week, a figure that placated even his Republican mother and relatives. Over the next sixteen years McDougall's irreverent cartoons became a staple of the new journalism.

It would be inaccurate to suggest that the *World* embarked boldly, or all at once, on its policy of illustrating the news. The first effort—a four-column cut of the Brooklyn Bridge—seemed almost to frighten Pulitzer.[14] At least he made no extravagant claims for what it portended. "The *Graphic* must not be alarmed by our efforts in the illustrated line," he wrote. "We have no in-

from which the paper emerges at, say two o'clock, with the result of the night's work in the shape of six accurate pictures."
[13] Walt McDougall, "Old Days on *The World*," *The American Mercury*, IV (January 1925), 21.
[14] *World*, May 22, 1883, p. 1.

tention of attempting rivalry in that direction. The *Graphic* is the one newspaper in New York which is *sui generis* and unapproachable. We concede the field."[15] As the months passed, however, the *World* confidently printed more and more cuts, and measured the response in a soaring circulation. The timid first efforts gave way to ever more grandiose projects, and at times even to a sort of self-parody. Not content with "X marks the spot" accounts of murder and rapine, it took to supplementing even casual interviews with diagrams showing the rooms the reporter passed through to reach his subject, where the principals sat, the arrangement of the furniture, and so on.[16] By the summer of 1884, on hearing that the *Herald* had imported its own artist, Pulitzer issued a revised estimate as to which dailies led the field in illustrated journalism. "The *Herald*'s pink eye has imported an artistic German Baron to make pictures for it, but the *World* still stands at the head of illustrated daily journals, closely followed by the *Graphic*."[17]

It would be useless to describe all the portraits and cartoons which appeared in the newspaper during the early years, but two categories of illustration deserve special mention. Together with the daily pictorial accounts of men and events in the news, they constituted the *World*'s great achievement.

During the summer and fall of 1884, Pulitzer committed the full resources of his newspaper to defeating the Presidential candidacies of James G. Blaine and Benjamin Butler. No weapon was used with deadlier effect than the multi-column, front page cartoons which the *World* published on an average of twice a week between August 10th and Election Day.[18] It is obviously impossible to measure with precision the effectiveness of each element in a national campaign, but the closeness of the vote in New York State suggests that the *World*'s cartoons, culminating with the famous portrayal of the "Feast of Belshazzar," con-

[15] *World*, May 23, 1883, p. 4.
[16] A good example are the four meaningless cuts which accompanied a *World* interview with Colonel Mapleson and Adelina Patti. *World*, December 10, 1883, p. 5.
[17] *World*, July 6, 1884, p. 4.
[18] During that period the *World* published twenty anti-Blaine cartoons, six anti-Butler cartoons, and one pro-Cleveland cartoon, a total of twenty-seven.

tributed significantly to putting Grover Cleveland in the White House.

The cartoon campaign of 1884 represented the first concerted effort by a newspaper to win the minds of men who could not or would not take opinions from the printed word. Just as Arthur Brisbane would later become the highest paid of all editorial writers while working for Hearst because of his ability to "talk politics and philosophy in the language of truckmen and lumbermen," McDougall's and Gribayedoff's drawings made sense to those barely able to decipher the meaning of a headline, or not enough concerned about public events to scan the articles available to them.[19] A drawing of Butler seated complacently on a heap of his ill-gotten booty, or Blaine shrinking from a cascade of Mulligan Letters, made its own point. Contemporaries were shocked that Pulitzer printed his political cartoons on the front page; nothing like it had ever been done before. They failed to understand that the innovation followed logically when the publisher decided to reach the masses of men with a political message.

Political cartoons have always been much more effective in a negative role—tearing down rather than building up. It is interesting that Pulitzer pre-empted the front page only once during the critical weeks prior to the election to portray his candidate in heroic pose. The notably bland effort by McDougall showed a svelte, determined-looking Cleveland receiving the plaudits of the crowd at a Democratic rally in Brooklyn.[20]

---

[19] The description of Brisbane's editorial style, by Will Irwin, is quoted in Helen M. Hughes, *News and the Human Interest Story* (Chicago, 1940), p. 42. The example she cites in evidence of the remark is interesting, for it is clearly an attempt to draw a cartoon in words.

> "Trusts and unions are both combinations, beyond question. But a pronounced difference distinguishes them, and we shall endeavor to make it clearer.
> "You see a horse after a hard day's work grazing in a swampy meadow. He has done his duty and is getting what he can in return.
> "On the horse's flank you see a leech, sucking blood.
> "The leech is the trust.
> "The horse is the labor union."

Brisbane's type of editorializing was only a variation on McDougall's and Gribayedoff's—a verbal drawing.

[20] *World*, October 17, 1884, p. 1.

Effort was far better expended on Benjamin Butler, who as the self-avowed candidate of the workingman threatened to draw off a critical number of Democratic votes. Each of the six cartoons devoted to him carried the same message: Butler is a fraud, he has done nothing to help labor, his candidacy is part of a corrupt bargain to steal the election for Blaine. One cartoon showed "The Modern Belisarius" sitting on a pile of Civil War loot, idly examining a diamond ring on his finger. Dana is haranguing a group of workingmen on the candidate's behalf, while in the background Reid and Blaine collapse into each other's arms in laughter.[21]

DANA—THIS GREAT WARRIOR, NOW REDUCED TO POLITICAL MENDICANCY, HAS ALWAYS BEEN THE FRIEND OF LABOR. CAN'T YOU WORKINGMEN GIVE HIM A LIFE?

WORKINGMAN—HIS APPEARANCE BELIES HIS PROFESSIONS. HE IS NOT ONE OF US. WHAT HAS HE EVER DONE FOR US? WHY SHOULD HE SOLICIT OUR SUPPORT?[22]

An even more famous cartoon on the same theme depicted Butler as a tattered beggar, a sign on his chest reading "I Am Blind." With one hand he clutched a little beggar girl, unmistakably Charles A. Dana, and with the other held out a hat for whatever votes might be dropped into it. The reader sees, however, that the outstretched hat has no bottom, and that Blaine has crawled between the beggar's legs to catch the votes which pass through it.[23]

James G. Blaine, possibly the most popular political figure of his time, represented a far more formidable adversary. His undeniable charm seemed to weigh heavier with Americans than his reputation for rascality, and a long career of "twisting the lion's tail" won him widespread support among immigrant voters, especially Irishmen, ordinarily considered safe for the Democratic candidate. Not surprisingly, the *World* marked Blaine as a prime target, attacking him in front page cartoons on twenty different occasions during the twelve weeks of the campaign.

[21] Of course Dana's presence testified to his support of Butler in the editorial pages of the *New York Sun*.

[22] *World,* August 30, 1884, p. 1.

[23] *World,* October 20, 1884, p. 1. The other anti-Butler cartoons appeared on August 17, 1884, p. 1; September 15, 1884, p. 1; October 5, 1884, p. 1; and November 1, 1884, p. 1.

It used those opportunities to undercut Blaine's appeal among New York City immigrants, making arch reference to the "Rum, Romanism, and Rebellion" remark,[24] or satirizing the candidate's equivocal stand on prohibition. A cartoon by Gribayedoff showed him skulking away from a polling place in Maine, rather than pass through opposing ranks of wets and drys to cast his ballot in a state referendum on the liquor issue.[25] Similarly, the *World* tried to make light of Blaine's reputation for dealing sternly with the British. In a cartoon entitled "Too Busy to Bother the British Lion," McDougall portrayed the former Secretary of State avidly clutching a sheath of bonds—securities in the Fort Smith and Little Rock Railroad, the Union Pacific, the Hocking Valley coal mines—while in the background British policemen clubbed American citizens of Irish descent and dragged them off to Kilmainham Jail.[26]

A second category of anti-Blaine cartoons hopefully depicted the disaster soon to overtake the Republican Party. Inspired by the recent sinking of the "Tallapoosa," Secretary of the Navy Chandler's self-appropriated government yacht, Republicanism was portrayed on several occasions as a boat adrift in a storm, sinking or about to sink.[27] On other occasions it was depicted as a bankrupt movement whose pretensions to public virtue would finally be stripped away on Election Day.[28]

The *World* always returned, however, to the theme of Blaine's personal dishonesty. In a cartoon entitled "The Flesh-Pots of Plunder," he was portrayed sitting on the "Widow Butler's" lap, admiring a stew rich with such delicacies as land grabs, river and harbor steals, bribes from monopolists, and so on. "What a beautiful vision that is, Jimmy," the Widow says. "How savory the odor and how inviting the feast!" "Yes, Widow," Blaine answers. "We will have at least four years of splendid picking. But what a long spoon you have!"[29] The newspaper worked the

[24] See the *World*, November 2, 1884, p. 1.
[25] *World*, September 13, 1884, p. 1.
[26] *World*, October 31, 1884, p. 1.
[27] *World*, August 31, 1884, p. 1; see also September 27, 1884, p. 1.
[28] *World*, October 10, 1884, p. 1; October 18, 1884, p. 1; October 28, 1884, p. 1.
[29] *World*, August 24, 1884, p. 1.

same vein with a drawing of Blaine's $150,000 mansion in Washington to show what could be managed after "Twenty Years in Congress" on a top salary of $3,000 a year;[30] or of Blaine and Logan as "Babes in the Woods," huddled in a tree trunk watching the falling leaves—labelled Mulligan Letters—harken an early winter;[31] or of the candidate lying in bed assailed by nightmare visions of past corruptions "The Night Before his Bosworth Field."[32]

By all odds the most effective cartoon of this sort, and probably the most effective of the campaign, was McDougall's and Gribayedoff's joint representation of "The Royal Feast of Belshazzar and the Money Kings." Blaine's ill-advised acceptance of an invitation to dine in New York City with a gathering of the wealthiest men in America, in order to raise last minute campaign funds, gave the *World* its opening.[33] Hoping to establish once and for all the corrupt relationship between Blaine and the money kings, it portrayed him seated at a table heaped high with drink and meat, surrounded from left to right by Aspinwall, Dillon, Evarts, Morton, Sloan, Field, Dows, Gould, Mills, Vanderbilt (wearing a crown), Elkins, Roach, Dowd, Depew, Davis, Hatch, Seligman and Sage, each of them sporting rock-sized diamonds as shirt studs.[34] In front of the table, a tattered couple with their

[30] *World*, September 6, 1884, p. 1.

[31] *World*, September 21, 1884, p. 1. The "Mulligan Letters" revealed that as a Congressman, Blaine had helped to secure a large land grant for the Little Rock and Fort Smith Railroad in Arkansas. In return for the favor, he was granted the privilege of selling the bonds of the railroad at a generous commission. Blaine obtained the letters from James Mulligan, their possessor, on a ruse, and refused to return them when asked. He also refused to submit them to a Congressional investigating committee, claiming that they were purely personal. Although he tried to undo some of the damage to his reputation by reading bland extracts from the letters into the *Congressional Record*, the incident haunted him throughout the rest of his career.

[32] *World*, November 4, 1884, p. 1. For still other comments on Blaine's record of corruption see August 10, 1884, p. 1; August 23, 1884, p. 1; September 14, 1884, p. 1; September 28, 1884, p. 1; October 4, 1884, p. 1; October 13, 1884, p. 1; and October 26, 1884, p. 1.

[33] The *World* not unreasonably referred to the date of the banquet—October 29—as Blaine's "Black Wednesday." That same morning he had received the delegation of ministers in his hotel suite which resulted in the catastrophic "Rum, Romanism, and Rebellion" remark.

[34] The cartoon is not entirely accurate. Vanderbilt is shown at Blaine's side, wearing a crown; in actual fact he did not attend. The fact that his name was on the guest list suggests that the artists drew the cartoon prior to the event.

small daughter beseeched the boisterous assembly for leftover scraps of food.[35]

The Dickensian quality of the scene—Oliver Twist begging for more porridge—gave it more influence, perhaps, than all the other cartoons put together. "That picture was a decided hit," the *World* exulted, "because it presented an appalling fact to the American people. It brought them face to face with the danger that is involved in Mr. Blaine's candidacy for the Presidency. Every copy of the edition of the *World* containing that picture was sold at an early hour and thousands of extras have been supplied. The congratulatory letters that pour in upon us from all quarters testify to its effectiveness. . . ." Typically, Pulitzer added a little homily to his message of self-congratulation: "It is the truth that is powerful always."[36] Whether his faith was altogether justified, a later, more simple statement—"our cartoons helped to cast out Blaine"—is almost beyond dispute.[37] Certainly the Republican candidate considered the cartoon a factor in his defeat. Walt McDougall recounted a conversation with Blaine years later, when the heat of the campaign was spent, and when men who liked each other could talk in peace. "He . . . informed me, . . ." the cartoonist wrote, "that he believed there were good reasons for the *World*'s claim that the celebrated Belshazzar's Feast cartoon, which the Democratic State Committee enlarged to enormous size and placarded all over the city, had of itself influenced the election of 1884 sufficiently to account for the eleven-hundred-odd votes that lost him the State of New York."[38]

[35] *World*, October 30, 1884, entire top half of p. 1.
[36] *World*, November 1, 1884, p. 4.
[37] *World*, December 11, 1884, p. 4.
[38] Walt McDougall, "Pictures in the Papers," p. 68.
While it strains credibility to maintain that a single cartoon played the decisive role in electing Cleveland President, it is not at all far-fetched to argue that the *World*'s campaign of three months spelled the difference between success and failure. The Democratic candidate won, after all, only because he carried New York State, and he carried it by the slim margin of 1,149 votes. Who is to say that the newspaper did not change that many minds? Certainly not Cleveland. Many years later, when the *World* celebrated its twentieth anniversary under Pulitzer, he dispatched a special message recalling the exciting year, and paying unique tribute to the paper's part in securing his victory. "I never can," he wrote, "lose the vividness of my recollection of the conditions and incidents attending the Presidential campaign of 1884—how thoroughly Republicanism was intrenched—how brilliantly it was led—how

One reason for the *World*'s effectiveness is that it allowed the cartoonists complete freedom to express themselves. "Nobody dictated what I should do or how I should do it, . . ." McDougall reported. "J. P. never placed the least check upon my energies and he never uttered one word of reproof or harsh criticism during all the years I was on the *World*."[39] On the contrary, Pulitzer and Cockerill rallied to their defense when they came under attack. McDougall told of the time that a slightly irreverent drawing evoked a bitter letter of protest from an uptown minister. Cockerill called the cartoonist to his office, handed the letter to him, and asked him to wait and drop the reply in a postal box. It read:

My dear Sir,—
    Will you kindly go to hell?

John A. Cockerill.

A second *World* contribution to the development of illustrated journalism contrasts sharply with its innovations in the field of political cartooning. Pulitzer and his staff used pictures as a device for entertainment as well as propaganda. Most notably in the Sunday editions, they ran a variety of cuts whose only justification was the fun of looking at pictures. In this sense, the *World* directly competed with, and eventually outstripped, the *Daily Graphic*. The correlation between the *World*'s expanding use of pictures for entertainment and the *Graphic*'s demise in 1889 is too direct to be coincidental.

---

arrogant it was—and how confidently it encouraged and aided a contingent of deserters from the Democratic ranks. And I recall not less vividly how brilliantly and sturdily the *World* then fought for Democracy; and in this the first of its great party fights under present proprietorship, it was here, there and everywhere in the field, showering deadly blows upon the enemy. It was steadfast in zeal and untiring in effort until the battle was won; and it was won against such odds and by so slight a margin as to reasonably lead to the belief that no contributing aid could have been safely spared. At any rate the CONTEST WAS SO CLOSE . . . it may be said without reservation that if it had lacked the FORCEFUL AND POTENT ADVOCACY OF DEMOCRATIC PRINCIPLES AT THAT TIME BY THE NEW YORK WORLD the result might have been reversed. (Quoted in *Two Anniversaries: The World, 1883-1903; The St. Louis Post-Dispatch, 1878-1903*, the *World* [New York, 1906], p. 8.) The statement is all the more remarkable, considering Cleveland's high dudgeon at the press in general, and the *World* in particular, for pursuing him to his honeymoon hideaway in 1886. (See p. 34, note 70.)

[39] *Ibid.*, p. 70.

The *World* realized almost from the beginning that most people would rather look at representations of faces or scenes familiar to them than be educated by glimpses of faraway people and places. Of course one's own picture in a newspaper had hypnotic fascination, but even the picture of an acquaintance or friend meant far more than of some stranger, however famous. The same logic determined that most men would rather admire an illustration of a familiar street scene than of the grandest pyramid in Egypt.

The *World* conscientiously satisfied this craving for the commonplace, and in doing so, upset a few shibboleths about journalistic ethics and public morality.[40] Week after week it presented for examination the bewhiskered countenances of local politicians,[41] judges,[42] policemen,[43] firemen,[44] financiers,[45] journalists.[46] Not even the blasé gentlemen of the press easily

[40] This point applies only to the early period. In later years, when illustration had ceased to be a novelty, Pulitzer cautioned his staff to run cuts only when they had obvious relevance to the day's news. "Quality not quantity," he demanded in August 1898. "Striking superiority *attracting attention* [his emphasis] is wanted—not ordinary average pictures that only waste space." He repeated the injunction the following year. "Mr. Pulitzer again cautions all the editors against repetitions of pictures of familiar faces of well-known men. No picture should be printed unless it is new; No faces unless such faces are news; unless a well-known man dies or is elected to some office etc. Pictures should be as much news as the text, and the picture that does not make a new impression, or give a new idea, or tell a new story, is space wasted." The public had grown accustomed to pictures, and a policy that suited the early 1880s was no longer appropriate to the late 1890s. *Pulitzer Papers*, Library of Congress.

[41] See, for example, the *World*, February 10, 1884, p. 1 for twenty-three one-column cuts of the Aldermen of New York City. Also February 17, 1884, p. 1 for twenty cuts of city bosses; April 13, 1884, p. 1; and December 21, 1884, p. 20, for cuts of the Albany legislators (including Theodore Roosevelt); and December 28, 1884, p. 11, for fifteen cuts of the new Board of City Aldermen.

[42] See the *World*, February 24, 1884, p. 1 for twenty-one cuts of police and civil justices; and July 27, 1884, p. 1, for thirteen cuts of judges on the State Supreme Court.

[43] See the *World*, April 6, 1884, p. 1, for a group portrait of fifteen ranking police officers.

[44] See the *World*, July 20, 1884, p. 1, for eleven cuts of some of the city's brave "fire laddies."

[45] See the *World*, June 1, 1884, p. 12; April 12, 1885, p. 23; April 19, 1885, p. 23; and May 3, 1885, p. 23, for thirty-nine cuts in all of "Wall Street Bloods."

[46] See the *World*, July 6, 1884, p. 9, for likenesses of twelve New York journalists, including Nym Crinkle.

adjusted to finding their faces staring at them from the morning newspaper. "The Sunday *World* is a curious looking object," the trade periodical concluded in 1884. "A recent number contained the so-called portraits of a number of New York journalists. They have been endeavoring to catch the expression credited to them in the illustrations, but they have not caught the combination so far."[47]

Nor did the newspaper restrict its attention to celebrities, or those who liked to think of themselves as such. Its extensive gallery of merchants—small ones and prosperous ones—set Pulitzer's detractors to speculating on his motives.[48] Leander Richardson thought that it must have something to do with force-feeding the newspaper's circulation.

> The *World* prints every Sunday a lot of pictures of obscure tradesmen, whose portraits are accompanied by brief biographies couched in the most fulsome terms. We are told of the genius of the one-horse tailors, the brilliant attainments of queer shoemakers, and the noble intellectuality of second-class butchers, bullet-headed bakers and wild-eyed candlestick makers. About one-half of the area of the *New York World* on Sundays is given up to this kind of thing. Every fellow who sees himself printed in this fashion immediately thinks immortality is staring him in the face, and he proceeds to circulate the paper among his acquaintances. When the portraits are secured, with an agreement to give them places in the columns of the *World*, a definite arrangement is made as to the number of copies which shall be taken by the people interested. This is one of the ways of accounting for the circulation of Jewseph Pulitzer's paper.[49]

The awkwardness of accounting for a tenfold growth in circulation in terms of the extra copies sold to "one-horse tailors" evidently never occurred to Richardson, for he sternly asked a few weeks later whether the arrangement did not constitute a fraud on advertisers. "The *World* is getting most of its advertising

[47] *The Journalist*, July 26, 1884, p. 2.

[48] For picture features on merchants in the city, see the *World*, October 12, 1884, p. 13; October 19, 1884, p. 13; November 9, 1884, p. 9; November 16, 1884, p. 9; November 30, 1884, p. 17; December 7, 1884, p. 22.

[49] *The Journalist*, November 8, 1884, p. 5.

on the pretense that its actual circulation is represented in the figures shown by these sales to vain men who want to see their features in print. It is a pretty hollow sort of an affair after all."[50] His inability to see that many people, friends and customers, shared the storekeeper's momentary brush with fame, and had reason to purchase the paper themselves, is eloquent testimony to the novelty of the technique.

In successive weeks and months the *World* printed portraits of men other New Yorkers knew personally or by repute, but who did not ordinarily qualify as celebrities. Ministers,[51] teachers,[52] doctors,[53] lawyers[54] naturally appeared in the gallery, but so did society figures,[55] hotel clerks,[56] theatre managers,[57] stage personalities,[58] artists,[59] even cooks.[60] Traditionalists argued that the process, if justified at all, had been taken too far:

> When it gets down to printing the pictures of a lot of cooks and scullions, the picture business is certainly pretty thoroughly played out. I never was much taken with the cut business for daily newspapers, anyway, excepting when it was used in connection with some prominent affair. People would naturally like to know what Fish of the Marine Bank looked like, and they would have some little curiosity as to the personal appearance of Ferdinand Wood. . . . On the whole, I am inclined to the conclusion that the matter of illustration in daily journalism had better be left to the *Graphic*.[61]

[50] *The Journalist*, December 6, 1884, p. 4.

[51] See, for example, the *World*, March 2, 1884, p. 1, for twenty-three cuts of Protestant ministers in New York and Brooklyn.

[52] A *World* picture on March 29, 1885, p. 18, paid tribute to "the women who are in charge of our future statesmen."

[53] For an example of a picture feature on doctors, see the *World*, June 22, 1884, p. 9.

[54] A typical picture feature on lawyers appears in the *World* on June 15, 1884, p. 9.

[55] See, for example, the *World*, March 30, 1884, p. 9; April 27, 1884, p. 1; August 10, 1884, p. 9; December 21, 1884, p. 21.

[56] *World*, September 21, 1884, p. 13; also September 28, 1884, p. 9.

[57] *World*, October 19, 1884, p. 9.

[58] *World*, June 29, 1884, p. 9; September 14, 1884, p. 9; April 5, 1885, p. 20.

[59] *World*, December 7, 1884, p. 21; December 14, 1884, p. 22; January 18, 1885, p. 19. Not to discriminate between the sexes, the *World* ran a picture feature about female artists on March 15, 1885, p. 17, gallantly headlining it: FAIR HANDS UNDER WHOSE TOUCH THE CANVAS GLOWS AND LIVES.

[60] *World*, May 4, 1884, p. 9.   [61] *The Journalist*, May 17, 1884, p. 5.

Pulitzer needed only to glance at the latest report from his circulation department to perceive the fallacy in their argument. He accepted the desirability of printing linecuts of men famous and infamous, and he did more than any publisher of his time to make such cuts part of the news-gathering process. But like a thoughtful host trying to include everybody in the conversation, he recognized that ordinary men crave their own share of immortality. It is significant that no category of faces appeared more frequently in the *World* than National Guardsmen, the one most likely to cut across sections and classes to strike a response in the majority of homes.[62]

Further evidence that illustrated features about ordinary men and women had wide popular appeal is provided by the *World*'s use of them to gain a foothold in such neighboring cities as Brooklyn, Newark, and Bridgeport. Astride a winner and knowing it, Pulitzer did not even change the categories of faces as he looked across the Hudson and East Rivers. Thus, for Brooklyn, the newspaper printed portraits of political figures,[63] socialites,[64] theatre managers,[65] policemen,[66] merchants,[67] and not least, National Guardsmen.[68] The other cities received less publicity, but essentially the same pattern held up.[69]

What seems now so innocuous, indeed a staple of journalism, aroused strong feelings when Pulitzer showed the way. In the early summer of 1884 the *World* ran a picture feature, embel-

[62] In a single year—between March 9, 1884 and March 8, 1885—the *World* devoted ten long picture features to National Guard members, past and present. This does not include similar features for the neighboring city of Brooklyn. See March 9, 1884, p. 1; January 18, 1885, p. 9; January 25, 1885, p. 9; February 8, 1885, p. 16; February 8, 1885, p. 20; February 15, 1885, p. 9; February 22, 1885, p. 17; March 1, 1885, pp. 17-19; March 8, 1885, p. 17.

[63] *World*, May 4, 1884, p. 13; June 15, 1884, p. 13; June 22, 1884, p. 13; July 6, 1884, p. 13; July 13, 1884, p. 13; July 20, 1884, p. 9; July 27, 1884, p. 12; August 3, 1884, p. 9; August 10, 1884, p. 13.

[64] *World*, May 11, 1884, p. 13; June 8, 1884, p. 9.

[65] *World*, June 29, 1884, p. 13.

[66] *World*, August 17, 1884, p. 9.

[67] *World*, August 24, 1884, p. 9; September 7, 1884, p. 9; December 7, 1884, p. 23.

[68] *World*, May 3, 1885, p. 22; May 10, 1885, p. 20.

[69] For Newark, see *World*, September 7, 1884, p. 9; September 14, 1884, p. 13; September 21, 1884, p. 13; September 28, 1884, p. 13; October 5, 1884, p. 14. For Bridgeport, October 5, 1884, p. 13; November 9, 1884, p. 13.

lished with fourteen cuts, on some of the pretty girls of Brooklyn, "ladies who grace and adorn the social circle."[70] Although it attempted to do no more than what the other features had done—advertise ordinary men and women to themselves—the initial reaction was one of shock and outraged propriety. Several irate citizens from the cloistered community across the East River spoke of horse whipping the scoundrels who had invaded their privacy, while Pulitzer's competitors rebuked him for his violation of journalistic ethics. The *Herald* termed the story "an invasion of private life," and *The Journalist* speculated about what it would do to the reputation of all newspapermen.

> The *World* made an error of no small magnitude when it published its series of Brooklyn Belles in last Sunday's issue. . . . Brooklyn is not used to these wild western methods of journalism.
>
> On Monday morning after the objectionable pictures appeared the studio of the photographer who made the pictures from which the drawings were obtained, was thronged by an anxious and angry crowd of fathers, brothers, husbands and lovers, all breathing dire vengeance upon the photographer. . . .
>
> It may be a mark of push and energy on the part of a daily paper to present to its readers the portraits of criminals, of politicians who are occupying a large portion of the public's attention, or of anyone who is either thrust forward or pushes himself before the public in a prominent manner, but it is a piece of glaring bad taste for a newspaper to invade the sanctity of the home circle and hold up to public gaze and mayhap ridicule the portraits of young ladies who in no wise court publicity, and in whom the public has no interest except as they are pretty women. . . .
>
> There is no legitimate excuse for holding these women up to the ridicule and ribald comments of the bar-room and the street. . . . It needs no arguments to prove that the affair was got up for what is known in newspaper parlance—a sensation—and as a sensation it was a success. It has, however, lowered the standard of the paper by publishing it, and has lost it many friends. . . . It is just this sort of journalism that fosters the idea in the minds of the general pub-

[70] *World*, June 1, 1884, p. 9.

lic that a newspaper man has no conscience, and that
when he enters the house it is a good time to lock up
the spoons.[71]

Pulitzer serenely weathered the storm, for he recognized two
things which escaped the attention of his more conservative contemporaries. First, whoever was beating at the door of the harried
photographer in Brooklyn, it clearly wasn't the flattered belles,
their proud families, or admiring friends. As Pulitzer noted, "in
the midst of all the newspaper interviewing, editorial twaddling
and legal flapdoodling touching the artistic presentation of a
number of Brooklyn's society belles in last Sunday's *World*, it
may not be out of place to say that we have received no complaints from the charming and worthy ladies whose portraits
graced our pages."[72] More important, the outraged citizenry could
not have been too outraged, since the *World*'s circulation soared
in Brooklyn and elsewhere, while the circulation of newspapers
which earnestly advised him on ethics lagged painfully behind.
As the editorial continued:

> The criticisms of able journalists touching the
> methods of their contemporaries are not, as a rule,
> valuable. If the *World* were conducted according to
> the ideas of George Jones, the intendant of the *New
> York Herald* and other journalists not identified with
> our payroll, the probabilities are that it would soon
> be in a condition as lamentable as that which distin-
> guishes a number of alleged newspapers in this
> vicinity.[73]

A related aspect of illustrated Sunday journalism consisted in
doing for street scenes what portraiture did for people. Again the
pivotal word is "familiar," for just as most men preferred to see
in their newspaper a picture of a friend rather than a statesman,
so they appreciated more a picture of a locale they knew rather
than of some faraway place. It is notable that an identical headline, FAMILIAR STREET SCENES, appeared over several of the
World's illustrated features.[74]

[71] *The Journalist*, June 7, 1884, p. 3.
[72] *World*, June 6, 1884, p. 4.   [73] *Ibid*.
[74] See, for instance, the *World*, November 16, 1884, p. 16; December 7,
1884, p. 20; December 21, 1884, p. 22.

While the newspaper paid regard to the obvious civic landmarks in features such as those on the Windsor Hotel, or on the burial grounds adjoining St. Paul's Church and Trinity Church, it more typically tried to focus on places of special interest to the masses of men.[75] For instance, it ran an illustrated article on Castle Garden, the "gateway of immigration" for tens of thousands of New Yorkers;[76] on the dime museums that cluttered the West Side;[77] on the great shopping center along 14th Street, which it called "woman's thoroughfare;"[78] on the police court and the people who regularly appeared in it;[79] on the various foreign restaurants downtown in the immigrant district;[80] on Inspector Byrnes' Detective Bureau in Central Headquarters, with its rogues' gallery and museum of curios from past crimes.[81] The choice of subject matter itself reveals much about the identity of the *New York World*'s readers. Sometimes the articles got away from buildings and places to depict sights commonly seen on the street. The *World*'s artists drew peddlers with "their warehouses on their backs," street corner vendors of caramels and bonbons, stage-drivers wending bulky vehicles through dense throngs, trained dogs entertaining for the pennies tossed on the sidewalk, traveling German bands.[82] Hardly the material to be researched on upper Fifth Avenue!

Of course only a small part of the cuts which appeared in the Sunday *World* over the months conformed to this neat pattern of illustrating ordinary men and places. Pictures soon became the most important single element in the Sunday edition, and the editors struggled to find new ways to work them in. Some of the features, thin even by *World* standards, clearly had only their suitability for illustration to recommend them. A long article headlined:

[75] For the picture feature on the Windsor Hotel, see the *World*, December 7, 1884, p. 20; for St. Paul's graveyard, February 8, 1885, p. 17; for Trinity's graveyard, January 25, 1885, p. 17.

[76] *World*, February 1, 1885, p. 17.   [77] *World*, January 18, 1885, p. 17.

[78] *World*, December 14, 1884, p. 21.

[79] *World*, November 23, 1884, p. 18.

[80] *World*, January 25, 1885, p. 20.

[81] *Ibid.*

[82] The examples cited appear, respectively, in the *World*, November 2, 1884, p. 13; November 16, 1884, p. 16; December 7, 1884, p. 20; December 21, 1884, p. 22; January 4, 1885, p. 20.

THE PAROXYSMAL EPOCH.
KISSES IN EVERY KNOWN AND UNKNOWN LANGUAGE
How It Is Done, and Generally
What Is Thought of It.

was one such.[83] The "scholarly" study consisted of little more than illustrations of pairs of lips meeting at different angles. Similarly, a *World* examination of the current craze for roller-skating became a vehicle for drawings of gangly figures falling or about to fall.[84] The newspaper's concern with the splendid ward-robe of President Arthur, his "lovely coats, charming vests and angelic trousers," led to an account replete with cuts of each garment on his back short of underdrawers.[85] Like a child with a new toy, the *World* sometimes did not even seek an excuse to print its pictures. In December of 1883 it ran a facsimile of the handwritten notes President Arthur spoke from at the previous year's Evacuation Day ceremonies. "The whole is given below," it solemnly explained, "so that the readers of the *World* may become familiar with the chirography of the President of the United States."[86]

The frenzied casting about for novelties to illustrate reached a climax of sorts when the *World* directed the attention of its readers to the new science of "noseology." The introduction filled the entire front page of the newspaper, and was suitably headlined.[87]

NOSEOLOGY.

HUMAN CHARACTER ILLUSTRATED BY THE HUMAN PROBOSCIS.

SOME MEN WHO ARE FAMOUS AND SOME WHO ARE NOT.

[83] *World*, March 8, 1885, p. 20.
[84] *World*, March 22, 1885, p. 20.   [85] *World*, April 20, 1884, p. 9.
[86] *World*, December 2, 1883, p. 9. At least one other journalist of note was excited by this unorthodox use of illustration. On December 31, 1883, shortly after the *World* ran the reproduction of President Arthur's notes, Edward Bok wrote a confidential letter to Pulitzer offering to make available his personal autograph collection for similar treatment. The publisher declined the offer. *Pulitzer Papers*, Columbia University Libraries.
[87] *World*, April 20, 1884, p. 1.

DISTINGUISHED NEW YORKERS WITH CELEBRATED NOSES.

HOW THAT ORGAN INDICATES STRENGTH AND MENTAL PECULIARITIES.

A SOLEMNLY SCIENTIFIC SUBJECT ARTISTICALLY ANALYZED.

Needless to say, each revelation about the mysteries of the human nose required, and received, a line drawing as example. The subject carried enough weight to warrant a sequel the following week on "feminine facial protuberances."[88] The spoilsports among Pulitzer's critics estimated that once had been too much. "Enterprise is the soul of journalism," the trade periodical conceded in its next issue. "But when Mr. Pulitzer recently filled a whole page of his paper with caricatured noses of local politicians, people of refinement dropped the paper in disgust and held their own nasal organs—figuratively speaking."[89] Pulitzer heeded critical advice on this occasion no more than he had previously. He returned the following spring with a related study of "speaking eyes and lips," more acceptable, perhaps, than what had gone before, but hardly the response of a penitent.[90]

It would be wrong to exaggerate the extent to which the newspaper resorted to frivolities in finding subjects for illustration. To do so is to overlook the professionalism of the men who did the drawings, and the men who supplied the words to go with them. On the whole, they succeeded admirably in mating pictures and prose to the benefit of both. A popularized (and slanted) review of former American Presidents, published at a time of the party conventions, was enhanced by portraits of the twenty-one men who had held the office.[91] Cleveland's inauguration suggested an article on the White House, which benefited from seven one-column cuts showing interior views of the building.[92] The news that General Grant might die at any moment led to an account of his rise from obscurity, an account rendered all the

88 *World*, April 27, 1884, p. 10.
89 *The Journalist*, June 28, 1884, p. 6.
90 *World*, March 15, 1885, p. 20.
91 *World*, July 13, 1884, p. 9.
92 *World*, March 15, 1885, p. 17.

more graphic by pictures of the houses he had lived in at various times during his life.[93] Obviously illustration was used most often in a way acceptable by modern standards, lending substance and depth to the words it accompanied.

Nor can the frivolous use of pictures be dismissed simply as evidence of inexperience. Illustration was still enough of a novelty (consider the popular song honoring Lydia Pinkham's vegetable compound) to warrant the fullest possible exploitation.[94] The public of the 1880s did not look at pictures with the same practiced eye as today, and a seemingly uninspired feature on "noseology" might at that time have seemed humorous and sophisticated.

Moreover, the newspaper's willingness to experiment put it well on the track to uses for illustration which achieved final acceptance in the twentieth century. Pulitzer's responsibility for the development of colored comic strips, which first appeared on Sunday, November 18, 1894, in the form of Richard Felton Outcault's "Shantytown," is familiar to any student of the press.[95]

[93] *World*, March 22, 1885, p. 17.

[94] Mrs. Lydia Estes Pinkham pioneered the portrait ad to sell her "Vegetable Compound for Female Complaints." Her motherly face, above a message addressed to the "Ladies of the World," could not help but inspire confidence. She promised to cure ovarian troubles, inflammations, ulceration, falling and displacements, spinal weakness, tumors in the uterus, faintness, headaches, sleepiness, depression, indigestion, and kidney complaints, as well as to ease change of life. With a compound eighteen percent alcohol, she probably did all of that. At least an anonymous poet thought enough of the cure to dedicate his talents to its marvels, and in passing, to comment on one form of newspaper illustration.

> "Then we'll sing of Lydia Pinkham
> And her love for the human race;
> How she sold her veg'table compound
> And the papers published her face."

The words were later set to music, and it became a favorite rowdy song.

[95] Outcault inaugurated a strip shortly afterwards called "Hogan's Alley," which had as its main character an odd-looking street gamin with no hair and just a single tooth jutting out of his perpetually grinning mouth. The Yellow Kid, as he came to be called after the color of his flowing robes, was so popular that he soon outgrew Hogan's Alley and became a comic strip in his own right. When Hearst arrived in New York City he hired Outcault to draw the "Yellow Kid" for the *Journal*, but the *World* retaliated by signing George B. Luks to keep the original strip going. Loud billboards throughout the city announced that New York had competing Yellow Kids. According to the accepted version, the popularity of a comic strip character also provided the name for what Pulitzer and Hearst were involved in: Yellow Journalism.

Not so familiar are the faltering first steps dating back to the early 1880s. In December of 1884, for example, the *World* adopted a comic strip format to illustrate the plot of a comedy currently playing at the Union Square Theatre entitled "Three Wives to One Husband."[96] Five sequential one-column cuts depicted the tribulations of a matrimony-minded artist's model. Although the line drawings were not in color, and not intended to be part of a continuing story that would appear week after week with established characters, at least the essential format of comic strips had been introduced.[97] The newspaper continued its experiment the next week with a strip in ten parts, each with a four-line stanza of verse beneath, offering a tongue-in-cheek plot for grand opera.[98]

Even the cartoons McDougall and Gribayedoff turned out, after their release from the campaign against Blaine and Butler, can be identified as prototypes of the Yellow Kid. Their earliest efforts resembled the political campaign technique: a single drawing, now on a humorous theme, stretched across several columns. One depicted the ritual of the Thanksgiving turkey at a boarding house, where the guests came equipped with everything from clubs and hatchets to vials of sulphuric acid to get at a bird which looked as if it had been riveted together;[99] another suggested the establishment of a United States Matrimonial Agency at Castle Garden, through which incoming maids and maidens might list their qualifications for prospective husbands ("can cook and play poker," "sings in Italian," "widow with experience and $6,000," etc.).[100] Later the artists branched out, and in doing so approached more closely what we now consider the comic strip

[96] *World*, December 14, 1884, p. 9.

[97] This is not intended to suggest that the format originated with the *World*. Four months previously, on August 16, 1884, the *New York Daily News* published six cuts in sequence to depict a humorous situation which it entitled "A Hat Off a Peg." (The strip appeared on a Saturday, the evening newspaper's equivalent day to Sunday for supplemental material.) Although I have been unable to discover any earlier date for such use of illustration, the possibility cannot be ruled out. Pulitzer's newspaper deserves credit for two things. It was among the very first, the *New York Daily News* notwithstanding, to use pictures to tell a story. Moreover, it did not abandon the device, but worked on it and developed it until the Yellow Kid resulted.

[98] *World*, December 21, 1884, p. 22.

[99] *World*, November 27, 1884, p. 1.

[100] *World*, December 7, 1884, p. 1.

form. They divided a single cartoon into several boxes, each of which delivered a gag on a common subject. Thus, Gribayedoff provided a mock calendar for the New Year in December of 1884 which suggested what New Yorkers might look forward to: in April, Russell Sage absentmindedly donating something to a beggar; in May, Queen Victoria ordering three more statues to the memory of John Brown; in November, a "cop" refusing a drink![101]

The subdivision of cartoons for purposes of humor was carried forward in 1885. A New Year's drawing included all the staple jokes, from wild celebrating the night before to hangover the morning after.[102] Walt McDougall asked WILL ROLLER-SKATING COME TO THIS?—and showed dogs and horses gliding on wheels, postmen completing their rounds before midday, absconding cashiers skating off to Canada, and so on.[103] The differences between such art and the sort developed by Outcault are too many to be minimized, but in the *World*'s increasingly flexible and varied use of illustration are implied the later developments which culminated in "L'il Abner" and "Dick Tracy" as expressions of American culture.

In the final measure, the *World*'s varied use of pictures, starting with a line-drawing of a bridge over a river timidly offered in 1883, had influence far beyond that newspaper's own success or failure. The real significance is what happened to the press as a whole, for Pulitzer's innovations could not long remain the property of one paper. *Harper's Weekly* recognized a revolution well underway when it noted in 1893 that "the question of 'cuts' in the columns of the daily newspapers, if not exactly a burning one, excites more animated comment than many of more importance. It has been settled in favor of their use now by every considerable morning paper in New York."[104] Journalists were just starting to appreciate what Pulitzer had seen ten years before, that illustration offered a great new dimension to the press, and vastly facilitated its mission to entertain and inform.

[101] *World*, December 28, 1884, p. 9.
[102] *World*, January 1, 1885, p. 1.
[103] *World*, January 25, 1885, p. 1.
[104] Anon., "Things Talked Of," *Harper's Weekly*, xxxvii (April 22, 1893), 367.

CHAPTER FOUR

SPORTS

Newspapermen have experimented with sensationalism, multi-column headlines, illustration, and a host of other devices to attract new readers, but not without realizing that their success or failure would depend in large measure also on the content of the inside pages. It is all very well to arrange an attractive front page, but as long as people are more interested in sports, fashions, comic strips, advice to the lovelorn, and the like, rather than hard news, an attractive front page by itself is only the beginning. The constant discovery of every poll, since scientific polling was first attempted, has been that a Presidential address or diplomatic conference runs a poor second to a championship prize fight in stirring reader interest.[1]

The seriousness with which people pursue their frivolities helps to explain why the popular journals usually excel in covering such subjects as sports or entertainment. Each paper caters to its own audience, and if the financial reports or book reviews in the *New York Times* are likely to be unequalled, the same can be said of the baseball coverage or gossip columns in the *New York Daily News*. Indeed, so seriously do people take their frivolities, and so expert do they become, that the specialized departments of the mass circulation dailies provide some of the most authoritative reporting in those dailies. Helen MacGill Hughes made the point when she commented that "no journal is 'yellow' in the departments; they are the most disciplined and intelligent part of a newspaper."[2] Men who have devoted years to following the

[1] See, for example, the Gallup Poll of 1930, which showed that the only features in a metropolitan daily read by more than forty percent of male readers were the political cartoon, weather report, pictures, lead sports story, and comic strips. The same percentage of women looked at pictures, the humor column, advice to the lovelorn, comic strips, and the serial story. George Gallup, "Evaluation of Reader Interest," *Proceedings of the American Society of Newspaper Editors*, VIII (New York, 1930), 230.

[2] Helen MacGill Hughes, *News and the Human Interest Story* (Chicago, 1940), p. 63.

fortunes of a local baseball team read with an expertise and sophistication equivalent to that of a financier pouring over the latest stock market quotations, and as equally demanding of satisfaction.

Joseph Pulitzer's recognition of the importance of the specialized departments in the drive for circulation constitutes an important part of the success story of the *New York World*. He contributed greatly to a compartmentalization of newspapers that had been in process since the end of the Civil War—into sports pages, women's pages, and so on—and did as much as any American publisher to win respectability for the notion that the press's function was not only to report the news, but to consider as news whatever the general populace wished to read about.[3]

The *World*'s coverage of sports provides one of the clearest indications of its determination to treat authoritatively, and in detail, the subjects that interested the masses of men. The press had been reporting major sporting events since the 1850s, but most of the articles dealt with horse racing, a pastime respectable precisely because it was patronized by the moneyed class. Any other events which might merit a stickful of type were assigned to nonspecialists on the city desk. "In the early 1850s," a pioneer sportswriter recalled, "the only member of the newspaper staff who in any way resembled the modern sporting editor was the 'turf' man."[4] The following decades saw the press pay somewhat greater attention to baseball and boxing, a trend started in 1862 when the *New York Herald* hired Henry Chadwick to report baseball news. But not until Pulitzer arrived in the city did any of the metropolitan dailies conceive of a separate sports department staffed by experts. One of Pulitzer's earliest moves, signifying the role sports would play in the new *World*, was to install H. G. Crickmore, an authority on horse racing, as editor-in-charge of the first such department.[5] "In the matter of

---

[3] William Randolph Hearst carried the logic to an extreme when he established the *New York Daily Mirror* in 1924 on a formula of ninety percent entertainment and ten percent news. Bernard McFadden's *Daily Graphic*, founded the same year, avoided so far as possible any news at all.

[4] *Editor & Publisher*, VI (January 12, 1907), 3.

[5] My source for crediting the *New York World* for being the first to establish such a department is Alfred McClung Lee, *The Daily Newspaper in America* (New York, 1937), p. 629.

turf and sporting news the *World* is without equal in daily journalism," an editorial justly boasted at that time. "It is the authority."[6]

Although it would be some years before the concept fully took hold, Pulitzer's imagination carried him one step further. He reasoned that just as newspapers concentrated all their editorials on a single page, and their financial news on another page, so would the growing army of sports fans appreciate a page, or several pages, of articles exclusively devoted to their interests. He urged his editors to find an expert in each category of sports, to arrange that they contribute articles on a regular basis, and to see that the articles were printed side by side. "The sporting should be grouped together most effectively, contiguously, compactly," he wrote in a long memorandum from Bar Harbor in October 1899. "The same idea mentioned above with respect to other matters of having experts on each branch should be systematized for all sports. In the case of each of the 40 different branches, whether it be fishing or golf or cycling or rowing, the foremost expert should regularly contribute to the *World* and one ought to be in every Sunday issue."[7] In such an informal way was the sports page born.

These instructions were based on a shrewd assessment of what caught the attention of the majority of men. The *World* rebuked competitors like the *Herald* and *Tribune* for assuming that because many New Yorkers were immigrants, their interest centered exclusively, or even primarily, on foreign affairs. "We have a large foreign population, it is true," an editorial declared, "but it is a population that is largely absorbed in local affairs, and it cares more for the account of a rattling glove contest than for the intricacies of Servian diplomacy, the health of the Nizam of Hyderabad or the griefs of the Begum of Mysore."[8] So aware

[6] *World*, May 27, 1883, p. 4.

[7] Memorandum from Bar Harbor to Charles M. Lincoln. Quoted in Don C. Seitz, *Joseph Pulitzer, His Life & Letters* (New York, 1924), p. 429. His editors were slow to respond to the idea, and Pulitzer harped on it in the following weeks. See his almost identically worded instructions on November 1, 2, and 3, 1899. "I repeat," he insisted on the latter occasion, "sporting should be unified, well classified, well arranged, well displayed. Two pages at least. Should not be scattered." *Pulitzer Papers*, Library of Congress.

[8] *World*, May 14, 1884, p. 4.

was Pulitzer's newspaper of the average man's priority of interests that it apologized on several occasions during the summer and fall of 1884 for the amount of space it devoted to the Cleveland–Blaine Presidential race. Cleveland's victory in November brought forth a sigh of relief, not only because the Democratic candidate had triumphed, but because the *World* could revert to its task of entertaining, as well as informing, the masses. Commenting three days after the election on a crowd of 7,000 that showed up at Madison Square Garden to cheer John L. Sullivan on to victory, the newspaper drew the obvious moral. The successful promotion, it argued, "demonstrates how easy it is to shift the popular mind from politics to fisticuffing. The people have had enough of the disturbance about the Presidency. They long for entertainment that is substantial and edifying. Let the games of the arena proceed. The Republic has been saved."[9]

The *World* not only catered to the taste of the masses by reporting sports, it encouraged such interests as manly and praiseworthy. A long editorial in the spring of 1884 reviewed the events scheduled for the months ahead: baseball ("more than ever our national game"), horse racing, tennis, track, football; and saw in them evidences of American vitality.

> Our people run to athletic sports. Why? Because they enjoy the contest of strength against strength. At a horse race, which is the highest order of sport, the spectator watches eagerly the struggle of the noble animals as they strain for victory. Men ordinarily humane and kind-hearted go to a boxing match because they love to see two powerful brutes contending for the mastery. . . .
>
> It is the height of folly to discourage or throw an impediment in the way of such popular enjoyments.[10]

Perhaps more important, the love of sport shared by tens of thousands of unpretentious men served to counterbalance what the newspaper detected as an effete strain in American life, symbolized by spinsterly poetesses and pale scholars.[11] It rejoiced in

[9] *World*, November 11, 1884, p. 4.
[10] *World*, May 4, 1884, p. 4.
[11] See Chapter Seven for a longer treatment of anti-intellectualism in the *World*.

a well-attended walking match at Madison Square Garden as "part of [the] reaction against over-intellectual concentration which was making dyspeptics and nervous wrecks of civilized men."[12]

The attention paid to sports is only part of the story, for in the stratified society of New York City in the 1880s rich man and poor man pursued their separate interests, rarely converging on the same arena to enjoy the same events. Of course some overlap of interest occurred. If yachting as a pastime belonged to J. P. Morgan and his set, the international aspect of a competition like the America's Cup races evoked a response from the tenement masses who hoped to see England defeated, just as Fifth Avenue attended Madison Square Garden in white tie and tails to watch a particularly well-publicized prizefight. But, in general, the interests of the classes diverged, with boxing, baseball, and walking races easily identifiable as lower-class sports, and football (a college man's game), yachting, and polo the pastimes of the wealthy.[13] In this respect, as in so many others, the *World* chose to address the tenement masses. Its pride in the comprehensiveness of its sports coverage required that all events receive notice, but emphasis was always placed on stories that would provide conversation for workingmen rather than their employers.

Generalizations about the class connotation of sports apply least to horse racing, which unlike the games men played and watched, had been a favorite recreation since colonial times.[14]

---

[12] *World*, May 1, 1884, p. 4.

[13] Much has been written on the correlation between class structure and sports. Thus, in modern England, a society with rather a more rigid class system than the United States, soccer is less of a gentleman's game than cricket, a fact attested by the respective number of cricketeers and footballers who are honored on the Queen's annual birthday list. The adoption of the Notre Dame football team by the so-called "subway alumni chapter" in New York City (and later the popularization of professional football through the exploits of such figures as Red Grange and Don Hutson), the construction of municipal tennis courts in less well-to-do neighborhoods, which resulted in a Mexican–American like Pancho Gonzales winning the championships at Wimbledon and Forest Hills, the proliferation of golf courses that brought the game to tens of thousands of clerks and laborers, all seem to denote a blurring of class lines in America, or what is perhaps a triumph of the middle class in the mid-twentieth century.

[14] For a while even horse racing was restricted to gentlemen. Daniel

---

More important, the turf offered opportunities for special excitement to rich and poor alike, whether to develop thoroughbreds and see them carry the family colors to victory, or to wager a few pennies on a long shot coming first under the wire. If any activity challenged baseball's claim to being the national sport, it was the annual seasons of racing at Sheepshead Bay, Monmouth Park, Saratoga, Brighton Beach, and Prospect Park. Under the leadership of H. G. Crickmore, the *World* covered those events exhaustively.

Some of the rivalries stirred almost as much excitement as the Presidential race between Cleveland and Blaine. Drake Carter's triumph in the Autumn Cup stakes at Sheepshead Bay in September 1884 found the *World* marveling at a climactic moment in American social history. "Yesterday's racing at Sheepshead Bay was the finest day's sport ever witnessed in this country," it declared in a separate editorial. "So many splendid horses were never seen before on an American track. The events were all first-class, and the crowd in attendance was large and happy. Even the 'losers' got the worth of their money."[15] Scarcely less exciting was the competition between Maud S., Jay-Eye-See, and Phallas for laurels as the champion American trotter. On four occasions in one month their rivalry received front page attention, notably when Jay-Eye-See brought the record for the mile down to 2.10 minutes, when Maud S. recaptured the record with a sprint of 2.00¾ minutes, and when in a much-heralded direct confrontation at the Prospect Park Fair Grounds the gelding Jay-Eye-See failed to wrest the championship from its larger and stronger rival.[16] William H. Vanderbilt's decision to sell Maud S. to Robert Bonner for $40,000 itself merited extensive cover-

---

Boorstin points out that in seventeenth century Virginia a member of the lower class who raced his horse for sport was guilty of violating colonial law. He cites a decision of the York County Court in 1674, fining one James Bullocke "one hundred pounds of tobacco and caske, . . . it being contrary to Law for a Labourer to make a race, being a sport only for Gentlemen." See Daniel Boorstin, *The Americans: The Colonial Experience* (New York, 1958), p. 104.

[15] *World*, September 7, 1884, p. 4.

[16] See the *World*, August 2, 1884, p. 1, for a report on Jay-Eye-See lowering the mile record to 2.10 minutes; August 3, 1884, p. 1, for Maud S. recapturing the record with a dash of 2.00¾ minutes; August 16, 1884, p. 1, for pictures of the three leading trotters; and August 29, 1884, p. 1, for a description of Maud S.'s triumph over Jay-Eye-See.

age on the front page.[17] Of course the premier event of thorough-bred racing, the English Derby at Epsom Downs, also belonged there, and in 1883, with the victory of St. Blaise, in the lead story slot.[18]

The *World* covered the turf more as a patron than a chronicler of contemporary sports. Two of its Sunday pictorial features in 1884, for example, were given over to what it called the KINGS OF THE TURF. MEN WHO MAKE A SPECIALTY OF THOROUGH-BRED HORSES, and an editorial that year introducing the start of a new season spoke with pride of a schedule one-third heavier than the previous year's.[19] It looked forward hopefully, and characteristically, to America soon overtaking Britain in the quality of its thoroughbreds. "The idea of any narrow-minded, bigoted crusade being made against horse-racing is absurd, . . ." an editorial declared. "The Turf is getting to be an American institution, and it is one which ought to be encouraged as it is in European countries."[20] Not least, it argued for a bill legalizing betting at the racetracks. An adverse vote by the state legislature in the spring of 1885 found the *World* urging that the matter be reconsidered. "If we want to keep up the sport," the newspaper argued, "to improve our magnificent breed of horses, to continue to show English racers the heels of our flyers and to give employ-ment to thousands of trainers, jockeys, stable hands and other employees, then we must have such a law as is now proposed at Albany and which allows men who go to races to bet on the horses under proper and entirely safe and sufficient restric-tions."[21] Even horse racing, it seemed, provided material for a proletarian and patriotic crusade.

The *World* thus demonstrated its determination to provide a sports coverage second to none, but it was in other areas, boxing and baseball particularly, that the appeal to the masses was most apparent. Boxing aroused an excited response in tenement neighborhoods (particularly with an Irish–American named John

[17] *World*, August 20, 1884, p. 1.
[18] *World*, May 24, 1883, p. 1.
[19] The pictorial features appeared on August 31, 1884, p. 9, and September 21, 1884, p. 9. The reference to a fuller racing calendar is in an editorial on June 30, 1884, p. 4.
[20] *World*, April 29, 1884, p. 4.   [21] *World*, May 6, 1885, p. 4.

— 124 —

L. Sullivan as heavyweight champion of the world) which the newspaper strived dutifully to satisfy. In the year and a half between Pulitzer's purchase of the *World* and the Sullivan–Ryan bout of January 1885, fight reports appeared on the front page on eighteen different occasions, most of them pertaining to the Boston strong boy, and on two other occasions multi-column pictorial features depicted what the newspaper unimaginatively, but with alliteration, labeled as MEN OF MIGHTY MUSCLE.[22]

This close attention to the violent world of the prize ring is all the more remarkable when taken together with the newspaper's oft-repeated concern over the low state to which boxing had fallen. It pretended to deplore the influence of John L. Sullivan, who—the *World* claimed—had reduced the manly and scientific art of self-defense to a mere display of brawn. "The recent battles, if they deserve the name," an article declared, "have been but farces when compared with many of those [in the past]. The advent of Sullivan inaugurated a new era in fighting, and the ring of bygone days, which was patronized by respectable people, has degenerated now until to be connected in any way with the manly art is considered to be beneath any man save roughs and thieves."[23] The newspaper argued in editorials ahead of their time that any sport dedicated to maiming an opponent, in which victory was measured by a concussion successfully administered, merited the severest scrutiny. "Every blow is given with the object of disabling and with a good prospect of killing

[22] *World*, May 15, 1883, p. 1; and May 16, p. 1 (on the Sullivan–Mitchell fight); August 6, 1883, p. 1; and August 7, 1883, p. 1 (on the Sullivan–Slade fight); January 11, 1884, p. 1 (on the Boyle–Wycherly fight); January 29, 1884, p. 1 (on the Goode–Norton fight); March 8, 1884, p. 1 (on the Sullivan–Robinson fight); March 27, 1884, p. 1 (on a fight staged between De Baum and Heiser before society folk at the Racquet Club); May 13, 1884, p. 1 (on the Mitchell–Edwards fight); July 1, 1884, p. 1, and July 2, 1884, p. 1 (on the fiasco when Sullivan showed up drunk for a fight with Mitchell); October 25, 1884, p. 1 (on the Dempsey–Henry fight); October 27, 1884, p. 1 (on the McDermott–Burns fight); November 11, 1884, p. 1 (on the Sullivan–Laflin fight); November 20, 1884, p. 1, and December 18, 1884, p. 1 (on a scheduled fight between Sullivan and Greenfield stopped by the police, and their subsequent acquittal in court); November 25, 1884, p. 1 (on the Mitchell–Burke fight); and January 20, 1885, p. 1 (on the Sullivan–Ryan fight). The pictorial features appeared on August 3, 1884, p. 1, and September 28, 1884, p. 15. Of course dozens of other fight reports appeared during that period on the inside pages.

[23] *World*, January 6, 1884, p. 10.

the person at whom it is aimed. It is a matter of wonder that these fights have not before now resulted in manslaughter."[24] And what of the people who attended the exhibitions? "When the sage moralist rubs against the reverend [sic] statesman and the illustrious encyclopedist at the side of the prize ring, even though blows are softened by hard gloves, [one] must conclude that there is a vast amount of barbarism still left in the sons of Adam, and [one] may well ask himself the question, 'Is our civilization a complete success?' "[25] It even proposed on one occasion that the sport be abolished. "We would suggest," an editorial argued, "that the police may very readily put a stop to the 'slugging' matches if they really feel so disposed. They are gatherings of a disorderly character which attract the worst ruffians and criminals in the city. . . . It cannot be very difficult to prevent such gatherings, or at least to make them unprofitable."[26]

Such statements seem to contradict the argument that the *World* uncritically accepted, and catered to, the interests of the masses. But their import is deceptive. The newspaper is much better likened to the individual who deplores the bloodlust which attracts him to boxing, but is nonetheless attracted. The page one articles which reported bloody encounters between relentless adversaries certainly were not composed by moralists. Consider how the headlines convey excitement rather than disapproval. Sullivan's third round knockout of Herbert A. Slade had as its head, THE MAORI VANQUISHED. THE VAST ASSEMBLAGE ALMOST FRENZIED WITH ENTHUSIASM.[27] A savage bout between Jack McDermott and Jim Burns brought forth BATTERED WITH BARE FISTS. FIGHTING IN THE OLD STYLE ON THE TURF—FIVE DESPERATELY FOUGHT ROUNDS FOR A SMALL PURSE, IN WHICH BOTH PUGILISTS WERE TERRIBLY PUNISHED.[28] Jack Dempsey's victory over Tom Henry, a fighter from Birmingham, England, was heralded with DEMPSEY WORSTS HENRY. THE BRUMMAGEM LAD DEFEATED AFTER SIX TERRIFIC ROUNDS.[29] The point is perhaps

[24] *World*, September 2, 1883, p. 4.
[25] *World*, May 16, 1883, p. 4.
[26] *World*, December 19, 1884, p. 4.
[27] *World*, August 7, 1883, p. 1.
[28] *World*, October 27, 1884, p. 1.
[29] *World*, October 25, 1884, p. 1.

more graphically made by a negative headline. The newspaper's words reeked contempt after a bout in which a California visitor failed to stand up to Sullivan's hard fists. AN IMMENSE AUDIENCE DISGUSTED WITH THE LATTER'S TACTICS—FOURTEEN FALLS IN ONE ROUND—'GOING TO GRASS' TO SAVE PUNISHMENT.[30]

The *World* revealed itself also in some of the uninhibited comments which followed exciting matches. The brief, but brutal, contest between Sullivan and Slade, for example, inspired an editorial comment much different from those penned in quieter moments. Once again the newspaper alluded to the brutish instinct of man, but with the heat of combat still upon it, the brutishness was something to accept, and even to revel in.

> It was a great exhibition and it showed the natural brutality of human nature. . . . A fierce joy thrilled in every breast and burned in every eye as the magnificent ruffian Sullivan delivered his powerful blows and knocked his helpless antagonist about the ring at his pleasure. It looked as if a yell of delight would have burst forth if he had given the poor wretch a death blow.
>
> When the unequal battle was over shouts went up as for a great victor and the vanquished dragged himself away unnoticed and left a bloody track as he went.
>
> After all, the world is not very different now from what it was when gladiators fought to the death in the presence of "gallant knights and ladyes faire."[31]

Its enthusiasm for prizefighting extended to using the editorial columns for proposing future matches. The possibility of a bout between Charles A. Mitchell, an Englishman noted for his boxing ability, and John L. Sullivan, the slugger, evoked an encouraging comment from the *World*. "There is a widespread interest among sporting men," it remarked editorially, "in the possible matching of Sullivan and Mitchell, and the interest is a genuine and excusable one. These two men may now be regarded

[30] *World*, March 8, 1884, p. 1.

[31] *World*, August 7, 1883, p. 4. Part of the bloodlust in that statement might reflect the fact that Slade was part Maori, and that in besting him Sullivan had upheld the "superiority" of the white race. The days when boxing promoters would devote their careers to discovering a new "white hope" were not far off.

as the best living exponents of the science of fisticuffs."[32] The "Letters to the Editor" column became a forum for Irishmen in New York City fiercely loyal to the champion. "I want to say that the opinion of your expert about Sullivan's want of mind and staying power is —— ——," wrote "Shorty" McCaull. "I will bet $100 to a cent that your expert is an Englishman, and I can lick him inside of nine minutes." D.H.D. grieved at the intolerance toward Sullivan shown by policemen and other public officials. "I hope you will leave me to say one word for as brave a man as ever split a cheek or stove a jaw. I have known John L. Sullivan for ten years and a braver man doesn't live. But he never has a show. Just as he gets warmed up the police or somebody else stop him. What's the use of having bravery if a man can't be left to show it?. . . Is this fair? Is this just? Is this treating a brave man right? But that's the way it always is with an Irishman. He has no show at all." For W. W., another anonymous correspondent, official ingratitude could only be redeemed by a vote of public confidence. "Why not open a box subscription for a statue of Sullivan?" he suggested.[33]

The enthusiasm for boxing carried over to baseball, a sport still in its infancy, but because of its warm reception among all segments of the population, already being referred to as the national game. The *World* good-humoredly likened it to the competition that had enthralled the country during the summer and fall of 1884. "The use of bases is essential to base-ball, and the game of politics is often put to base uses. Players are frequently caught out in both games. . . . There are 'fouls' in both games, though vastly more in politics than in base-ball. In both, the better a player runs, the more successful he is. . . . In a word, the national game of baseball is making a heavy strike to excel in importance the national game of politics."[34] Such levity was a token of appreciation, but it did not intrude on the newspaper's serious reporting of each day's games. Thus, an article describing a superlative pitching performance in a game between the New York and Cleveland professional teams, in which "the New York

[32] *World*, May 28, 1884, p. 4.
[33] The letters all appear in the *World* of August 10, 1883, p. 6, and reflect the tremendous interest stirred by the Sullivan–Slade bout.
[34] *World*, January 25, 1885, p. 4.

pitcher caused consternation in the Buckeye ranks by striking out thirteen men," captured the drama with a headline that read: WELCH'S PUZZLING CURVES. THE CLEVELAND MEN STRIKE AT THE SUBSTANCE AND HIT THE SHADOW.[35] When 100,000 cheering fans joined a torchlight procession welcoming the New York Metropolitans back to the city after having won the American Association Championship, the *World* reported the event in its lead story slot. THE CHAMPIONS WELCOMED proclaimed the headline over an article which sang the praises of Gotham's newest heroes.[36]

Baseball also provided material for feature articles in the Sunday edition. A pictorial feature on the BOLD KNIGHTS OF THE ASH depicted fourteen mustachioed heroes grouped in a circle around a pair of crossed bats and two baseballs.[37] The public marveled at articles reporting that an ace pitcher on a professional team might earn more in seven months of playing a child's game than many college professors earned in a year. "With the changes in the style of pitching have come higher wages for the players," the *World* announced, "until now a base-ball team is an expensive institution. New York has the two men who are paid more for playing ball than any others in the world. They are Ward and Ewing, and each receives a little over $3,000 for the present season."[38] Such salaries substantiated the *World*'s claim for baseball as the coming national game, and justified its being regarded as a major item of news in a mass circulation daily.

The unlikely pastime of marathon walking races also merited extensive coverage, largely because the contestants were primarily Irishmen, and heroes of New York's Irish–American community. The great race of April 1884, which developed into a duel between Rowell and Fitzgerald, and was finally won by Fitzgerald when he covered 610 miles round and round the track in six days, appeared on the front page of the *World*, in lead story position, for eight consecutive days. The newspaper's readers could not get too many details, which meant that the race received far more intensive coverage than any event during the first

[35] *World*, August 29, 1884, p. 2. [36] *World*, October 28, 1884, p. 1.
[37] *World*, October 12, 1884, p. 16.
[38] *World*, October 5, 1884, p. 12.

three years of Pulitzer's proprietorship, including the climactic moments of the Cleveland–Blaine contest. The articles, with illustrations, always filled at least two full columns, and during the final days, as Fitzgerald and Rowell came down to the wire each still in contention, they were jumped to page two and filled five or six columns.[39] HURRAH FOR FITZGERALD! the newspaper proclaimed in headline on the last day, HE WINS THE GREAT MATCH BY COVERING 610 MILES.[40] The *World* could provide no clearer indication that it would regard as significant news whatever the masses of people made significant.

The recognition of sports reporting not only as a device to raise circulation, but to address a particular audience, is apparent in still another respect. Boxing, baseball, walking races were all regarded as major items of news. Even roller skating matches, again dominated by Irish contestants, found an important place on the front page.[41] But when Yale defeated Harvard for the national football championship before 8,000 cheering spectators on a field just outside of New York City, the report was buried in an inconspicuous place on page five.[42] College men and their games were hardly the concern of the tenement house population of lower Manhattan. The *World* commented occasionally on the role sports should play in the college curriculum, but discovered little that was edifying in the spectacle of polite young men "deporting themselves as hooligans." "The young Apaches of Yale and Princeton," it declared in an editorial dripping with contempt, "can come together in gangs, pit themselves against each other in phalanxes, fight, kick, punch, gouge, bite, scratch and macerate in one wild and riotous rough-and-tumble until they are covered with blood, and this will pass muster under the eyes

[39] The first story, previewing the race, appeared in the *World* on April 27, 1884, p. 9. They filled the front page thereafter as follows: April 28, 1884, p. 1 (with thirteen illustrations); April 29, 1884, p. 1 (with four illustrations); April 30, 1884, p. 1; May 1, 1884, pp. 1 and 2; May 2, 1884, p. 1 (with seven illustrations); May 3, 1884, pp. 1 and 2 (with five illustrations); May 4, 1884, pp. 1 and 2 (with three illustrations); and May 5, 1884, p. 1, reporting the contestants' day of rest after the conclusion of the race.
[40] *World*, May 4, 1884, p. 1.
[41] The *World* reported the start of the six-day roller skating race on March 2, 1885, p. 1. The account of Donovan's victory, after rolling 1,090 miles, appeared on March 8, 1885, p. 1.
[42] *World*, November 30, 1883, p. 5.

of sensitive women and discriminating men as an unexceptionable outdoor sport."[43] The *World* was obviously no place for middle- and upper-class graduates of Ivy League institutions to follow the "old school's" triumphs.

The same logic which required that the *World* devote dozens of columns every day to sensational or frivolous material, and which put political cartoons on the front page, was also responsible for the emergence of the sports page. Pulitzer's decision to address the largest possible audience was a noble one, for it is better to read any reliable newspaper than no newspaper at all. The decision also meant, however, that the *World* would accept the style that popular taste dictated for it. The result was neither altogether good nor altogether bad. If gentlemen journalists had reason to damn the paper for its obsessive interest in scandal, or its garish headlines, they also paid it the compliment, at least in later years, of adopting many of its techniques. Not the least compliment lay in regarding an exciting pennant race, or a championship prizefight, as events worthy of attention.

[43] *World*, November 29, 1884, p. 4.

CHAPTER FIVE

A NEWSPAPER FOR WOMEN

It has already been noted that the *New York World*, and papers like it, represented a response to changes which occurred in American society after the Civil War. The fundamental change was America's coming of age as an industrial nation. The triumph of the machine meant that tens of thousands of men and women, both foreign born and native, congregated in cities and worked long hours of the day, six days a week, to earn enough to subsist. They were ill-educated, unsophisticated, and hungry for stimulation. Many of them had never before purchased newspapers on a regular basis. Their presence, and their condition, contributed to the rise of what contemporaries called sensational journalism, and what critics in later years scorned as Yellow Journalism.

During the same period, a movement that antedated even the first textile mill in Lowell, Massachusetts (although industrialization gave it momentum), also started to work great changes on the society. Its influence was felt in areas as disparate as politics, education, literature, and homemaking. Not least among the institutions affected was the press. Pulitzer and his colleagues had to come to terms with the fact that American women in the second half of the nineteenth century were on the verge of winning a struggle they had waged for generations on behalf of equal rights. In the old days it had been assumed that the feminine mind was focused exclusively on the eternals of child-rearing and housekeeping, and that only men gave thought to matters of public interest. Newspapers reflected that assumption by filling their pages with politics, stock market quotations, and business notices, pages as sturdily masculine in nineteenth century terms as the upholstery at the Lotus or Century Clubs. With the recognition that a status revolution, elevating wives and daughters from their role as household pets to something approaching equal place in the society, was almost won, the traditional policy no longer made sense.

Most of the great dailies in the United States rose to the challenge. They wooed women with short stories, recipes, beauty hints—all of the features that have long since become staple elements in the newspaper. It is not surprising that Pulitzer was among the leaders in developing those techniques. He aspired to lead the nation in circulation, and he could hardly do so by ignoring half of the population. The vital role that he played in ridding the New York press of its masculine orientation is partly explained by his presence in the city at a critical time. Even more important, however, is the fact that as a pioneer in popular journalism, anxious for a readership in the hundreds of thousands, he had to be among the first to recognize the drift of social change.

The interesting point about the *World*'s coverage for women is not that it existed, but that it was sensitively tuned to honor old prejudices while recognizing new realities. A newspaper that addressed an audience composed largely of immigrants and tenement-house dwellers could not help but be influenced by a movement so sweeping as female emancipation. At the same time, that audience was most likely to be grudging in its concessions to the movement, and most insistent upon upholding traditional values. Pulitzer's great achievement is that he successfully walked a tightrope between modernism and conservatism. It would have been fatal to ignore feminism, and fatal to endorse it. He managed—a considerable and subtle feat—to do neither.

Certainly no one could deny that women had improved their status in the postbellum period. The impact of reform could be seen in all sorts of areas, even one so mundane as housekeeping. Domestic chores became less time-consuming as urban families moved into apartment buildings, and were further simplified by such inventions as the sewing machine, the carpet sweeper, and the electric flat iron.[1] Commercial laundries at least partially

[1] See Richard Morris, ed., *The Encyclopedia of American History* (New York, 1953), pp. 537-38, for the dates of those inventions. Kate Wells dis-

relieved housewives of their washday blues, and canned and pre-packaged foods of the task of preparing meals.[2]

More dramatic gains were registered on other fronts. The courts increasingly took exception to the common law doctrine of woman as a creature to be held in the palm of man's hand, and accorded her equal rights before the bench.[3] Education for girls as well as boys ceased to be an unrealistic aspiration. Only 1,378 women received bachelor's degrees in the United States in 1870, about one to every six men. Twenty-five years later their number had grown to 4,383 (about one to every four men), with another 210 earning master's degrees and 25 doctorates or the equivalent.[4] Still more thousands of women insisted upon a different sort of equality, the chance to earn their own living at jobs of their own choice. Not content to be seamstresses and kitchen maids, not even content to accept the easy title of "school marm," they entered dozens of new occupations and stayed there. Almost before the Old Guard recognized that its ramparts had been breached, they were doctors, lawyers, journalists, librarians, lecturers, artists.[5] The impact was measured in dozens of different ways, as women married later, had less children, divorced more frequently, even achieved sexual equality.[6] Clearly a revolution of such dimensions must have influenced the press, not only by awakening it to women's potential as newspaper

---

cussed their impact upon family life in "The Transitional American Woman," *Atlantic Monthly*, XLVI (December 1880), 817-23.

[2] Between 1870 and 1894 the domestic consumption of canned goods rose from 30 million a year to 700 million. See Chauncey M. Depew, ed., *One Hundred Years of American Commerce*, 2 vols. (New York, 1895), II, 399.

[3] See Matilda J. Gage, *Woman, Church and State* (Chicago, 1893), for a review of changing legal attitudes toward women by a contemporary of Pulitzer's.

[4] *Historical Statistics of the United States* (U. S. Government Printing Office, Washington, D.C., 1960), Series H 327-38, pp. 211-12.

[5] Annie (Nathan) Meyer, ed., *Woman's Work in America* (New York, 1891), reviews the progress of the sex in securing equal job opportunities.

[6] See Carroll D. Wright, *Marriage and Divorce in the United States: 1867-1886*, First Special Report, Commissioner of Labor (Washington D.C., 1889). for an authoritative summary of changing social and sexual mores during that period. For more popular treatments of the same subject, see Lewis Dio *et al.*, "The Health of American Women," *North American Review*, CXXXV (December 1882), 503-24, and John S. Billings, "The Diminishing Birthrate in the United States," *Forum*, XV (June 1893), 467-77.

readers, but by determining that its content for women would include more than recipes and fashions.

The traditional role of housewives as managers of the family budget, together with the development of new principles of retailing, also helped to modify the attitude of newspapers. Before the rise of merchants like A. T. Stewart in New York City, and John Wanamaker in Philadelphia, almost all selling was carried out by small shops competing vigorously for a minuscule share of the market. The best any merchant could hope for was a growing trade within the blocks immediately surrounding his shop or pushcart. On special occasions customers might travel some distance to shop in an area, such as the Washington Market on Vesey Street, but not to patronize particular establishments. There was no reason for merchants to hire space in the daily press to advertise their wares.

The great contribution of Stewart and Wanamaker lay in rationalizing the retail side of business to keep pace with production. They used new selling techniques—uniform and clearly marked prices, honesty in guaranteeing the quality of the merchandise, low pressure salesmanship—to win the goodwill of customers, and by dealing in volume offered goods in a variety and at a price beyond the ability of small shopkeepers to compete. The great department stores which resulted owed their existence in part to extraneous factors, such as the influence of the Civil War in encouraging men to buy their clothing off the rack, but above all they measured the vision of a handful of pioneering merchants.[7]

Their innovations had an immediate and profound influence upon the press. Unlike the small shopkeepers of old, content to serve an area of several blocks, these princes of retailing looked to the entire city as their market, and relied upon full-page displays in the newspapers to reach it. "What his rivals called his audacity or foolishness," Frank Presbrey wrote of Wanamaker, "was grounded in a supreme faith in the effectiveness of adver-

[7] Although A. T. Stewart opened his famous store in 1823, and by 1852 could advertise it as the largest of its kind in the world, the great era of such merchandising began at the close of the Civil War.

tising. What he wanted to see a few years ahead he felt sure could be made real by the uses of publicity. For dull times, or even panicky times, the remedy was an increase in advertising."[8] Starting in the late 1870s, he took entire pages in the newspapers to advertise a sale, and by his success, forced rival department store proprietors to follow suit. Within a year or two the display ad had become an accepted tool of merchandising.[9]

So heavy was the demand for space that newspapers put out massive Sunday editions, and subscribed to feature syndicates, to maintain even a rough parity between editorial content and advertising. Even so, the rule-of-thumb ratio of 70–30 dropped to 50–50, and even lower. The industry willingly made itself over because advertising revenue soon overshadowed subscriptions and newsstand sales in determining whether the ledgers would be written in red ink or black. Wanamaker and his colleagues relied upon the press for their survival, but increasingly, particularly as the costs of labor and equipment rose, the press in turn relied upon them.

Two considerations loomed large in the minds of publishers and merchants as they considered this relationship. First, advertising had point, and was worth paying for, in proportion to the number of potential buyers who saw and were influenced by it. Although the statement has to be qualified, since a paper's reputation as an advertising medium generally, or for a certain type of ad, might exist apart from its number of subscribers, the obvious pressure upon publishers was to boost their circulations in order to attract advertising accounts. There were several ways to do so. They could appeal to immigrants, still an untapped audience, or to depressed workingmen, but the most obvious

[8] Frank Presbrey, *The History and Development of Advertising* (Garden City, 1929), p. 329.

[9] Robert Park drew particular attention to the part played by Sunday journalism in the rise of the department store. As he put it, "the department store is, in a sense, a creation of the Sunday newspaper. At any rate, without the advertising that the Sunday newspaper was able to give it, the department store would hardly have gained the vogue it has today. It is important in this connection that women read the Sunday paper before they did the dailies. The women are buyers." Robert E. Park, "The Natural History of the Newspaper," reprinted in Robert E. Park, Ernest W. Burgess, and Roderick D. McKenzie, *The City* (Chicago, 1925), p. 95.

group were the tens of thousands of women who had previously been lost by default to a few magazines and specialized journals. The popular press courted them simply because they were there.

Just as important as the number of people who read the ads in a newspaper was the type of people. The advertising profession, just being born, had already discovered a few axioms. It knew, for example, that a vendor of quality merchandise would do better to hire space in the *Tribune* rather than the *World*, because the smaller audience in this case was also the audience most likely to buy. It knew with even greater certainty that whatever her retiring disposition otherwise, the woman of a household had most to do with spending the family income, and that advertising, to be effective, had to be addressed to her. Nathaniel C. Fowler, a Boston newspaperman, expounded the wisdom in several advertising manuals published during the 1880s and 1890s. As he wrote on one occasion:

> The better the woman, the more directly she is interested in her husband's stockings, his hats and other things. If a certain color or new style of necktie becomes the fashion, the woman will know of it at least a week before her husband has learned anything about it. If the woman doesn't like the wearing quality of her husband's underwear, she will hunt up a store where better underwear can be bought.
>
> The woman can buy better articles, from spool cotton to ulster overcoats, for less money than the average man can buy with more money.
>
> The average man doesn't know about those things that he thinks he knows about.
>
> Although substantially all men are readers of advertisements, and are directed by advertising argument, an advertisement has not one twentieth the weight with a man that it has with a woman of equal intelligence and the same social status.
>
> A woman who would not read advertisements would not be a woman, consequently all women read advertisements.
>
> Woman buys, or directs the buying of, or is the fundamental factor in directing the order of purchase, of everything from shoes to shingles.[10]

[10] Quoted in Presbrey, *History and Development of Advertising*, pp. 317-18.

This insight carried an obvious corollary for newspapers. If women more than men comprised the desirable audience for advertisers, then the same motives which urged a large circulation required that a goodly part of the circulation be female. John Wanamaker was not interested in describing his dry goods to the sort of readership attracted by the *Police Gazette*. In order to assure him, and other clients, that their message would reach more appropriate eyes, publishers had to provide articles and features that women would enjoy.

Although no individual was responsible for the circumstances that made the fair sex so important to newspapers, it was a matter of individual choice how to respond to those circumstances. Joseph Pulitzer, a man whose genius lay not so much in pure inventiveness as in an ability to respond quickly to the needs and opportunities of the moment, helped to set the standard for the industry. He recognized that the modern challenge was to develop a newspaper that had no gender, and brought all his skill and imagination to bear in shaping the *World* along those lines.

Mostly this meant discovering and publishing stories that would appeal to adults of both sexes. The most striking characteristics of Pulitzer's newspaper, its sensationalism and imaginative use of illustration, were appreciated by women as well as men. There is nothing particularly masculine about a lively story dealing with murder or thwarted romance, and no reason why one sex more than the other would be fascinated by pictures.

Even in writing directly for women, the *World* followed the principle that the way to interest them was simply by running interesting articles. The result was that much of the material on the Woman's Page had a wider appeal than the location suggests. Both sexes, for example, were presumably diverted by the features which compared the New York City girl with girls from other cities and other countries, always to the benefit of the domestic specimen.[11] The newspaper quoted with approval the

[11] Although the *World* laid on flattery with a trowel, and obviously hoped thereby to win the goodwill of female readers, it is also true that the century

comment of a visiting European aristocrat, that American girls "say original things and have original ideas, while the French miss always refers everything to mamma."[12] Certainly, they had it all over Englishwomen, as the *World* heatedly pointed out in answer to Sir Lepel Griffin's slanders. "If he prefers the red faces, pronounced jaws, flat waists and big feet of the women one meets on Regent Street, to the animated countenances, graceful forms and exquisite features of the women on Broadway, that is his misfortune."[13] The *World* staff must have carefully culled British publications to find instances of insult, for frequent editorials answered the charges in tones not altogether good-humored. Whether it was the *London World*'s comment, that the American girl's "voice is harsh and loud, her accent . . . outrageous and her nasal twang unbearable," or the one in another publication, "that it requires all the finesse and firmness of the British aristocracy to keep the American lady from eating peanuts at the Queen's reception and throwing the shells over the steps of the throne," one answer sufficed to meet them all.[14] "This is not humor. It is good, stolid English conviction handed down from remote generations, and nothing can disturb it, not even the fact that the British aristocracy shows a marked tendency to improve its stock and its manners by marrying American girls."[15]

---

held women as objects of special devotion. Thomas Beer noted caustically that Daniel Sickles made public reference to "our world conquering and enlightened womanhood" a few days before shooting down his wife's lover in the nation's capital, and that public men argued for and against women's suffrage by citing their greater purity. (See Thomas Beer, *The Mauve Decade* (New York, 1926), p. 27.) "The Era of Women has dawned," Benjamin Orange Flower rejoiced in *The Arena* magazine, "bearing the unmistakable prophecy of a far higher civilization than humanity has ever known before. It is an uncontestable fact that woman is ethically, infinitely superior to man; her moral perceptions are firmer and stronger, her unselfishness far greater, her spiritual nature deeper and richer than that of her brothers." ("Editorial Notes," *The Arena*, IV (August 1891), 382.) James Bryce could but agree, adding quietly that "the community at large gains by the softening and restraining influence which the reverence for womanhood diffuses." James Bryce, *The American Commonwealth*, 2 vols., (revised ed.; New York, 1891), II, 611.

[12] *World*, September 15, 1883, p. 4.

[13] *World*, February 2, 1884, p. 4.

[14] The comment about the "unbearable nasal twang" of American girls was quoted in the *World* on September 7, 1884, p. 10; the comment about eating peanuts at the Queen's reception on September 14, 1884, p. 4.

[15] *World*, September 14, 1884, p. 4.

The *World* soberly considered why this superiority should be, and discovered the reason in political institutions as well as racial heritage.

> There is no country where woman is so esteemed and accorded her proper position with such graceful gallantry as this, and therefore our women are more independent, more self-confident, more self-reliant, and more brilliant in society than those of any other nation. History does not tell of such a race of splendid women as have grown up under the expansive and ennobling ideas of domestic life that prevail in the United States and that are due not only to the primal disposition to deal justly with women that had its origins with our Saxon ancestry, but to the liberality of our political institutions. . . . It is in our free America where woman has an undisputed empire and where her distinctive and lovable attributes blossom out in their most charming fullness and perfection.[16]

As surely as American girls had it all over their sisters in Europe, so did the girls of New York City out-dazzle those from out-of-town. The *World* detected a clue to the special qualities of Gotham's women (for to the newspaper feminine charm was a complex subject, and one worthy of the deepest analysis) in the fact of their living in the greatest city of the New World. According to a long article in the Sunday edition of October 26, 1884, environment worked on them to create God's ultimate female.

> What the New York woman of the higher order is likely to have as her special denotement is style. . . . Out of a hundred New York society women, nine-tenths of them will have more or less style. Out of a hundred women from other cities, not one-tenth will have any style, and the style of the women here will bear a more delicate flavor, a more subtle significance, than the style of the women elsewhere. . . .
> Her complexion is apt to be clear, bright, smooth, thanks to her excellent and varied diet, her habits of life and the sea air which she constantly breathes. . . . She meets a variety of men and women and has manifold experiences; she sees the same things at different

[16] *World*, October 26, 1884, p. 10.

— 140 —

angles and learns to discriminate between reality and sham. . . . She has not the passion for "culture" that marks her Boston sister, and she is not so subject to fads of diverse kinds. She is not likely to be severely intellectual or burdened with scholarship. But she is intelligent, discriminating, socially round and full of tact; and tact is the jewel of the feminine soul.[17]

Only once did the *World* waver in its devotion to the home-grown breed, and then in the midst of a campaign to raise circulation in Brooklyn. It admitted that some observers found the girls across the East River to be prettier, and suggested that if the judgment was fair, the awful things New York City women did to themselves to be fashionable explained it. "Cosmetics and strained corsets are the unseen hands that drive away the bloom of nature for the artificialism of the toilet chambers."[18]

Of all the subjects of interest to both sexes, although ostensibly classified as women's reading, none was more interesting than sex itself. Pulitzer's fine instinct for popular journalism is revealed in a long memorandum to the Managing Editor of the *World*, written some years after his retirement. He seized on the furor surrounding Gorki's visit to the United States with his common law wife, and suggested that the incident be used "as a sort of text or peg to . . . refer to the different standards in different countries in Europe. Also George Eliot, living with Lewes as husband and wife without being married. George Sand's living with everybody. Byron living not with his wife but Countess Guiccioli, and with everybody else's wife, and so many other genii. Goethe has housekeepers; Voltaire the Marquise du Chatelet." Pulitzer went on to warn that although the article "could be made very interesting by these historical illustrations," it would have to be handled with discretion. "Don't be cocksure, rather pick up the thoughts and suggest them rather than clubbing it into the heads of the readers. Suggest rather than make bold assertions."[19]

Pretty much the same formula—sex discreetly handled—ruled

[17] *World*, October 26, 1884, p. 10.
[18] *World*, April 26, 1885, p. 20.
[19] Memorandum from Bar Harbor, October 1899. Quoted in Don C. Seitz, *Joseph Pulitzer, His Life & Letters*, p. 432.

during the years of his active proprietorship. The *World*'s numerous articles on models who posed in the nude, for example, denoted a fascination more than aesthetic. Between April and December of 1884, the newspaper repeatedly assured its readers, and perhaps itself, that no immorality attached to disrobing in the service of art. "For the model the painter is not a man no more than the former is a woman for the painter," it declared. "During the pose both live in an ideal world in which the sexes do not exist and in which matter is revealed, so to say, to the eyes of the soul rather than to those of the body. But let an intruder knock at the door of the studio and the model flees in a fright and hides behind a curtain. Modesty, that virtue dormant in every woman, awakens at the approach of a profane step near the temple."[20] Having made the point, the *World* felt obliged to repeat it on several occasions, the last time rebuking those who thought the point needed to be made at all. "To many of our puritanic, straitlaced nation," we read finally, "this must seem positively shocking, hideously immoral, absolutely corrupting. . . . The reason is that they have not the true eye of art, or indeed any sympathy with art."[21]

If nudity in the service of art was noble, the newspaper considered semi-nudity in the service of fashion altogether ignoble. As already noted, it conducted a long and detailed campaign against women who appeared at the opera or other evening functions in dresses with plunging necklines. "The Metropolitan Opera House was built in the interest of good taste," it declared in a statement which combined punning with high moral purpose: "The extremely low necks are, however, barely in good taste."[22]

The *World* had clearly discovered an issue to exercise many of its readers. Letters of moral outrage filled the Letters to the Editor column for days afterwards. "A Mother" wrote in to say that she was "absolutely shocked at the exhibition of semi-nudity that greeted" her at the opera, and "Another Mother" to describe "shuddering" at the thought "of the temptations that are

[20] *World*, August 6, 1884, p. 10.
[21] *World*, December 7, 1884, p. 18. See also June 22, 1884, p. 10.
[22] *World*, December 24, 1883, p. 4.

placed before [her sons] in fashionable society."[23] At the same time, the newspaper's close attention to the etiquette of décolleté fashion, and its interest in the mechanics of keeping off-the-shoulder dresses above the danger zone, suggest that this was a subject not to be exhausted by periodic pleas for modesty. It interviewed dressmakers at length to discover who might properly lower the neckline. "The general rule," one of them revealed, "is, in the case of a debutante, to so cut an evening dress as to just suggest the contour, for an older society girl we allow the bosom to be well-defined, and for a matron or chaperone there is no particular or decided limit."[24] Its attempt to achieve a consensus on the most important question—what would happen if the shoulder strap gave way—came to nothing, but not for lack of effort. An early authority testified gloomily that "these are made to fit so tightly that the dress cannot slip, but if they should happen to break—well disastrous consequences might follow."[25] Several weeks later a second designer argued more confidently that "this idea that the whole waist depends for support on the straps is the height of absurdity, and as for the waist falling down if they gave way—it is impossible."[26] Not least, the newspaper gave serious thought to which celebrities showed a cleavage to best advantage. Pointing out that "the Queen herself in her best days was never alarmingly reluctant as to the extent of her own display of these womanly charms with the possession of which she is in no small degree accredited," and that the Queen's daughters also left "little to the imagination," it singled out one member of the family for special praise. Princess Louise, the *World* declared, "can hardly be blamed for not seeking to conceal one of the most rounded, plump and satiny necks and pairs of shoulders and the most billowy of bosoms in the United Kingdom; and that is saying a good deal."[27]

Sex figured importantly in a variety of other feature articles and editorials. The double standard came under review in the celebrated case of Lieutenant Simpson, who had been discharged

[23] *World*, December 21, 1883, p. 4; and December 23, 1883, p. 4.
[24] *World*, December 23, 1883, p. 5.
[25] *Ibid.*
[26] *World*, January 6, 1884, p. 9.
[27] *World*, July 6, 1884, p. 11.

from the Army for "conduct unbecoming an officer and a gentle-man" when he married the woman with whom he had, until then, been living. An angry editorial in the *World* deplored the morality which allowed an officer to remain a gentleman while keeping a mistress, but stripped him of that status when he solemnized the relationship at the altar.[28] The same theme was explored in an article describing a midnight mission in the city for "fallen women." The newspaper printed a poignant letter from an alumna of the institution, pleading with the *World* to take the lead in urging that women no longer bear the full onus for a misalliance. "I believe that the injustice that the unprotected woman has to submit to here and elsewhere at the hands of men will never cease, never be even lessened, till the great power, the newspaper, takes up the subject of making man, as well as woman, accountable to society for the breaking of society's moral laws. 'Fallen women' indeed! Who makes them fall? Who discards them after they have fallen? And where is the society that shuns the man, shuts the door on him?"[29]

In a lighter vein, the *World* scolded those ministers who com-plained that attendance at their Sunday evening services had dropped because young couples used the time for courtship. "When courtship or church-going is the alternative," it asked, "what young man or maid will hesitate in the choice?"[30] It greeted the announcement of an important genetic discovery, by which the sex of an unborn child could be predicted, with a long and straight-faced report.

> The great discovery is the law that "sex is deter-mined by what I shall designate as the superior parent; also that the superior parent produces the opposite sex;" that is to say, that if the husband is superior to the wife the family will consist mostly of girls, and vice versa. . . .
>
> Dark complexion is superior to light. . . . A square forehead and prominent veins are "superior," a large prominent eye (which "indicates conversational pow-er") is the reverse. But the best indication of superi-

[28] *World*, October 7, 1883, p. 4. [29] *World*, January 9, 1884, p. 4.
[30] *World*, November 11, 1883, p. 4.

— 144 —

ority is a large and prominent nose, Roman or aqui-
line, full a third the length of the face. . . .

Philosophers, lawyers, editors, poets, literary men
and brain workers generally have a large excess of
daughters. Wine merchants, tavernkeepers, small retail dealers, orators, physicians and musicians have a
preponderance of boys. Clergymen appear just to
struggle through the ordeal without incurring the
stigma of inferiority, being equally intelligent, sober
and moral with their wives and producing an equal
number of boys and girls.[31]

The article carried as its headline: A NEW SCIENTIST WHO IS
LIKELY TO CAUSE THE GREAT DARWIN TO BE FORGOTTEN.

Pulitzer did not win a female following solely by discoursing
on subjects of general interest, for he knew that it is the business of popular journalism to persuade individual groups of people
that the newspaper contains material specifically for them. Just
as the sports page acknowledged an area of masculine interest,
hundreds of articles appeared in the *World* tailored solely or
primarily to the concerns of women. The publisher never
doubted his ability to please the sex on its own terms. He
mocked the suggestion of Mrs. Henry Clews that the way "to
cultivate a taste for the news of the day" among women was by
establishing special clubs which would hire people to read to
them. The idea that they had to be dragooned into enjoying
newspapers, he declared, "may be called the most wonderful discovery of the age. It will be found out next that the American
ladies do not eat custard pie and take no interest in diamonds
and Dandy Dinmonts."[32]

If the *World* did not share that prejudice, its own prejudice
was at least as revealing. Most of its special features reflected
the traditional notion that a woman's place was in the home, and
that her interests were primarily domestic. It relied heavily on
fashions, etiquette, recipes, and the like, or on traditionally

[31] *World*, November 4, 1883, p. 10.
[32] *World*, December 1, 1884, p. 4. Dandy Dinmont refers to a breed of
terrier dog, named after a character in Sir Walter Scott's *Guy Mannering*.

"feminine" subjects, to enlist the loyalty of the distaff side. Thus the newspaper kept its readers fully informed on matters of style, whether at lawn tennis parties, at the seaside, or on the street during the various seasons.[33] During the fall of 1884, fashion dictated that "cloth dresses for street wear . . . be heavily braided. This fashion seems to be universal, almost the only variety being the combination of cloth with plain velvet or plush."[34] Necklines that season also showed a change. "The fashion of cutting demi-toilet dresses square or V-shape in the neck seems to be more than ever the vogue, and now comes the rumor that the bonnet strings are to be removed."[35] The paper even considered the part played by dress in the feminist movement. It ran a long, and on the whole, respectful report about a reform exhibition attended by a Mrs. Stow, in which the feminist appeared in the "Triple S" suit, consisting of a cutaway coat, a pair of silk trousers, and a silk shirt falling to just below the knees.

> Before the exhibition proper Mrs. Stow read a paper in which she asserted that, whereas woman's legs are useful members of her body, and capable of much attractive dressing, they should, and in the near future, be displayed without any of the silly prudishness which now insists upon their never being mentioned, and always hidden by clumsy bags. "The legs may be encased," said Mrs. Stow, "either in trousers, leggings or stockings, according to time, place and occupation. . . . Women will very soon as fearlessly display their legs—properly dressed—as they now do their arms."[36]

Other traditional areas of female interest received similar attention. Beauty articles advised women on a variety of problems, from the proper use of cosmetics to ways of removing facial

[33] See, for example, the *World*, June 10, 1883, p. 5; June 17, 1883, p. 5; and March 7, 1885, p. 9, for articles on women's fashions. The thoroughness with which the *World* reported such matters does not contradict earlier assertions about it being a paper primarily for members of the poor and lower middle classes. Women, like men, achieve vicarious pleasure in reading about things they would like to own, but could never afford. This explains a fashion article on January 13, 1884, p. 11, describing in detail a dress designed to retail at $30,000, one surely beyond the means of all but a handful of women in the metropolis.
[34] *World*, September 28, 1884, p. 14.
[35] *World*, October 12, 1884, p. 10.   [36] *World*, September 16, 1883, p. 12.

hairs.[37] Long dissertations appeared on how to brew a cup of coffee, on new uses for catfish in making soup, on the versatility of the tomato and onion, and so on.[38] Almost every issue of the paper carried helpful hints on problems in interior decoration. The conscientious housewife read in the fall of 1883, for instance, in an article headlined THE CHIC IN FURNISHING, that:

> The popular wood this season . . . is unquestionably rosewood. Ebony is not so much employed as heretofore, and mahogany has taken a second place since the revival of rosewood. . . .
> Fashion requires that the modern parlor shall avoid all appearance of uniformity in its furniture. In a word, every piece is expected to have some characteristic not possessed by its neighbor. . . .
> The materials employed in upholstery this season are varied. Heading the list of materials for the parlor are silk velours. . . . Plush and satin are also in style for parlor covers.[39]

But of all the articles in this genre, none were more common, nor better received, than those on etiquette. Arthur M. Schlesinger suggests one reason why this should be, when he points out that the American concern for correctness fostered a minor industry between 1870 and 1917, as thick volumes on etiquette appeared off the printing presses at the rate of five or six a year.[40] Corroborative evidence comes from Edward Bok. He reported in his autobiography that a single column on social usage in the *Ladies' Home Journal*—"Ruth Ashmore's Side Talk With Girls" —drew 158,000 letters in sixteen years.[41] They came "from

[37] *World*, July 1, 1883, p. 5; and September 22, 1884, p. 9.
[38] *World*, February 18, 1884, p. 4; and November 9, 1884, p. 11.
[39] *World*, October 21, 1883, p. 11.
[40] Some of the books were simply compilations of previously published articles (e.g., Dr. Robert Tomes', *The Bazar Book of Decorum* [1870], *The American Code of Manners* [1880], taken from the *American Queen* magazine, and *Social Life* [1889], taken from the *Delineator*). Others represented original efforts by authors, usually women, who had the name or background to qualify as social experts. John A. Logan's widow, Grover Cleveland's sister, and Julia Ward Howe's daughter each took advantage of their names to become arbiters of correct behavior. See Arthur Schlesinger, Sr., *Learning How to Behave, A Historical Study of American Etiquette Books* (New York, 1946), especially pp. 30-35, for a discussion of the American concern with etiquette.
[41] Edward Bok, *The Americanization of Edward Bok* (New York, 1920), pp. 169-71.

young ladies in the West and East; . . . from young men who are rising in the world; . . . from elderly people to whom fortune has come late, but whose children begin to wish to know how to take their places in the gay world; from all parts of the country, in fact."[42]

Although Mrs. Elizabeth M. Gilmer's column for the *New Orleans Picayune*, which she inaugurated in 1896 under the by-line "Dorothy Dix," is commonly taken as the first regular newspaper feature of its kind, the *World* anticipated Mrs. Gilmer by more than a decade with a column that appeared regularly for several months in the form of "letters" from Edith to her country cousin, Bessie.[43] The series began in November 1883, with a letter from Edith honoring her "agreement to write . . . about some points of social etiquette in New York, so that when you move to the city next year from your lovely country home you can be *au fait* at once."[44] She embarked immediately on one of the thorniest problems: how to call on acquaintances and leave a calling card. This, she told Bessie, is "the first and most important social duty." Succeeding weeks brought advice on how to give an afternoon tea;[45] how to entertain at a small dinner;[46] proper behavior when attending a ball;[47] and the etiquette of New Year's visits.[48] Edith also shared with her cousin the current gossip-about-town, and sought her advice on possible changes in social convention. Would it not be possible, she asked early in 1884, for a reform to be affected which would allow a gentleman to escort his partner back to her seat after the dance instead of being stuck with her?[49]

[42] Remark attributed to the editor of *American Queen*; quoted in Schlesinger, *Learning How to Behave*, p. 32.

[43] The fact that the letters appeared in a New York City daily, even one so irreverent as the *World*, undoubtedly contributed to their importance. Arthur Schlesinger points out that "as America's commercial capital, New York inevitably became also America's social capital, elbowing aside Washington, which had served as the court of last appeal for the preceding generation. Etiquette writers needed only to cite Manhattan's latest fashions in order to establish their right to speak with finality." Schlesinger, *Learning How to Behave*, p. 30.

[44] *World*, November 18, 1883, p. 10.
[45] *World*, November 25, 1883, p. 10.
[46] *World*, December 2, 1883, p. 11.
[47] *World*, December 9, 1883, p. 9.
[48] *World*, December 30, 1883, p. 10.   [49] *World*, February 3, 1884, p. 14.

The articles aroused a keen response among readers of the *World*. Letters poured into the editor's office praising them, and asking that they be continued. "I want to thank you for publishing the letter from a city belle to her country cousin in today's paper," Annie Austin wrote. "At home in the country we didn't think much about etiquette, . . . but now that I have been in the city some time it seems to me quite possible that a man should be straightforward and sensible, and at the same time wear the proper kind of coat." "High Society" remarked that it "has created considerable interest among both sexes," while E. H. Gould asked that it "be followed by other articles of a similar character."[50]

One might wonder what expositions on the proper use of calling cards, on the latest fall fashions, on the techniques of giving an intimate supper, had to do with the bedraggled wives and daughters of workingmen in the tenements of lower Manhattan. The answer is that they were valued precisely for their Cinderella qualities. Although most of the women who read the newspaper might be lucky to purchase a dress every third autumn, and when they did it was for use rather than style, this made them all the more avid to partake at least vicariously of a world they could never join.

The Letters to the Editor column amply establishes that the lists of those who worried about correct behavior included more than the sophisticated few.[51] "A constant reader" asked if it was "a polite thing for a lady to come in and sit at the table without removing her bonnet when she has been in the house at least an hour and has no idea of going out again."[52] The *World* thought not, but begged indulgence for the offender since removing the

[50] The letters quoted appeared in the *World* on November 20, 1883, p. 4. See also January 16, 1884, p. 4, for a forlorn plaint from "C.H.C." when the letter failed to appear in one issue. "I noticed with much regret that your paper of yesterday (January 13) did not contain one of the customary letters from 'Edith.' Are we to have no more of them?"

[51] For examples of letters seeking advice on questions of etiquette, see the *World*, January 13, 1884, p. 4; February 15, 1884, p. 4; September 14, 1884, p. 4; and October 19, 1884, p. 4. By 1885, such letters had become so common that the *World* made a special feature of them, and answered them under the headline SOCIAL ETIQUETTE. See February 15, 1885, p. 18; March 8, 1885, p. 16; March 15, 1885, p. 20; and May 3, 1885, p. 19.

[52] *World*, January 13, 1884, p. 4.

hat would probably upset her hairdo. Several readers wanted to know if a gentleman writing a note to a young lady, and requesting a reply, should enclose a stamped, self-addressed envelope.[53] "It was highly improper to inclose a stamp, . . ." the editor decided. "If a young lady cares enough about a gentleman to answer his notes she will be only too happy to provide her own postage stamps." D. H. Babcock asked "if it is possible for a young lady to 'flirt' with a gentleman with whom she is acquainted."[54] "It certainly is possible," came the reply. "The idea that a lady can only carry on a flirtation with a stranger is preposterous." In answer to "a friend's" question, how to break the conversational ice at an evening sociable, the newspaper suggested "a few references to the weather or the latest piece of interesting news in the day's *World*. If an acquaintance, get off a joke about roller-skating. On being presented to a lady it is always in order to compliment her on her complexion or the fit of her dress. After that the conversation will drift pleasantly."[55] A young lady, who styled herself "ignoramus," worried whether it was proper to answer in kind when a gentleman said "Happy to have met you."[56] "It depends entirely upon the relative degrees of happiness experienced by both," the *World* suggested reasonably. It seemed clear that quite aside from the desire to read about the gracious life as others lived it, even the relatively unsophisticated folk who patronized the *World* wished to attain their own graciousness, and appreciated articles which would help them.[57]

Edith's letters about correct behavior were supplemented by a series of columns touching on other areas of female interest. They are revealing because they represent the newspaper's re-

[53] *World*, September 14, 1883, p. 4.
[54] *World*, December 10, 1884, p. 4.
[55] *World*, March 10, 1885, p. 4.
[56] *World*, May 3, 1885, p. 19.
[57] The advice about correct behavior served another purpose as well. New York City was, and still is, a cold, impersonal, aloof place, particularly for those who had come from foreign lands, or who had been trapped in the degrading flux of the tenements constantly moving from flat to flat. The *World* could do little to help them emotionally, but in features such as this it supplied at least a touch of what they missed: warmth, intimacy, neighborliness.

sponse to a new age in which women sought identification and status. The *World* was not ready to antagonize its tenement house following by endorsing the most radical manifestations of feminism, but neither could it risk being blind to the evidences of a revolution in progress. The columns, and the articles that supplemented them, offered a convenient basis for compromise, for in them liberal thoughts could be expressed without committing the newspaper to a liberal course.

Perhaps the most popular of those columns was "Jenny June's Melange," which appeared weekly for several months in the form of chatter over the breakfast table. Sometimes Jenny June merely elaborated on conventional and rather frivolous subjects. A piece on dieting headlined HOW TO GET RID OF ADIPOSE TISSUE, for instance, pointed out that "the principle of the cure was largely based upon diet, which was at first nitrogenous but variable, afterwards farinaceous and absolute. The liver is attacked and brought into line by a safe and special remedy; hot water is used; hot medicated foot baths, and the number of meals at once reduced."[58] But often the conversation at breakfast veered to the serious problem of how women could best take their place as equal members of the society. Jenny June spoke highly of the custom in Amsterdam and other cities in Holland of establishing special hotels for female travelers to which "the other sex" would not be admitted. "Such homelike hotels are more needed by women travelling in this country than in any other that is civilized on the face of the earth, . . ." she declared. "It is very rarely . . . that they can pay high prices, or fling money about as men do; rarely that they are able to travel unless with their fathers or husbands or brothers; and when they do it is with a hundred small fears and anxieties born of their limited experience, their habit of depending upon others for direction that men know nothing of."[59] She urged her well-to-do readers to resist the blandishments of luxurious living which made them "hot-house plants of a feebler growth than ever."

> The husband gives the orders, the janitor receives the
> supplies and sends them up to the cook and the lady

[58] *World*, October 21, 1883, p. 9.
[59] *World*, October 28, 1883, p. 9.

of the "apartment" is not required to lift her hand, or open her mouth unless she wishes to do so. . . . Timidity is the obstacle against which women have constantly to contend—and ignorance and isolation tend to increase it.[60]

Those same women, if they enjoyed private incomes, would do well to consider the pitfalls involved in turning the incomes over to their husbands. "If the wife furnishes all the money she naturally expects the attention and companionship of her husband, who lives upon it, and views him after a time very much as a sort of lackey or upper servant—paid to perform a certain kind of service. If he takes possession of the funds and uses them as his own he learns to consider them so, and the wife is obliged to ask as a favor for a moiety of that which belongs to her."[61]

The column eventually ceased to appear, but in its place came new ones, variously entitled "The World of Women," "Doings of Women Folk," "Doings in High Society," "Movements in Society," and archest of all, "Grandma's Wise Advice."[62] They covered a wide range of subjects, from chronicling the movements of the rich and near-rich, to describing the activities of First Ladies, to castigating that most traditional of all villains, the husband who buried his nose in a newspaper at the breakfast table.

The significant thing about them is that they pushed out the limits of the "World of Women" and provided a platform for other articles that came close to discoursing seriously on serious issues. It is true that the issues were usually "feminine" ones—that is, concerned with home, or children, or woman's status—but by appearing at all they helped to dispel the illusion of the sex as scatterbrained and helpless. A good example is the series on housing which considered the problems posed as middle class families began to leave the white, clapboard houses they had once occupied and move into great, multi-unit apartment buildings.[63] The reason for the exodus had to do primarily with

[60] World, November 18, 1883, p. 9.

[61] World, November 11, 1883, p. 10.

[62] See, for example, the World, May 25, 1884, p. 11; August 31, 1884, p. 10; October 19, 1884, p. 10; December 7, 1884, p. 18; January 20, 1884, p. 10; and January 27, 1884, p. 12.

[63] The first such building went up in 1870 at 142 East 18th Street, just off Irving Place. Couples of the most impeccable social standing applied for ad-

money, or the lack of it. Despite the popular prejudice against sharing one's roof with strangers, most families found it increasingly difficult to maintain a private home. The rentals on decent sized structures (minimum standards were considerably more generous in those days[64]) varied from $1,500 to $2,000 a year, or up to one-half of a professional man's income. Rather than sacrifice other luxuries, the young-in-heart willingly abandoned the outmoded biases of a previous generation and made their home on a shelf. It became almost a badge of chic modernity to announce an apartment address.

The *World* heartily endorsed this further evidence of New York's vitality. In an article headlined THE WONDERFUL BUILDING GROWTH OF THE EMPIRE CITY, it spoke rapturously of the luxuries urbanization had brought. "It is a rare thing to find a suit [sic] of apartments in an ordinary flat now that does not include bathroom, ranges, dumb-waiters, icebox and stationary wash-tubs, luxuries heretofore enjoyed only by the wealthier classes. Apartments of this description may be had for $20 to $30 a month rent, and for tenants able and willing to pay more the improvements range from French-plate mirrors to the latest application of electricity."[65] At the same time, the newspaper pointed out that progress exacted a toll, and that urban living grew more complicated in proportion as it grew more comfortable. Some of the problems could be passed off as inevitable concomitants of the modern age. For example, New Yorkers

---

mission, for all the uncertain morality of living above and below other families. No small credit goes to the fact that Rutherford Stuyvesant, one of the distinguished names in the city, commissioned the building, and Richard Morris Hunt was its designer. Other landlords soon imitated Stuyvesant's example. A dreary succession of apartment buildings went up on both sides of the island north of 42nd Street, by the hundreds each year after 1880, as the middle class came to the same decision en masse.

[64] According to William Dean Howells, who set down in depressing detail the problems of Mr. and Mrs. March as they searched for an apartment, the "New York ideal of a flat . . . was inflexibly seven rooms and a bath. One or two rooms might be at the front, the rest crooked and cornered backward through increasing and then decreasing darkness till they reached a light bedroom or kitchen at the rear. It might be the one or the other, but it was always the seventh room with the bath; or if, as sometimes happened, it was the eighth, it was so after having counted the bath as one." William Dean Howells, *A Hazard of New Fortunes* (New York, 1889), p. 73.

[65] *World*, September 16, 1883, p. 11.

— 153 —

tucked into their vertical buildings had to adjust to far less spacious rooms than they had once known. A comic feature in July 1883, attempted to predict what the final result would be:

> The reporter looked into a little closet, about five feet by three in size.
> "How do you manage to sleep in it?" said he.
> "It is easy enough after you get used to it," replied the happy tenant. "I sleep with my knees crooked. This room, two by four, is the kitchen. When we want to pump water we open the hall door, so as to give the pump-handle room to move it."
> "You like living here?"
> "I wouldn't live anywhere else."[66]

Worse yet, the tenants no longer enjoyed the privilege of speaking in a normal voice to each other without inviting the whole neighborhood to participate. The consequences could be dire indeed!

> The Genteel Flat house is slowly but surely under-mining the character of the New Yorker. . . . The first three months in a Genteel Flat is said to produce depression. At the end of six months melancholia sets in, then confirmed misanthropy and deep-seated hatred of all things that are. A patient investigation of the evil has led to the discovery that all this springs from the thinness of the walls and flooring in these houses.[67]

In other instances, the *World* considered the impositions unnecessary, and printed angry comments in which wives and mothers could see their grievances expressed. The greatest problem lay in the age-old antagonism between landlords and children, an antagonism that resulted in many middle class couples, who refused to take an oath of celibacy, being unable to live in neighborhoods commensurate with their incomes. The newspaper suggested the folly of such a situation, particularly in a society that had "acquired the disgraceful habit of having children."[68] It urged that considerably more buildings be constructed for use

66 *World*, July 29, 1883, p. 5.
67 *World*, February 1, 1885, p. 9; see also June 24, 1883, p. 5.
68 *World*, September 2, 1883, p. 4.

rather than show. "Let some good genius of an architect invent a genteel flat where children can be made comfortable and will not be regarded as nuisances. A little less zinc on the cornice, not so much sculptured brown stone on the entrance, a trifle less fresco and ground glass, but bigger courts, thicker walls and larger sleeping rooms, and then—an open invitation to tenants with children."[69]

Women also recognized the voice of reason and sympathy in articles deploring the tyrannical power of janitors, who not only greeted requests for service with a snarl, but frequently earned under-the-table commissions by announcing to tenants which merchants they would patronize. Few families dared to ignore advice from men who wielded powers of retaliation equivalent to those of a Captain Bligh. The janitor "now shakes his keys at thousands of helpless tenants and lords it over their families with his arbitrary rules and regulations. . . . He must be placated, fed or fought. To fight him is fatal, for he holds the strategic position of the front door."[70]

This was relatively mild stuff for a crusading journal, but it did represent a problem series with women in mind. Equally noteworthy were the articles that considered the activities of various female celebrities: artists, Cabinet wives, socialites.[71] They were chatty accounts, telling women what they wanted to know about other women. PEN-PICTURES OF THE WOMEN WHO RECEIVE DISTINGUISHED VISITORS AT THE WHITE HOUSE AND IN THE HOMES OF THE CABINET MINISTERS, the headline on one announced. HOW THEY LOOK, ACT AND WHAT THEY WEAR.[72] Despite the gossipy tone, they delivered an important moral about the competence of the sex. The newspaper pointed out in describing some of the personalities active in the nation's capital that "everyone knows the traditional effectiveness of women in political intrigue, and, whether this be well founded or not, it is

[69] *World*, August 2, 1883, p. 4.
[70] *World*, September 2, 1883, p. 4; see also February 3, 1884, p. 10; and April 20, 1884, p. 4.
[71] See, for example, the *World*, July 20, 1884, p. 11; and November 9, 1884, p. 10.
[72] *World*, March 29, 1885, p. 18.

at least a fact that some of the shrewdest politicians of Washington are of the gentler sex."[73]

Other features went on to explore the progress of women in achieving equal job opportunity. An account which developed into a catalogue of all the occupations in which they participated bore the triumphant headline: WOMAN WINNING HER WAY. PROGRESS MADE IN CONQUERING THE BUSINESS WORLD. THE DOWNFALL OF BELLES AND THE INCREASE OF DUDES A RESULT PREDICTED BY WORKING WOMEN. To its credit, the newspaper did not settle for huzzas, but went on to single out the great reform still to be won. "The question of wages is now the most serious question. In nearly all kinds of work women are paid less than men."[74] It worked the same vein the following year by printing extensive extracts from Emily Faithfull's lectures in England on the achievements and problems of American working women.[75] As if to underline its support for this aspect of women's rights, the *World* also ran a long article by Eliza Archard, the feminist, rebutting a recent piece in the *Contemporary Review* which had argued that the sex was unfitted by temperament to serve in the ministry. Miss Archard dismissed the logic as the outgrowth of a Bible written by men for men.[76]

[73] *World*, November 9, 1884, p. 10.

[74] *World*, May 28, 1883, p. 8.

[75] *World*, June 15, 1884, p. 11.

[76] *World*, February 24, 1884, p. 11. Her reply is worth quoting at length as an example of feminist militancy during the late nineteenth century. Professor Godet, she wrote,

> reminds us how woman is weaker than man, more easily tempted, &c., &c., and that sin came into the world by a woman. It is no such thing! Observe! It took the devil himself to make the woman fall. It only needed the woman to tempt the man and make him fall. We do not find it on record either that the man made any great opposition to falling. On the contrary, it looks rather as though he was dying to be tempted all the time.
>
> Then Adam turned about and blamed the woman for it. He wasn't very gentlemanly, to say the least. . . . Another important point most people lose sight of is this: men wrote the Bible and made it to suit themselves. If women had written it they would have made it very different. If, for example, Eve had been permitted to tell her side of the story, she might have thrown a light on the question which would have changed the complexion of theology for all time. . . .
>
> The Professor tells us how the fine, ardent, imaginative, emotional, vivacious, &c., &c., nature of woman makes her liable to 'easier seduction' into the ways of error than man. It does, does

Even the most militant feminists, those who rebuked the *World* for its unwillingness to carry reform to the logical conclusion, hailed such articles for acknowledging that femininity no longer implied helplessness. "Accept our thanks for the page in the Sunday *World* devoted to the enlightenment of the people upon what women are doing," Maria C. Arter wrote to the Editor. "You may not directly advocate giving us the ballot, but you are letting your readers know that a large number of women are entering upon careers that fit them for exerting an influence for good in any field."[77]

The essential point about these features is that they represented the *World*'s compromise between women's changing status and the traditional notion of femininity still adhered to by the immigrant and lower income groups who comprised so large a part of the newspaper's readership. The old-fashioned idea of the female as essentially a plant of domestic growth determined the emphasis upon household matters in editing the Woman's Page. But the realization that the new American woman had successfully challenged tradition determined that the columns written for her would at least pay lip service to the fact of her emancipation. Although the columns were rather timid by modern standards, evidently neither the *World* nor its readers regarded them as such. The "World of Women" column of May 25, 1884, referred enthusiastically to the new role the sex had carved for itself, and to the column's part in heralding that role:

> It is gratifying to note the many compliments the *World* Woman's Column is receiving. Evidence increases that it is growing in favor and fame. . . . This modest department was established in the belief that

---

it? Is it woman or man, pray, who gets drunk, who fills workhouses and penitentiaries, who goes in for ward politics and becomes an Alderman or Street Commissioner . . . ?

Whenever a woman has uncommon mental ability and strong common-sense men say she has a 'masculine' intellect. There isn't any sublime self-conceit in this compliment, is there . . . ?

Woman's proper place is whatever and wherever she can make it. . . .

Ought woman to preach? They ought to do exactly as they please about it.

[77] *World*, April 25, 1884, p. 4.

the female sex of our time cared for something more than fashions and crochet work. Women in our happy time are broadening their interests, educating themselves and engaging in industrial occupations as they never did before. . . . It is a supreme satisfaction to know that the evolution of the feminine half of the race has reached the point that the Woman's Column of a newspaper means something more than darned net and venerable recipes for making sweet pickles.[78]

⸻ ◦ ◦ ⸻

The question arises, if the feminist movement was mainly one of the middle class, and the *World* predominantly a paper of the lower-middle and lower classes, why the accumulating evidences of a status upheaval received any acknowledgement at all? Part of the answer is that it had to, because even lower class wives and daughters, if only by virtue of contributing to the family income, participated in it. Moreover, as shall be seen, the homage paid to the real substance of feminism—the right to vote, the right to an equal education, the right to practice a profession— was never more than minimal. The *World* thought it proper that young ladies should aspire to read romantic poetry, but altogether improper that they should use their reading ability to study medicine. The articles it published for women were on subjects which the most conventional of them might enjoy.

It is hardly surprising, in that case, that while acknowledging the fact of emancipation the newspaper also continued to address a traditional female: domestic, gentle, refined. All sorts of features paid homage to the sex's role as the great civilizer in American society, the patron of art and literature. The *World* was among the first, for example, to publish fiction in the Sunday edition on a more or less regular basis.[79] The stories provided

[78] *World*, May 25, 1884, p. 11.

[79] The first story appeared in the Sunday edition of May 20, 1883, p. 10. Contributed by "an artillery officer," it was entitled "Our Doctor." The *World's* experiments with fiction became thenceforth ever more ambitious. In less than a year, on January 27, 1884, it devoted an entire page (p. 14) to a tale by General Felix Agnus, publisher of the *Baltimore American*, entitled "A Woman of War. A Story of Love and Daring." A separate editorial the day before praised the "original romance" as abounding "in stirring war scenes and love episodes. . . . This is one of the best products of [General Agnus'] facile pen." See the *World*, January 26, 1884, p. 4.

escape from humdrum lives, but they also affected to serve a literary or aesthetic function. Invariably they told of fair ladies and gallant gentlemen, of love foiled but ultimately triumphant. Colonel Leslie Grahame, the hero of one such saga, had lost his love to another because he was too shy to declare himself. He returns from his sad exile a hero, a holder of the Victoria Cross, to discover that the loved one is now widowed and once more available. The story concludes on the following note:

> It is well that the drooping branches of a weeping-willow have made a little secluded bower of the landing-place; well, too, that the gardener, coming down to moor the boat, does not arrive a minute sooner or his astonished eyes might have seen what Queenie afterwards mysteriously reports, "My mommie crying and Colonel Grahame comforting her, as mommie does me when I tumble down, holding her head on his shoulder and stroking her hair."
>
> For Leslie Grahame's long-repressed tale of love has been spoken at last and the little playfellow of early days—the prize which he gave up in bitter self-denial to his boy friend, has whispered to him the "Yes" which, had he been more farsighted, might have been spoken long ago and have spared him years of self-inflicted exile.[80]

The *World*'s poetry sustained this vision of a sweeter and gentler universe. Once again the maidens were shy, and the heroes, finally at least, resolute. John W. Dafoe's "Sometime" illustrates the romantic and idealized tone of the verse.

> Sometime, sweetheart, our paths will cross again
>   And I will look once more into thine eyes,
> And feel no more the sorrow and the pain,
>   While soft and sweet will sound thy sweet replies.
>
> Sometime, dear heart, sometime, though ocean's foam
>   And mountains rise between us, we will meet;
> Thy heart will find within my heart its home,
>   And all my bitter life will turn to sweet.[81]

Lines like these expressed essentially feminine sentiments in words the century had conditioned the sex to prefer. That the

[80] *World*, September 16, 1883, p. 10.
[81] *World*, January 25, 1885, p. 17.

poems were written primarily for women, and honored their greater sensitivity and civilizing mission, was made more clear in a subsequent piece published in the newspaper. According to the last stanza:

> Yes, a woman! Brightest model
> Of that high and perfect beauty.
> Where the mind and soul and body
> Blend to work out life's great duty.
> Be a woman: naught is higher
> On the gilded crest of time;
> On the catalogue of virtue
> There's no brighter, holier name.[82]

It is also noteworthy that although the *World* ran relatively few book reviews, the great majority of those which did appear discussed books of particular interest to the fair sex. Mrs. John Sherwood's *Manners and Social Usages* was endorsed as "valuable to all classes," mainly for proposing an etiquette not entirely borrowed from Europe.[83] Several months later the newspaper reviewed *Three Visits to America* by Emily Faithfull, the English feminist, and commended it in headline for paying A SENSIBLE TRIBUTE TO OUR SOCIAL FREEDOM AND OUR GIRLS.[84] "Nym Crinkle's" columns, meanwhile, shared with the *World* readers personal impressions and gossip about the theater. Written in short, disconnected sentences, similar to the style of Broadway columnists of a later era, they touched on a wide variety of subjects, but mainly on those women would enjoy.[85] The earliest one, for example, discussed Lily Langtry's beauty, the rivalry between prima donnas at the Metropolitan Opera House and Academy of Music, and the charms of Mme. Sembrich, perhaps the greatest diva of her time.[86]

Of all the articles that catered to women's appetite for culture, none appeared more frequently, nor stirred greater interest, than

[82] *World*, February 15, 1885, p. 18. The *World* identified Montague Marks as composer of the poem, but a letter to the Editor three days later from Mr. Marks emphatically disclaimed responsibility for it.

[83] *World*, June 8, 1884, p. 11.

[84] *World*, December 16, 1884, p. 17.

[85] See "Nym Crinkle's" column in the *World* for May 3, 1884, p. 20, for an illustration of how the author anticipated later journalistic practice by bringing together a series of short and unrelated items under one heading.

[86] *World*, January 13, 1884, p. 5.

those on the great seasons of opera which commenced with the construction of the Metropolitan Opera House in 1883. Partly the interest reflected the sex's traditional role in fostering musical development in the United States.[87] ("I do not think," Walter Damrosch remarked some years before he assumed the directorship of the Metropolitan, "that there has ever been a country whose musical development has been fostered so exclusively by women as America."[88]) Much more important, for tenement wives as well as the ladies of the middle class, was the drama of watching the wealthy struggle for social primacy.

The music, and the rivalry, captured the *World*'s attention from the beginning. Its lead story on October 23, 1883, described the glitter and pomp as both houses began their seasons on the same evening. "The new Opera House with its brilliant assemblage presented a dazzling sight," the newspaper reported. "No such audience had probably ever been seen in America. The triple rows of boxes were all filled. Diamonds flashed all the way round from one pole of the great horseshoe magnet to the other, and costumes of the richest material shone in every hue."[89] It was less enthused, however, by Joseph C. Cady's design for the Metropolitan.

> Enough money has been spent on this structure to make it a monument and a valuable architectural addition to our city. It is in reality one of the most conspicuously ugly of the many ugly buildings that disgrace our good taste. There appears to have been no sense of decorative obligation to the community whatever. The Opera House is ill-designed, antiquated and altogether inharmonious in its plan and proportions, and not only poverty-stricken but absolutely painful in its embellishment. A more amazing

[87] Their contribution was evidenced in a variety of ways. They turned out in force for concerts (with or without their husbands); they made up the major portion of music teachers and students; and they saw to it that piano practice for children became one of the ordeals of growing up. Although the credit devolves mainly upon women of the middle class, music was identified as a female concern, and a newspaper which wrote for women—of whatever class —was obliged to report on developments in that field.

[88] Quoted in Charles A. and Mary R. Beard, *The Rise of American Civilization*, 2 vols. (New York, 1927), II, 457.

[89] *World*, October 23, 1883, p. 1.

example of wealth working without taste or conviction or public spirit was never seen.[90]

The competition between the two companies, as they spent
lavishly to lure artists from all over the world, proved to be
critically expensive for both. Although the *World* described brilliant evenings of Italian opera at the Academy of Music, with
Adelina Patti the reigning artist, the challenge from uptown soon
proved to be overwhelming.[91] In the spring of 1885, the Academy's impresario finally laid down his checkbook. "I cannot
fight Wall Street," Colonel James H. Mapleson declared, as he
announced that henceforth there would be no more opera at 14th
Street. The Metropolitan attempted meanwhile to overcome a
$600,000 deficit during its first year by engaging Dr. Leopold
Damrosch, who had been director of the New York Symphony
Orchestra, to put the company on a sustaining basis. Damrosch's
admiration for Wagnerian opera, at the time largely unperformed
in this country, suggested an obvious solution. The *World* regarded as "hardly credible" the earliest rumor that German casts
would be imported to balance the Metropolitan's books. "The
attempt to make the stockholders of the Metropolitan put up with
it in the place of Italian opera would be about as successful as the
attempt to get English Opera into the Academy."[92] It changed its
tune, however, when the impresario persevered and returned
from Europe with a cast of Wagnerian artists. "There is no artistic reason, . . ." the newspaper declared some weeks later, "why
Dr. Damrosch's venture should not meet with as much popular
favor as the form of lyric drama which has hitherto been accepted
as the proper thing."[93] By November it was running illustrated

[90] *World*, October 28, 1883, p. 4. For another criticism of the architecture,
see November 10, 1883, p. 4.

[91] A typical review praising the Academy's offerings appeared in the paper
following the premier presentation of the 1884 season. See the *World*, November 11, 1884, p. 5. Such articles carried a built-in hint that they were written
primarily for women: approximately half of the lineage was devoted to a list
of the dowagers present at the opera house, and what they wore.

[92] *World*, August 16, 1884, p. 4.

[93] *World*, September 21, 1884, p. 4. See October 5, 1884, p. 4, for another
optimistic statement. Dr. Damrosch's death early the next year merited a long
and respectful obituary on the front page. See February 16, 1885, p. 1.

articles on THE IMPRESARIO AND HIS TROUPE OF SONG BIRDS,[94] and reporting effusively on the "triumph" of German opera.[95]

The *World*'s news content for women reflected the further assumption (still prevalent today) that aside from "culture" the feminine mind centers on questions of marriage and morals. In October 1883, for example, an American actress beloved for her portrayal of goodness and chastity in light drama created an international incident by allegedly snubbing the Prince of Wales when he requested an introduction. It seemed that the Prince's widely publicized affairs with various disreputable women offended Mary Anderson's sense of decency. The *World* reported her reluctance to meet the philanderer as a lead story on page one, under the headline MARY ANDERSON'S TRIUMPH. "A great deal of comment has been passed in high quarters," it declared, "and society circles profess themselves to be profoundly astonished at the lack of spirit shown by the Princess of Wales in honoring Miss Anderson with her presence at one of her representations."[96] An earlier editorial on the same subject suggested that while her countrymen might be proud of Miss Anderson's spirit, her rudeness was probably unnecessary.

> To the sensitive feminine mind the questions are propounded: Why should virtue have anything to fear from the courtesies due to men in exalted positions; or why should an actress imagine that an introduction to a Prince could sully her reputation independent of her own conduct? Do not some of the best and purest women in England notice His Royal Highness occasionally without fear of moral ruin?[97]

Similarly, the newspaper used its contacts in Democratic circles to answer a question in women's minds since Grover Cleveland entered the White House. It took occasion in the year preceding his marriage to lay to rest rumors that the President would soon

[94] *World*, November 9, 1884, p. 12.
[95] *World*, November 19, 1884, p. 5.
[96] *World*, October 28, 1883, p. 1.
[97] *World*, September 15, 1883, p. 4. The *World* cynically suggested in the same editorial that inasmuch as Miss Anderson's press agent had supplied the Prince of Wales with photographs of the star without his request, the episode had many of the overtones of a carefully managed publicity stunt.

give up his bachelorhood. "Considerable amusement has been created at the White House, and especially among the ladies of the President's family, by the persistency with which it is declared that the President is about to be married shortly. . . . To put a stop to all such stories the *World* correspondent is permitted to state, upon the best authority, that matrimony is not included among the President's intentions. He finds other business more pressing and is still fond of his bachelorhood."[98] The news of a social revolution in Chicago, which saw the sexes swimming together in the same pool, also merited attention. Headlined INAUGURATION OF MIXED NATATORIAL GYRATIONS, the report recognized the enormity of the experiment while commending the discretion of those who took part.

> Some of the young ladies were at first a little shy of entering the water before strangers and in the company of male companions, and upon leaving their dressing-rooms looked dubiously at their rather scanty attire. When once in, however, this feeling wore away, and those who were the most timid in the start became the boldest before the clanging of the big bell announced the close of the lesson. . . . The girl with a poor form had no business there, for once wet the thin bathing suit clung to the person as closely as a glove on the hand. The ladies' suits consisted of a short tunic and tight-fitting breeches of a length consistent with the modesty and beauty of the limb of the wearer. Some of the more audacious young ladies would lounge carelessly about the steps when exhausted with swimming. . . .
> Everything was conducted in a proper manner and there was nothing that could be called in the least improper or immodest.[99]

Nor was the *World* ever "improper or immodest" in its general approach. Whether addressing immigrants and depressed natives in the tenements of lower Manhattan, or slightly more prosperous families settled in brownstone flats uptown, it correctly judged them to be conservative on such social questions as

[98] *World*, March 20, 1885, p. 5.
[99] *World*, September 16, 1883, p. 12.

— 164 —

female emancipation.[100] Whatever their politics otherwise, they believed in the verities about man being head of the household, and woman his loyal helpmate and mother of his children. They were not the group to take the lead in supporting the plea of feminists for the vote or the right to practice a profession. God had prepared women to bear children, which meant that He had endowed them with natures more gentle than man's, but also less fit to understand and succeed in the world of affairs. The evidence of magazines like the *Ladies' Home Journal* and *Ladies' Home Companion* suggests that wives as well as husbands shared those prejudices. "From my earliest years I have ever believed in woman," Edward Bok announced in a full page editorial in the *Ladies' Home Journal*. "That belief was instilled into me by my mother." But he added that "women of good judgment and refined feelings" did not want the responsibility of voting, since they reigned by their own "birthright—womanly, gentle, loving and true."[101] The circulation of the magazine continued to prosper.[102]

[100] Although the American Federation of Labor supported women's suffrage from the beginning, its motivations were unique, and not really representative of working class sentiment. The Federation hoped that since women were active in a variety of reform movements, their presence at the polls would make it easier to enact pro-labor legislation.

[101] Edward W. Bok, "At Home With the Editor," *Ladies' Home Journal*, IX (August 1892), 12.

[102] Most people—men and women—shared Bok's point of view. Francis Parkman took leave from Montcalm and Wolfe in 1879, for instance, to pen a scathing denunciation of the suffragettes in the *North American Review*, pointing out that it would be "madness," particularly in the large cities, to make bad government worse by allowing women to interfere in politics. Francis Parkman, "The Woman Question," *North American Review*, CXXIX (October 1879), 303-21. The political placards in New York State compressed the sentiment into a nice slogan: STAND BY THE WOMEN. WOMAN'S RIGHT IS THE RIGHT OF FREEDOM FROM POLITICAL DUTIES. At least two explanations can be cited why even women who were active in community affairs looked down on the suffragettes. The movement hurt its own cause by making the battle for the ballot part of a larger battle between the sexes. A probably apocryphal remark by Mrs. Oliver Hazard Perry Belmont symbolized the attitude. "Brace up, my dear," she told a sobbing suffragette, facing a jail sentence for vandalism, "Just pray to God. She will help you." Quoted in Clifton Fadiman, ed., *The American Treasury, 1455-1955* (New York, 1955), p. 124. In her mannish tweeds, with severe hat and still more severe expression, the unsexed suffragette asked of women more than they were willing to give. Furthermore, the demand for political rights represented a break with previous tradition, while agitation against drink and other varieties of sin had been a feminine pastime since

— 165 —

The *World*, careful always to reflect the bias of the people who patronized it, used the many features and editorials prepared for women not only to entertain them, but to draw an image of ideal femininity not unlike that which father and grandfather before had cherished. Incidents and figures prominent in the news became the dramatis personae of a contemporary morality play which depicted the "good" woman in a way that must have pleased the majority of the paper's readers.

She was first of all uncomplaining. An editorial on the passing of Mrs. Anna Ottendorfer, owner of the *New York Staats–Zeitung*, pointed out that the deceased had never participated in "any of the clamorous movements of the more restless of her sex," because society willingly granted to her all the privileges she desired without agitation. "She was never heard demanding her rights and complaining of the wrongs inflicted by men. For men and society appear to have accorded to her all the rights that her stanch [sic] industry and her brave spirit wanted."[103] Charles Stewart Parnell's mother, on tour in the United States to raise funds for Irish independence, exemplified the nobility of women who dedicated themselves to the cause of their men. "The mother of Mr. Charles Stewart Parnell is a model woman. Quiet and unpretending, she is yet enthusiastic in the cause so dear to her son. . . . It would be a good thing if our American women were equally patriotic and unselfish. They might accomplish some good for their country if they would abandon the agitation of [sic] woman's rights and urge the people to rescue the Government from the hands of a dishonored and dishonest party."[104] The young lady who drove a student at Bellevue Medical College to suicide because he could not satisfy her appetite for finery demonstrated how wrong it was for the sex to be demanding of material things. "If the fiancee of the young student had remembered that to a good wife whose husband's means are limited the wearing of homespun is 'prouder than rustling

---

early colonial times. The one type of reform instinct was much more radical than the other.

[103] *World*, April 9, 1884, p. 4. The news story reporting her death appeared on p. 2.

[104] *World*, August 15, 1884, p. 4.

in unpaid for silk,' she would not have been so anxious that he should 'hurry up and get rich,' and the letter found in the dead man's pocket would never have been written."[105] Above all, it was woman's highest mission to remain chaste in body and thought, however great the temptations set before her. The *World* rejected the plea of a New York cleric that the double standard be abandoned, and that women no longer be punished alone for the sins they shared with men. "Monsignor Capel, we think, takes a superficial view of the matter. It is not the thing we vaguely call society that propounds these laws, but the conservative instincts of mankind which look to its own preservation and are not always the dictates of morality. Infidelity in a woman, judged entirely by this standard, is more injurious both to the individual and to the race than infidelity in a man, and it is that fact and that alone that has caused it to be visited by a heavier penalty."[106]

The newspaper urged women to turn their minds from frivolous things and devote themselves to the great calling of marriage and motherhood. "The futile attempts to open new professions, new branches of unwomanly slavery, will not improve matters," it declared at the end of an article listing the new positions they filled. "The women's rights movement seems to be on the wrong track. It is home woman wants."[107] A young health cultist who undertook to lecture her sex on beauty techniques received similar advice from the *World*. "Miss Thomas among other rash things set herself up as a model of physical beauty in some respects, and called attention to her waist, which she proudly said was twenty-seven inches in circumference. She also announced that a child to be healthy must be free from nicotine and alcohol. There is but one remark to make to Miss Thomas, and it is that a woman with a waist twenty-seven inches round ought to be producing healthy children and not going round the country talking about them."[108] The newspaper could not understand the "extraordinary spasm of morality" in Paris which forbade a baby-show, since the point of such an exhibition

[105] *World*, September 23, 1883, p. 4.
[106] *World*, November 19, 1883, p. 4.
[107] *World*, August 31, 1884, p. 11.
[108] *World*, December 1, 1884, p. 4.

was to show women fulfilling their natural function. "Why should not maternity be publicly praised and its fruits admired? . . . What is there immoral in the exhibition of that which is the evidence of a noble duty rightfully performed?"[109]

If the womanly virtues were loyalty, patience, good humor, and chastity, and the womanly responsibilities marriage and motherhood, the day's news also demonstrated what common failings the sex shared. The *World* did not catalogue those failings because it wished to reform women; it would hardly have risked antagonizing the very readership it was trying to attract, and the way the comments were tempered with humor suggests that it considered the failings part of their charm. The list is interesting, rather, because it reveals to what extent the newspaper hung onto the stereotyped conception of women as lovable but scatterbrained, prey to a host of specifically feminine weaknesses. Thus, they were presumed to be the talkative sex, unable to keep silent even when it meant betraying a confidence. The *World* did nothing to dispel the image in editorials praising the integrity of Miss Rebecca Jones, a housemaid who went to prison for contempt of court rather than testify in a will suit against her former employer. "The mere fact," it declared, "that there is one woman in the United States and the world who can keep a secret is of inestimable value at this time, when mankind has ceased to believe in the existence of such a person."[110] They were also hopelessly emotional and sentimental creatures. The outpouring of fruit and flowers and proposals of marriage which descended upon a condemned killer named Rugg as he awaited execution for his crimes suggested to the newspaper that strange verdicts would result if females were allowed to serve on juries. "One thing is very certain: this abnormal exhibition does not speak encouragingly for the administration of absolute justice when women shall have an equal voice in dispensing it."[111] It was a truism that the sex had no sense of practicalities. A house-

[109] *World*, October 13, 1884, p. 4.

[110] *World*, May 21, 1884, p. 4. Miss Jones' reticence fascinated the *World*. For another statement on her good conduct, see February 19, 1885, p. 4. She was released from prison on March 27, 1885, after spending almost a year behind bars.

[111] *World*, April 27, 1884, p. 4.

holder in Brooklyn, who refused to obey a court order granting the right of eminent domain to an elevated railway company, and who had to be carried bodily from her home, demonstrated what most people already knew.

> It is doubtful if a woman ever understands how to fight the inevitable. She always expects a grand-trunk railroad to change its time-table so that she can fix her hair, and she always tells her husband, who has the affairs of the universe on his shoulders, that if he does not lay them aside and come to the matinee with her he does not love her. As a rule, men very low down in the scale bow to the authority of an officer; but who ever heard of a woman in the same scale who did not fight a whole platoon of policemen and compel them to tie her, hand and foot, and put her in an express wagon? The picture of Mrs. Elsinger, of Brooklyn, standing on her flagstone and defying the Elevated Railway Company is in evidence.[112]

Most important, they could not be expected to think logically, or to make significant contributions to the fund of human learning.[113] The *World* took notice of a critical biography of Thomas Carlyle written by Gail Hamilton, in which she not only spoke disparagingly of the historian's personal life and habits, but suggested that his monumental work on the French Revolution was overrated. It seemed evident to the newspaper that the personal criticisms must have influenced the intellectual ones, and that only a feminine mind could be responsible for such a perversion of logic. "She measures him with a pudding-stick, which is the handiest thing she had; she cannot forget that he got up cross one morning and bellowed at Mrs. Carlyle. For this reason the 'French Revolution' is necessarily weak and untrue. We have to thank the Female Critic for this new system of adjustment. It could never have been conceived by a man."[114] An incident at the

[112] *World*, April 18, 1884, p. 4.
[113] The brightest of women were apt to concede their inferiority to men. Even Beatrice Webb, who lived to regret her foolishness, signed a manifesto in 1889 against the enfranchisement of her sex, and blurted out at a luncheon that "I have never met a man, however inferior, who I do not consider to be my superior." Beatrice (Potter) Webb, *My Apprenticeship* (London, 1926), p. 355.
[114] *World*, December 30, 1883, p. 4.

height of the 1884 Presidential campaign found the *World* no more sanguine about the sex's thought processes. "Elizabeth Cady Stanton and Susan B. Anthony combined," it declared, "ought to be able to prove, in spite of the popular notion, that women can at times be logical. But their proclamation to the members of the National Woman Suffrage Association in favor of Mr. Blaine rather strengthens the popular notion."[115]

None of these weaknesses were cause for alarm so long as the sex confined itself to womanly pursuits and looked to man for advice and protection. The *World* even regarded good-humoredly the spectacle of young ladies attending college, or their mothers engaged in local reform movements, if they did not thereby presume to usurp man's traditional role of leadership. A *World* reporter who attended the Vassar commencement ceremonies in 1883 found "to his great astonishment and intense satisfaction . . . that the young ladies, far from being made aggressively smart or in any manner less fascinating by their arduous course of studies, were preserved in all the bloom and attractiveness of bouncing, piquant girlhood.

> Not one of them, so far as he discovered by personal inquiry, had a mission or desired to have one. Most of them, when asked what they intended to do with all their learning, tossed their heads and replied that they intended to get married with it. An answer which, the *World* representative thought, embodied in a terse and lucid phrase all the wisdom and philosophy of a girl's lifetime. The report . . . helps to establish the fact that Vassar is not flooding the country with professional women whose acquirements are too varied and whose independence is too great to permit them to undertake one of the chief and noblest duties and responsibilities of life.[116]

The same logic enabled the newspaper to view with equanimity Oxford's decision in 1884 to permit women to take Honors examinations.[117] It pointed out that Cambridge already had 150 in residence, and that "they have proved themselves to be none

[115] *World*, August 2, 1884, p. 4.
[116] *World*, June 17, 1883, p. 4.
[117] It would be several more years before Oxford awarded degrees to women.

the less womanly for being the more learned. They are still what true women always will be, 'modest, gentle, unassuming'—far more so, indeed, than many of our pushing, ostentatious society women."[118]

The married matrons who busied themselves with a variety of causes to fill their idle hours exposed the contradictory strain in the newspaper between political liberalism and social conservatism. It considered such women to be somewhat comic, and did not attempt to conceal its amusement. But as a journal dedicated to its own crusades it could hardly refrain from endorsing the crusades of others. The result was reports which managed to be at once respectful and patronizing. The *World* praised an organization engaged in sending missionaries to France, but under the headline: TO SAVE HEATHEN FRANCE. THE PORTENTOUS WORK IN WHICH CERTAIN LADIES ARE ENGAGED.[119] A much more significant group, which had played a major role in policing stockyard violations on the East Side of Manhattan, was identified as the BEEKMAN STREET VIGILANTES.[120] The paper understood and appreciated their work in eliminating unsanitary and cruel practices, but the lead paragraph of its story describing a tour of inspection conveyed the impression of five fussy females out for a stroll:

> Five fashionably dressed ladies of middle age and an equal number of young men issued from a brownstone residence on Beekman Hill in East Fifty-first Street yesterday forenoon, promptly at 10 o'clock. They lingered for a few minutes on the sidewalk. The ladies busied themselves by adjusting their new spring wraps and in giving their Easter bonnets the proper poise. . . . Before the little procession reached Forty-eighth Street their coming was heralded by a small boy with powerful lungs, who proclaimed, "There comes the Smelling Committee!"[121]

[118] *World*, May 11, 1884, p. 12.   [119] *World*, April 24, 1885, p. 5.

[120] An authority on the development of sanitary regulation in New York City gives primary credit to those women, organized as the Ladies' Health Protective Association, for eliminating the vile stockyard practices that had demoralized the section of Manhattan on the East Side between 41st and 47th Streets. See Gordon Atkins, *Health, Housing, and Poverty in New York City 1865-1898* (Ann Arbor, 1947), pp. 201-202.

[121] *World*, April 25, 1885, p. 1.

If the *World*'s attitude toward coeds was permissive, and toward reform-minded matrons of the middle class at least tolerant, it had nothing but contempt for the aggressive, benighted females who persisted in agitating for the vote. The great objection to them, of course, was that by demanding a voice in the conduct of public business they belittled the noble mission of staying at home and rearing children. A frivolous editorial in November 1883, commenting on a change-of-sex case in Wisconsin, made not too veiled allusion to all the women who defied their own nature and tried to emulate men. "Miss Frank Dubois, . . ." it declared, "by marrying Gertrude Fuller has demonstrated that the female body, no less than the female mind, when aroused to a full sense of its rights, can defy the puerile restrictions of nature very much as it defies the obsolete laws of reason. . . . The only working hypothesis is that the advanced female intellect is able to assume all the signs and all the functions of men."[122] The *World* rejoiced at rebukes to the suffragette movement delivered in Connecticut[123] and New Jersey,[124] but its harshest words, and lengthiest pronouncements, waited until the spring of 1885, when the issue came to a vote before the New York state legislature. It urged all the traditional arguments against admitting women into the polling places. The law, as proposed, violated New York's constitution. It "may save the strong-minded females who want ballots because they have no babies a great deal of fruitless trouble, to remember that the Constitution of the State confines the elective franchise to 'male citizens of the age of twenty-one years.' A law giving females the right to vote without an amendment of the Constitution would be so much waste paper, and it is not probable that a proposition to make such a change in the fundamental law would prevail."[125] Normal women had no interest in politics, and the practical consequence of the reform would simply be to double the number of Democratic and Republican voters. The *World* cited in evidence a letter from Mrs. W. M. Coggswell on the experience of Wyoming. "Not two women in the Territory would vote for a Republican if her hus-

[122] *World*, November 3, 1883, p. 4.
[123] *World*, March 28, 1884, p. 4.
[124] *World*, April 2, 1884, p. 4.   [125] *World*, March 30, 1885, p. 4.

band were a Democrat, or vice versa, and indeed most women take their tickets from their husbands and never look at them at all but cast them in."[126] Most important, the men of New York owed it to their wives and sweethearts to protect them from the sullying influence of politics. "The male citizens of the Empire State yield to none in their gallantry and in their respect and affection for the opposite sex. But they prize the ladies too highly as domestic treasures to be willing to convert them into brawling politicians." That women themselves appreciated such protection was evidenced by the delegation which waited on the legislators with banners inscribed BABIES, NOT BALLOTS. "These ladies assure our learned legislators that they would rather rock cradles than run conventions, and that the fire-side is more precious to them than the franchise."[127]

The vote which narrowly defeated the measure brought a cry of triumph from the *World*. "It is evident," the newspaper exulted, "that our legislators, a very large majority of whom are married men, would rather see women rocking the cradle than running the caucus." Reason and tradition had prevailed, and it was only proper that the sensible females who contributed to the victory be rewarded in the traditional way. "We congratulate the interesting ladies who reject both pantaloons and politics on the effect of their protest against the Suffrage bill. As a recognition of their good sense, their husbands, fathers or brothers, as the case may be, ought to present each and every one of them with a love of a spring bonnet."[128] Dozens of editorials were subsumed in that single, patronizing sentence.

The *World* had scored a very considerable achievement in its policy toward women. Social and commercial developments in the 1880s dictated that a mass circulation daily take cognizance of change as it occurred by addressing itself equally to both sexes. At the same time, the masses of men, and probably the masses of women, strongly distrusted movements likely to upset

126 *World*, April 10, 1884, p. 4.
127 *World*, March 30, 1885, p. 4.
128 *World*, April 9, 1885, p. 4.

CHAPTER SIX

A GOSPEL OF WEALTH

A popular newspaper cannot succeed unless it shares in large measure the attitudes of the people it addresses. If it aspires to circulate in the hundreds of thousands it must be like a mirror, reflecting back to the public the inarticulate public philosophy.

Such a newspaper can, on occasion, hold out against the popular will and provide leadership in a direction it thinks is wiser. Pulitzer did so in 1895 when he helped to avert a pointless war with Great Britain over the boundary between Venezuela and British Guiana. His action required considerable courage, since the clamor for war on both sides of the Atlantic was intense, and self-seeking politicians were offering themselves as messiahs who would lead their nations to victory. It is true also that popular journals engage in a certain amount of pandering when they print what they know the public wants to read about, rather than what they think is important. Pulitzer's justification for the *World*'s sensationalism as necessary if he was to "talk to a nation, not to a select committee," is a case in point.

The argument nevertheless holds that a newspaper addressed to the John Does of a society must share many of their attitudes and assumptions. A basic agreement on fundamentals cannot be faked for long, nor can a mass circulation daily expect to find a following among people who do not share its convictions. When asked the secret of his success as a syndicator of feature material, S. S. McClure explained that the articles which appealed to him seemed to appeal to most people. This is the genius of popular journalism: to combine a point of view that is common with an altogether uncommon ability to project that point of view.

As much as any other newspaper in America, the *World* had this facility for being uncommonly common. Its rapport with the masses of men is illustrated in many ways, but none better than in its tortured love/hate attitude toward the captains of industry in American life. The newspaper, like the people who read it, did not know whether to admire those newly emerged eminences or to oppose and condemn them.

The confusion is explained by the contradictory pressures operating on the society in the 1880s. On the one hand, it was a time of social ferment, when class lines were starting to harden, and when reformers who wished to mitigate the worst inequities of industrial capitalism looked to Rockefeller and Vanderbilt and the rest as the enemy. Henry George would come within a hair of being elected Mayor of New York City in 1886, and the same year a riot in Haymarket Square in Chicago would herald the nationwide scope of discontent. The story of those events, and of tenements, sweatshops, strikes, privation, is the story of enmity between rich and poor.

At the same time, in the buoyant atmosphere of the nine-teenth century, when the job of building a nation had not yet been completed, and when nothing seemed beyond human aspiration, the men who had parlayed daring and vision and enterprise into princely fortunes stood out as heroes for others to emulate. They were the latest exemplars of a success cult in America which had a lineage back to *Poor Richard's Almanac* and Emerson's invitation to "Hitch your wagon to a star." The admonition to succeed was repeated in the *McGuffey Readers*, in the popular prose of magazines, in the warmed over rhetoric of June commencements. Proverbs glorified it ("You can't keep a good man down," "There's always room at the top"), and writers developed it into a minor industry. Horatio Alger wrote the same novel 135 times and never lost his audience. William Makepeace Thayer churned out reams of nonfictional material, from a biography of Lincoln (*The Pioneer Boy and How He Be-came President*) to assorted manuals of self-help (*Turning Points in Successful Careers*; *Aim High: Hints and Helps for Young Men*; *Men Who Win*).[1] Orison Swett Marden came forth

[1] Thayer's titles are strikingly similar to Norman Vincent Peale's. Instead of *Aim High: Hints and Helps for Young Men*, we get *A Guide to Confident Living*; instead of *Men Who Win* we get *You Can Win*. The cult is evidently still in full flower. It probably explains why Hemingway's *The Old Man and the Sea* so perplexed George Humphrey. "Why would anybody be interested

with inspirational volumes of his own, as well as a monthly periodical entitled simply: *Success*. By the turn of the century, *Successful American* had appeared in New York, *Success: An Illustrated Magazine for the People* in Baltimore, *Eternal Progress* in Cincinnati and Chicago. "We live in a country," Edward Bok rejoiced, "where every success is possible, where a man can make of himself just what he may choose."[2] More than being unnecessary, even shameful, failure was almost un-American. "I say, get rich, get rich!" Russell Conwell pleaded in *Acres of Diamonds,* and true to his sermon, he earned an estimated $8,000,000 by repeating the exhortation six thousand times.[3]

Most Americans joined those evangelists in worshiping at the

---

in some old man who was a failure and never amounted to anything anyway?" Eisenhower's Secretary of the Treasury is reported to have asked. Quoted in Eric Goldman, *The Crucial Decade: America, 1945-1955* (New York, 1956), p. 239.

[2] Edward Bok, "The Young Man in Business," *Cosmopolitan*, XVI (January 1894), 338.

[3] I have relied heavily in this paragraph on Merle Curti, *The Growth of American Thought* (New York, 1943), pp. 644-50. The urgency of success helps to explain why hard work has been an American fetish since early colonial times, when Massachusetts and Virginia enacted laws to contain the innocent pleasures of berry pickers and poetizers. *McGuffey's Eclectic Readers* handed down the commandment to generations of school children. The tale of "The Idle Boy Reformed," for instance, told of a youngster who disliked work, and asked his animal friends to play with him. "No, I must not be idle," they each replied. "What, is nobody idle?" the story concluded. "Then little boys must not be idle. So he made haste and went to school and learned his lessons very well, and the master said he was a good boy." (Quoted in Foster Rhea Dulles, *America Learns to Play: A History of Popular Recreation, 1607-1940,* [Gloucester, Massachusetts, 1959], pp. 203-204.)

The ethic was reflected in New York City's bustle during the 1880s and 1890s. More than earning a living, or exorcising the demon sloth which preyed within their Protestant souls, the middle classes strained to prove that they were up-standing, go-getting, on-the-toes competitors in a game which had no place for laggards. The terrible urgency to succeed, to be getting some place, to be "not just liked, but well-liked," made daily labor an ordeal. And once aboard the merry-go-round, desperately clutching for the brass ring, they could not get off. Work became the stuff of which neuroses are made, no longer a pleasure or necessary part of life.

All sorts of signs pointed to the no-nonsense motivation of life in American cities. Arthur Schlesinger notes that the American *Who's Who*, unlike the British, does not include the recreations or hobbies of the notables listed there. Americans invented the rocking chair (to be on the move while sitting still); their candidates "ran" rather than "stood" for office; they played games with a "grim determination" to have fun. See Arthur Schlesinger, *Paths to the Present* (New York, 1949), p. 9.

shrine of what William James called the bitch-goddess success.[4] The immigrant dreamed of leaving the slums, the poor news-boy of returning a millionaire's wallet and being rewarded for his honesty with a vice presidency in the firm, the timid clerk of persevering and advancing and one day addressing his boss by first name. They could all look up to the nabob as one who had achieved their dreams.

As a spokesman for its time, the *World* was buffeted by these conflicting pressures. Its political liberalism and crusading zeal alienated it from the robber barons who had achieved great wealth by exploiting those weaker than themselves. Its materi-alism, and faith in success, and conviction that success was spelled with a dollar sign, lured it back to them. The two atti-tudes found simultaneous expression in a newspaper uncertain of what it felt, knowing only that the rich could not be ignored.

Contempt for the money men was expressed in a variety of ways. The *World* likened them to royal monarchs, and feared what they would do when ultimate power resided in their hands. "Like kings, they derive their revenues from taxes on the people. Like kings, they control legislation. Like kings, they are masters of the will and of the work of tens of thousands of their fellow-men. The chief distinction is that our kings are much richer and more powerful than some of the kings they have over in Europe. . . . It is alarming to think what the result will be if they gain as much in the next twenty years as they have done in the last twenty."[5] The glitter of monarchy tarnished, and gold turned to brass, when the majesty of the individual kings was objectively evaluated. Gould accumulated his great fortune, for instance, not as a reward for daring and enterprise, but because he thought nothing of prostituting the laws of the land for his personal enrich-ment. "It does not require any extraordinary amount of courage

---

[4] James objected as much to the meaning of success in America as to its importance. "The moral flabbiness born of the exclusive worship of the bitch-goddess SUCCESS. That—with the squalid cash interpretation put on the word success—is our national disease." William James, Letter to H. G. Wells (1906). Quoted in Clifton Fadiman, ed., *The American Treasury* (New York, 1955), p. 26.

[5] *New York World*, August 22, 1883, p. 4.

and brains when in control of a corporation to double or quadruple its stock and to divide up the plunder when the laws, secured for the purpose, authorize the operation. It does not even demand much boldness to purchase Congresses and Legislatures, for our Government is a Government of lawyers and our peculiar system winks at the acceptance of large fees from corporations by the lawyer who happens to be at the same time a Senator, a Congressman or an Attorney-General."[6] Extreme wealth did not make them benevolent monarchs. "It was about time for Rockefeller to do something religious," the *World* sneered on hearing that John D. Rockefeller had donated $40,000 to the Chicago Baptist Theological Seminary.[7] Nor did wealth endow its possessors with more grace than they had before. An editorial entitled "Wealth and Vulgarity" considered how the millions of dollars squeezed from passengers on the New York Central Railroad had simply confirmed William Henry Vanderbilt in his boorishness. "What respect is due to a man who counts his wealth by the hundred million and spends it wholly for the gratification of his own whims and pleasures? . . . Who in the coarse and vulgar language of a horse jockey extols his son, not for his culture, not for his virtues, not for his industry, not for his patriotism or public spirit, but for his sharpness in Wall Street gambling and because 'he never squeals.' "[8] The Commodore's son convicted himself when he blurted out, "The public be damned!" in reply to a question on railroad policies put to him by reporters in Michigan City on October 8th, 1882.[9] The words, Pulitzer's editorial declared, "are as appropriate to him as bristles to a hog. All the dollars in the world cannot remove innate vulgarity. They can only make it more offensive by coating it over with insolence and swagger."[10]

[6] *World*, October 21, 1883, p. 4.

[7] *World*, June 2, 1883, p. 4.

[8] *World*, October 14, 1883, p. 4. The expression "squeal" refers not to informing, but to a way of testing the quality of a hunting dog. "A stableboy seizes the dog's tail or ear between his teeth, and holds the animal suspended thereby. If he 'squeals' he is a mongrel. If he bears the punishment without squealing he passes muster."

[9] Extensive extracts from the interview are quoted in Wayne Andrews, *The Vanderbilt Legend.* (New York, 1941), pp. 190-94.

[10] *World*, January 31, 1884, p. 4.

Vanderbilt and his railroad became the special targets of a *World* crusade which lasted for almost a year. Headlines like THE VANDERBILT FRAUD,[11] HOW THE NEW YORK CENTRAL PLUNDERS THE PEOPLE,[12] OUR RAILROAD CANCER,[13] EXPOSING THE FREIGHT DISCREPANCIES OF THE CENTRAL ROAD,[14] A MALIGN RAILROAD,[15] THE SCURVEY RAILROAD,[16] MONUMENTAL MISMANAGEMENT,[17] THE RAILROAD BLACKMAILER,[18] and so on, heralded the newspaper's relentless pursuit of its quarry. The New York Central was indicted for ignoring the comfort and safety of its passengers, for exploiting its workers, for charging exorbitant rates, for corrupting legislatures, for all the sins a nineteenth century railroad could be guilty of.[19] It did those things for the sake of profit, in order that a steady 8% dividend could be paid on $90,000,000 worth of stock, at least $50,000,000 of which represented water, "based on nothing but the stroke of a pen in the hands of the Vanderbilt dynasty."[20]

So violent was the assault that Pulitzer's enemies wondered what motivated the publisher. *The Journalist* saw a possible explanation in two unrelated, but well established facts. Jay Gould and William Vanderbilt were business rivals; Pulitzer had purchased the *World* from Gould. Was it possible, Leander Richardson wondered, that Gould had not surrendered his entire interest in the newspaper, that he still influenced its editorial policies?[21] The truth, of course, was more simple. In his liberal phase Joseph Pulitzer distrusted great fortunes in private hands, just as his business sense forced him to envy and admire the entrepreneurs who had amassed such fortunes. The *World* reprinted in November 1883, a series of statistical observations by John Swinton as to what William H. Vanderbilt's $200,000,000 for-

---

[11] *World*, June 1, 1883, p. 4.   [12] *World*, June 12, 1883, p. 1.
[13] *World*, June 9, 1883, p. 6.   [14] *World*, June 13, 1883, p. 6.
[15] *World*, June 14, 1883, p. 4.   [16] *World*, June 16, 1883, p. 1.
[17] *World*, June 11, 1883, p. 4.   [18] *World*, January 20, 1884, p. 4.

[19] For still more articles and statements condemning the New York Central, see the *World*, June 6, 1883, p. 5; September 14, 1883, p. 1; February 10, 1884, p. 4; February 15, 1884, p. 4; February 16, 1884, p. 4; February 17, 1884, p. 4; March 26, 1884, p. 4; and March 28, 1884, p. 4.

[20] *World*, January 20, 1884, p. 4.

[21] *The Journalist*, April 7, 1884, p. 7. See pp. 12-13 for a prior discussion of Richardson's suspicions.

tune entailed. Converted into gold, the wealth would become an ingot weighing 350 tons. It would require 7,000 strong men to lift that amount, 25 freight cars to haul it, 1,400 horses to pull it, 70 elephants to carry it. "We were long ago convinced," the newspaper concluded, "that Mr. Vanderbilt had more money than one man could safely enjoy, but we never had the fact brought home to us with Cyclopian blows until Brother Swinton and his able artist took hold of it."[22]

Nor was it only Vanderbilt who offended the newspaper's liberal spirit. The entire system by which great fortunes were accumulated—stock manipulation, secret deals, cornering the market—smacked of fraud and piracy. "This is the most pernicious kind of gambling. It is a game played by combined capital against consumers and small dealers, in which the stakes are the daily necessaries of life. The profits of the gamblers are taken directly out of the pockets of the masses of the people. It is the power of combined wealth creating a monopoly of articles which every citizen is compelled to purchase, and the price of which is raised above the legitimate standard fixed by supply and demand in order to enrich the gambling monopolists."[23] Indeed, the game was worse than gambling, for the reckless men who played it created millions in fictitious values upon which they then declared dividends for themselves. Early in 1885 the newspaper quoted *Poor's Manual* to the effect that the railroad capital of the United States included some $4 billion of watered, or worthless, stock. "Is it not time," the *World* asked, "that these railroad corporations should be taught by restrictive laws that they no longer hold the executive, judicial and legislative branches of the Government in their control?"[24]

The question was given added point by the great Wall Street panic of May 1884, which grew out of the collapse of the investment house of Grant & Ward. Ferdinand Ward, a Wall Street shark, had persuaded former President Grant to invest most of his fortune, and Ulysses Grant, Jr., his name, to a partnership in which each would wax wealthy through speculation

[22] *World*, November 12, 1883, p. 4.
[23] *World*, October 3, 1883, p. 4.
[24] *World*, January 18, 1885, p. 4.

in the stock market. Ward proceeded to weave a complicated financial web, running up debts of $14,000,000 on false or non-existent collateral to keep his creditors at bay while grimly plunging for the speculative killing. His downfall spelled catastrophe for the brokers who had been drawn in and brought panic to the street. James D. Fish, President of the respected Marine Bank, participated in Ward's schemes (he claimed because of Grant's assurances that Ward could be trusted), for almost $1,000,000 of bank capital, none of it secured. When the bubble burst the Marine Bank was forced into receivership. To compound the crisis, John C. Eno, President of the Second National Bank, was responsible for a run on that institution when the news leaked out that he had embezzled $4,000,000 to finance his own speculations. Every bank and brokerage firm in the financial district which had overextended itself, or cut corners, or even placed funds on deposit with those that had, felt the effects of the tremor, and several collapsed.[25]

The accumulating evidence of sordid, amoral practices on Wall Street aroused the *World* to full fury. It printed bitter articles on how the bank failures affected poor people who had trustingly deposited their life savings for others to manipulate. MANY LARDERS EMPTY AND THE WOLF OF HUNGER COMING TO THE DOOR, the headline on one of the articles proclaimed.[26] It reproached all of those involved, even General Grant, now a bankrupt and the object of widespread sympathy. "Grant has always been a money-lover," the newspaper charged, "a man of greed and a man of rather vulgar associations. These facts are against him just now."[27] Or again, "his offense is in his disregard of the high dignity of his position as the first citizen and the first soldier of the Republic. He has degraded his title, and in so doing has degraded the nation. What claim has such a man on

[25] The panic received detailed coverage in the *World*. See May 7, 1884, pp. 1-3; May 8, 1884, pp. 1-2; May 13, 1884, pp. 1-2; May 14, 1884, p. 1; May 15, 1884, pp 1-2; May 16, 1884, pp. 1-2; May 17, 1884, p. 1; May 18, 1884, pp. 1, 9; May 22, 1884, p. 1; May 25, 1884, p. 1; May 26, 1884, p. 1; May 27, 1884, pp. 1-2; May 28, 1884, pp. 1-2; May 29, 1884, p. 1; and May 30, 1884, p. 1.
[26] *World*, May 19, 1884, p. 1. See also June 3, 1884, p. 5.
[27] *World*, May 31, 1884, p. 4.

the sympathy of the people?"[28] Above all, the *World* demanded that justice be meted out to the primary culprits. "The preservation of law and order, the preservation of property and liberty, the safety of the country, demand that these criminals shall go to Sing Sing for as many years as the law allows."[29] A series of editorials warned the District Attorney's office that a double standard of justice just then between rich and poor man would arouse "a sullen spirit of discontent" among the tenement masses.[30] Fish's conviction the following year on twelve counts of embezzlement did much to appease the *World*'s wrath, but it pointed out that justice would still not be served until he received the full sentence allowed by law.[31] "There is no question as to the justice of the verdict. . . . The prisoner deserves, and we believe will receive, the punishment the law imposes. There is hardly a redeeming feature in his crime or in his career."[32]

The newspaper took other occasions that year to express contempt for the mentality and practices of Wall Street. On January 5, 1884, its lead story, which ran over to fill four complete columns on page two, reported Henry Villard's declaration of bankruptcy and resignation as President of the Northern Pacific Railroad. The fallen titan announced that he had signed over title to a still uncompleted mansion on Madison Avenue in order to make good on a debt of several hundred thousand dollars owed to the Oregon Railway and Navigation Company, which he had formerly headed. For one newspaper in New York, the announcement was cause for moralizing rather than sympathy. "The *World* alone," an editorial declared, "of all the journals in the city, has withheld its tribute from the famed railway gambler whose collapse is a great moral lesson—a warning to all men to avoid speculative enterprises. . . ."

> Why this sycophantic adulation of a man who at best was but a mushroom in the muck-heap of speculation? . . . In what way did his fortune, so soon got and

28 *World*, May 18, 1884, p. 4. See also May 29, 1884, p. 4.
29 *World*, May 28, 1884, p. 4.
30 For example, see the *World*, May 23, 1884, p. 4.
31 The report of his conviction appeared on April 12, 1885, p. 1.
32 *World*, April 13, 1885, p. 4.

so soon lost, benefit humanity? . . . His example has been vicious and demoralizing, because it has turned scores of men into the vortex of speculation, to be stranded as he is himself. While the *Herald* extends its sympathies to this fallen chieftain of Mammon, ours go out to the men who have been ruined by his example, to the widows who have been made homeless by him, and to the laborers in the icy Northwest who are toiling for unremunerative wages because of his extravagance.[33]

It called upon men everywhere to heed the lesson of Villard's downfall. "Beware of Wall Street! . . . Shun the temptation of the Wall Street gambling table. . . . Do not dream of becoming a Money King as soon as you secure a gilt gingerbread crown and a brass sceptre. . . . You may not drive golden spikes and build Madison Avenue palaces, but you will not fall suddenly and drag your friends down with you."[34]

The end of the year brought a harsh jibe in cartoon form at all the speculators who had seen fortunes made of paper shrivel away during the 1884 panic. McDougall's drawing took up two-thirds of a page to portray the embarrassment of the money men. Vanderbilt and his associates appeared as rats in a cage (a label put their stock losses at $49,000,000); Gould as a gnome in shrunken clothes watering a wilted, potted plant (his stock losses $41,600,000); Villard as a buzzard perched on the headstone of the Northern Pacific (its losses $15,700,000); Eno and Ward and Fish as birds flying the coop, and so on.[35] It was a

[33] *World*, January 5, 1884, p. 4. See pp. 1-2 for the report of his bankruptcy.
[34] *World*, January 6, 1884, p. 4. Years of so advising his readers came back to plague Pulitzer in 1896. After pressuring the Cleveland administration to replenish the gold reserve by floating a $100,000,000 bond issue directly to the public (the previous year $64,000,000 to purchase bullion had been raised by selling the entire issue to J. P. Morgan and Co. at 104½, who resold it at 120 on the market), Pulitzer instructed his broker to purchase $1,000,000 worth at the going rate. To his chagrin, he realized an immediate profit of $50,000 as the market value rose. Don Seitz describes the sequel. "Mr. Pulitzer was deeply concerned as to how he could rid himself of the unearned increment. A council was called of all the wise heads in the office to advise him. . . . Finally, after two hours of wearisome debate, the business manager remarked, speaking for the first time: 'Why not keep it?' This advice was duly presented to the agitated gentleman at Lakewood—and accepted!" Don Seitz, *Joseph Pulitzer*, p. 209.
[35] *World*, December 21, 1884, p. 17.

declaration by a liberal newspaper against the foremost symbols of nineteenth century finance capitalism.

If the *World* did not admire how those men accumulated their fortunes, it admired still less what they did with them. The moneyed elite embarked on an orgy of display during the 1880s, almost as if a Thorstein Veblen had been anticipated and defied. They found partial outlet for their millions in the construction of ever more grandiose castles on Fifth Avenue, commissioning French chateau to rise side by side with Florentine palazzo in an uneasy truce of style and period. William K. Vanderbilt, for instance, engaged the services of Richard Morris Hunt in 1879 to design a chateau of approximately fifteenth century style on the corner of 52nd Street. The $3,000,000 building, two years in construction, used gray limestone throughout, initiating the movement away from the brownstone facades of lower Fifth Avenue.[36] Its rooms were solemnly given over to antique furniture and tapestries, and suits of armor lent charm to the long hallways.[37] The effect evidently impressed enough people to ease the way for Vanderbilt and his wife Alva to be accepted into Mrs. Astor's inner circle of society. As for Hunt, a society architect first, he had fulfilled his assignment by providing the ostentation

[36] Visitors to New York City often felt let down by the homes below 42nd Street. They were uniformly of brownstone, in the worst of Victorian design, announcing their magnificence with funereal solemnity. The material had been used in earlier decades, because of its cheapness, to surface the rear of buildings, but on the street side it gave the impression of so many monks in somber convention.

[37] Vanderbilt's daughter, Consuelo, recalled the pleasures of growing up in a well-furnished home. "How gay were the gala evenings when the house was ablaze with lights and Willie and I, crouching on hands and knees behind the balustrade of the musicians' gallery, looked on a festive scene below—the long dinner table covered with damask cloth, a gold service and red roses, the lovely crystal and china, the grown-ups in their fine clothes. The dining room was enormous and had at one end twin Renaissance mantel-pieces and on one side a huge stained-glass window, depicting the Field of the Cloth of Gold on which the kings of England and France were surrounded with their knights, all not more magnificently arrayed than the ladies a-glitter with jewels seated in high-backed tapestry chairs behind which stood footmen in knee breeches. Next to this big dining room was a small breakfast room adorned with Flemish tapestries and Rembrandt's portrait of the Turkish Chief. Then came a white drawing room hung with a fine set of Boucher tapestries; here were the beautiful lacquer secretaire and commode, with bronzes chiseled by Gouthiere, made for Marie Antoinette. Next door our living room, a paneled Renaissance salon, looked out on Fifth Avenue." Quoted in Christopher Tunnard and Henry Hope Reed, *American Skyline* (New York, 1953), pp. 180-81.

his client demanded. "The first thing you've got to remember," he advised his son, "is that it's your client's money you're spending. Your business is to get the best results following their wishes. If they want you to build a house upside down standing on its chimney, it's up to you to do it, and still get the best possible results."[38]

George B. Post, one of Hunt's pupils, took his inspiration from Fontainebleau for the Cornelius Vanderbilt residence at 57th Street. It boasted a marble reception hall conspicuously larger than the Supreme Court's, and a still larger ballroom which could be converted into a full size private theatre. Directly opposite it, on the southeast corner, stood the gray-stone palazzo of Collis P. Huntington, noted for its red-brocaded drawing room. J. P. Morgan enlisted the services of Stanford White for the Italian Renaissance design of the Metropolitan Club on 60th Street, a gleaming white, colonnaded structure, with severely classical lines. Immediately adjoining it, Richard Morris Hunt designed a pink, gingerbread ornamented French chateau for Elbridge T. Gerry.

The Pompeian conceit of the wealthy, reflected as much in the pose of lordly superiority they affected as in the uninhabitable buildings they commissioned, aroused the *World* to some of its most bitter editorial philippics. On the first Sunday under Pulitzer's proprietorship, an editorial described the would-be American aristocracy as "a caricature of the original. It has about it the odor of codfish and not of the mustiness of age." The newspaper argued that aristocracy "ought to have no place in the republic—that the word ought to be expunged from an American vocabulary."[39] A man's credentials in the New World depended upon character and talent, not breeding. "It is to such men as Abraham Lincoln, and Jefferson and Jackson and Franklin, all most lowly born, that we owe most of our greatness as a nation. They made themselves new units in the social problem and out of poverty and ignorance carved honor and renown. This is the

---

[38] Quoted in Russell Lynes, *The Tastemakers* (New York, 1954 [Universal Library edition]), p. 131.
[39] *World*, May 13, 1883, p. 4.

— 186 —

proudest fact in our history. We make men, we do not inherit them."[40]

The great objection to the display on Fifth Avenue was that it represented a throwback to what Americans had rejected in Europe. "It is certainly false Americanism to foster class distinctions, to create an aristocracy of wealth and to show a distaste for the customs of a Republic and a passion for the obsolete follies that prevail under a monarchical form of government."[41] The newspaper admitted that under normal circumstances people had a right to make themselves as ridiculous as they pleased, but insisted that some folly demanded rebuke:

> When a set of wealthy noodles set themselves up as an "aristocracy," when they parade self-made coats-of-arms in public after the fashion of European royalists and aristocrats; when they flaunt the follies and vices and airs of a foreign and largely criminal "nobility" in the faces of a republican people, they invite criticism and deserve ridicule.[42]

They became fair game for ridicule partly because in aping the manners and customs of Europe they rejected, at least by implication, the conventions of their own country. To do so was hardly patriotic, and patriotism always weighs heavily with a mass circulation daily. Just as important, the *World* feared that their pretensions might influence the continuing struggle in American history between Federalism and Republicanism:

> This growing luxury and extravagance, this steady departure from Republican simplicity is dangerous. The passion for foreign habits, foreign luxuries, foreign sloth, is hardly compatible with love of liberty and equality. It creates a passion for special privileges and bogus aristocracy which cloaks itself under a pretended desire for a "stronger" centralized government. It is old-fashioned Federalism over again, intensified by modern wealth.[43]

[40] *World*, April 30, 1884, p. 4. For further comments on the affectations of the wealthy, see January 27, 1884, p. 4; and April 23, 1884, p. 4.
[41] *World*, December 16, 1883, p. 4.
[42] *Ibid.*
[43] *World*, June 6, 1883, p. 4.

Although it rebuked Mrs. Astor and her circle for toadying indiscriminately to foreign aristocracy, what galled it most was the worship of things British. New York City society had carried on a love affair with British aristocracy since pre-Revolutionary times. The Prince of Wales' visit in 1860 endures as probably the most exciting single event in the social life of the city, and Jennie Jerome's marriage to Lord Randolph Churchill in 1874 thrilled ambitious mothers for years after with the thought of what might be. Loving the British aristocracy for its style and poise, Fifth Avenue welcomed its representatives and tried as much as possible to be like them. "They have indeed out-heroded Herod," Arthur Montefiore wrote in 1888, "and the mashers and aesthetes who have been almost laughed out of England bloom with exotic luxuriance in New York society. No English covert-coats are shorter, or walking-sticks thicker, or trousers baggier than those which are provided for these dudes by their 'custom tailors.' "[44]

This rampant anglomania seemed symptomatic to the *World* of a general decline in patriotic feeling among the monied elite.

> There is in this country, outside of the immediate confines of Dudedom, a widespread British spirit manifest in the everywhere epidemic Anglomania— a development precisely proportionate to the decline of American patriotism in our low upper classes. It is seen in the far-off aping of an English aristocracy with such outward signs as coats-of-arms for grand-fatherless families, liveried servants, English ways and clothes and the use of the worst Cockney phrases and words.[45]

The newspaper responded predictably when a group of socialites, gathered at Delmonico's to celebrate the 100th Anniversary of British withdrawal from New York City, concluded the festivities with a rendition of "God Save the Queen." "It may have been within the limits of international courtesy to propose the health of Queen Victoria at a celebration of the evacuation of

[44] Arthur Montefiore, "New York and the New Yorkers," *Temple Bar*, LXXXIV (1888), 346; quoted in Bayrd Still, *Mirror for Gotham* (New York, 1956), p. 221.
[45] *World*, April 27, 1885, p. 4.

— 188 —

New York by the British, but to sing—yes, sing in grand American chorus—'God Save the Queen'—was that not a little too much like European royalty worship? . . . What were our prominent Delmonico banqueters celebrating, anyway?"[46] It referred to the incident in the same issue as an example of Fifth Avenue's contempt for the spirit which won the Revolution:

> New York under Cornwallis, Tryon and Clinton was not half as British as it is under the Union Club, the Murray Hill regime and the worship of British lords and the Prince of Wales. There was no Coaching Club here in 1783; no fox-hunting clubs; no Piccadilly paper collars or Prince Albert coats. The natives did not drop their h's and the American ladies did not try to ride to hounds or marry English titles. English ways were unpopular, English poodles were not the fashion, and English actors were scarce.[47]

The snob appeal of British names for hotels and apartment buildings compounded the insult. "We give our hotels such names as the Westminster, Clarendon, Victoria, Buckingham, &c. . . . This in spite of the fact that our fair land abounds in the sweetest and most musical of Indian names. It is a matter of fact that but one flat house in the city has been honored with an Indian name —the new Dakota."[48]

The newspaper blamed English influence for the palaces along Fifth Avenue, which it regarded as pitiful monuments to the folly of men and women who thought that within the marble walls they could become aristocrats.

> We are getting to be a remarkable and, in modern times, unprecedented sort of a Republic. A Republic full of shoddy aristocrats without the titles which make the European aristocracy. . . . A Republic, not aping in monkey clothing alone the fashions of the English exquisites who come to the United States mainly on matrimonial ventures, but imitating Europe intellectually, morally and mentally in its tastes, pursuits, amusements and vices. . . . Our swell houses must be palaces, with foreign decorations, foreign

[46] *World*, November 28, 1883, p. 4.
[47] *World*, November 28, 1883, p. 4.
[48] *World*, April 11, 1884, p. 4.

mantel-pieces, foreign frescoing, foreign pictures and foreign servants and English liveries. Our carriages must bear English crests and coats-of-arms stolen from the English College of Heraldry. . . . Our yachts must be ocean steamers, even if they are only used to carry our wealthy brokers to and from their business. Our paupers of to-day who grow into millionaires to-morrow, either through Wall Street or politics, the Governorship or by some other questionable means, become at once the most rabid victims of the Anglomania disease.[49]

Nor did pretension, and the newspaper's response to it, stop there. High society's infatuation with lineage and heraldry inspired a series of articles that should have made all but the most thick-skinned ashamed to display their crests in public.[50] HOW THE ARMORIAL FOL-DE-ROL OF ARISTOCRATIC ENGLAND IS IMITATED IN DEMOCRATIC AMERICA, one of the headlines proclaimed.[51] Or again, THE FOREIGN FLUMMERY OF CITIZENS OF A REPUBLIC,[52] OUR MUSHROOM NOBILITY,[53] OUR SHODDY NOBLEMEN,[54] CITIZENS OF A REPUBLIC REPUDIATING AMERICAN IDEAS.[55] All of the grievances about pomposity, and lack of patriotism, and rejection of republican values, were symbolized by the fad of wearing a crest to announce one's worth. "It is a false and foolish pride," an editorial remarked, "which prompts our people to

[49] *World*, June 6, 1883, p. 4.

[50] The first families had started to show a marked interest in genealogy, which taught them what they had always suspected but were never sure of, that their roots went back to the British kings. The Reverend Charles Nichols performed his most useful function by chronicling the royal descent of some highly unlikely New Yorkers. "Mr. J. Pierpont Morgan, Mr. E. D. Morgan, and Mrs. Herbert Livingston Satterlee," he wrote, "are the scions of a dynasty of Welsh kings, the founder of which was Gynned Cymric, king of all Wales, 605 A.D. Mr. Morgan can by right use eighteen quarterings on his shield, but by choice shows only twelve. Mrs. John Jacob Astor, one of the most far-descended as well as beautiful leaders of the ultra-smart set in the United States, derives her patrician cast of family type. Ogden Mills, Mrs. Vanderbilt, Mrs. Oscar Livingston, Mrs. James Francis Sullivan of Philadelphia, Mrs. Frank S. Witherbee, Lispenard Stewart, James Laurens Van Alen, Mrs. Royal Phelps Carroll and Mrs. Vanderbilt descend gracefully from kings." Charles Nichols, *The Ultra-Fashionable Peerage of America*, quoted in Dixon Wecter, *The Saga of American Society* (New York, 1937), pp. 394-95. (It was Nichols who descended Mrs. Vanderbilt gracefully from kings twice in the same sentence.)

[51] *World*, December 9, 1883, p. 1.   [52] *World*, December 16, 1883, p. 1.
[53] *World*, January 6, 1884, p. 1.   [54] *World*, January 13, 1884, p. 1.
[55] *World*, December 30, 1883, p. 1.

— 190 —

borrow or invent coats-of-arms and to display them as they are displayed in England as an evidence of blue blood and long descent. There is about it a false pretense as well as an apeing of foreign airs which, while seemingly a mere personal weakness, is in fact an insidious spirit against democratic simplicity and earnestness."[56]

Even more deplorable was the practice of marrying heiresses off to impoverished noblemen, a not inexpensive way of buying into a title. Aside from the obvious democratic objections, and the embarrassing coincidence that those love matches always included a healthy dowry from the bride's parents, certain questions of a more personal nature intruded. "When American parents," the newspaper asked, "ambitious for a title for their children, wed them to the miserable scions of foreign aristocracy, do they ever pause to reflect on the misery of a cold, loveless, monotonous home?"[57] Indeed, did the girls recognize the moral implications of allowing themselves to be sold? "A girl who sells herself or allows herself to be sold for a title without love or affection sacrifices the best attributes of womanhood. What has she a right to expect except a cold, calculating life, full of frivolity or of abuse?"[58] The *World* took some comfort that the public would probably be spared a new round of matchmaking when a delegation of titled Koreans arrived in New York City. "Some of our fair daughters and title-hunting mothers-in-law will perhaps be checked by the nonappearance of a handle to the Korean names, such as Earl, Marquis, Viscount or even 'Sir.' . . . The mothers-in-law would be unable to talk about 'My daughter, the Countess of Ik,' or 'My darling child, the Viscountess Sik.' "[59]

So strongly did the newspaper feel these sentiments that on occasion it found itself in the unique position of praising Astors and Vanderbilts. Caroline Astor's marriage to Orme Wilson in 1884, easily the brightest social event of the season, represented one such occasion. "The true attractiveness of the affair," the

[56] *World*, January 6, 1884, p. 4.
[57] *World*, May 11, 1884, p. 4; see also August 14, 1883, p. 4.
[58] *World*, November 21, 1883, p. 4.
[59] *World*, September 19, 1883, p. 4.

World decided, "was the fact that the daughter of one of our wealthiest, most prominent and oldest citizens had made a love match, and that her heart had chosen for its mate a plain American. . . . All honor to her."[60] Even more remarkable, particularly in light of its repeated attacks on the New York Central line, were the good words it had early in 1885 for William H. Vanderbilt:[61]

> Mr. Vanderbilt has a few qualities we like. He does not own yachts and put on aristocratic airs. . . . We do not believe that the coat-of-arms on his carriage is as big as a full-sized hand. His servants do not wear yellow tags and cockades. We never saw Mrs. Vanderbilt nursing a poodle. He has not sought to buy European gingerbread titles for his daughters, as he could have done with his large wealth, and as many of our vulgar moneyed aristocrats do. The young Vanderbilts, male and female, have all married plain Americans.[62]

Those few instances when the *World* waxed mellow only underlined its implacable hostility to pretentious wealth. "We have been accused of being bitterly opposed to the wealthy," an editorial declared. "That is generally untrue. We respect wealth when it is made the instrument of good. . . . We despise wealth when it accumulates in the hands of money lords who seek to establish an aristocracy of dollars; . . . when it is prostituted to shoddy display and to the gratification of coarse and vulgar tastes."[63] Of course on those terms the *World* detested most of the monied class.

Pulitzer and his staff did not lack for evidence in drawing the major indictment, that Fifth Avenue set itself above the common man's love of country. The nabobs contributed neither time nor money to the great Evacuation Day parade of 1883, although— as we have seen—they serenaded Queen Victoria at a Delmonico's banquet that evening. "Where will the money kings

---

[60] *World*, November 19, 1884, p. 4.

[61] The *World* would have been less pleased with Vanderbilt's son, William K., who in 1895 arranged the most famous of the transatlantic marriages. He paid the Duke of Marlborough $10,000,000 to make his beloved Consuelo, the Commodore's great-granddaughter, a Duchess of the Realm.

[62] *World*, January 13, 1885, p. 4.   [63] *World*, October 14, 1883, p. 4.

and our shoddy aristocracy be found in to-day's parade, celebrating the most patriotic and glorious event in New York's
history?" It knew the answer:

> They will not be in the procession. They would not
> even contribute out of their enormous wealth to the
> expenses of those who will march in the line. But if
> the celebration should have been held in honor of
> Kings and Princes, and if Dukes and Marquises and
> Earls were to be received at the Battery, how they
> would have poured out their cash, and how eagerly
> they would have contended for the prominent posi-
> tions in the procession![64]

William Vanderbilt incurred the hisses of the marchers as they
filed down Fifth Avenue (even though he married his sons and
daughters to "plain" Americans) for failing to adorn his block-
long mansion with a single banner or emblem. "It is possible,"
the newspaper conceded, "that the sullen gloom of the Vanderbilt
palace may have been due to thoughtlessness, or at most to indifference. But is it not likely that it will by many be construed
into a studied insult to the day?"[65]

The *World's* campaign to raise funds to put a pedestal under
the Statue of Liberty further justified the accusations. Money
poured in from all sides when Pulitzer asked the city for
$100,000, but except for a $1,000 check from Pierre Lorillard,
Fifth Avenue ignored the plea. "The wealthy part of the community has treated the project with more than Pecksniffian contempt," the newspaper editorialized.

> It will always remain a matter of reproach to them
> that while the working men, women and children of
> the country were straining every nerve to raise this
> money they looked on with an apathy that amounted
> to contempt. We say this deliberately and advisedly.
> In the opulent city of New York there is enough
> money wasted every day in licentiousness, folly, and
> shame to build this Pedestal. And it is because the
> luxurious classes, whose dollars are given without
> stint to every ephemeral appeal to their vanity, show
> by their attitude at this time that an enduring pa-

[64] *World*, November 26, 1883, p. 4.
[65] *World*, November 28, 1883, p. 4.

triotic sentiment makes no impression on them and arouses no feeling of emulation, that we make these remarks. . . . It is simply disgraceful that the wealthiest city on the continent let the people scratch this money together, when an hour's attention to it on the part of the rich would see the task consummated.[66]

Walt McDougall bitterly reproached their miserliness in a cartoon showing Vanderbilt, Field, and Gould—their arms heavy with moneybags, and diamond studs glittering on their shirt fronts—unable to see a contribution box for the Statue fund because of the silver dollars imbedded in their eye sockets.[67]

It wasn't only patriotic appeals that resounded hollowly in the deaf ears of the rich. Any suggestion that philanthropy might be in order seemed to have the same result. A Sunday feature article late in 1884 pointed out that with but few exceptions—notably the Astor and Lenox Libraries which had been willed to the city in 1848 and 1878 respectively, and Peter Cooper's endowment of Cooper Union—New York's millionaires had proved to be as tightfisted dead as they were alive. "Every few weeks some very rich man dies who could easily leave a million or two as an endowment to a college, library, hospital or art gallery without wronging any of his kinsmen. But he does not leave a dollar in that way. Everything goes to swell coffers already swollen, to add to the greed of the very greedy."[68] They did not begrudge final expenditures from the grave, but only for what the *World* termed their "curious tombstone vanity," stone mausoleums—rivaling those of the pharaohs—for posterity to remember them by.[69]

The final irony is that they remained immune to the softening influence of culture while wandering restlessly between frescoed rooms on Fifth Avenue. To be sure, the railroad and banking barons had started by the 1880s to ransack Europe and buy up its art treasures, spending millions to fill their marble mansions with booty from the public galleries and indigent homesteads of every likely land. Financiers who confined their reading to the stock market ticker bought books by the shelf-full, concerned

[66] *World*, May 1, 1885, p. 4.
[67] *World*, April 12, 1885, p. 1.
[68] *World*, December 14, 1884, p. 18.
[69] *World*, November 25, 1883, p. 9.

only that the bindings harmonize with an already arranged color scheme. Tough-minded manufacturers decorated their walls with Tintorettos and Rembrandts, contented because the pictures told a story.[70] They had been seized by the urge to collect, and they satisfied it with contemptuous ease.

Whatever the cultural gain from importing vast stocks of canvases and statuary, the evidence seemed to show that it had little effect on the people who did the buying. A few of them acquired "cultivation," or at least believed that they did. Andrew Carnegie brought Matthew Arnold to America as his guest, and enjoyed well-publicized friendships with Lord Bryce, Herbert Spencer, and John Morley. But most of the others must have yearned for a rocking chair and a Currier & Ives print. Years later, Henry Frick was remembered "sitting on a Renaissance throne under a baldacchino holding a copy of the *Saturday Evening Post*."[71] Or as Charles Francis Adams recorded in his autobiography, sparing no one, "I have known, and known tolerably well, a good many 'successful' men—'big' financially— men famous during the last half century; and a less interesting crowd I do not care to encounter. Not one that I have ever known would I care to meet again, either in this world or the next; nor is one of them associated in my mind with the ideas of humor, thought or refinement."[72]

In coveting art for reasons of status, the collectors of the late nineteenth century gave little encouragement to contemporary artists. They became patrons of the dead rather than the living. According to Arthur Montefiore, it was far easier to meet successful American painters in London or Paris than in New York.

[70] As Charles Beard wrote, "Even the Orient was forced to yield up graven goddesses of mercy and complacent Buddhas to decorate the buildings of men absorbed in making soap, steel rails, whiskey, and cotton bagging and to please the women who spent the profits of business enterprise. The armor of medieval knights soon stood in the halls of captains of industry whose boldest strokes were courageous guesses on the stock market or the employment of Pinkerton detectives against striking workingmen; while Mandarin coats from Peking sprawled on the pianos of magnates who knew not Ming or Manchu and perhaps could not tell whether their hired musicians were grinding out Wagner or Chopin." Charles A. and Mary R. Beard, *The Rise of American Civilization*, 2 vols. (New York, 1927), II, 386. See also Aline B. Saarinen, *The Proud Possessors* (New York, 1958).

[71] Quoted in Curti, *Growth of American Thought* (New York, 1943), p. 513.

[72] Charles Francis Adams, *Autobiography* (Boston, 1916), p. 190.

"The millionaires of the New World . . . prefer spending their money in the markets of the Old," he wrote in 1888, "thereby depreciating the American school, as a school, and discounting the American artist as a producer."[73]

The *World* took pains to remind its readers of those facts. "Our newly made millionaires," one of the earliest editorials declared, "who graduate from trade or from the broker's board, consider it their sacred duty to society to buy pictures just as much as to buy carriages, to put their coachmen and footmen in livery and to invent coats-of-arms. They know nothing about art any more than about Chinese vases. But they are excellent judges of gilded picture frames!"[74] The fact that "money does in most not bring with it artistic taste and culture" could more easily be forgiven than the corollary, that money in the New World did not culturally enrich the society which produced it.

> As a rule [the "best society" of New York] does not throw its mahogany doors open to struggling talent. It has not recognition for those geniuses whose ideas or labors command the respect of princes in other countries, and whose title as poet, actor, painter, preacher or inventor breaks down all barriers of caste.
>
> Take it altogether, some of our good society, when measured by the demands of the community in which it lives, is a very selfish and barren society.[75]

Such statements had a significance beyond measuring the social contribution of a handful of nabobs. The newspaper hoped, by showing that the emperor wore no clothes, to dissuade tens of thousands of New Yorkers from slavishly conceding the superiority of one class over another. It hoped to prevent the rise in the New World of a peasant mentality inherited from the Old. It hoped to forestall, if not class consciousness, at least class war. They were important aims at a time when unchecked immigration and wracking poverty made one-half of the city strangers to the other.

[73] Montefiore, "New York and the New Yorkers," *Temple Bar*, pp. 352-53; quoted in Bayrd Still, *Mirror for Gotham*, p. 227.
[74] *World*, May 12, 1883, p. 4.
[75] *World*, December 23, 1883, p. 4.

The surest way of deflating the self-appointed aristocrats was to make them seem ridiculous, something easily enough accomplished so long as money dominated the cultural marketplace. The events leading to the construction of the Metropolitan Opera House, a showcase which came into being because two factions of New York's monied class (roughly new wealth and old) could not agree on how to honor each other's pretensions, provides a case in point.

Until 1883, the only place to hear Grand Opera was at the old Academy of Music, on 14th Street. Music lovers filled the orchestra and stalls of the Academy, enjoying an unobstructed view of the stage, while the wealthy patrons of opera looked down in regal isolation from their reserved boxes, symbols of social success. It became a matter of some urgency for those who had already earned millions, but not yet bought acceptance, to sit beside them in restless homage to culture. Unfortunately, the Academy of Music had only eighteen boxes, and the reigning gentry (led by August Belmont) coldly refused to have more added.[76] When persuasion and bribery both failed (including an alleged offer of $30,000 for one box), the nouveau riche joined together to build their own opera house, one which would outshine the Academy and provide pews for all deserving millionaires.

William K. and Cornelius Vanderbilt, whose wives put the same energy into social climbing that their father reserved for railroads, assumed leadership of the fund-raising drive, with notable assistance from William Rockefeller, Jay Gould, George F. Baker, and Collis P. Huntington. The $2,000,000 building which went up at 39th Street and Broadway was ugly inside and out, but Joseph Cady, the architect, fulfilled his primary mission by cramming it with boxes, 122 of them grouped in two tiers of

[76] The list of box holders at the Academy of Music provides an interesting clue to established wealth in the city, as opposed to parvenus like the Vanderbilts, Rockefellers, and Goulds. It includes the families of August Belmont, William R. Travers, Pierre Lorillard, Henry G. Stebbins, Sheppard Ganday, S. L. M. Barlow, Isaac Townsend, Isaac Bell, Robert L. Cutting, and Louis Hoffman, as well as Messrs. Lazarus, Coles, Heckscher, Dinsmore, Garner, and Lukemeyer. The Astors and Roosevelts belonged on the list by right, but since they had never bothered to subscribe they were available to lend precious social tone to the newly established Metropolitan Opera.

equal social prominence. Reporters soon dubbed them the Golden Horseshoe, and estimated that $540,000,000 of wealth congregated there at any single performance.

The opportunity was too good for Pulitzer's irreverent *World* to ignore. Nym Crinkle gave society fair warning when he wrote that "never was there a time in our history when the burlesquer, the pamphleteer, the satiric moralist had stretching before him such a national harvest from which to gather . . . all the feculent fruitage of selfishness, hollowness and hypocrisy to adorn his picture of the new regime of money-makers."[77] The age called for satire, and if Pulitzer's *World* was not best equipped for the task, at least it filled a gap until more sophisticated candidates came along.

The spectacle of distraught society figures trying to decide whether they should be seen on opening night at the Academy of Music or the Metropolitan Opera House provided an early opportunity for laughter.

> Now to be in both places at once is physically impossible, and not to be in both places subjects one to the risk of not being in the right place. In other words, the fearful responsibility is put upon the high art patrons of music of deciding which house they will appear in on the opening night.
>
> This is not an easy choice, for no one at this moment can tell which is to be the accepted place. . . . What a fatal and crushing misfortune it would be if my lady Cheesly Butterworth elected to go to the Academy, and then found that all the swell people were at the other shop! There is only one way out of this difficulty. Let the ladies have a caucus on behalf of high art and resolve which house they will serve in advance.[78]

Of course, and society might have known it, the "best people" followed the Vanderbilts to the new building on 39th Street. The *World*'s blue-blooded correspondent, "Van Somerindyke," brought back a careful description of what transpired that night. He assured the newspaper's readers, just as he had assured an

[77] *World*, March 1, 1885, p. 18.
[78] *World*, October 14, 1883, p. 4.

anxious matron between acts, that the financiers who had paid so dearly to import bassos and sopranos from foreign lands would never allow a crass commercial spirit (or musical taste) to defile New York's most recent temple of culture.

> I was there.
> I had to be. It was understood in our set that not to be there would put a fellow out of the swim, don't you know. . . .
> By Jove, when our governors put on airs about music it makes me sick. It's all too thin. We didn't build the Metropolitan Opera House because we know anything about music. The idea was to fix up a place where the first families could come together socially in good clothes and talk. We couldn't do it at the Academy because there were a lot of old muffs who had made a closed corporation of that barracks. The first families must come together somewhere, mustn't they? . . .
> It makes me sick to hear the Fourteenth Street fellows talking about it's not paying. Who ever said it would pay? . . .
> Mrs. Stevens said to me, "Good Heavens!" said she, "you don't think it will pay! Do you?"
> I calmed her. "Madame," says I, ". . . there is not the slightest danger. It will never pay, except when we pay for it."
> "So glad," says she. "I was afraid they were going to debase a divine art to a commercial standard. The Opera is the only place left where we can sanctify our lives by losing money. Let us keep it pure and undefiled!"
> That's the kind of Roman spirit that animates our women.[79]

The purity of dedication that built the Metropolitan did not deter the *World* from commenting on some of the more curious theatre-going customs to be seen there. It could not imagine what motivated the nabobs to bring valets with them to the opera, unless they needed help to make sense of the performance.

> It was reported yesterday that all the stockholders at the Metropolitan were to have these attachments

[79] *World*, October 24, 1883, p. 4.

> last night, and the rumor had two noticeable effects. It produced a sudden rise in the price of musical valets at the Intelligence Offices. Good men who knew Wagner's music were in lively demand. The old Italian school of lyric valet commanded a good price, and valets of the English or oratorio school were held quite firmly. The other effect of the rumor was to create the general impression at the Opera House last night that the young swells who stood all the way round the tier were valets.[80]

Nor did the newspaper particularly appreciate the "very Frenchy" habit, on display at the Metropolitan as elsewhere, of young fops dressed in swallow-tail coats and flaring vests, rising from their seats in the orchestra between acts to scan the audience with their lorgnettes. It suggested an effective, if radical, remedy for the rudeness. "A squad of active young men in the gallery provided with putty-blowers might curb the antics of the oglers and mashers in the front orchestra chairs."[81]

The *World*'s criticisms of the wealthy families in New York City, finding fault both with how they made their money and what they did with it, stemmed from its liberal political bias. Reform meant changing the conditions of life and labor which men like Vanderbilt, Gould, and Villard had created, and which they did most to perpetuate. A newspaper like Godkin's *Evening Post* made an aesthetic judgment when it deplored the vulgarity of the nabobs, but for Pulitzer and his staff, criticizing their values was but another way of attacking them as political foes.

The different motivation caused the *World* to be if anything, more stern than a Godkin in detecting signs of pretension, and more outspoken in urging the populace to reject material values. An article about a woman whose husband married her for her fortune was appropriately headlined: WEALTH A CAUSE OF MISERY.[82] Men whom it suspected of dancing to the music of the pied pipers of industry read of their disgrace on the newspaper's editorial page. "What a materialistic age this is becoming!" the *World* declared on learning that Charles Francis Adams and Jay Gould would sit together on the same railroad board of directors.

[80] *World*, October 25, 1883, p. 4.   [81] *World*, October 27, 1883, p. 4.
[82] *World*, July 12, 1884, p. 12.

How must the old-fashioned ideas of high honor
have changed, how must the standard of self-respect
have been lowered, when we find the direct descend-
ant of the Adamses who filled the Presidential office
given over to money-making, embarking in railroad
corporation schemes with Jay Gould, and while denying that he is that tarnished operator's tool, boasting
that he is in general harmony with this venal associate and fellow-director!

This is a materialistic age. Family renown, personal character, a high sense of honor are more or
less suspended. Money is the attraction, the modern
craze and power in this age, and this is why we find a
Charles Francis Adams, the great-grandson of Washington's successor and grandson of another President,
bent on making money with apparently as much
eagerness and "in general harmony" with Jay
Gould.[83]

But there was another side to the newspaper's philosophy.
If political principle caused it to reject the nabobs and all they
stood for, its sensitivity to the values of the time made it grudg-
ingly respect them for having succeeded in the way most people
measured success. The *World* as an organ, and Joseph Pulitzer
as an individual, were profoundly influenced by the Horatio
Alger mythology of American life. They shared the popular vision
of a pot of gold at the end of the rainbow which men could secure
through their own efforts. It was right that they should, for the
genius of popular journalism is to express in a striking way attitudes that in themselves are ordinary.

The ardor with which Pulitzer coveted wealth is beyond
dispute. In September 1883, the *World* printed a list of the
millionaires currently residing in New York City. Along with it
went an arch reminder that new names would soon be added.
"We find the names of only three or four newspaper publishers
in the magnificent array. By this time next year, as things are
going, the list will be beautified with the names of at least a half-
dozen journalists. We could name them now, but modesty for-
bids."[84] Pulitzer intended to become wealthy himself, just as the

[83] *World*, March 8, 1885, p. 4.
[84] *World*, September 30, 1883, p. 4.

majority of his readers regarded wealth as the ultimate form of success.

It was natural in that case for the newspaper, ever responsive to popular attitudes, to report in detail on who the rich were, and how they lived. The natural political enemies of the *World* also became a favorite subject for respectful treatment. Many years later, when Pulitzer administered the paper through memoranda to his managing editors, he suggested a typical article for the Sunday edition. "I think it would be a good idea, an interesting feature," he wrote, "to give a full list of all the partners of J. P. Morgan & Co., with a little personal description of each, a little condensed history of their rise to prominence; . . . the specific work of each partner—their age; individual wealth of each."[85] But the technique was applied long before Pulitzer's blindness forced him to abdicate direct control of the newspaper.

The *World* admitted in an editorial reply to a society lady from Morristown, New Jersey, who had written in to complain about the amount of space devoted to the activities of the "lowest classes," and to invite coverage of a forthcoming event involving "ladies and gentlemen," that it was indeed interested in chronicling the activities of the rich. "We do not recognize 'classes' in the mere matter of going to the seashore or giving parties, and we are not devoted to the work of exalting snobs and cads. Still, it would not be surprising if we detailed a special reporter to go out to Morristown on the 17th to record the performances of the fine ladies and gentlemen who are advertised to illuminate the Tournament with their presence."[86] The reply seems to be sarcastic, as if the only motive for sending a reporter would be to discover new material for social satire. If such was the intent it is misleading, for the *World* specialized in covering society's various functions. Its careful descriptions in word and picture of the rich at play enabled thousands of readers to participate at least in their imaginations. DIAMONDS FLASH AND SILKS SHIMMER proclaimed the headline over an article describing a ball at the Metropolitan Opera House the previous evening. WHO WERE THERE

[85] Memorandum from Pulitzer to Charles M. Lincoln, dated March 8, 1911. Quoted in Seitz, *Joseph Pulitzer*, pp. 426-27.
[86] *World*, September 8, 1884, p. 4.

AND WHAT THEY WORE. The two-column account included four-teen illustrations depicting the celebrants whirling about the dance floor.[87] A VAST CROWD IN FANCY COSTUMES AND DOMI-NOES—THE BALL A GREAT SUCCESS, the newspaper wrote of the twentieth annual "Circle de l'harmonie Ball,"[88] Three days later a headline described the GORGEOUS UNIFORMS OF THE MEN AND THE BEAUTIFUL COSTUMES OF THE LADIES MAKING EVER-CHANGING PICTURES IN THE BALLROOM at a National Guard event.[89] An evening of Shakespearean drama, followed by dining and dancing, was described as BRILLIANT ENTERTAINMENT AT THE RESIDENCE OF WM. C. WHITNEY.[90] The annual festivities at the Bay Liederkranz Ball were conducted IN MASKS AND DOMI-NOES. ALL THE BUILDING BECOMES GAY WITH LIFE AND ANI-MATION.[91] The Great Purim Ball evoked A BRILLIANT SCENE IN THE ACADEMY. FANCY COSTUMES TRIP ON THE FLOOR, WHILE BEAUTY, IN RICH APPAREL AND BLAZING WITH JEWELS, OCCU-PIES THE BOXES.[92]

The *World* outdid itself in December 1883, on the occasion of a grand ball at the home of William K. Vanderbilt. The event topped the social calendar for that year, and received exhaustive coverage in a newspaper responsive to the interests of the masses. A long article on the morning of the festivities described the grandeur of the Vanderbilt mansion, the floral decorations which had been provided, the people who would attend, and most important, what the ladies would wear. The headline called it a scene of MAGNIFICENCE UNSURPASSED.[93] The next morning the *World* devoted three full columns to recreating what had gone on, under SCENES OF DAZZLING SPLENDOR AT THE GREAT MANSION. "The great Vanderbilt ball," according to the lead sentence, "about which society has been in such a flutter of expectation for months past, has come and gone and now is a matter of social history, where it will rank pre-eminent as the most brilliant private ball which has ever been given in this city, and probably in the United States." The newspaper's reporters strolled through great halls adorned with the art of the centuries,

[87] *World*, January 7, 1885, p. 5.   [88] *World*, January 20, 1885, p. 2.
[89] *World*, January 23, 1885, p. 3.   [90] *World*, February 5, 1885, p. 2.
[91] *World*, February 18, 1885, p. 5.   [92] *World*, March 13, 1885, p. 5.
[93] *World*, December 11, 1883, p. 5.

and decorated for the occasion with bowers of roses and blossoms of more exotic growth. But none of it matched the splendor of the human peacocks on display. "The costumes of many of the ladies present, both in beauty of design and richness of color, may be said to have fairly eclipsed the pictured fancies of the painter and, taken as a whole, the sight was one which will be witnessed only once in a lifetime."[94]

Nor was it only society on the dance floor which assumed a fairy tale aspect. The *World* devoted two-thirds of its front page on May 25, 1884, for example, to a report on the Coaching Club's annual spring parade down Fifth Avenue. FAIR WOMEN AND BRAVE MEN AT THE COACHING CLUB'S SPRING PARADE, the headline enthused. A KALEIDOSCOPIC SCENE OF BRILLIANCY AND BEAUTY ON FIFTH AVENUE - THE FLASHING OF SPRING COSTUMES AND CLINKING OF SILVER HARNESS AND THE MUSIC OF THE HORNS STARTLE CENTRAL PARK - THIRTEEN COACHES IN LINE - WHO DROVE AND WHO WERE GUESTS.[95]

The great social event that year occurred in November, when Orme Wilson took as his bride Miss Caroline Astor, in a ceremony conducted at the home of her parents. Once again the *World*'s coverage was unsurpassed. The news story, with descriptions of the Astor house, the genealogy of the two families, the gifts presented, the guests in attendance, and of course, the ceremony itself, took up five complete columns on page one, and four more columns on page two. Gribayedoff contributed a four-column, front-page illustration to the account, depicting the couple as they kneeled to take their vows before an assemblage of the most eminent names in New York society. It seemed almost uninspired to headline an affair so grand SOCIETY'S GREAT WEDDING.[96]

The fascination with wealth extended to the men who had earned the money to purchase such display. Jay Gould was the target of repeated criticism on the *World*'s editorial page, but the newspaper—without embarrassment—also made him the subject of an interview on how to get ahead in business. An

[94] *World*, December 13, 1883, p. 5.
[95] *World*, May 25, 1885, p. 1.
[96] *World*, November 19, 1884, pp. 1-2.

article headlined CHATS WITH FINANCIERS reported admiringly that although the market value of his holdings had fallen between $40,000,000 and $50,000,000 during 1883-1884, the financier continued to receive dividends estimated at $6,000,000 annually.[97] The striking thing about the articles in this genre was their almost exclusive focus on the incomes the individuals earned. They were day-dreaming rather than do-it-yourself accounts, entirely uninformative when it came to suggesting how to turn small investments into large profits, but wonderfully precise on the rewards accruing to those who knew the secret. The failure to be more specific could not much have grieved the inhabitants of tenements and brownstone flats, who had enough to do in meeting their household expenses without embarking on projects in competition with the bulls and bears of Wall Street. Day-dreaming was all they could manage. The fact that the articles were often little more than lists of names and the incomes which went with those names suggests how thoroughly men had been gripped by the dream of wealth. It takes a special motive, or special obsession, to plough through prose not unlike that of the Manhattan telephone directory.

The catalogues of success came in many varieties. Sometimes, as suggested, they were little more than lists of names and numbers: of 400 estimated millionaires in New York City,[98] or of women in the city who had inherited millions.[99] More often the newspaper divided its subjects into categories, and considered each category separately. Several of the articles dealt with what the *World* called "Wall Street Bloods," men who controlled the banks and brokerage houses in the financial district. As with all of the articles of this type, the subjects were portrayed in one-column cuts, while short paragraphs described their personalities and estimated their annual incomes.[100] The treatment was applied to attorneys whose fees totalled between $10,000 and $30,000 a year,[101] to medical men earning over

[97] *World*, December 26, 1884, p. 5.
[98] *World*, October 1, 1883, p. 3.
[99] *World*, November 5, 1883, p. 5.
[100] See, for example, the issue of February 3, 1884, p. 1; May 11, 1884, p. 9; May 25, 1884, p. 9; and May 10, 1885, p. 22.
[101] *World*, June 15, 1884, p. 9.

$10,000[102] (and in a separate article, between $20,000 and $50,000[103]), to the various MERCHANT PRINCES in the metropolis,[104] and even to millionaires sitting in the United States Senate.[105] Alternatively, the newspaper's gaze went afield to regard millionaires in other cities,[106] and more specifically, to list the wealthy women not only of New York,[107] but of Washington, D. C.,[108] Chicago,[109] and Cincinnati.[110]

Two things stand out about such features. The amount of attention devoted to wealthy women reveals again that the articles did not so much represent entrepreneurial reporting as an attempt to describe a fairy tale world in which every inhabitant was a prince or princess. The *World* was a newspaper published for women as well as men, and both sexes enjoyed the romance as an escape from the tedium of their own lives. The articles are also a striking demonstration of the journal's faith in the Horatio Alger mythology of the time. They told not only of rich people, but of people who had achieved riches through their own efforts. A feature on THE LEGAL FRATERNITY OF NEW YORK—MEN WHO HAVE WORKED UP FROM THE RANKS delivered the moral with admirable succinctness: "Investigation shows that most of the leading attorneys started life under great difficulties, and owe their success either to favorable incidents or to their own endeavors."[111] Even the headlines over the articles expounded on the gospel of Success. They identified their wealthy subjects as GO-A-HEADATIVE MEN,[112] MEN OF MARK AND PUSH,[113] MEN WHO GRASP AT FORTUNE AS SHE FLIES,[114] and summed up the creed

[102] *World*, December 2, 1883, p. 10.   [103] *World*, June 22, 1884, p. 9.
[104] *World*, October 5, 1884, p. 9. See also October 26, 1884, p. 13.
[105] *World*, April 13, 1884, p. 9; also January 11, 1885, p. 9. "'There is no objection to wealth in such a position," the *World* declared in a separate editorial, "provided it has not been made out of official jobbery or that the possessor does not owe his seat to its use. . . . When we find, however, that there is no question relating to public lands, railroads, telegraphs, or any other great enterprises, which does not involve the personal interests of many Senators who are to pass upon them, we cannot help wishing that the Senate had some poorer and more honest men than at present." *World*, April 14, 1884, p. 4.
[106] See *World*, May 10, 1885, p. 18, for an article on Baltimore millionaires.
[107] *World*, March 8, 1885, p. 18.
[108] *World*, February 22, 1885, p. 18.   [109] *World*, April 12, 1885, p. 18.
[110] *World*, April 26, 1885, p. 18.   [111] *World*, December 16, 1883, p. 15.
[112] *World*, November 2, 1884, p. 9.
[113] *World*, November 23, 1884, p. 12.   [114] *World*, April 26, 1885, p. 23.

which inspired them in the simple line, SUCCESS THEIR MOTTO.[115]

The escapist quality of such literature, and its meaning for women as well as men, can be seen again in the extensive articles the *World* published on the homes of the wealthy. More than providing another glimpse into a world without airshafts, dark hallways, and crowded rooms, they appealed to a homemaking instinct among women which later editors would exploit in much the same way as Pulitzer. Edward Bok credited the success of the *Ladies' Home Journal*, whose circulation swelled from 440,000 to an unprecedented 1,000,000 within a few years of his taking control in 1889, to its interest in making middle class homes more attractive. In his autobiography he described meeting a woman at a friend's funeral who barely knew the grieved family. "I'll be perfectly frank," she replied when he asked what brought her there. "I am going to the funeral just to see how Mrs. S——'s home is furnished. She was always thought to have great taste, you know, and whether you know it or not, a woman is always keen to look into another woman's house."[116] The editor immediately acted on the hint by running a long series of photographs under the heading of "Inside a Hundred Homes." It became one of the *Journal's* most popular features.

Bok's editorial judgment is self-evident, but the *World* anticipated him by about ten years with its own series on elegant homes. Some of the articles described in word and picture the mansions of the very wealthiest of New York society: James Stebbins;[117] Commodore Vanderbilt;[118] William K. Vanderbilt;[119] Mrs. Ogden Goelet;[120] Cornelius Vanderbilt;[121] Mrs. Mark Hopkins;[122] William Astor, Mrs. Paran Stevens, and William C. Whitney;[123] Jay Gould;[124] and so on.[125] Others reported on the

[115] *World*, November 23, 1884, p. 13.
[116] Edward Bok, *The Americanization of Edward Bok* (New York, 1922), p. 243.
[117] *World*, May 11, 1884, p. 12.   [118] *World*, May 18, 1884, p. 11.
[119] *World*, May 25, 1884, p. 11.   [120] *World*, June 8, 1884, p. 11.
[121] *World*, April 5, 1885, p. 19.
[122] *World*, January 18, 1885, p. 17. Mrs. Hopkins' mansion was located in Great Barrington, Massachusetts. She owned another one in California.
[123] *World*, March 29, 1885, p. 17.
[124] *World*, June 15, 1884, p. 11.
[125] For further articles of the same sort, see the *World*, December 30, 1883, p. 10; and April 12, 1885, p. 21.

homes of celebrities. The newspaper visited the residence of Sarah Bernhardt in France;[126] and of Thomas Edison in Gramercy Park;[127] as well as those of A. S. Hatch and J. C. Eno,[128] George I. Seney,[129] Colonel Fred Grant, and Ulysses Grant, Jr.,[130] men prominent in the Wall Street panic of 1884. A few articles—such as the one on the "Dalhomaje" Apartments on 59th Street—even considered gracious living at the upper middle class level. "Mr. S. G. Hyatt is the agent for these buildings," the *World* declared, "and we do not think he will have much difficulty in renting them."[131]

Of course hardly any of the newspaper's readers could hope to borrow ideas from the furnishings and decorations described in those articles. Jay Gould's home was noted for its wonderful, hand-carved woodwork; Mrs. Goelet copied her salon from the Palace at Versailles; William K. Vanderbilt's doors of solid bronze cost a fortune in themselves, and his floors were of inlaid tile in Venetian style; James Stebbins had accumulated a treasure in paintings, statuary, and rare bric-a-brac to decorate his mansion on Madison Avenue. But it did not matter if the wealth that went into such homes made them irrelevant to the house-proud women of poorer means. It was still enjoyable to read about how the fortunate few lived, and the very inaccessibility of their style made them more than ever like figures out of a familiar and well-beloved fairy tale.[132]

The fascination with wealth knew no limits. The *World* took to printing tax rolls to show what the nabobs paid for their property in New York City; Newport, Rhode Island; and other favorite locations.[133] On August 3, 1884, for example, it devoted

[126] *World*, March 2, 1885, p. 2. [127] *World*, June 1, 1884, p. 11.
[128] *World*, May 24, 1884, p. 5. [129] *World*, June 1, 1884, p. 16.
[130] *World*, June 2, 1884, p. 5. [131] *World*, November 9, 1884, p. 5.
[132] Pulitzer pointed out to Don Carlos Seitz, in a letter dated February 22, 1901, that all classes were interested in the homes of the wealthy. "Take a double page," he suggested, "and give the pictures of the exteriors of say 20 houses, the finest in New York without exaggeration as to cost. Then have a series from Sunday to Sunday of the interiors of these houses, one each Sunday. Carefully and reliably done so as to touch the imagination not only of the poor but of the rich, not only society but the socialist. All will be interested to see exactly the luxuries & beauties of each." *Pulitzer Papers*, Library of Congress.
[133] See the *World*, October 14, 1883, p. 2; August 3, 1884, pp. 13-14; and April 26, 1885, p. 19. The last article gives property valuation in Newport.

seven complete columns on page thirteen, and two more columns on page fourteen, to listing everybody in the city whose property was assessed at $100,000 or more. (The lists served a joint purpose, since the newspaper was also engaged in a crusade to have those in the upper income brackets bear a heavier share of the tax burden.) Similarly, it went back in history to report who owned wealth during the Revolutionary period,[134] or during the decade immediately preceding the Civil War.[135] So obsessive was the interest that gold in its pure state became a subject for feature treatment in the *World*. An article on the sub-treasury vault on Wall Street described how millions of dollars in specie and legal tender was stored and safeguarded. With it went nine full-column cuts and two half-column cuts, depicting among other things a straw basket containing $20,000,000 in cash, a vault crammed with gold, and a heap of new and used bills of various denominations.[136] Once again the newspaper had come dangerously close to parodying itself.

An odd discrepancy is apparent. The *World* attacked the titans of Wall Street as buccaneers, and their style of living as unsocial and vulgar. At the same time, it glorified them as living symbols of the American dream of success. If the paper contradicted itself with almost every issue it delivered to the newsstands, the contradiction was part of its appeal. It did no more than reflect the idealism and crassness of the community that produced it, which is another way of saying that it was a paper of and for the people.

[134] *World*, December 16, 1883, p. 15.
[135] *World*, November 25, 1883, p. 10.
[136] *World*, February 19, 1885, p. 9.

CHAPTER SEVEN

JINGOISM AND ANTI-INTELLECTUALISM

The *World* strived, through its news content and opinions, to speak for the masses of men who had previously read newspapers only sporadically, if at all. It attempted to influence as well as inform and entertain them, using the editorials on page four in particular as weapons in a self-declared war against privation and privilege. But the special relationship between the *World* and the previously inarticulate people who patronized it operated in both directions. The men and women who daily received lectures on the need for reform, and how to achieve it, exerted their own influence by imposing upon the journal ideas unrelated, and often contradictory, to those put forward in the crusading editorials. The *World* repeated many of the platitudes and fallacies they wished to hear in order to win their confidence and make them susceptible to more enlightened thought.

Once again, the first rule of popular journalism, as it is an axiom of politics, is that the preconceptions of the people must be honored. They can be influenced and led, but not in ways radically different from those they are accustomed to, and not without constant assurance that their present attitudes are essentially wise. Pulitzer was fortunate, as perhaps any popular journalist would have to be, in sharing many of his readers' ideas and values. We have seen that he was a man of the time in his attitude toward the captains of American industry, admiring them for their material success, and resenting how they achieved that success. His immigrant background and dominating personality fitted him for the delicate task of acknowledging the justice of the women's rights movement while resisting the most radical demands of that movement. He could not have made of the *World* what he did without such broad areas of rapport between himself and the general public.

But no individual is a perfect microcosm of his age, and obviously in many other respects Pulitzer's instincts were different from those of the great body of Americans. A few such differences could be tolerated, and even respected, just so long as they did not become too many, and did not infringe upon questions of basic controversy. In the final analysis, the publisher's success depended as much upon the way he adapted to ideas not his own as his skill in expressing ideas he shared with the majority of men.

Two of the emotions that men at the time were most susceptible to, in the United States as elsewhere, were jingoism and distrust of intellectuality. Popular thought on a question like women's rights evolved over the years, but the people's thrilled response to a call to arms, and their idea of scholarship as something alien and frequently ridiculous, remained fairly constant from one decade to the next. It is noteworthy that in almost every country where a popular press functioned, the newspapers of largest circulation were usually also the ones that played upon those emotions.

The argument that an important element in Pulitzer's success was the extent to which he partook of popular ideology becomes more complicated in regard to jingoism and anti-intellectualism, for they are not traits one would ordinarily associate with the publisher of the *New York World*. Pulitzer was a man of vast learning who sought learned men for companionship, the very opposite of an anti-intellectual. He was also a sophisticate, and, as he demonstrated in 1895 at the time of the Venezuela boundary dispute with Great Britain, one well able to withstand the emotionalism and fervor which carries men to war. The best description of the publisher comes from Alleyne Ireland, who spent about a year as his private secretary, conversing with him, reading to him, and keeping him informed on developments in the arts, literature, and politics. Ireland was constantly amazed by the breadth and profundity of Pulitzer's insights. "To an extraordinary flow of language," he writes, "[Pulitzer] added a range of information and a vividness of expression truly astonishing. His favorite themes were politics and the lives of great men. To his monologues on the former subject he brought a ripe wisdom, based upon the most extensive reading and the shrewd-

est observation, and quickened by the keenest enthusiasm."
When his nerves allowed, the publisher liked to sit with his
secretaries for an hour after dinner, discussing recent books, or
lecturing to them on events out of history. He picked out the
"high lights," according to Ireland, "in pregnant phrases of
characterization, in brilliant epitome of the facts, in spontaneous
epigram, and illustrative anecdote. . . . Every sentence was
marked by the same penetrating analysis, the same facility of
expression, the same clearness of thought."[1] Pulitzer as thus
described would seem to be distinct from Pulitzer the popular
journalist. At least his editorials in the *World* expressed a more
simplistic notion of scholarship and patriotism than was typical
for a man of his erudition.

In part, this is simply to say that he could not afford the
luxury of contradicting his audience on questions so deeply felt.
He had great influence upon hundreds of thousands of people,
but the people in turn influenced him. Like any other popular
journalist, at some point he had to follow the path of least resis-
tance in determining his editorial policy.

The real trick was to follow it with conviction. A newspaper
cannot make a habit of expressing what it does not believe, at
least not do so effectively, and sooner or later it must either convert its audience or be converted itself. More specifically, it must
be capable of doing both. The chapters to follow consider areas
in which the *World* stood squarely on principle, and served as a
beacon for the city, lighting the way to reform. Its statements
regarding jingoism and anti-intellectualism demonstrate the
opposite art, the ability to move in the direction that popular
will demanded. The one trait was as vital as the other in determining the newspaper's success.

But how does one resolve the apparent contradiction between
Pulitzer the individual, scholarly and judicious by temperament, and Pulitzer the popular journalist, who became one of the
foremost spokesmen for opinions the very opposite of scholarly
and judicious? It makes little sense to argue that he uncon-
cernedly prostituted himself and his beliefs for the sake of ex-

[1] Alleyne Ireland, *Joseph Pulitzer, Reminiscences of a Secretary* (New York,
1914), pp. 168-70.

pediency. Pulitzer did not achieve his great name through a career of journalistic streetwalking, nor in all likelihood would he have been effective in that role. Rather, he was able to engage in a dialogue with the masses of men, to be influenced as well as to influence, because he contained within himself many of the seeds which in other breasts sprouted into plants of more ugly growth. He was not a jingoist, for example, but he had enough of the jingoist's combative temperament to satisfy the passion in the pages of his newspaper. He was certainly not an anti-intellectual, but as one who had made his own way in the world, often in the face of cruel harassment, he understood and appreciated the popular distrust of those who styled themselves "learned." He was uniquely qualified, in short, to publish a newspaper for the common run of men and women, because even when he disagreed with them, he understood better than most what they thought, and sympathized enough to honor their thought when he could do so without sullying his own.

The clearest indication that the pages of the *World* recorded a dialogue rather than a monologue is seen in its chauvinistic response to challenges from overseas. The unsophisticated public had little patience with theories of diplomacy that urged the wisdom of avoiding controversy whenever possible. It regarded challenges in the international sphere as not much different from personal challenges, and expected the State Department to face them in a way befitting the national honor. Anything less than a truculent, chip-on-the-shoulder response was liable to be construed as cowardice. The *World's* credentials to speak for as well as to the masses of men rested at least in part on the lip-service it paid to this convention. Although the *New York Journal* exploited patriotic mania much more blatantly fifteen years later with black headlines that thrilled a city, and completed the work of making all men newspaper readers, it did so only after Pulitzer had established the appeal of bellicose rhetoric. The *World's* columns are a storehouse of proof that the confident American public appreciated nothing more than a fight or threat of a fight —at least until blood was shed.

To be sure, certain similarities are evident between the Joseph Pulitzer of 1883, a guardian of national honor, and the

Pulitzer of 1895, who won the plaudits of sensible men everywhere for his part in averting a needless war between Britain and America over the Venezuela boundary, and who in a speech accepting a joint award from several peace organizations, referred to "that false and perverted patriotism called jingoism."[2] He resisted an appeal from Washington during the last year of the Arthur administration for naval construction, pointing out that the country stood in no imminent peril of war, and that in all probability the appeal concealed a last-ditch Republican scheme for feeding at the public trough.[3] Similarly, he argued that the United States had nothing to fear from a French-built canal across the Isthmus of Panama. The canal, he wrote, "is the great necessity of the age," and nothing in its construction by European capital violated the Monroe Doctrine.[4] When Representative William Dorsheimer, a Democrat from the Seventh District of New York, rose in the House on January 17, 1885, to advocate that the country immediately embark on a competing route through Nicaragua, since the activity of the De Lesseps Company constituted "a cause for serious disquietude," Pulitzer described the speech as "Fourth of July style of oratory." He saw the military implications of the French canal in much more simple terms. "In peace, all nations would enjoy equal privileges in the navigation of this short cut between the great oceans by whomsoever it might be built. In case of war, the canal, like Providence, would be on the side of the heaviest battalions. . . . Does not this expose the folly of all this grandiloquent talk about the military aspect of the Isthmus Canal question?"[5] Pulitzer in this frame of mind welcomed any influence which contributed to better understanding between nations. He even spoke benignly on occasion of the good work done by touring theatrical troupes, which usually meant English troupes, in breaking down suspicion between peoples. "Art is defying the limitations of geography and tongue," he exulted, "and rapid communication of thought and

[2] Address delivered on June 5, 1896. Quoted in James Wyman Barrett, *Joseph Pulitzer and His World* (New York, 1941), p. 162.
[3] See, for example, the *World*, May 3, 1884, p. 4.
[4] *World*, December 19, 1884, p. 4.
[5] *World*, January 20, 1885, p. 4.

feeling is linking the intelligence of all nations into one brother-hood of good taste."[6]

But the publisher did not often forget in this way his own combative temperament, or the predilections of the people who sponsored him. Leander Richardson noted sourly in 1884 that the *World's* criticisms of James Blaine for his history of "tak[ing] a hitch in the British lion's tail and twist[ing] that useful appendage to the fullest extent of his muscular ability" did not come from a particularly appropriate source. After all, Richard-son pointed out with justification, "not so very long ago the *World* was the most emphatically 'jingo' newspaper published in America."[7]

Whether the adversary was Count Otto von Bismarck, or the most obscure leader of a Central American banana republic, the *World* allowed no affront to the national dignity to go un-answered, and ended usually by threatening the most extreme forms of retaliation. Bismarck landed in the newspaper's bad graces early in 1884 when his government banned American pork from the German market on the suspicion that it carried trichinosis. The action represented a serious blow to farmers in this country, but the *World* seemed as worked up by the re-flection on U.S. livestock as by the commercial implications. It suggested a boycott on German wines until the American pig was exonerated. "It is within the range of reason," an editorial declared, "to expect the German authorities to change their views of the American Hog when they find that the question is seriously affecting the export of their native wines."[8] The dispute heated up a few weeks later when Bismarck intercepted a reso-lution from the United States House of Representatives to the German Reichstag, transmitted through Minister Sargent in Berlin, expressing regret at the death of one of the Chancellor's political rivals. When Secretary of State Frelinghuysen attempted to appease ill feelings by recalling Sargent from Berlin, the *World* angrily rebuked him for his timidity. "Such an occasion demanded a message to the German government which would

[6] *World*, March 11, 1885, p. 4.   [7] *The Journalist*, July 19, 1884, p. 5.
[8] *World*, January 10, 1884, p. 4.

have sounded as a trumpet call and have sent a thrill through every heart which beats for liberty. . . . But flabby diplomacy wades through long, tortuous, meaningless sentences and sneaks through a hole it itself makes for its escape."⁹ It called upon "the American people . . . to drive from power an Administration cringing and cowardly in its foreign policy."¹⁰ Calmer voices, which argued that perhaps Bismarck was justified in resenting the resolution as an intrusion in Germany's domestic affairs, that in any case the matter had best be dropped, aroused the *World* to new fury. "The intense satisfaction betrayed by the *New York Times* over Bismarck's 'straight-faced mockery' of the American House of Representatives is worth noting. . . . There can be no doubt that the *Times* shares with Bismarck a feeling of loathing and contempt for the American Congress and the American people it represents."¹¹ A usually unoffending journal to the north set off still another explosion. "*The Boston Herald* advises the House of Representatives to calmly pocket Bismarck's insult," the *World* noted. "Bismarck has successfully bullied all Europe, but he will hardly be able to rub his fist under the nose of the entire United States without hearing the eagle scream."¹²

Although England and the Empire were a particular bane of the *World's*, they did not offer it frequent opportunities for bombast. It manufactured an occasion late in 1884, however, when Sir John MacDonald, the Prime Minister of Canada, proposed an imperial alliance between England, Canada and Australia as "a sort of police to keep the peace of the world and to league together for offense or defense in time of danger." On the whole, the *World* received the idea good-humoredly, but not without suggesting that the three English-speaking nations carefully weigh its merits. "We hope never to have the slightest difficulty with our amiable Canadian neighbor," an editorial declared. "But if such a necessity should be forced upon us, England would be very loath to send her regiments to Canada to be gobbled up by the Yankees. Besides, if ever there should be a disturbance of the friendly relations of the world, how mortified the great 'Im-

---

⁹ *World*, March 12, 1884, p. 4.
¹⁰ *World*, March 28, 1884, p. 4.
¹¹ *World*, February 23, 1884, p. 4.
¹² *World*, February 19, 1884, p. 4.

perial Alliance' would feel to see our government tuck one of its 'police' under its arm and carry it off to Yankeeland!"[13]

The great arena for jingoism during the late nineteenth century was not across the Atlantic, but south of the border, where a host of unstable governments offered rare opportunity for American economic and political penetration. A scarcely disguised racism, the assumption that some ill-defined superiority carried in the national bloodline, justified American efforts to make its influence predominant even in areas where the American flag did not fly. The *World* shared many of the symptoms of this expansive nationalism. An incident in Tampico, where Mexican authorities boarded an American vessel and lowered its flag because of alleged port violations, led the newspaper to offer a revealing prescription for dealing with the offenders. "If any Mexican greaser pulls down the American flag," it urged, "beat him over the head with the flag-staff!"[14] On another occasion it noted complacently that "duelling is looking up. Two Mexicans have actually succeeded in mutually slaughtering each other on the field of honor. This sort of thing should be encouraged—in Mexico."[15]

Jingoism and racism of this sort influenced much of the *World*'s comment on Latin America. Cuba, for example, was already marked out fifteen years before the sinking of the *Maine* as a likely prize to be seized in the name of manifest destiny. A recurrence on the island of insurrection against Spanish authority showed how quickly the journal could shift from relative pacifism to a stance more pleasing to the mass of its readers. On April 16, 1884, in one of its earliest comments on the subject, it carefully disclaimed any intention on the part of the United States of becoming involved in the struggle. "The people of the United States," an editorial declared, "feel but little interest in the revival of the troubles in Cuba. We naturally sympathize with any people struggling for their freedom, but we do not forget the American policy of minding our own business and avoiding foreign complications."[16] Its tone changed with the

13 *World*, December 20, 1884, p. 4.
14 *World*, May 7, 1884, p. 4.
15 *World*, March 24, 1884, p. 4.
16 *World*, April 16, 1884, p. 4.

very next issue. On April 17, responding to a rumor that Consul-General Badeau had resigned his position at Havana because Spanish authorities had insulted him when he protested the mistreatment of American citizens, the newspaper delivered the sort of ultimatum that would become more familiar in the days of McKinley. "This feeble Republic has been insulted by the Spanish robbers in Cuba for about fifteen years and it is almost time to put a stop to it."[17] In May and June it ran news stories announcing negotiations for the imminent sale of Cuba to the United States. THE SPANISH BANTLING TO BE TAKEN UNDER THE EAGLE'S WING, the headline on the first of those reports proclaimed.[18] When two Cuban newspapers which reprinted the articles found themselves suspended for twenty days, the *World* abandoned any pretense of neutrality regarding the future of that unhappy island. "It strikes us," the paper declared, "that when journals are not permitted to copy the *World*'s news with due credit it is time for a revolution. We are for Free Cuba from this time henceforth."[19]

Pulitzer's concept of a Free Cuba was not precisely what the Cubans themselves had in mind, for with his jingoistic response to real or imagined Spanish slights went an equally jingoistic concept of America's future in the Caribbean. By 1885, rumors abounded that the United States would purchase Cuba for $150,000,000. The publisher suspected jobbery in the transaction, and urged that the negotiations be suspended. He opposed the purchase as likely to enrich a combination of unworthy speculators, but added "that it is only a matter of time when Cuba will fall into our hands naturally, and that, too, without any great cost."[20]

Other countries south of the border also became objects of the *World*'s expansive nationalism. In Guatemala, a dictator named General Rufino Barrios had seized power, and was currently engaged in using the armed forces to bring Honduras, Costa Rica, Nicaragua and San Salvador into federation with his country. Again the *World* was initially inclined to a hands-off policy.

[17] *World*, April 17, 1884, p. 4.
[18] The stories appeared on May 21, 1884, p. 1; and June 4, 1884, p. 3.
[19] *World*, June 12, 1884, p. 4.
[20] *World*, May 8, 1885, p. 4.

Commenting on reports of bitter fighting between troops from Guatemala and San Salvador, the newspaper declared that it "is of no conceivable consequence to any one but those immediately concerned. . . . Least of all does it concern the people of the United States, who now have no Garfield Cabinet and no Secretary of State eager to muddle himself and his country by meddling in South American affairs."[21] Within days, the editorial tone changed. Secretary of State Bayard's assurance that the United States would not allow Barrios to jeopardize the life or property of American citizens, and speeches in the Senate accusing France of encouraging the Guatemalan dictator in order to forestall an American canal through Nicaragua, inspired the *World* to a more positive statement about this nation's rights and responsibilities in the troubled area. "It is evident," an editorial declared with prideful patriotism, "that our Government feels equal to a 'tussle' with the Guatemalan tyrant and that it will tolerate no nonsense at his hands."[22]

A rebel group in Panama, which threatened to obstruct transit across the Isthmus, received similar warning. "There will be no fooling about the matter," the *World* promised, "and the parties interested may as well make up their minds that every dollar's damage done to American property will have to be fully repaid."[23] The announcement that a contingent of marines would be sent to Panama to protect American investment there was greeted by the newspaper with rejoicing. Pulitzer must have realized that the military expedition benefited the same economic interests he fought so arduously at home, but nothing appealed more to the masses, and hence to the *World*, than an opportunity for aggressive patriotism. "Our marines who are ploughing to Panama may encounter fevers and malaria," the newspaper wrote, "but it is worth something to serve notice on mankind that the flag of the United States cannot be insulted with impunity even in a torrid climate."[24] Evidence that the contradiction disturbed Pulitzer appeared in an editorial two weeks later,

[21] *World*, March 13, 1885, p. 4.
[22] *World*, March 18, 1885, p. 4. The news article reporting the State Department's tough policy appeared in the same issue, on p. 2.
[23] *World*, April 5, 1885, p. 4.
[24] *World*, April 9, 1885, p. 4.

which drew an unconvincing distinction between jingoism and Jacksonian firmness. "Jingoism finds no favor with the present Administration," the *World* maintained. "But foreign powers will ascertain that when American interests are threatened or the rights of any American citizen, native or naturalized, are in question, there will be a Jacksonian promptness in applying a forcible and effective remedy."[25]

The *World*'s jingoism was predicated on a style of patriotism, unashamed and undiscriminating, which has largely disappeared in the twentieth century. Shortly after Pulitzer assumed control, the newspaper ran an article by ex-Lieutenant Governor William Dorsheimer describing his tour across the American continent. "No one who reads [the article], . . ." the newspaper declared in a separate editorial, "will thenceforth regard the most glowing tribute to the greatness of the American republic as boastfulness and self-glorification. . . . With such a picture before him, who can doubt the words of the song, that of all the nations of the earth the 'glorious Yankee nation is the greatest and the best?' "[26] That conviction encouraged the newspaper into such positions as predicting the imminent decline of tourism when Americans discovered the superiority of their own country over Europe. "In fifty years from the present the weight of fashionable travel will be from the other side."[27] It led to sober thoughts on the purity with which Americans spoke their language. "The best and purest English spoken anywhere in the world is in the United States. . . . English scholars of two centuries and more ago would find themselves perfectly at home in this country; but it is doubtful if Shakespeare would understand a line in one of his own plays if Irving were to read or recite the play."[28] Most notably, it inspired rhetoric which would be interpreted as satire were not the subject so sensitive. Replying to a reader who asked for an

[25] *World*, April 22, 1885, p. 4.

[26] *World*, May 21, 1883, p. 4. This is the same William Dorsheimer who was elected to the House of Representatives in 1884, and whose objections to a French canal through Panama were dismissed by the *World* as "Fourth of July style of oratory." See p. 214.

[27] *World*, March 30, 1884, p. 12.

[28] *World*, November 23, 1884, p. 4. The reference is to Sir Henry Irving, manager of the Lyceum Theatre in London, and leading man to Ellen Terry in many memorable Shakespearean productions. He was the first English actor to be knighted.

aesthetic judgment about the American flag, the *World* had this to say:

> There is no flag, banner, gonfalon or oriflamme in existence so beautiful as the ensign of the American Republic. Its colors are the most beautiful to be found in the rainbow. Its combination is aesthetic. Our flag is to all other flags what the rose is to the botanical kingdom and the eagle to the ornithological species. Our bosom not only swells with pride when we behold the emblem of our country, but our artistic sense is lulled to sweet repose.[29]

As often happens, extreme patriotism toward the mother country went together with xenophobic disdain for other countries. The *World* airily dismissed French pride in Voltaire, Rousseau, and Hugo as the great figures of modern literature, and symbols of national enlightenment, by noting that "[you can] expect to extract sunshine from a cucumber before you hope to dislodge this gross ignorance from the French cranium."[30] It announced Crown Prince Frederick William's state visit to Spain with the front-page headline, FRITZ'S COOL RECEPTION, only months before threatening Bismarck for his disrespect of the House of Representatives.[31] It referred to King Alphonso as a "pitiful little specimen of inherited rule" the year after delivering an ultimatum to Spanish authorities for their alleged insult of Consul-General Badeau in Havana.[32] Three days later the newspaper elaborated on the theme when it described the King as "a nonentity—brainless, characterless and worthless. . . . He is of doubtful paternity, and cannot even show a clean record of corrupt Bourbon blood. . . . Still he is a King, and, considering his origin and bad breeding, is 'as good as could be expected.' He might have been a tramp."[33]

Much the most popular target for ridicule was the British royal family and British institutions generally. Not even periods of national mourning restrained the *World* from its savage assaults. It referred to Victoria as "a Queen whose mind is tinged

[29] *World*, July 24, 1884, p. 4.   [30] *World*, April 27, 1884, p. 11.
[31] *World*, November 24, 1883, p. 1.
[32] *World*, January 15, 1885, p. 4.   [33] *World*, January 18, 1885, p. 5.

with melancholic madness over the loss of an offensive gillie" when she mourned the death of her son, the Duke of Albany.[34] The Duke's memory fared no better. "He was scrofulous, epileptic and paralytic, but the immediate cause of his death was a severe spree, which was quite too much for his frail frame and weaker brain."[35] The *World* pretended mock concern in March 1884, with the sudden death of Prince Leopold, Victoria's youngest son. "It will not be surprising," an editorial noted, "if the blow should aggravate the hereditary brain disorder which has been slowly manifesting itself in the Queen since Prince Albert's death."[36] As for Prince Leopold, "he was a wholly inconsequential personage, who with his royal descent inherited also unfortunately the taint that attaches to that scrofulous breed."[37]

The newspaper took a particular delight in the stories that circulated about Queen Victoria's strange relationship with her late body-servant, John Brown. During February 1884, it printed copious extracts from a recently published version of a diary she kept between 1862 and 1882, in which Brown figured prominently. On one occasion, when she confided in the diary her concern at a leg injury he had sustained, the *World* accompanied its text with line drawings of what the leg might have looked like.[38] The series also afforded opportunity for a snide comment on the aged Queen's morality. "If a widow in private life were to have the picture of her lusty manservant hung in her chamber and his statue erected before her window how busily scandal's tongue would wag. But, then, the Queen, despite her deplorably bad ancestry, is a very moral old lady, and nobody can say anything against her reputation."[39]

Other members of the royal family fared as badly. In an article headline A PRECIOUS LOT OF GOOD-FOR-NOTHING PRINCES AND DUKES, the *World* delivered the following judgments:

[34] *World*, October 7, 1883, p. 9.
[35] *World*, April 24, 1884, p. 4.
[36] *World*, March 29, 1884, p. 4.
[37] *World*, April 10, 1884, p. 4; see also March 30, 1884, p. 12.
[38] Extracts from the diary appeared in the *World* on February 12, 1884, p. 1; February 27, 1884, p. 5; and February 28, 1884, pp. 1-2. The illustrations appeared in the latter issue.
[39] *World*, October 8, 1883, p. 4. For a similar series of comments see February 28, 1884, p. 4.

> There are enough truths of a discreditable character to be laid at [the Prince of Wales'] door to disgrace the names of a dozen other men. . . . The Duke of Edinburgh . . . is cold, selfish and miserly. . . . His wife . . . is proud, arrogant and domineering. . . . The Duke of Cambridge . . . is the Commander-in-Chief of the British army. That he is utterly unfit for the position has been painfully demonstrated on more than one occasion, going back, indeed, to the Crimean War, when he showed the white feather in a way that would have ruined another man.[40]

The condemnations were part of a continuing series exposing what the *World* took to be the moral decadence of British aristocracy. A typical article bore the headline: ENGAND'S HOUSE OF LORDS. SPENDTHRIFTS, LIBERTINES, WIFE-BEATERS AND DRUNKARDS AS RULERS OF GREAT BRITAIN.[41]

Much of this venom can be explained in terms of the newspaper's larger crusade against privilege and pretension wherever it existed, in the United States as elsewhere. But the equal spirit with which the *World* rebuked Englishmen far from the seats of the mighty suggested that it had an xenophobic aspect as well. The London poor, for example, received little more respect than their titled compatriots. "If the New York poor could get clean, decent, healthy apartments at cheap rates," an editorial declared, "they would respect themselves and live in a decent manner. . . . But the London poor, even in a fairly habitable apartment, would stuff the broken windows with rags, lie on dirty straw and wallow in filth, gin and degradation."[42] The *World*'s judgments of British artists and writers was equally disparaging. A complaint from Oscar Wilde's mother that the American press had not treated her son fairly during his lecture tour of the United States evoked a bad-tempered reply from the paper:

[40] *World*, October 12, 1884, p. 10; another such article appeared on February 18, 1885, p. 4.

[41] *World*, January 13, 1884, p. 11. The British aristocracy was a favorite *World* target, as illustrated by articles and comments on September 30, 1883, p. 9; April 6, 1884, p. 11; September 28, 1884, p. 12; November 30, 1884, p. 19; December 5, 1884, p. 4; January 12, 1885, p. 4; and January 30, 1885, p. 9.

[42] *World*, February 24, 1884, p .4. See also September 29, 1884, p. 4; and June 23, 1883, p. 4; for variations on the same theme.

> Inasmuch as the divine sunflower apostle took several thousand dollars out of this country and left nothing but the memory of a very ugly young man with a profusion of hair, a wealth of cheek and an insane pair of legs, it would seem that he ought to feel like congratulating himself and that his ma ought to be happy. But naturally, having inflicted an injury upon us the family will never forgive us.[43]

The newspaper had greater hopes for Matthew Arnold. "If the gifted gentleman would only stay in America long enough and stop lecturing long enough to take a few lessons we would undoubtedly make a good practical, common-sense citizen of him, and he would sooner or later own a potato patch in Minnesota or Texas and be independent."[44]

However flippant on occasion, these statements do reveal a deep anglophobia, undoubtedly in part encouraged by Irish-American sensibilities, and in part by the shared language and institutions (as well as America's cultural dependence) which made British presence a constant and oppressive reality. The other countries of Western Europe did not become as much the objects of xenophobia because they were more remote. The dark suspicion with which the *World* greeted a proposal from Washington to lease dry dock facilities at Pensacola to the British Navy confirms that xenophobia, rather than heavy-handed bantering or dislike of aristocracy, was the operative word. "As this is the only Government dry-dock on our Gulf coast," an editorial declared, "we trust the Government will not permit its sale, at least to a power who may utilize it for docking warships to ravage our coast should possible complications arise from the Panama Canal matter."[45]

The last corollary of jingoism, implied by the word and revealed in the newspaper, was the willingness to accept war as a natural extension of diplomacy. Obviously, since violence was so often threatened, the thought of making good on the threat could not have been a fearful one. Although the United States was barely

---

[43] *World*, December 17, 1883, p. 4. For comments on British provincialism generally, see January 13, 1884, p. 4; January 18, 1884, p. 4; and July 16, 1884, p. 15.
[44] *World*, January 6, 1884, p. 4.
[45] *World*, March 10, 1884, p. 4.

one generation removed from its Civil War, a rising birthrate and expanding economic power encouraged an almost cavalier attitude toward further conflict. The *World* properly urged that all avenues be explored to reach a peaceful settlement when fighting threatened to break out in 1885 between England and Russia, but at the same time it betrayed utter lack of feeling for what war would mean in terms of suffering and death. Analyzing the implications of the impending struggle for the United States, it pointed out that "if war is inevitable the British Navy cannot proceed to pay its respects to the great Russian seaports too soon. And the sooner they are closed the better the price of American wheat."[46]

The jingoistic tone which pervaded so many of the newspaper's comments on foreign affairs is only one measure of its commitment to the biases and predilections of its readers. Even more typical than truculence toward foreign nations was the popular suspicion of intellectuality and scholarship at home. The masses of men tended to glorify common sense, which in turn meant that they tended to underestimate the possibility of uncommon wisdom, and to resent its claim to respect. The result was often anti-intellectualism, a disdain for qualities assumed to be either pretentious or un-American. Pulitzer's willingness to honor this bias, his statements on behalf of instinctive and practical wisdom over wisdom theoretical and abstract, determined as much as any other factor his right to serve as spokesman for the most numerous class of Americans.

That the *World* itself drew a distinction between the "we" and the "they," between uneducated wise men and overeducated fools, is clear from an editorial joshing the *New York Times* for cutting its price to two cents. It reprinted a comment from the *Denver Tribune* which argued that the reduction was a mistake since the *Times* appealed to a better class of people, and satirically agreed. "This is undoubtedly true," the *World* admitted. "Nearly all its readers are aristocratic people, . . . and it is necessary that they should understand Greek and Latin and be familiar with the classics in order to thoroughly appreciate the paper. . . . The drolleries of the [humorist] are usually pitched

[46] *World*, April 10, 1885, p. 4.

— 225 —

in such a lofty key that none but skilled collegians are able to drift along with him. . . . It should have raised its price to ten cents and put another encyclopedical Harvard College Graduate at work on the editorial page with a stylus."[47] Clearly, the conceits of those who knew a few phrases in a dead language, and happened to have memorized some irrelevant facts in a fancy college, were not enough to impress the tough-minded editors of Pulitzer's journal.

The *World*'s more practical attitude toward education was set forth in a series of editorials that discussed what learning was for, and how it should be pursued. They argued that the point of going to college was mainly to earn more money.

> The majority of the sensible students in any college will prefer the more liberal education which the *Transcript*—more justly than it intends—calls a "practical money-getting use." That is exactly what we educate the majority of our young men for—to prepare them for the successful, remunerative, practical pursuit of whatever profession or calling they may adopt. . . . For the coming active life colleges which now offer a truly liberal education extend advantages in the modern languages, the sciences and other elective studies, worth infinitely more than the old musty, monastic curriculum of bygone ages, precisely because they fit young men not merely for getting money, but for getting on successfully in whatever they undertake.[48]

Lest educators balk at this businesslike view of their responsibility, the *World* offered a cogent reminder of the reality that had invaded their ivy-covered citadels. "One thing is certain—and this practical view of a practical education should commend itself to the trustees, faculty and all who are interested in the success of any particular institution—those colleges which have adopted the enlarged and more liberal system of optional studies find a gratifyingly corresponding enlargement in the number of students."[49]

---

[47] *World*, September 30, 1883, p. 4. A similar disdain for intellectualism was apparent in the newspaper's reply to criticisms of its grammar. See, for example, December 1, 1884, p. 4; and January 24, 1885, p. 4.

[48] *World*, February 20, 1885, p. 4.

[49] *World*, March 1, 1885, p. 4.

The *World's* "practical view of a practical education," as opposed to learning for its own sake, determined its stand on all manner of academic questions. It urged in several editorials, for example, the wisdom of consolidating the colleges which were springing up throughout the country into a single college in each state, on the grounds that America did not need as many graduates as it turned out, and that the proliferation of degrees awarded annually served only to satisfy the vanity of those so honored. "The country is full of noodles and nobodies," the newspaper complained, "who tack D.D. or L.L.D. to the tails of their otherwise inconspicuous names, getting their warrant for doing so from colleges that are of no more importance than they themselves are. A single real college or university in each State would be sufficient."[50]

Much more pointed was the *World's* concern about exposing women to the rigors of philosophy and literature and other disciplines unsuited to the feminine mind. By its own standards the concern made sense, for so long as learning was not its own justification, but was valuable only in order to gain entry into the professions or to increase one's earning power, then women who looked forward to careers as wives and mothers would do better to devote themselves to cooking and sewing. Moreover, the immigrant groups in New York City who constituted so large a part of the *World's* audience, as well as lower class readers generally, were by and large those most resistant to female emancipation. Few spectacles offered greater cause for disquiet than that of young ladies leaving their homes to absorb "occult" doctrine in such places as Vassar, Radcliffe, and Mount Holyoke.

The newspaper's comment on the June commencement ceremonies at Vassar in 1884 deftly exploited these deep-felt prejudices. Fearing partly for the girls, and partly for the country, it wondered what would result when future mothers were taught to be scholars.

> There is something appalling in the amount
> of transcendental erudition which Vassar College
> poured out at its Commencement. A deep study of

[50] *World*, February 25, 1884, p. 4. For further editorials on the same subject, see October 17, 1884, p. 4; and January 29, 1885, p. 4.

Nihilism was made by sweet eighteen, and "Imagination in Mathematics" was the title of an address by a beautiful creature of nineteen summers. "Are physical and vital forces correlative?" asked a blushing damsel, and a ravishing creature in lawn discussed the sociological forecast of the Irish in America. We look in vain over the long list for an essay on the proper method of clothing children in fall and spring. There is not a single gleam of scientific knowledge shed upon the vexed problem of whose baking powder is safest, and one finds not a suggestion of how the great American pancake is to be successfully evolved.

We very much fear that these charming Hypatias will become gray at twenty with too much useless learning.

What does the country want? Girls who can reply to Henry George and Huxley? . . . Go to! We want sensible, intelligent wives and mothers, not transcendental philosophers.[51]

Its report on the commencement the previous June had been more hopeful, but only because it seemed then that the girls did not take their scholarly pursuits too seriously. A *World* correspondent returned from Poughkeepsie in 1883 with the good news that the typical member of the graduating class had no ambition beyond finding a husband and having children.[52] Not even the most determinedly anti-intellectual members of the community could find fault with such an attitude.

A similar distinction between useful knowledge and that which is effete and unnecessary colored the *World*'s statements on secondary school education. It strongly opposed, for example, a bill introduced in the State Assembly by Isaac L. Hunt to make physiology and hygiene compulsory courses in the public school system. The newspaper did not argue on pedagogic grounds, but simply pointed out that "the average infant of our day, as a rule, knows too much [already], either for his own good or the good of the country." It mocked the suggestion that the national welfare depended upon youngsters absorbing a multitude of unnecessary

51 *World*, June 13, 1884, p. 4.
52 *World*, June 17, 1883, p. 4. The visit is discussed on p. 170.

facts, and indeed questioned whether racial virility did not somehow depend upon maintaining a state of relative ignorance.

> Mr. Hunt . . . labors under the pleasing delusion
> that the more a small boy and a tender girl know
> about their assimilation, secretion and cellular tissue
> the better able they will be to uphold the palladium
> of our liberties. This is a hallucination on the part of
> Mr. Hunt. . . . The preservation of our inalienable
> privileges does not depend altogether on a knowl-
> edge of physiology. . . .
> To cram every department of human knowledge
> into the soft heads of the rising generation would be
> to convert the race into learned and sickly cranks.[53]

An editorial the following year called upon the Board of
Education to alleviate "the competition of scholars and the over-
stimulation and strain put upon them," which it claimed had
resulted in "anemic faces, neuralgic nerves and morbidly active
sensibilities of the pupils. . . ." The newspaper went on to warn
that "in many cases [children] have dwarfed all their vital functions in the development of their memories."[54]

With scant respect for scholarship as a good in itself, and alive
to the value of practical learning for practical ends, the *World*
could be expected to regard with favor that most practical of all
pursuits, vocational training. The first occasion for an editorial
statement came in September 1883, in commenting on the testimony of John Brewster, a businessman, before the Senate Committee on Labor and Education. Brewster had dismissed the
"theories" (a pejorative word used by the *World*) of the wit-
nesses who preceded him, and offered instead the "common
sense" view that "there should be less piano playing and more
practical instruction." The *World* heartily endorsed this view,
and praised Brewster for his distinguished performance before
the Committee. "The great trouble with the American people,"
it argued, "is want of discipline." Young women could do with
less instruction in the arts, and more in "sewing on a button or
darning a stocking." As for young men, "one means of meeting

[53] *World*, January 25, 1884, p. 4.
[54] *World*, March 30, 1885, p. 4.

[the] difficulty is to be found in the establishment of industrial schools. Early subjections to manual discipline, and the acquirement of the invaluable faculty of obeying and patiently waiting for slow results, are the advantages of an industrial education."[55] Of course the newspaper did not mean that all youth should be restricted to vocational training, but it implied that society had paid a heavy price for instilling useless knowledge in the minds of the young when they could be much better employed tending lathes and operating the machinery of industry.

Such a no-nonsense concept of learning was bound to have concomitants in the newspaper's judgments on art and literature. Then—as now—the last group to accept avant-garde movements in the arts, and the first to reject them as meaningless or obscene, was the group that had least place for the arts in its daily life. The *World*'s judgments of contemporary painters and authors reveal all the bias of an organ which spoke for those who distrusted scholarship as an ideal, and the art work valued by scholars as a fulfillment of the ideal.

A surprisingly large number of artists came under the newspaper's gaze. Thus, of America's foremost painter-in-exile, it noted that "the alleged artist, Whistler . . . amazes and amuses London as much by his crank sayings as he does by his queer combinations of color."[56] The country's most respected essayist was identified as "the late-lamented Billy Emerson, the minstrel."[57] As for the author of *Leaves of Grass*, the *World* remarked airily that "Walt Whitman may well congratulate himself upon the publication at Dresden of a translation of his alleged poems into German, since it may prompt some enterprising American to translate them into English."[58]

Such comments, while revealing, are also clearly attempts to inject humor into the otherwise arid pages of a too-serious newspaper. But humor ceased to operate, and with it whatever critical faculties the *World* possessed, when the editors responsible for

[55] *World*, September 30, 1884, p. 4.
[56] *World*, August 12, 1884, p. 4.
[57] *World*, July 6, 1884, p. 4.
[58] *World*, May 30, 1884, p. 4. In fairness, a year later the *World* ran a feature article on Whitman which was complimentary. See April 19, 1885, p. 19.

surveying literature detected immorality in the works they reviewed. Émile Zola's brand of realism proved a particular trial to the newspaper. "Zola is very fond of narrating how near he once came to absolute starvation," it remarked, "and some of the readers of his florid filth almost wish he had quite arrived."[59] In a more sober estimate several months later, the *World* reviewer hazarded that "Zola's mistake seems to be that he has undertaken to find his subjects in the slums of social and moral life, while he possesses the power to delineate its higher and nobler phases."[60] The newspaper could say no less while honoring the stern moral principles of its readers.

Mark Twain's *Huckleberry Finn* came in for much more severe criticism when it appeared early in 1885. The newspaper revealed most of its displeasure in a headline which read in part: WIT AND LITERARY ABILITY WASTED ON A PITIABLE EXHIBITION OF IRREVERENCE AND VULGARITY. It could not forgive the author for finding humor, or meaning, in the adventures of a bad boy, and seriously wondered whether Mark Twain's reputation could survive a work so obviously tasteless in concept, and slovenly in execution.

> Were Mark Twain's reputation as a humorist less well founded and established, we might say that this cheap and pernicious stuff is conclusive evidence that its author has no claim to being ranked with Artemus Ward, Sydney Smith, Dean Swift, John Hay, or any other recognized humorist. . . . *Huckleberry Finn* is the story (told by himself) of a wretchedly low, vulgar, sneaking and lying Southern country boy of forty years ago. . . . The humor of the work, if it can be called such, depends almost wholly on the scrapes in which the quartet are led by the rascality of the imposters. "Huck's" lying, the Negro's superstition and fear and on the irreverence which makes parents, guardians and people who are at all good and proper ridiculous. That such stuff should be considered humor is more than a pity. Even the author objects to it being considered literature. But what can be said of a man of Mr. Clement's [sic] wit, ability and position

[59] *World*, October 18, 1884, p. 4.
[60] *World*, February 22, 1885, p. 20.

deliberately imposing upon an unoffending public a piece of careless hack-work in which a few good things are dropped amid a mass of rubbish?[61]

The offense was serious enough for the *World* to make it the subject of a long editorial two weeks later. Noting complacently that the Library Committee of Concord, Massachusetts, had rejected the novel as "trashy and vicious," the newspaper warned Mark Twain that not even his popularity could survive many more Huckleberry Finns. "Mr. Clements [sic] has been fortunate," it declared, "in publishing several popular books, in some of which it has been hard to find anything approaching humor. . . . But nobody seems to have told 'Mark Twain' that no vein is so easily overworked and completely worked out as the vein of humor, especially when it comes to being forced fun or wit worked up to order. Perhaps 'Huckleberry Finn' is about to convey this valuable information for the first time to the heretofore sometimes humorous 'Mark Twain.'"[62] Once again the mentality which suspected art was deceived by its own suspicions into serious misapprehensions about the intent and achievement of the works it scrutinized.[63]

The *World*'s popular taste is revealed as much by the authors it praised as those it condemned. Victor Hugo was singled out on the occasion of his eighty-third birthday as the great man of contemporary letters, superior to Zola, Maupassant, Tennyson, Browning, Eliot, Meredith, Hardy, James, Twain. An editorial

[61] *World*, March 2, 1885, p. 7.

[62] *World*, March 18, 1885, p. 4. Other authors who became the objects of *World* wit or criticism were William Dean Howells (July 27, 1884, p. 4), Algernon Swinburne (November 9, 1884, p. 4), Alfred Lord Tennyson (December 3, 1884, p. 4), and Henry James (May 3, 1885, p. 23).

[63] It is also true, however, that Twain's masterpiece was received unfavorably in many quarters in 1885. Louisa May Alcott dismissed it by saying that "if Mr. Clemens can not think of something better to tell our pure-minded lads and lasses, he had best stop writing for them." (Quoted in Thomas Beer, *The Mauve Decade* [New York, 1926 (Vintage Books edition)], p. 25.) "We are glad to see that the recommendation to this sort of literature by its publication in the *Century* has received a check," the *Literary World* commented on hearing that the book had been banished by the Concord Library. (*Literary World*, XVI [March 21, 1885], p. 106). *Life Magazine* found it "coarse and dreary fun," while *Critic* reprinted an editorial from the *Springfield Republican*, terming it "no better in tone than the dime novels that flood the blood-and-thunder reading population." *Life Magazine*, V (March 12, 1885), p. 146; *Critic*, III (March 28, 1885), p. 155.

cited him "as leader in the successful war of the romanticists against the classicists," and added irrelevantly that he "is and always has been eminently a man of the people."[64] Still more revealing was the newspaper's praise for Mrs. Emma South-worth, which appeared in the same article that condemned Zola as a purveyor of filth. Noting with approval that "she has built up a well-earned fortune" from her forty-nine novels, the *World* found them to be "characterized by spirited movement, easy diction and well-constructed and dramatic plots."[65]

Literature, it seems, was to be judged by standards not too different from those applied to newspaper feature articles. It should tell a story, and in doing so use all the tricks of plot development and lively prose to hold the reader's attention. Just as important, if the story happened to deal with wickedness or immorality, it should be made a parable to show that the sinner is always bereft in his sinfulness. The standards were primitive, but not altogether blameworthy in a newspaper addressed primarily to men and women whose preference in reading, if they read at all, was for unsophisticated tales which diverted them temporarily from themselves.

A clear distinction must be drawn here between Pulitzer and the newspaper he published. Every evidence suggests that the man, despite his lack of formal education, was erudite, scholarly by temperament, and cultivated in taste. The newspaper, on the other hand, faithfully reflected in areas such as those just considered the biases of people doomed, by economics if not natural causes, to almost utter lack of erudition. And that is precisely the point. In seeking to address a mass audience, and to influence it in the direction of reform, the *World* had first to win the loyalty of that audience. It did so by becoming like the people it wished to lead. The newspaper and its readers ended by influencing each other, partly no doubt to their mutual benefit, partly perhaps to their mutual loss.

[64] *World*, February 26, 1885, p. 4.
[65] *World*, February 22, 1885, p. 20.

CHAPTER EIGHT

THE IMMIGRANT

Newspapers in the United States have generally been in-effective in leading social reform. This is partly explained by the fact that the press is better equipped to report "events"—a race riot, a strike, an act of violence—than to describe the social conditions which form the background and explain the reasons for those events. The result of reporting on the criminality of the poor, while ignoring the circumstances which make the poor turn to crime, is not likely to be crusading zeal. Moreover, as papers prosper they tend to become more removed from their readers, and hence less responsive to their needs. A publisher managing a property worth hundreds of thousands, or millions, of dollars, can only with difficulty imagine the problems and share the interests of the anonymous people whose pennies contributed to his fortune.

One of the most remarkable achievements of the *New York World* under Pulitzer is that it overcame those limitations, and championed as its own the men and women caught in the vortex of urban growth. Other newspapers also showed sporadic concern for the poor, but none so consistently and ardently as Pulitzer's *World*.[1]

The editor's strength lay in his recognition that success carried with it certain risks which might prove debilitating unless the individual took care to protect himself. In the fall of 1883 he soberly evaluated the testimony of a witness before the Senate Committee on Education and Labor, that "it is the general opinion of the laboring classes that the press of this country is subsidized by capitalists." Pulitzer denied the charge if it meant that most publishers could be persuaded by subsidy or bribe to

---

[1] It might be noted that Jacob Riis received his early training as a student of the slums while a reporter on the *New York Tribune* and later the *Evening Sun,* and that Lincoln Steffens graduated to other expressions of social protest after a stint on the *Evening Post.*

slant their journals' news coverage to suit a small moneyed group, but he conceded that the same result often came to pass in less sinister ways.

> It is a great misfortune that with all its enterprise, with all its ability, with all its honesty, the press of this city and of this country is not entirely on the side of the people in all great social questions. . . .
>
> But the personal influences of some rich proprietors are stronger than the claims of the people. Some proprietors and editors not only belong to the capitalist class, but are identified in sympathy and ideas not with the class from which they sprang, but with the class to which they have risen. We do not blame them for it too severely. They cannot help it. It is only human nature. Man is greatly controlled by his environment. His sympathies, affections, aspirations, are most directly influenced by those nearest him.

Recognizing the peril, Pulitzer refused to succumb to it. "There is one [paper in this city]," he concluded, "not controlled nor in any way swayed or influenced by the side of capital. . . . That is the *World*."[2]

Far from deferring to the rich, the newspaper adopted a set of principles that aligned it solidly with the depressed element in the city. The earliest announcement came on the first day of Pulitzer's ownership, in a statement over his signature which declared that "there is room in this great and growing city for a journal that is . . . dedicated to the cause of the people rather than that of the purse-potentates— . . . that will serve and battle for the people with earnest sincerity. In that cause and for that end the new *World* is hereby enlisted and committed to the attention of the intelligent public."[3] Pulitzer carefully distinguished in the same issue between independence and indifference. "An intelligent newspaper must be independent," he wrote. "But it must not be indifferent or neutral on any question involving public interests. If it is a newspaper with the people and for the people, it must maintain those broad principles on which universal liberty is based, and oppose those abuses and evils the destruction of which was the mission of free institutions."[4]

[2] *New York World*, September 9, 1883, p. 4.
[3] *World*, May 11, 1883, p. 4.   [4] *World*, May 11, 1883, p. 4.

The *World* did not pretend to be an impartial journal, for impartiality would suggest that all classes in the class-ridden society had equal power behind them, and presented their claims with equal justification. Aware that such was not the case, it chose to side with those who most needed help. "Its sympathies go out to the lowly rather than the Money Kings and watered millionaires and shoddy aristocracy. The many, however poor and humble, ought to prevail over the few, however rich and powerful." Such a credo carried with it an extensive commitment to crusade in a city only obliquely reflecting the American dream of unlimited opportunity for all. The *World* summarized its mission in the same editorial, demanding "justice and equal rights and privileges for all, of whatever color, class, race or condition."[5] Almost two years later, when Pulitzer had laid the foundation for his own fortune, he returned to this theme of the press's role in a free society.

> The *World* will continue to fight error, to vindicate truth, to expose frauds and shams, to protect the weak, to maintain the rights of all the people, to resist the abuses and aggressions of corrupting wealth and power, to expose demagogism, venality, fraud, and lawlessness—to give its readers a newspaper of honest, intuitive convictions, which in news, character and general tone shall not be excelled anywhere. . . . Our ambition is to make the *New York World* a newspaper possessing not only the greatest circulation and the greatest prosperity, but the greatest character of any journal published in the English language, and rendering the greatest public service to the people.[6]

This was not empty rhetoric, for Pulitzer believed (or so he professed) that the *World*'s devotion to principle had determined its stunning success in competition with older and more established dailies. He credited its large circulation in 1885 to the fact that "at the end of two years we can reproduce the promises we made to the public when we took charge of the *World*, with the

[5] *World*, December 7, 1883, p. 4.
[6] *World*, May 10, 1885, p. 4.

proud consciousness that we have fully and faithfully lived up to their spirit and their letter."[7]

The occasions for self-congratulation followed many months of crusading on behalf of the depressed classes who huddled in the manmade hell that was Manhattan below 14th Street. There were dozens of causes to be won—better housing, fairer working conditions, improved schools, hospitals, and social services—but none more fundamental than the right of all Americans, native and foreign-born, to take their place as equal members of the society. It was not a principle easily achieved. Most of the men and women who populated the city's slums, and who labored long hours in sweatshops and construction gangs to earn barely enough for subsistence, were either immigrants themselves, or the children of immigrants.[8] They had come to America as pilgrims, in search of a land of opportunity and freedom. Sometimes just the fact that they were foreign prevented them from completing the quest, for America was also a land suspicious of strangers. The *World*'s greatest crusade, and its most notable fulfillment of early promises, consisted in tendering welcome to the immigrants, and in urging their right to share in the privileges which earlier immigrants, ancestors of native America, had declared for all men.

Although an increasing number of the men and women who debarked during the 1880s came from hitherto unrepresented lands—Russia, Poland, Hungary, Italy—the transition from the "old" immigration to the "new" had not yet gone on long enough to bring the two into anything approaching numerical parity. Only about eighteen percent of the total immigration to the United States during that decade represented Catholics from Mediterranean countries, or Jews fleeing Czarist oppression. As

[7] *World*, May 10, 1885, p. 4. Pulitzer issued a similar statement in 1884, in response to a rumor that the *Herald* might drop its price to one penny. "We believe," he wrote, "that the principles of the *World* had more to do with its success than its price." See June 9, 1884, p. 4.

[8] Commissioner of Labor Carroll D. Wright estimated in his 1894 report on housing in four major cities that 95.23% of the inhabitants of slum buildings in New York City were either first or second generation Americans. Carroll D. Wright, *Slums of Baltimore, Chicago, New York, and Philadelphia*—7th Special Report, Commission of Labor (Washington, D.C., 1894); quoted in James Ford, *Slums and Housing*, 2 vols. (Cambridge, Massachusetts, 1936), I, 184.

the table below demonstrates, the bulk of the new arrivals continued to be Irishmen and Britons, Germans and Scandinavians.[9]

PERCENTAGE OF IMMIGRATION OF CERTAIN NATIONALITIES
TO TOTAL IMMIGRATION FOR SUCCESSIVE PERIODS.

	1831-1840	1841-1850	1851-1860	1861-1870	1871-1880	1881-1890	1891-1899
Irish	35%	46%	35%	19%	16%	12.5%	10.1%
British	13	15	17	26	19	14.5	9.7
German	25	25	37	34	26	28	15.5
Scandinavian				5	8	11	8.8
Russian and Polish						5	14.8
Hungarian						7	15.2
Italian						6	16.4

But to note that the immigrants of the 1880s shared roughly the same ethnic and cultural backgrounds as the original stock which populated the country is not to minimize the hostile, or at best, cool reception they received on arrival. The slogan "America for the Americans" long antedated the coming of southern Catholics and eastern Jews, who in later decades would feel its full force.[10]

Part of the reason for the mounting dislike of foreigners during the 1880s is simply that more of them were in evidence than ever before. The United States had experienced periods of great influx during the late 1840s, and again during the decade following the Civil War, but never on the scale seen by Pulitzer's generation. Prior to 1880 the number of total immigrants had reached 400,000 on only one occasion—in 1854—while in eight

[9] The chart appears in Robert W. DeForest and Lawrence Veiller, eds., *The Tenement House Problem*, 2 vols. (New York, 1903), II, 80. The same point emerges by listing the year of maximum immigration into the country for each national group.

Ireland 1851	Italy 1907
Germany 1882	Austria–Hungary 1913
Scandinavia 1882	Russia 1924
Great Britain 1888	

Information for the list is taken from U.S. Department of Commerce, *Historical Statistics of the United States* (Washington, D.C., 1960), Series C 88-114, pp. 56-57.

[10] Oscar Handlin makes the point that the great surge from southern and eastern Europe arrived many decades after Know-Nothingness as a political movement had spent its force. See Oscar Handlin, "The Immigrant and American Politics," in David F. Bowers, ed., *Foreign Influences in American Life* (Princeton, 1944), pp. 93-98.

of the following ten years the total soared considerably above that figure:

1881	528,545	1886	329,529
1882	648,186	1887	482,829
1883	522,587	1888	538,131
1884	453,686	1889	434,790
1885	353,083	1890	445,680[11]

Just as important, the majority of immigrants made New York City their port of arrival, which in turn meant that a considerable proportion tended to remain in the metropolitan area. The city's total of foreign-born residents rose by almost fifty percent between 1880 and 1890, by which time two out of five New Yorkers remembered a different land as their place of birth.

FOREIGN-BORN POPULATION IN NEW YORK CITY[12]

Place of Birth	1880	1890
England, Scotland, Wales	39,276	48,114
Ireland	198,595	190,418
Germany	163,482	210,723
Denmark, Norway, Sweden	5,183	10,139
TOTAL	406,536	459,394
Italy	12,223	39,951
Austria–Hungary	16,937	47,514
Russia and Poland	13,571	55,549
TOTAL	42,731	143,014
All Others	29,403	37,535
GRAND TOTAL	478,670	639,943

Add their children to the equation and the impact of immigration upon the city comes into focus.

A movement of such dimensions, demanding great adjustments on the part of natives as well as aliens, was bound to cause a certain degree of tension. While the individual immigrant may not have anticipated that he would live with the wisecrack, the snub, the calculated cruelty as the stuff of his daily existence, he could learn to bear them. Far more serious were the emotions which not even goodwill could dispel, and which finally lay at the

[11] *Historical Statistics of the United States*, Series C 88-114, pp. 56-57. The figures are adjusted to take account of those who emigrated back to Europe.
[12] The chart appears in DeForest *et al.*, *Tenement House Problem*, II, p. 83.

bottom of anti-immigrant sentiment. Workingmen feared that their jobs would be usurped, businessmen that their shops would be taxed out of existence by the O'Callaghans in City Hall (or perhaps blown up by radicals), racists that America would be mongrelized by castoffs from the gutters and alleys of Europe. In each case the fears were deeply felt and beyond easy assurance, the raw material for an atmosphere of hate.

The fact that the newcomers went directly from steerage quarters aboard ship to slum quarters ashore, as shown by the correlation between statistics on immigration and slums, made a bad situation even worse. According to Kate Claghorn's report for the New York State Tenement House Commission, Manhattan had 22,000 tenements with a population of 500,000 in 1881, 32,000 with a population exceeding 1,000,000 in 1888, and 40,000 with approximately 1,300,000 occupants in 1895.[13] The numbers by themselves are but a skeleton; considered in terms of flesh and blood they describe the rise of neighborhoods like Jew Town and Little Italy, spreading inexorably over the city, and so foreign that they almost seemed to flaunt their foreignness. To the nativists each slum building filled with human cargo just brought in from Europe was a personal affront, a reminder that the unwanted immigrants were among them. Each building refuted the Melting Pot myth, for how could the immigrants possibly learn the ways of the New World when they lived in ghettos which preserved all the ways of the Old? Not least, each building confirmed in its poverty what native America had long contended, that the immigrants were hopelessly European, for surely poverty could not be blamed on the land which had received them. "In the great 'dumbell' tenements," Allan Forman exclaimed in *American Magazine*, "in the rickety old frame buildings, in the damp, unwholesome cellars, on the sidewalks and in the gutters reeking with filth and garbage, is a seething mass of humanity, so ignorant, so vicious, so depraved that they

[13] Kate Claghorn, "Foreign Immigration and the Tenement House in New York City," *The Tenement House Problem*, II, 77-78. Corroboration for her report comes from the New York State Tenement House Commission of 1884, which estimated 26,000 tenements in the city that year. Cited in Ford, *Slums and Housing*, I, 179.

hardly seem to belong to our species. Men and women; yet living, not like animals, but like vermin!"[14]

As the immigrants lived apart, so did they work apart. Whether the example be the Italian and his padrone, the Jew and his sweater, the Irishman, the German, the Swede, most of them left domestic ghettos at dawn to earn their bread in a commercial ghetto. They generally worked among their own people, for foremen who had only preceded them to America, in a language they had brought from Europe. Contact on a larger scale between the old Americans and the new might have helped to dispel the fears which feed on ignorance, but the city's increasing compartmentalization by nationality prevented it.

Although native laborers shared the prejudices of the rest of the community, they had a personal reason for distrusting the presence of foreigners. Immigration meant cheap labor, and cheap labor meant unemployment (or so it seemed) for men who could not or would not work for substandard wages. H. H. Boyesen, himself an immigrant from Norway, characterized the imported workers as "a disturbing element, an unexpended surplus in the labor market which unsettles all economic relations."[15]

Union leaders who successfully petitioned Congress to abolish contract labor, and who tried unsuccessfully to stiffen immigration requirements, admitted that the real wages of American labor had steadily risen, if slowly. But they argued that the improvement was only a small part of what could have been, and, more important, that because of immigration, labor had not gotten its fair share of the increasing national wealth. Industrial development in the postbellum period had provided palaces for Rockefeller and Carnegie, and shanties for their workmen.

Still other groups, usually professional men with a strong sense of national heritage, worried about the impact of aliens upon American institutions. The fears expressed in newspaper and

[14] Allan Forman, "Some Adopted Americans," *American Magazine*, xv (November 1888), 48.

[15] H. H. Boyesen, "Dangers of Unrestricted Immigration," *Forum*, iii (July 1887), 533-34. See also Washington Gladden, "The Problem of Poverty," *The Century*, xlv (December 1892), 245-56.

magazine articles about the political power of the Irish in large cities offers a case in point. Responsible men agreed with Lord Bryce's observation, that "the government of cities is the one conspicuous failure of the United States," and did not hesitate to ascribe a reason.[16] "Let it be borne in mind," a letter reprinted in *Littell's Living Age* warned in 1886, "that nearly the whole two million of Irish now in the United States reside in the cities and towns, where they can most easily organize and bring their strength to bear on American politics and obtain offices and party spoils. . . . They are notoriously the most active, elbowing, pushing, grasping politicians in our country."[17] Or as John Paul Bocock put it, much more succinctly: "New York has ceased to be an interesting study for municipal experts. It is clean given over to Irish domination."[18]

Part of the reason for objecting to power in the hands of Irishmen or other immigrant groups was the fear that they would use it to impose unfair taxes on property owners. "Having secured the taxing power," the same letter in *Littell's Living Age* maintained, "their constant effort everywhere is to increase the 'rates' on the taxpayers, in order to raise [municipal] salaries higher, and find places for more Irish office-holders. A constant struggle is going on in all our Northern cities between the American taxpayers and the Irish 'tax-raters,' as they are usually called, and it is a struggle for existence on the part of the American element."[19]

Native America suspected also that religion disqualified Catholics from participating in the democratic process, since Roman thought had little in common with American thought. The great spokesman of Main Street and Sagamore Hill, who mirrored so faithfully the tensions and aspirations of the group that produced him, expressed his concern in private comments to a friend. "The Catholic Church," Theodore Roosevelt said, "is

[16] James Bryce, *The American Commonwealth*, 2 vols. (revised ed.; New York, 1891), I, 608.

[17] "Power of the Irish in Cities," *Littell's Living Age*, LVI (November 6, 1886), 383.

[18] John Paul Bocock, "The Irish Conquest of Our Cities," *Forum*, XVII (April 1894), 188. See also Henry Childs Merwin, "The Irish in American Life," *Atlantic Monthly*, LXXVII (March 1896), 289-301.

[19] "Power of Irish in Cities," p. 383.

in no way suited to this country and can never have any great permanent growth except through immigration, for its thought is Latin and entirely at variance with the dominant thought of our country and institutions."[20]

If middle class Protestants worried about the dual loyalty of Catholic immigrants, a loyalty divided between Pope and country, businessmen somewhat inconsistently worried about the radicalism of those same immigrants. A few scraps of anarchist literature, together with a bomb at Haymarket Square or a demonstration by twenty or thirty bearded zealots at Union Square, convinced the fearful that the republic was in peril. And always the blame fell on immigrants. The myth of wild-eyed foreigners debarking at Castle Gardens, petitions in one hand and bombs in the other, achieved wide currency during the 1880s. *Puck*, for example, published a double-page cartoon on May 11, 1887, entitled "The Evolution of the Anarchist." The first frame showed the immigrants as they arrive, quiet men with hands clasped in prayer, thanking God for delivering them to America. The second—"As We Find Him Six Months Later" —had them demonstrating at an anarchist rally, arms waving and hair askew. "Down with the beasts of law and order!" the sign on their podium read. "Down with Government. Anarchist Group No. 101. Meeting Every Sunday. Free Beer!"[21]

Even the arts recognized a moment for patriotism. Thomas Bailey Aldrich composed "Unguarded Gates" in 1892, and explained why in a letter to George E. Woodberry.

> I went home and wrote a misanthropic poem called "Unguarded Gates" . . . in which I mildly protest against America becoming the cesspool of Europe. . . . My Americanism goes clean beyond yours. I believe in America for the Americans; I believe in the widest freedom and the narrowest license, and I hold that jailbirds, professional murderers, amateur lepers . . . and human gorillas generally should be closely questioned at our Gates. Or the "sifting" that

[20] Quoted in Charles and Mary Beard, *The Rise of American Civilization*, 2 vols. (New York, 1927), II, 399-400.

[21] Charles Jay Taylor, "The Evolution of the Anarchist," *Puck*, XXI (May 11, 1887), pp. 180-81.

was done of old will have to be done again. . . . Rud-
yard Kipling described exactly the government of
every city and town in the . . . United States when he
described that of New York as being "a despotism of
the alien, by the alien, for the alien, tempered with
occasional insurrections of decent folk."[22]

Incipient racism, not so fully developed as it would be in the
next decade, but still unmistakable in form and import, also
contributed to the bedevilment of the immigrant. The middle
class proved to be highly receptive to ideas about the special
virtues and responsibilities of the Anglo-Saxon, perhaps (as historians have suggested) because they offered a welcome anchor
for men and women who had just experienced the upheavals at-
tendant upon industrialization.[23] This meant evil tidings for the
immigrants, for if God intended the American people to be colo-
nizers because He made them racially pure, then it followed that
those who did not partake of such purity must forever be out-
casts. The same suppositions which a decade later justified the
United States keeping the Philippines first turned inward to condemn the newcomers. In 1889 the weekly *America* expressed the
fears of many when it decried "the pollution of our national lifeblood by the stream of ignorance, misery and vice pouring into it
from the lowest strata of European life."[24]

[22] The letter, written on May 14, 1892, is quoted in Vernon Louis Parrington,
Main Currents in American Thought, 3 vols. (New York, 1927, 1930), III,
58-59. Aldrich's poem expressed the same sentiments more grandly. It begins:

> Wide open and unguarded stand our gates,
> And through them presses a wild motley throng—
> Men from the Volga and the Tartar steppes,
> Featureless figures from the Hoang-Ho,
> Malayan, Scythian, Teuton, Kelt, and Slav,
> Flying the Old World's poverty and scorn;

The last lines are presumably prophetic:

> Have a care [he is addressing "Liberty, White Goddess!"]
> Lest from thy brow the clustered stars be torn
> And trampled in the dust. For so of old
> The thronging Goth and Vandal trampled Rome,
> And where the temples of the Caesars stood
> The lean wolf unmolested made her lair.

[23] The "status revolution" thesis is expounded most notably in Richard
Hofstadter, *The Age of Reform; From Bryan to F.D.R.* (New York, 1955),
particularly Chapter Four.

[24] *America*, I (March 28, 1889), 3.

It was but a short step from condemning immigrants for what they were, to condemning them for what they believed. Thomas Beer shed his typical good humor to describe a flotilla of "titanesses" descending upon one of Grover Cleveland's assistants to secure Presidential approval for a bill excluding Catholics from West Point and Annapolis.[25] The example is more than matched by incidents out of Joseph Pulitzer's career. Leander Richardson's vendetta against the publisher, already referred to, resulted in expressions of anti-Semitism unknown today outside of the sewers of subterranean hate literature. "He is a smart businessman because he is a Jew," Richardson conceded, "and has the commercial instincts of his race very sharply developed within him."[26] But the fact of his Jewishness mocked Pulitzer's position on Park Row, and suggested where he more properly belonged. "As a business manager of a clothing establishment somewhere in the direct vicinity of Chatham Street, Jewseph Pulitzer would be an honor to his race and a glory to his surroundings."[27] The owner of the *World* did not have to imagine the plight of immigrants in a hostile America; he was an immigrant himself, and of a background more scorned than most.[28]

This is not to say that by their very presence the newcomers became a target for calumny and abuse. It was a subtler pressure most of them faced, compounded partly out of the very fact of being alien and alone, partly out of the assumed superiority of native Americans toward anyone different, partly out of poverty,

[25] Thomas Beer, *The Mauve Decade* (New York, 1926), p. 145.

[26] *The Journalist*, August 16, 1884, p. 5.

[27] *The Journalist*, November 8, 1884, p. 5. See *ibid.*, July 12, 1884, pp. 1-2, for a longer, and much more vicious, torrent of anti-Semitic abuse.

[28] The result of dozens of such articles, spewing out filth and mistaking it for criticism, was an order from David Sutton, the city editor, banning *The Journalist* from the *World* offices. Leander Richardson took note of the directive, and found it not only an imposition on men's right to read what they pleased, but "foolish and silly" besides. Mr. Sutton, he declared, "has given orders that nobody shall be allowed to bring a copy of this paper into the *World* office on pain of dismissal, and he has otherwise shown a disposition to quarrel with *The Journalist*. Aside from the fact that Mr. Sutton has no right whatever to say what his reporters shall or shall not read, his conduct is foolish and silly in several other directions. This course is occasioned simply by the fact that *The Journalist* has upon certain occasions spoken rather briskly of Jewseph Pulitzer and his personal and business methods. Mr. Sutton hopes by excluding *The Journalist* from the *World* office to curry favor with his master." *The Journalist*, January 3, 1885, p. 4.

and partly out of uncertainty as to how to improve their condition. They needed a champion, and at a time when few were willing to enter the lists, the *World* came forward. The timing of its support, as much as the support itself, is what endeared it to the tens of thousands of people who asked nothing more dramatic than the right to be accepted on their own merits.

The newspaper did even more, for its humanity was combined with a peculiar acceptance of the immigrants' own prejudices. More than one observer has noted that the individual ethnic groups, prey to bigotry themselves, become some of the most outspoken bigots against others (in the manner of Studs Lonigan and his Irish gang in Chicago, who waylaid Jewish boys and paid them back for "killing Jesus"). The Irish looked down on the Germans; the Germans looked down on the Italians; the Italians looked down on the Jews; and presumably the Jews looked down on all of them. The *World*'s pro-immigrant sentiment embraced all nationalities, but not without consideration for their respective numbers and influence. It had far more good to say about Irishmen and Germans, for example, people numerous enough to be worth cultivating, than about Italians and Slavs. The newspaper's relatively jocular attitude toward the "new" immigrant groups, who were still a decade away from challenging the supremacy of the "old," endeared it all the more to the O'Callaghans and Schmidts.

Basic to its position, the cavilling comments about particular nationalities notwithstanding, was a strong sense that America owed its vitality to the infusions of blood it had received from many different lands. "Our greatest merit," an editorial declared, "as it should be our greatest boast, is that we have assimilated all that is vital from every available stock, and, utterly disregarding the class distinctions of the past, have given Nature a new freedom to work out a new race. . . . What [the immigrants] bring us is strong blood and unlimited possibilities."[29] A report that 1,500 people had arrived the previous day at Castle Gardens caused the newspaper to exult. "They were sturdy Belgians, Englishmen, Scotchmen, Welshmen, and Irishmen with their families,

[29] *World*, January 27, 1884, p. 4.

promising to add good healthy blood to our population. . . . Such additions to our numbers are welcome."[30]

Convinced that immigration was a blessing, the newspaper responded strongly to the proposals of those who would limit its scope or effect through various legal devices. It attacked a court decision which delegated to the Commissioners of Immigration the authority to determine which individuals or families were to be regarded as "paupers," and so sent back on the steamships that brought them.[31] The *World* stated that it did not trust the discretion of the Commissioners to make such a decision.

> We do not intend to let English and Irish parishes ship to our shores their chronic paupers who are unable to support themselves. But we recognize no man as a pauper here who has the power and the will to work for a living. He may land on our shores with his passage paid by his government and without a dollar in his pocket to buy a meal or pay for a lodging. But if he has the God-given capital of a sound constitution, a stout arm, brains in his head and honor in his heart, he is welcome to the Republic, free to labor for a living and entitled at the proper time to the equal rights guaranteed to all citizens by the Constitution.[32]

Movements to stiffen the qualifications for citizenship received no more sympathy. The *World* derided General Grant's suggestion, that immigrants be required to "speak and write the English language" and prove a sound moral character before they achieve citizenship, as a denial of American principle, as well as a formula for bureaucratic anarchy. "If knowledge of the English language is to be a *sine qua non*," an editorial asked, "why not offer a premium to have the language spoken with grace and elegance?" The second proposal raised a still more cogent question. "What is to be the precise moral stand for the foreign-born gentleman who desires to begin the process of voting along with Negroes and native-born imbeciles? . . . It would be unfair to establish a constitutional test of morals, and yet if the matter were left to localities a social leper might slip into citizenship

30 *World*, May 7, 1884, p. 4.
31 *World*, August 4, 1884, p. 4.
32 *World*, June 27, 1883, p. 4.

in Colorado who would be utterly loathed in the pious, piney sections of Vermont."[33]

In welcoming all immigrants to America, the *World* responded angrily to those who would distinguish between them, and deny some because of their religion. A letter from a subscriber in Asbury Park, New Jersey, protesting the publication of an illustrated article on the Catholic Church, with twelve cuts of prominent clergymen, was answered in scornful style.[34] "This is a fine exhibition of bigotry," an editorial declared. "Three weeks ago the *World* printed an entire page of portraits of the eminent Protestant divines of this city. We received no protest from Catholic readers. The *World* has no prejudices. . . . It is a pity that the intelligent gentleman at Asbury Park doesn't possess some of our charity and fairness."[35] The paper rebuked with equal vehemence arguments circulating just prior to the national party conventions which dismissed General William Sherman as a candidate for the Republican nomination because his wife was a Catholic.[36]

The newspaper's great opportunity for crusading against religious bigotry, while at the same time undermining the fortunes of a political enemy, came at the height of the Cleveland–Blaine contest. Throughout the summer of 1884 a series of articles appeared, prominently displayed, recounting James Blaine's complicity in the Know-Nothing movement in Maine during his period as editor of the *Kennebec Journal*, and his probable responsibility for the Madrigan circular, an anti-Catholic tract mailed to Protestant voters in the Fourth District of Maine during the election of 1875, which was instrumental in defeating the candidacy of James Madrigan for Congress.[37] Simply to associate

[33] *World*, May 9, 1884, p. 4.

[34] In fact there were two such articles: March 16, 1884, p. 1, with portraits of twelve Catholic priests; and March 23, 1884, p. 9, with ten more portraits. Both articles appeared in the Sunday edition.

[35] *World*, March 26, 1884, p. 4. The exchange illustrates one of Pulitzer's favorite techniques. He would print a letter expressing sentiments opposite to his own—often expressing them badly—then use the editorial columns to reply.

[36] *World*, March 14, 1884, p. 4.

[37] The articles and editorials included evidences of Blaine's participation in the Know-Nothing movement (August 13, 1884, p. 5; and September 16, 1884, p. 4); recitals of what the movement stood for (July 27, 1884, p. 4; and July 28, 1884, pp. 1, 4); instances when contempt for foreigners had also

the Republican candidate with the policies and methods of the Know-Nothing movement was condemnation enough.

The joint crusade against religious intolerance and Blaine's candidacy reached a climax on October 30, 1884, with the first report of the Reverend Dr. Burchard's ill-advised reference to "Rum, Romanism and Rebellion." Although Blaine organs like the *Tribune* and *Herald* tried to minimize the damage by pretending that the incident never happened, the *World*'s loud and repeated protests defeated their conspiracy of silence. "Mr. Blaine and his friends," an editorial on October 30th charged, "in their eagerness to clutch at every chance of making political capital, have not hesitated to inflame religious prejudice and to drag creeds into politics. . . . The offense is the more serious because the insult came from a minister of the Gospel."[38] Subsequent news stories and editorials, which ran to Election Day, took special pains to keep the remark foremost in the consciousness of Irish voters. CATHOLIC CLERGYMEN INDIGNANT, a headline blared, while editorials repetitiously reminded just who had been insulted.[39] "The party of Fraud, Fanaticism and False Pretense, which in the eleventh hour of the campaign thus exposes its bigotry and intolerance, has been striving to win Democrats of Irish nationality to its candidate, and has been pinning its hope of success on the 'defection' of Catholics from the Democracy. Will the People submit to this insult?"[40]

The fact that Blaine's mother and grandmother had both been Catholics made it more difficult to tar him with the brush of anti-Catholicism, and encouraged the *World* to contribute its own dirt to a notably dirty campaign. Just as it had earlier used innuendo to suggest that Blaine's marriage to his wife had been a shotgun affair, printing all the details only after the story broke in the *Indianapolis Sentinel*, it maintained a pose of rectitude while

---

brought Know-Nothings into contempt for the law (August 28, 1884, p. 4, for a discussion of the Madrigan circular; and September 8, 1884, p. 8, for a report on how Maine Know-Nothings assaulted a Catholic priest); and philosophizing about the implications of the movement in a democratic society (July 19, 1884, p. 4; August 7, 1884, p. 4; and July 29, 1884, p. 4).

[38] *World*, October 30, 1884, p. 4.

[39] The headline appeared on November 3, 1884, p. 7.

[40] *World*, October 31, 1884, p. 4.

repeating gossip about the candidate's rejection of his grand-mother's religion. A headline which had appeared in a Waynes-burg, Pennsylvania, newspaper was reprinted in a prominent place for *World* readers to contemplate. BLAINE'S INGRATITUDE. TREATS HIS GRANDMOTHER GILLESPIE'S REMAINS, INTERRED AT WAYNESBURG, WITH CONTEMPT, ON ACCOUNT OF HER BEING A CATHOLIC. Having delivered the gossip, the newspaper sancti-moniously cleansed itself in the very next sentence. "We have not read the article, do not feel attracted to it and will not re-publish any matter of that sort."[41] A similar attempt to take the journalistic highroad while stirring up the Catholics of New York City occurred earlier in the summer, when the *World* innocently reported the denial of a Congregational minister, which appeared in a letter to the *Tribune*, that Blaine had at any time as an adult worshiped in the Roman Church. "The reverend gentleman . . . says that James G. Blaine 'has never been a Catholic since coming to man's estate,' and adds: 'If as a little child he took his mother's hand and walked with her to church, why there is a good Protestant day of judgment coming which will no doubt purify as by fire the touch of that mother's hand.' "[42] The newspaper had found for itself a Burchard from the north woods, and could piously mouth the hope that "after this . . . the question of Mr. Blaine's religion will be dropped," knowing all the while that the opposite was inevitable. The response came three days later in a letter from an irate subscriber. "Of all the cowardly, villainous, blasphemous statements I have ever read this caps the climax. A Catholic mother's 'touch' to require the fire of judgment day, and of a Protestant judgment day, too, whatever that is! I verily be-lieve that if the *Tribune* thought it necessary for Blaine's success in the coming election, it would stab that mother in the dark."[43] The *World* felt now justified in reminding its readers in several editorials that "Mr. Blaine was silent under this insult to his mother's religion."[44]

Hopefully, such condemnations of James G. Blaine could be

[41] *World*, October 1, 1884, p. 4.
[42] *World*, June 27, 1884, p. 4.
[43] *World*, June 30, 1884, p. 4.
[44] See, for example, the *World*, October 31, 1884, p. 4, from which the quotation cited comes.

translated for the foreign-born into larger condemnations of Republicanism as a movement. A letter from a Republican with the wonderfully appropriate name of Elihu B. Winthrop provided one opportunity. "I shall not quarrel with you at all," Mr. Winthrop wrote, "if you convince your Irish friends that it is their duty to remain with the Democracy, for that is where they properly belong. . . . I will say frankly that I am not friendly to the Irish mob, and I would prefer to see the Republican Party get along without it. The moment we admit it into our ranks that moment we lower the standard of the Republican Party and give encouragement to what I believe to be an uncongenial and dangerous element."[45] Of course the point of singling this letter out for publication, among hundreds received daily, was its usefulness as a vehicle for rebuttal, and as a base upon which to make broad judgments about the nature of the Democratic and Republican Parties.

> Mr. Winthrop—whose name has a Puritanical resonance—doubtless represents a large percentage of the intolerance and bigotry of the Republican Party when he says that he does not like the idea of Irishmen voting for Blaine. . . .
> Every intelligent foreigner knows that the Democratic Party is the party of equal rights. It has bravely stood always as a barrier between the foreign-born citizen and the wrath of the "Native American." It has protected him from the Republican intolerance which seeks ever to curtail his liberties, regulate his personal habits and prescribe his religion. . . . Sensitive Irishmen are not likely to ally themselves with an organization largely controlled by elements which deride, condemn and insult them. They would hardly feel at home in the company of Mr. Winthrop and his "holier than thou" associates.[46]

The pro-immigrant views of the *World* had a positive as well as negative aspect. More than merely refuting the charges of those who deplored the presence of foreigners on American soil, more even than manipulating evidences of prejudice to the advantage

[45] *World*, August 23, 1884, p. 4. Mr. Winthrop so ideally suited the *World*'s purposes that one may well wonder whether the newspaper created him.
[46] *World*, August 27, 1884, p. 4.

of the Democratic Party, the *World* self-consciously took sides with the newcomers on the issues that concerned them. Unlike the righteous reformers of the middle class just starting to descend on the slums, for example, the newspaper saw no reason to impose prohibition on people who did not share the Puritan dread of drink.[47] "Intemperance is a great evil," an editorial admitted. "But Prohibitionism is no cure. As a remedy it is worse than the evil itself. It is unconstitutional, revolutionary, fanatical; it crushes the rights of the minority; it is destructive of liberty and true self-government."[48] The issue proved to be a stout weapon against Blaine during the campaign of 1884, since the candidate had avoided taking a stand on the prohibition law in his own state and in the other Republican strongholds of Kansas and Iowa. The *World* strived mightily to convince foreign-born voters in the city that the Grand Old Party was also a party of dries.[49] "Its insolent assumption of a superior morality up to the standard of which it desires to bring the habits, appetites and even the amusements of the people by oppressive sumptuary legislation, are in our opinion the worst features of that now thoroughly corrupt organization."[50]

The right to imbibe freely became something more than an academic issue for New Yorkers in 1885 when Mayor William Grace disapproved legislation by the Board of Aldermen, allowing beer to be sold on Sundays between 10 A.M. and 2 P.M. The *World* spoke on behalf of the tenement house population generally, but more specifically on behalf of the immigrants who did

[47] This is not meant to imply that anti-prohibitionism was solely, or even primarily, a workingman's cause. Professor Julian S. Rammelkamp of Albion College, to whom I am indebted for a close and perceptive reading of this manuscript, notes that the *St. Louis Post-Dispatch* campaigned just as ardently against prohibition as the *New York World*. It would distort logic to suggest that the *Post-Dispatch* was to that extent a working class organ. The campaign in St. Louis is better described as a middle class gesture on behalf of property rights, since a victory for the "dries" would have wreaked havoc upon the St. Louis brewing industry. The point is not whether other groups shared the feelings of the tenement house population about prohibition—as of course they did—but whether the *World's* stance put it squarely on the side of the poorest people on an issue that concerned them.

[48] *World*, September 25, 1884, p. 4.

[49] See, for example, the *World*, August 18, 1884, p. 4; and August 23, 1884, p. 4.

[50] *World*, August 30, 1884, p. 4.

not concede immorality in drink, when it disputed Grace's authority to reserve Sunday mornings exclusively for worship. "Strict Sabbatarians," it declared, "who enjoy their warm firesides, their good dinners, their fine wines and the playing and singing of their family and friends on Sunday evenings have no just right to say that the workingman who labors all the week shall not be allowed to enjoy his beer and music in a public garden on the only day of the week not given up to toil."[51]

Sabbatarianism as a broader issue also found the newspaper on the side of those who did not share the Protestant custom of immunizing the day from all pleasures. "The sum and substance of all the remonstrances is that Sunday is held by certain classes to be a sacred day in a purely ecclesiastical sense, and therefore all other classes should be deprived of the recreation and pleasures that they can only obtain on that day; and this is not a winning argument in such a metropolis as ours in the nineteenth century."[52] It urged not only that museums and other cultural places be open for those who wished to attend them on the Sabbath, but that the individual be allowed to decide for himself whether to engage in such broader pleasures as sports or outings. "The Sabbatarian who wants to shut himself up in his house all Sunday has a right to do so," the *World* declared. "He has no right to insist that his neighbor shall do the same thing."[53]

The newspaper most clearly defined its sensitivity to immigrant needs, and distinguished itself from the ordinary run of middle class reformers, by opposing that shibboleth of nineteenth century liberalism, competitive civil service examinations.[54]

[51] *World*, February 3, 1885, p. 4. At the same time, the newspaper did endorse a bill under discussion in the Missouri Legislature requiring that instruction on the evils of alcohol and nicotine be provided in the schools. "In this way what ill-advised fanatical reformers vainly attempt to accomplish by force may come about naturally in due time through popular education." *World*, February 20, 1885, p. 4.

[52] *World*, July 22, 1884, p. 4.

[53] *World*, December 31, 1883, p. 4. See also December 24, 1883, p. 4; July 6, 1884, p. 4; and May 8, 1885, p. 7.

[54] Again a word of caution is in order. Of course foreign-born Americans were not the only ones to resent the emphasis of the patrician reformers upon civil service reform. It was a form of elitism, contrary to the Jacksonian vision of democracy, and bound to weigh heavily upon any man who had not completed a high school education. Eric Goldman notes, for example, that the Populists who convened in Omaha in 1892 had little use for the reform, since

Clearly, if government positions were to be assigned on the basis of written tests, so that a man's knowledge of such subjects as composition, civics, and history determined his fitness for service, all but the most alert or privileged immigrants would find themselves critically handicapped. However admirable in concept, civil service examinations carried a built-in bias which the *World* could not accept.

> We favor real, genuine Civil-Service Reform as heartily as the Governor, the *Boston Herald*, or the most profound mugwump in existence. But we call the competitive examination hobby an unwholesome excrescence on real Civil-Service Reform which ought to be dropped. . . .
>
> The high offices in the Government are not subject to "competitive examination." But the subordinates —clerks, messengers, letter carriers and scrubwomen —must undergo a school-room ordeal. Is this Democratic? Is it just? Is it common sense? Does it fit the framework of a Republican government?[55]

This was an embarrassing position to take, for the newspaper could hardly reject the underlying principle without lending comfort to the political machines all reformers were expected to abhor. It equivocated by denying that it opposed every sort of competitive examination. "On the contrary, we desire that every candidate for public office shall be very thoroughly examined as to his fitness for the duties he seeks to undertake. Only the examination should be practical and sensible, not 'literary' and theoretical. . . . If we needed a porter to lift heavy loads we should measure the breadth of his shoulders and not the capacity of his brain."[56] The formula was not calculated to cause imaginative ward heelers excessive concern, but better that they survive a while longer than that immigrants be subjected to more hazards than they already encountered.

---

it seemed to promise a permanent and self-perpetuating ruling class in America. (Eric Goldman, *Rendezvous with Destiny* [New York, 1952], pp. 48-49.) The point nevertheless holds that immigrants had more reason than most to resent this sort of progress, and that they discovered in the *World* an organ to represent them.

[55] *World*, January 4, 1885, p. 4.

[56] *World*, January 26, 1885, p. 4. See also December 25, 1884, p. 4.

Of all the immigrant groups, none was so favored by the *World* as the Irish. It printed material specially tailored for their interest, and espoused their cause with an ardor that had Pulitzer's detractor, Leander Richardson, despairing for the British. "There was nothing that could be done by the British government in connection with Ireland that did not meet with the most violent demonstrations of disapproval on the part of the *World*," he wrote. "The paper was Irish all over, and it thirsted for British gore with a thirst that passed all understanding. It even went so far as to secure the services of a celebrated Fenian leader as its Paris correspondent."[57]

Richardson's observations in this instance were more accurate than usual, although malice caused him to distort their significance. The *World* did support the Irish cause abroad as well as at home, and undoubtedly the prospect of enlisting readers from within the city's large Gaelic community encouraged it in doing so, but the opinions thus expressed in no way violated the newspaper's principles or integrity. It was but a short progression, for instance, from criticizing the British for their aristocratic institutions to criticizing them for their treatment of the Irish nation. The newspaper's comments in part reflect an anglophobic streak that was widespread and more than respectable in the United States of the 1880s. Moreover, the fact that it took sides in a dispute across the ocean, partly to please immigrants in New York, did not prevent the *World* from lecturing to the Irish when it believed a lecture warranted.

The response to a report in 1883 that the British had executed an American-born nationalist named O'Donnell, who had been found guilty of assassinating an informer, was typical. The *World* did not justify political assassination, nor did it necessarily dispute the jury's verdict, but it protested bitterly against England's refusal to honor a request by Secretary of State Frederick T. Frelinghuysen for a delay in carrying out the sentence until all of the alleged errors in courtroom procedure had been examined. "England's treatment of our application . . . was a discourtesy and an injustice," the newspaper thundered. "It was the more discourteous and unjust because the answer to our

[57] *The Journalist*, July 19, 1884, p. 5.

— 255 —

request was so timed as to prevent any further communication with our Government before the execution."[58] Pulitzer willingly debated the issue in print with Charles A. Dana, who took occasion several weeks later to justify Britain's procedure. "Our contemporary's position may be gratifying to English snobs . . . but it will be offensive to all American citizens who possess proper amount of self-respect."[59]

Still more opportunities to favor the Irish came in 1884 during the campaign against Blaine. Of course the *World* exploited Blaine's record on questions important to foreign-born voters mainly to defeat his candidacy, but in identifying what it took to be wrong policy it delivered an unspoken moral about right policy. The attempt to so cultivate favor within the immigrant community sometimes had a ludicrous aspect, as when the *World* printed a letter protesting the Republican candidate's appearance at a reception in which several flags had been used as decoration, but not the Irish flag.[60] It found weightier material in the roster of Irishmen who had been arrested by British authorities during Blaine's tenure as Secretary of State. The newspaper hounded him for the obsequious tone of a letter he had written as Secretary to the editor of the *Irish World*, promising to appeal to "the friendly benevolence" of the British Government for the release of Michael Boynton, an American citizen seized by the British for his Irish nationalist activities.[61] Daniel McSweeny, who also ran afoul of the Coercion Act at the time Blaine ran the State Department, took to the stump to campaign actively against him, and again the *World* cooperated with lavish publicity, expressing horror not only that a public official could so neglect his duty, but that Englishmen could so abuse the citizens of a captive nation.[62]

Irish readers were charmed by articles praising the brave sons

[58] *World*, December 19, 1883, p. 4. The story of O'Donnell's execution appeared in a special edition on December 17, 1883, p. 1. See the same day's editorial page (p. 4) for an earlier criticism of British behavior.

[59] *World*, February 18, 1884, p. 4.

[60] *World*, September 28, 1884, p. 4.

[61] The letter is reprinted in an editorial on July 30, 1884, p. 4.

[62] The *World* first raised the McSweeny issue in an editorial on August 30, 1884, p. 4. His speeches against Blaine were reported on October 13, 1884, p. 2; and October 18, 1884, p. 2.

and daughters of the Emerald Isle, but they appreciated even more those which condemned the alien rulers of that isle. In this respect the *World* established its credentials from practically the first week of publication under Pulitzer. Its comments, as we have seen, ranged from sharp criticisms of the royal family and peerage generally, to predictable judgments about the respective merits of British and American women. The newspaper doubtless appreciated that such articles would set Celtic heads to nodding in sober agreement, just as evidences of British goodwill toward a figure in American politics was tantamount to slander. Blaine's strongest suit among the Irish-born voters in New York City was his reputation for jingoism, a trait which many of them assumed would discomfit the British were he to become President. It was a reputation the *World* worked hard to discredit. "We confess that we cannot find that Mr. Blaine has done anything to injure England," it noted early in the campaign.[63] The following month it reported darkly that as Secretary of State he had absented himself from the Yorktown Jubilee of 1881 because "he was . . . afraid of offending the British Lion."[64] Even more sinister, one of Blaine's warmest supporters, Cyrus Field, had erected a monument to the memory of Major John André, the British agent who conspired with Benedict Arnold during the Revolution to betray West Point.[65] The *World* delivered what it hoped was a coup de grâce when it informed its Irish readers of an interview in the *New York Tribune* in which Sir John A. Macdonald, Prime Minister of Canada, foolishly endorsed Blaine's candidacy. "It must not be forgotten," the newspaper pointed out, "that Sir John is a loyal subject of Her Most Gracious Majesty Queen Victoria. All of Sir John's friends in Canada are British subjects. The *Tribune* must feel proud to have an aristocratic Britisher, such as Sir John, testifying to the love entertained for Blaine by Queen Victoria's most loyal subjects and indicating a political policy for the people of the United States."[66]

[63] *World*, June 15, 1884, p. 4.

[64] *World*, July 18, 1884, p. 4.

[65] *World*, October 14, 1884, p. 4. The information was supplied in response to an inquiry from a subscriber named Pat Malloy.

[66] *World*, October 9, 1884, p. 4. There is poetic justice in the fact that four years later the Republicans contributed mightily to Cleveland's defeat by using

To report that the *World* consistently took the Irish side in the long quarrel with Great Britain is not to suggest that it did so indiscriminately, or at the price of surrendering its editorial integrity. The newspaper sternly rebuked the misguided nationalists who waged war on England by planting dynamite in public places. Not only did terrorism set back the cause of Irish independence, it violated moral law by killing innocent and guilty alike. "We deplore the use of dynamite by the Celtic enemies of England as a destructive, cruel, senseless crime," an editorial declared, "for it accomplishes nothing but the slaughter and maiming of innocent persons."[67] Or again, "the employment of this dreadful agent in the indiscriminate killing of innocent people is, if persisted in, going to hurt the cause of Ireland more than anything else."[68] Although a front-page cartoon in January 1885 made light of an incident in which British policemen confiscated a case of Boston beans, suspecting it of containing explosives, the business of blowing up people was not considered a subject for humor.[69] A more typical cartoon depicted several of the terrorists —Rossa, Short, Phelan, Joyce, Ford—as devils roasting in the flames of hell, their crime illustrated by a drawing of dead and mangled children lying at the base of the Tower of London, the site of a recent explosion.[70]

As an organ consciously devoted to the Irish cause, and anxious to attract Irish readers, the *World* naturally printed a variety of articles of purely ethnic interest. They included the columns written from Paris by James Stephens, a leading

---

the same strategy against him. They publicized a letter written by Sir Lionel Sackville-West, the British Minister to the United States, answering a request for advice by an ex-British, naturalized citizen on how he should vote. Sir Lionel vaguely, and foolishly, endorsed Cleveland's candidacy.

[67] *World*, April 15, 1884, p. 4.

[68] *World*, April 24, 1884, p. 4. Richard Short's acquittal by a New York jury after having inflicted multiple wounds on a fellow terrorist in a knife fight aroused the *World* to similar expressions of anger. "A suspicion is abroad," an editorial remarked, "that the jurymen were afraid to convict Short, lest they all and severally subject themselves to the fiendish vengeance of the terrible secret organization which protects and employs him. At all events there has been another shameful miscarriage of justice, and it is one that will bring fresh discredit to our city." May 7, 1885, p. 4.

[69] The "Boston bean" cartoon appeared on January 8, 1885, p. 1.

[70] *World*, February 8, 1885, p. 9.

Fenian; a dispatch from Michael Davitt in Dublin, expounding at great length his views on the Land League question; and innumerable reports on Irishmen meeting in conventions in New York City to damn the English.[71] Other stories had somewhat wider interest, although again it did not require a sociologist to determine that the sons of Erin would enjoy them most. The illustrated features on the Catholic Church already mentioned fell into that category, as did—for obvious reasons—the front-page coverage of marathon bicycle and roller-skate races won by contestants named respectively Fitzgerald and Donovan. Referring to Donovan's feat of rolling around Madison Square Garden for 1,090 miles in six days, the *World* judged it "unquestionably the greatest distance ever travelled by a human being depending solely on leg-propulsion. . . . Altogether Old Ireland holds a proud championship."[72] On the other hand, its lead story coverage of the Prince of Wales' visit to Ireland, another subject with obvious appeal, turned out rather badly. An editorial early in the tour praised the populace for making him welcome. "The fact is, Irishmen are generous and hospitable. They smother their hatred of England and pay honor to the heir to the British throne because he comes to them confidingly, as a guest."[73] Unfortunately, the rest of the tour consisted of demonstrations, black flags, and vegetables thrown with embarrassing accuracy. The *World* refrained from further editorial comment, and settled for front-page accounts of each riot as it occurred.[74]

The newspaper's equivocal attitude toward minority immigrant groups is particularly interesting in light of its great regard for the Irish and other "established" nationalities.[75] Although the

[71] For examples of Stephens' columns, see the *World*, May 11, 1884, p. 12; or April 20, 1884, p. 9. Michael Davitt's dispatch appeared on June 4, 1884, p. 9. For an example of the *World* reporting Irish conventions, see August 14, 1884, p. 1.

[72] *World*, March 8, 1885, p. 4.

[73] *World*, April 9, 1885, p. 4.

[74] Accounts of the riot appeared in the *World* on April 14, 1885, p. 2; April 15, 1885, p. 1; and April 16, 1885, p. 1.

[75] Although the *World* was particularly friendly to the Irish community, it attempted to cater to other national groups as well, notably the Germans (many of the editorials against prohibition were addressed to them). Not surprisingly, Pulitzer also demonstrated more sympathy for Jewish immigrants than the average publisher. He was embarrassed in 1884 when a subscriber pointed out that a police court report had included the sentence, "The Jew

World crusaded on behalf of Italian laborers by opposing the padrone system, it seemed to have little respect for them as people. The execution at Sing Sing of a convict named Angelo Cornetti provided opportunity for an uncharacteristic bit of philosophizing. According to an editorial the day following, it "was a fresh illustration of a peculiarity of the Italian temperament. We refer to the painful contrast between the promptness and decision which an Italian exhibits when he is about to kill somebody, and the vacillating and temporizing spirit which he shows when somebody is about to kill him."[76] Even more remarkable, the *World* borrowed a page from its bitterest enemies by arguing that the Italians who lived in slum conditions did so by their own perverse choice. An article describing some of the vilest rookeries in the city—shanties built under manure heaps at the bank of the East River in which "a foul liquid from the manure trickled down constantly on the heads of the tenants"—pointed out complacently that Italians occupied them, and seemingly without discomfort. ITALIANS FIND A NUMBER OF NEW AND VERY CHEAP RESIDENCES, the headline announced. LIVE HAPPILY AND CONTENTEDLY IN THE MIDST OF FILTH AND FOUL ODORS.[77] Indeed, such poverty was material for humor, as evidenced by a pun in the Christmas Day issue of 1883: "The poor Italians who are shovelling snow in the streets are having a happy Christmas. Their stockings may be said to be full."[78]

Other groups fared as badly. Demonstrating that he was not immune himself to the racial theories just starting to gain favor, Pulitzer asserted in an editorial that "the modern Greek is a treacherous, drunken creature. . . . To call a man a 'Greek' is equivalent to branding him a liar and a cheater."[79] When a sub-

---

is accused of having assaulted him." An editorial admitted that the wording was offensive. "It is the standing order in the *World* office—as in all intelligently conducted newspaper establishments—that no distinctions of race or creed are to be made in presenting the news. Occasionally, through oversight, something of the kind complained of above slips into the *World*, but it is rare indeed. We assume that the nationality and the religious beliefs of persons who fall into the newspaper can be of no particular interest to the public." February 14, 1884, p. 4.

[76] *World*, May 12, 1883, p. 4.   [77] *World*, March 25, 1885, p. 1.
[78] *World*, December 25, 1883, p. 4.
[79] *World*, February 15, 1885, p. 4.

scriber named Nicolaides understandably took issue with that judgment, the publisher stood his ground by stating that "no race in Europe shows such marked degeneracy and such bad traits. . . . For four hundred years Greece was under the heel of the cruel Moslem. Some of the worst national traits may be the result of the long years of oppression and degradation to which they were subjected by their haughty conquerors."[80] Pulitzer admired Slavs no more than Greeks. He resented the fact that some newspapers confused the Slavic immigrants who worked as scabs in the coal mines of Pennsylvania with Hungarians. "It might be well to explain that these foreigners, who, it is said, 'work for fifty cents a day and live like hogs,' are not Hungarians. They are Sclavs [sic]. They simply come from Hungary, but they are hated as intensely by the true Magyars as they are by the Pennsylvania miners."[81] Again a racial theory explained their inferiority. "These people are not Hungarians. They are . . . Asiatic invaders."[82] The same could certainly be said of the Chinese, as Pulitzer made clear when asked by a reader to explain why recent editorials had protested against the barbarity of French arms in slaughtering them. "The *World* may sympathize with the Chinese so long as they remain at home and attend to their own business. We do not want them here, but that is no reason why we should uphold the French in [shooting them down]. . . . We never indorse injustice of any kind, even though barbarians are the victims."[83]

However paradoxical it may seem, such statements do not indicate an anti-immigrant mentality. On the contrary, they reveal that the *World* shared not only the aspirations, but the prejudices, of the majority of immigrants in New York City. They result from the newspaper steeping itself too much in immigrant ideology. Irishmen, Germans, and Scandinavians made up the vast bulk of the city's foreign-born population; it was the mark of their insecurity that they sought still more vulnerable

[80] *World*, February 21, 1885, p. 4.
[81] *World*, April 18, 1884, p. 4. Pulitzer had a personal reason for making the distinction between Magyars and Slavs. He was born in Hungary himself, of Magyar–Jewish descent on his father's side, and Austro–German on his mother's.
[82] *World*, September 6, 1884, p. 4.
[83] *World*, September 3, 1884, p. 4.

groups to despise.[84] By the next decade, when Italian immigration had assumed significant proportions, comments of the Cornetti sort would no longer appear on the *World*'s editorial page, for by then Italians would be the new important underdogs to support. It is perhaps no more than a statement about human nature that we should measure the newspaper's commitment to the causes it espoused by the shortcomings as well as the virtues of that commitment.

[84] The *World* also honored the bias of lower class whites in its editorial policy toward Negroes. Although it claimed that "no distinctions of race or creed are . . . made in presenting the news" (see note 75 above), the newspaper followed journalistic convention by carefully identifying the race of a culprit if he happened to be nonwhite. Headlines such as ASSAULTED BY A NEGRO (May 23, 1884, p. 5), ATTACKED BY A NEGRO (July 25, 1884, p. 8), A NEGRO FIEND CONFESSES (September 7, 1884, p. 3), ROBBED BY A BURLY NEGRO (November 28, 1884, p. 1), HUNTING A NEGRO FIEND (December 6, 1884, p. 2) were common. In part, at least, the discrepancy reflected Pulitzer's own bias. He seemed to be pulled in two directions, believing as a matter of principle in equality of opportunity, yet sharing a common prejudice against Negroes. The tension is not altogether surprising, considering that he spent his formative years in the United States in the border city of St. Louis. One wonders what influence his wife had in this respect. In 1878 he married Miss Kate Davis of Washington, D.C., a distant relative of Jefferson Davis.

CHAPTER NINE

DISCOVERING THE POOR

New York City was a place of great charm in the 1880s. It is true that the city was growing at a hectic pace, and that already a physician had coined the word "neurasthenia" to describe the nervous complaint brought on by too much bustle and excitement, but in retrospect this concern about life's pressures seems somewhat self-conscious. Families could still gather around the piano to sing songs, or go on picnic outings to the farms of upper Manhattan, or if the weather was right, skate to band music on Central Park pond. Decades later old men would think back fondly to what they called the good old days. They would remember quiet neighborhoods with substantial homes and tree-lined streets, and recall that even the traffic jams caused by landaus, coupes, victorias and broughams as they piled up at Union Square were not so terrible as the blaring horns and reeking exhaust pipes of a later era. Above all, they would reminisce about the flavor life had then. Their thoughts would go back to the old Irish woman who sold apples and smoked a clay pipe; to the Negro who came by in the evenings with "hot co-o-orn"; to the ragpickers with their pushcarts, cowbells jingling as the cart moved; to the newsboys hawking extras; to the knife grinder ringing a bell as he passed by; to the Jewish peddler with a notion store around his neck; to the milkman and his one horse dray, ladling milk from a large can for the housewives as they came running down to meet him; to the mustachioed organ grinder who stood on the street corner with his monkey cranking out the latest melody by Edward Harrigan.

This was the New York City of charm and comfort, and the only New York many of its citizens knew. They celebrated it in song and story, and when it was past they cherished the memory. Only the poor knew about the other New York, a city of buildings given over to filth and decay, and of streets fouled

— 263 —

with heaps of refuse and swill that sent up a stink to offend the noses of the uninitiated. (The poor could not do much with their garbage in the years before the Department of Sanitation set up a system of daily or weekly pickups except let it fester.) The people Jacob Riis called "the other half" lived lives of quiet despair in the city below 14th Street, only rarely disturbing the smooth complacency of the families who inhabited the spacious streets uptown. They were the people, and theirs was the cause, which the *New York World* championed when Joseph Pulitzer arrived to establish his new journalism.

Their exact number is difficult to determine, since in any generation the definition of "slum" depends so much upon the attitude of the spokesman about the minimum standards needed to maintain self-respect. Commissioner of Labor Carroll D. Wright's report on housing in four major cities for President Cleveland in 1894 put the number of New Yorkers who lived in slums at about 360,000.[1] Somewhat less encouraging was a Board of Health census the year before, which stated that 1,332,773 persons, or 70.46 percent of the population, lived in multi-unit dwellings, and that only about 20 percent of those inhabited buildings of a better sort, termed for convenience "apartment houses."[2] Charles M. Robinson relied on the Board's report when he wrote that "about eight-fifteenths of the population . . . of the city live in tenements, in the common meaning of that term, as this leaves out of the count the tenants of the higher class of flats."[3]

The noted New York State Housing Commissions of 1884, 1894, and 1900 tried a different approach. They avoided a tricky exercise in semantics by choosing to study the "tenement house problem" rather than the "slum problem," using the legal definition of a tenement as "any house occupied as the home or residence of three families or more, living independently of each

[1] Carroll D. Wright, *Slums of Baltimore, Chicago, New York, and Philadelphia*, Seventh Special Report, Commissioner of Labor (Washington, D.C., 1894), p. 12.

[2] Cited in James Ford, *Slums and Housing*, 2 vols. (Cambridge, 1936), I, 187.

[3] Charles Mulford Robinson, "Improvement in City Life," *Atlantic Monthly*, LXXXIII (April 1899), 530.

other, and doing their cooking upon the premises."[4] The commissions realized that a definition that applied as well to the luxurious Dakota apartments on Central Park West as to the foulest rookery on Hester Street had obvious limitations, but they saw little point in restricting the meaning further when the aspirations of the poor only approximated what the rich already enjoyed. In any event, they estimated in the 1900 report that at least two million of the 2.4 million inhabitants of legally defined tenements depended to some extent upon public safeguards for "their health, protection against fire, and social environment."[5]

The men who tried to educate the nation about the need for reform spoke with one voice in describing the horrors to be found in the city's tenement districts. Most obvious was the fact of overcrowding. John I. Davenport reported in 1884 that "Philadelphia, with its 129 square miles of area, housed, in 1880, its 847,000 population—nearly 400,000 less than that of New York—in 146,412 dwellings, or double the number which were inhabited in New York."[6] The Commissioner of Labor's report on slum housing for President Cleveland included similar data from the Census of 1890. He noted that the slums of Baltimore had 7.71 persons to a dwelling, in Philadelphia 7.34 persons, in Chicago 15.51 persons, and in New York 36.79 persons.[7] "New York has the . . . most terrible congestion in the world," Charles Mulford Robinson wrote in 1899. "The nearest approach to New York is in the plague-ridden districts of Bombay. In all of Europe there is only one city district, a small part of Prague, that is even half as crowded as are parts of New York."[8] He might, if he wished, have been more specific. According to the Tenement House Committee of 1894, New York's Sanitary District A averaged 986.4 people to the acre for 32 acres, or

---

[4] Robert W. DeForest and Lawrence Veiller, eds., *The Tenement House Problem*, 2 vols. (New York, 1903), I, 37.

[5] *Ibid.*

[6] John I. Davenport, *Letter of John I. Davenport, Esq., on the Subject of the Population of the City of New York, Its Density, and the Evils Resulting Therefrom* (New York, 1884), quoted in James Ford, *Slums and Housing*, I, 166.

[7] Wright, *Slums*, p. 12.

[8] Robinson, "Improvement in City Life," p. 530.

about 30,000 people in a space of five city blocks. Bombay suffered the second most crowded section at that time, with 659.9 people to the acre, and the Josefstadt district of Prague, the worst in Europe, with 485.4 to the acre.[9]

Most of the other evils associated with the slums followed from those statistics. Normal standards of privacy, whether within the family or between families, could not be maintained. Profanity was commonplace, drunkenness something to be accepted, vice and degeneracy a fact of life. The poor inhabited flats that were ill-ventilated and ill-lit, and in them often neglected even rudimentary habits of hygiene. Their toilets and indoor washing facilities were fouled beyond redemption, their airshafts littered with garbage discarded through open windows, their hallways sheathed in darkness and rancid with a hundred smells.[10] Disease stalked through the tenement districts, death never more than a step behind. Infants and adults succumbed to the same conditions that, in Jacob Riis's phrase, made life hardly "seem worth the living."[11] An article in *Harper's Weekly* in 1879 reported that 70 percent of the deaths in New York City occurred in the quarter where the very poorest classes sought shelter, with more than half of the deaths among youngsters under five years of age.[12] The result, according to the Ladies' Health Protective Association, was a citywide death toll in 1882 of 31.6 per thousand of population, as opposed to 21.4 in London and 26+ in Paris, Berlin, and Rome.[13]

Here was a situation tailor-made for journalistic crusading. If almost half the city suffered from substandard housing, if (as investigation established) the situation could be traced at least

[9] "Report of the Tenement House Committee of 1894," *Assembly Documents*, 118th Session, Vol. IX, No. 37 (Albany, 1895), 11.

[10] These conditions are described in the reports already cited of the 1894 and 1900 Tenement House Commissions. See also the "Report of the Tenement House Commission of 1884," *Senate Documents*, 108th Session, Vol. V, No. 36 (Albany, 1885), and the *Annual Reports* of the New York Association for Improving the Condition of the Poor.

[11] Jacob Riis, *How the Other Half Lives* (New York, 1890), p. 162.

[12] Anon., "Tenement Life in New York," *Harper's Weekly*, XXIII (March 29, 1879), 246.

[13] Ladies' Health Protection Association, "Slaughter Houses in the City of New York" (New York, 1885), cited in Gordon Atkins, *Health Housing, and Poverty in New York City, 1865-1898*, pp. 202-203.

in part to the profiteering of landlords, and if tenants feared the consequences of making protest to the proper authorities, then clearly a newspaper could both win favor and perform a vital public service by publicizing and condemning the abuses as they occurred. Joseph Pulitzer, by background an immigrant, by conviction a reformer, accepted the challenge. While a newspaper like the *New York Tribune* blamed squalor in the lower part of Manhattan on the moral degeneracy of the people who lived there, and from that wisdom discouraged hopes that things could ever become better, the continuous crusade of the *World* stemmed from its refusal to accept the intolerable.[14] It was this spirit, communicated daily to tens of thousands of New Yorkers, together with the work of churches, settlement houses, and middle class reform movements, that brought at least a partial victory over the slums in the early decades of the twentieth century.

The *World* fulfilled its primary mission just by considering the plight of the poor to be news. It gave extensive coverage to the reports of the various Tenement House Commissions and related agencies, and on at least one occasion played a part in having an investigation launched. Professor Felix Adler's series of lectures on the "Tenement-House Problem," delivered in Chickering Hall in 1884 before the Society for Ethical Culture, were reported almost verbatim in the newspaper, a point of some significance since the controversy aroused by his talks resulted in Albany naming the Tenement House Commission of that year.[15] A lengthy excerpt from the Sanitary Aid Society report of 1885 offers further example of publicity used to underwrite a personal crusade. "To get into pestilential human rookeries," the report stated,

> you have to penetrate courts and alleys reeking with poisonous and malodorous gasses arising from accumulations of sewage and refuse scattered in all directions, and often flowing beneath your feet. You

[14] For examples of the *Tribune*'s position, see the editorial on February 6, 1884, p. 4, arguing that squalor was a normal condition for the most ignorant and brutalized classes; or the editorial on February 19, 1884, p. 4, declaring of high rents in the slums that it was the price landlords exacted from tenants in return for the privilege of converting the buildings into pigsties.

[15] Lengthy reports on the lectures appeared in the *World* on February 4, 1884, p. 8; February 18, 1884, p. 8; and March 3, 1884, p. 8.

have to ascend rotten staircases which threaten to give away beneath every step, and which in some places have already broken down, leaving gaps that imperil the limbs and lives of the unwary. You have to grope your way along dark and filthy passages swarming with vermin. Then, if you are not driven back by the intolerable stench, you may gain admittance to the dens in which thousands of human beings herd together. . . . Should you have ascended to the attic, where at least some approach to fresh air might be expected to enter from open or broken windows, you look out upon the roofs and ledges of lower tenements, and discover that the sickly air which finds its way into the room has to pass over the putrefying carcasses of dead cats or birds, or viler abominations still.[16]

Not content with reporting the discoveries of others, the *World* carried forward the work in dozens of articles which might have been prepared directly for the attention of the State Legislature. "In the rear of No. 31 Essex Street an old tenement emitted terrible odors," one news story began. "The stairs could only be ascended by feeling one's way, and as the upper stories were reached the heat and smell became unbearable, creating nausea. The windows of this place were kept closed because the odors from the yard, where horses, chickens and geese lived together was even worse than that which clung to the tenement."[17] An account of conditions in the Mulberry Bend area concluded with the observation that "nothing can blot out the fact that our tenement houses are pest holes, badly ventilated, wretchedly sewered and made the hot-houses of disease and immorality."[18] Even the headlines over these stories vibrated with rage. A PITIFUL SORE IN THE HEART OF THE GREAT CITY, described one of the buildings on Mulberry Street. WHO IS RESPONSIBLE AND WHO IS TO BLAME?[19] The *World* reporter who accompanied Sanitary Squad officers on their tour of Baxter Street returned with PICTURES OF POVERTY AND DEGRADATION IN CROWDED DISTRICTS.[20] TENEMENT-HOUSE SQUALOR was the terse comment

[16] *World*, April 23, 1885, p. 3. [17] *World*, July 4, 1884, p. 2.
[18] *World*, September 20, 1883, p. 4. [19] *World*, June 23, 1883, p. 1.
[20] *World*, August 25, 1883, p. 6.

over another account, pointedly run in the Independence Day issue of 1884.[21]

In one way, at least, the newspaper's contribution was unequaled. There is a tendency among the most charitable societies to consider poverty a statistic, something which can be defined by a number. Only those with the pen and soul of an artist—a Dickens in England, or Riis in America—seemed able to recreate vividly what poverty meant to the poor. The *World* understood it as well, and succeeded in communicating that understanding to a city badly in need of education. In the summer of 1883, for example, a young woman of the slums named Kate Sweeny suffocated in her sleep when a sewer overflowed and engulfed her. The horror of her death made the story worth a few lines in most newspapers, but only a few lines since hardly anybody knew of her and even less cared. The *World* was the exception, for it saw her as a symbol of the suffering of a whole class of slum dwellers. "In [No. 35 Mulberry Street]," its report began, "Kate Sweeny was found on Wednesday—dead."

> She had lay down in the cellar to sleep, and the sewer that runs under the house overflowed and suffocated her where she lay. No one will ever know who killed Kate Sweeny. No one will ever summon the sanitary inspectors. There will be no pallid ghost haunting the Inspector of Buildings. Who Kate Sweeny was or where she came from it is almost impossible to tell. There has been no obituary written. You will search the papers in vain. Nobody seems to have thought it worth an investigation.[22]

Of course the *World* did think it worth an investigation, and Kate Sweeny's obituary became a condemnation of the conditions that killed her, not a bad obituary as such things go.

The Christmas following her death brought another assault on middle class complacency. Men and women still digesting their holiday dinner opened the newspaper to see this headline:

POVERTY'S CHRISTMAS

[21] *World*, July 4, 1884, p. 2.
[22] *World*, June 23, 1883, p. 1.

HOW THE DAY WAS SPENT IN CHEERLESS CELLARS AND GRIMY GARRETS.

Harrowing Tales of Struggles to Obtain,
Not Turkey and Plum Pudding, but Bread
and Tea and Fire to Keep Out the Cold.

The story that followed did not equivocate about its intentions:

> In order to more vividly set before the readers of the *World* the manner in which some of our poorer citizens spent Christmas, a *World* reporter yesterday visited several families residing in the tenement-house districts. It would be hard to adequately describe the scenes encountered, but misery and wretchedness, uncloaked and undisguised, were met with in every case. Many instances there were where the families had no money to buy provisions, and others who had, but being necessarily obliged to buy of the smallest retailers, were compelled to pay prices which must have made an exorbitant profit for the dealer, who bought at wholesale.[23]

Nor did the newspaper have words of comfort for the gentry who considered their polite perspiration during July and August evidence of suffering. "It makes me smile," it quoted a doctor as saying, "when I hear the people on the broad avenues complaining of the summer nights' heat. They have spacious rooms. Every breeze is caught. They have ice-water and fans and gauzy covering and bath-tubs. . . . Down in those old-fashioned tenements that are banked up along the streets, . . . the miserable wretches are worse off than the veriest savages. . . . It is all very well to talk about improving the condition of these tenants. The only possible way to do it is to tear down the houses. When it is thoroughly understood how much evil they are responsible for I believe they will be torn down in the interest of humanity."[24] The hard fact is that the crowded cubicles below 14th Street became almost unbearable as summer heat blanketed the city. A witness before the 1900 Tenement Commission estimated that at least one-third of the slum dwellers habitually spent the night on rooftops or fire escapes, even in parked wagons, during the

[23] *World*, December 26, 1883, p. 2.
[24] *World*, July 6, 1883, p. 5.

— 270 —

sweltering months.[25] According to Jacob Riis, the police considered it routine business in some districts to cart away the bodies of those who had rolled off roof ledges in their sleep.[26]

The *World* spoke with ill-concealed bitterness against the private and public complacency which allowed fellow human beings to undergo slow torture in the heat, unnoticed and unassisted. "Ill-ventilated, vermin-infested quarters," an editorial declared, "some of them heated like ovens by the tin roofs overhead and the refraction from the adjoining buildings, are made still worse by the deprivation of water which they almost invariably suffer at such time. . . . The stranger who would see a novel phase of New York life and is too philosophic to suffer from the smells and noises, should walk through Essex, Suffolk or Norfolk Streets at evening while the hot wave pours."[27] As for the efforts of the Board of Health to at least contain epidemics by dousing the buildings with disinfecting fluid, the *World* found it "very much like pouring cologne into a sewer."[28]

Perhaps the most terrible aspect of summer in the slums was the toll it took on infant children. The newspaper reported in July 1883, that of 716 reported deaths the previous week, 392 had been among children under five years of age.[29] Its interview with the doctor helped to explain why:

> I suppose that nine-tenths of the little ones suffer from prickly heat. They are irritable and cross, and the mothers take them to the roof or down into the street where the air can blow on them.
>
> You will find the streets thronged with women carrying babies. They walk till they are tired out, then they sit down on the cool stone steps, or throw them-

---

[25] DeForest and Veiller, eds., *The Tenement House Problem*, I, 416. Many artists considered the rooftop dormitories a novel subject for illustration. Charles Graham's "On the Roof of a Tenement House" appeared in *Harper's Weekly*, along with the observation that "it is an interesting sight to see a roof which covers a whole block and is two acres in extent turned into the playground or the resting place of the hundreds of men, women, and children who lived under it." For the comment, see Charles Graham, "A Summer Resort on the Roof," *Harper's Weekly*, XXIX (August 1, 1885), 491; for the illustration, "On the Roof of a Tenement House," *op.cit.*, p. 496.

[26] Riis, *How the Other Half Lives*, pp. 166-67.

[27] *World*, September 10, 1884, p. 4.

[28] *World*, September 11, 1884, p. 4.

[29] *World*, July 3, 1883, p. 5.

selves upon the drays and trucks that are standing in the street. . . .

But you must understand that the heat has other disadvantages. Perhaps one of the greatest is the vermin. If you know anything about these places you must know that with the hot nights, the domestic parasites which infest the houses swarm with terrible virulence.[30]

As a result, each summer brought similar headlines: HOW BABIES ARE BAKED,[31] LITTLE ONES DYING OFF,[32] LINES OF LITTLE HEARSES,[33] DEAD AND DYING INFANTS,[34] KILLING THE LITTLE ONES,[35] PESTILENCE NURSERIES.[36] Sometimes the accompanying stories conveyed the horror by understatement.

"Is there a little baby dead here?" inquired the reporter of the bare-limbed child.

"Which one do you mean—the one in the rear or the one on the corner?" she replied.[37]

At other times they were unabashedly emotional.

Further down on the door-step of one of the most rickety houses sat a woman, holding in her lap an attenuated form that was the remains of a once healthy child.

"What ails the baby?" the reporter asked.

"I don't know," she replied sadly, but she gently turned the wasted form so that the livid skin became more apparent. "The doctors say that if the warm weather lets up the baby will get better," and gathering it up she walked down to the pier and sat down, alternately gazing at the water and the child.[38]

In both cases the *World* did not have to summon outrage, for the facts unadorned showed a divided city: New York uptown a center of wealth, culture and sophistication, and downtown, a Dantean vision of purgatory.

Infant mortality during the summer months only emphasized that the ultimate reckoning on slum conditions came in the form of statistics relating to disease and death. "While from the private

[30] *World*, July 6, 1883, p. 5.
[32] *World*, July 3, 1883, p. 5.
[34] *World*, July 16, 1883, p. 5.
[36] *World*, June 11, 1883, p. 2.
[38] *World*, July 16, 1883, p. 5.

[31] *World*, July 6, 1883, p. 5.
[33] *World*, July 9, 1883, p. 1.
[35] *World*, March 26, 1885, p. 8.
[37] *World*, July 3, 1883, p. 5.

dwellings that contain the other half of New York's population only 8,832 persons died out of a total of 37,924 last year," a *World* report soberly stated, "the number of deaths reported from the tenements was 20,690, and that from the hospitals and institutions that draw nine-tenths of their patients from the tenement population, 7,528."[39] A similar tone pervaded the newspaper's interview with Dr. John T. Nagle, Registrar of Vital Statistics, on the toll for the previous seven days. "Last week there were 716 deaths reported. Over one-half that number— 392—were children under five years of age, while 412 were those who died in tenement houses."[40] The *World* meant to stir its readers to action. It repeated Felix Adler's description of the two blocks at the bend of Baxter and Mulberry Streets in which 633 people had died in three years, and the single building at No. 31 Baxter Street from which 11 corpses had been taken in twelve months, and suggested the only recourse that remained. "Sooner or later, . . ." it declared, "the sanitary safety of a great community will have to ignore the greed and parsimony of the owners of these houses, as well as the temporary inconvenience of the inmates, and insist upon the eradication of the structures."[41]

Just two weeks after that editorial a situation came to light which put the problem in still more vivid terms. Inspectors from the Board of Health discovered a tenement on West 32nd Street in which typhus fever had been raging for weeks, claiming the lives of several tenants and bringing many more to the verge of death. Shocked headlines in the *World* described ambulances busy throughout the day "carrying filthy, dirt-incrusted people to the hospital on Blackwell's Island"; the death of a parish priest who had entered the hovel to bring comfort to its occupants; the incredible decay which had gone unchecked by health authorities until tragedy resulted.[42]

> From off the roof of Deely's Foundry, next east of the tenement-houses, workmen yesterday shovelled two huge cartloads of filth that had been thrown out of the tenement-house windows. . . . It lay on the

[39] *World*, June 11, 1883, p. 2.
[40] *World*, July 3, 1883, p. 5.
[41] *World*, December 18, 1884, p. 4.
[42] *World*, January 7, 1885, p. 1; and January 8, 1885, p. 1.

roof directly under the windows of the tenants, and so much had been thrown out that it was banked up against the window sills of the third story. . . . The [toilet] closets [in the cellar] became so foul that the tenants had to stop using them because they could not get to them, the refuse having flowed over the cellar. McNamara, janitor of the building, whose wife died of typhus, refused to clean the closets, claiming that it was the filth of the tenants of No. 555, and they refused to do it because they said they cleansed them last. So between them there was nothing done and the inspectors never did anything.[43]

The conditions in No. 557 might have made a case study for one of the Tenement House Commissions: "The waste pipes were stopped up and the filth from the closets ran over the floor. Foul matter of all sorts, decayed meat, vegetables and ashes were heaped in noisome little mounds in the dark, damp cellar. . . . The waste water ran even into the bedrooms, and a liberal portion of every shower came through the roof."[44]

The *World* made this building an object of special attention, an introduction for one-half of the city to the other half, a basis for editorials pleading that the misery found therein might soon be only a subject for historians. It impressed bluntly upon the privileged part of the population that the problem was everyone's. "When it is remembered that our great system of sewers connects the homes of the rich with the tenements of the poor the danger to public health in maintaining such pests will be apparent."[45] It indicted the Board of Health for its incompetence in allowing such a horror to pass unnoticed in a city presuming to share in the progress of civilization.

> Every one at all familiar with the crowded quarters of the New York poor knows very well that in almost every precinct there are rookeries where human beings are packed in every condition of uncleanliness and surrounded by every condition of disease. . . . If complaints are ever made they are made to a perfunctory agent who has but one duty to

[43] *World*, January 10, 1885, p. 2.
[44] *World*, January 8, 1885, p. 1.
[45] *World*, January 8, 1885, p. 4.

perform, and that is to collect the rents. The victims themselves are too ignorant or apathetic to go to the Health authorities. And it is to meet exactly this case that we have sanitary inspectors whose duty is supposed to be to the community at large.

The Board of Health's real value to the community lies not in its tardy spasms of energy, but in its increasing watchfulness, its thorough supervision of the dangerous pest-houses of New York, and a rigid holding to account of the property-owners who make their money out of the poor.[46]

Not least, the *World* posed the inescapable argument to a complacent people that the tragedy uncovered on West 32nd Street would happen again—and often—unless the community acted now to improve the housing of the poor:

Take a lot 25 feet front and 100 feet deep, and erect a building 25 by 80 on it, with accommodations for four families on each of its five or six floors, and you are simply making a trap to smother people. It is impossible that under such conditions there can be sufficient light and air for the occupants, and it is no wonder that the mortality in such places is excessive, and yet there have been many such buildings erected during the past year and a great ado has been made about "model" tenements. These are the best, perhaps, that there are, but the best is bad enough. When, however, you come to the old-fashioned rookeries, where the crowding is much greater, the condition becomes frightful.[47]

Reform was necessary in another area as well if New York hoped to bring its death rate down to a figure commensurate with that in other great cities. The sprawling food markets in the tenement districts presented colorful spectacles of pushcarts leaned against the curbs in solid rank, of peddlers raising their voices to announce the day's bargains, of distracted housewives wrapped in shawls debating inwardly how best to spend their pennies, but all the sounds and sights could not conceal that the food retailed there was in large measure contaminated and

[46] *World*, January 9, 1885, p. 4.
[47] *World*, January 11, 1885, p. 6.

impure.[48] According to the reports of the Medical Society of the State of New York, bread often contained sulfate of copper and inferior flour, as well as grit from ovens and machinery; meat crawled with parasites; canned goods were contaminated with copper and tin, with chemical preservatives and excess water; butter with copper, excess water and salt, and sometimes curd; lard with caustic lime, alum, starch, cottonseed oil, and water.[49] Unscrupulous dealers turned a profit by purchasing livestock infected with disease at sacrifice prices, and retailing the resultant "case" meat among unwary buyers. "Bob" veal—the meat from a calf less than four weeks old—caused particular problems since it relieved hunger pangs without providing nourishment, and ended up in the stomach as an undigestible mass. "A child's stomach is quite unable to cope with a piece of bob veal," a member of the Board of Health wrote in 1886; "in its violent efforts to remove the offending substance nature not infrequently removes the little sufferer."[50] Children also fell victims to adulterated candies, which often contained a variety of toxic chemicals to provide coloring or flavor.[51]

The most serious violations of State health laws occurred in the distribution of adulterated and impure milk. Although the law forbade adding water or other foreign substances to milk to increase its bulk, Board of Health inspectors could not hope to examine enough of the supply coming into the city to check the practice. The easiest device, and one widely used, was simply to add water. "I have frequently had in my possession," Dr. Cyrus Edson wrote, "toads and small snakes found in milk by the inspectors in New York, showing indisputably that the adulter-

[48] Jacob Riis described the Pig Market (so named because it sold the Jewish residents on Hester Street everything but pork) as follows: "Bandanas and tin cups at two cents, peaches at a cent a quart, 'damaged' eggs for a song, hats for a quarter, and spectacles, warranted to suit the eye, at the optician's who has opened shop on a Hester Street door-step, for thirty-five cents; frowsy-looking chickens and half-plucked geese, hung by the neck and protesting with wildly strutting feet even in death . . . are the great staples of the market." Riis, *How the Other Half Lives*, p. 115.

[49] See Mazyck P. Ravenel, ed., *A Half Century of Public Health* (New York, 1921), pp. 210-11.

[50] Cyrus Edson, "Poisons in Food and Drink," *Forum* reprint, p. 577, quoted in Atkins, *Health, Housing, and Poverty in New York City, 1865-1898*, p. 169.
[51] *Ibid.*

ator had stopped at some road-side pool and filled his cans!"[52] More clever violators of the law evaded the results of a lactometer test by adding salt, borax or soda, as well as water, thereby causing the milk to retain its original specific gravity, or by raising the specific gravity by skimming off the cream and then adding water. Milk dealers openly admitted that such practices were nearly universal, and argued that the economics of the industry demanded their use. A witness before the State Dairy Commissioner in 1884 testified that the widespread use of water "was rendered necessary in consequence of the consumers' demand for low prices."[53] It took more disinterested observers to record the social price paid in terms of mortality and sickness. The State Charities Aid Association reported in 1883 that the infant death rate of "forty-five per cent under five years of age [and] thirty-five per cent under one year of age" could largely be attributed to impure milk, and that these statistics did not represent all the suffering since "many a sickly and deformed bodily frame, and many a warped mental and moral nature—conditions worse than death—may be traced to the same source."[54]

The *World* campaigned against the milk scandal with more than usual vigor. It sought first to fix the responsibility for the excessive markup between what farmers received for their milk and what consumers paid.[55] Not much would be accomplished by eliminating health law violations if the result was to put the price of milk beyond the means of tenement house families.

> Ten cents a quart for pure milk would be cheaper and better than half that price for poor and adulterated milk.
>
> But the increased cost is a serious misfortune to the poorer and middle class. Cheap milk is almost as much a necessity to them as cheap bread. It is very desirable that the most stringent laws should exist and

[52] *Ibid.*, p. 576, quoted in Atkins, *Health, Housing, and Poverty in New York City, 1865-1898*, p. 158.

[53] "Tenement House Commission," *Sanitary Engineer*, x (June 19, 1884), 48.

[54] State Charities Aid Association, "Pure Milk and Infants' Food in Tenement-Houses," No. 34 (New York, May 1883), p. 17, quoted in Atkins, *Health, Housing, and Poverty in New York City*, p. 158.

[55] About 500,000 quarts of milk were retailed daily in the city at that time, at prices ranging from six to ten cents a quart. Farmers received two to four cents a quart for the same milk.

be enforced against the sale of impure milk. But of
what value is this protection if the cost of the article
is to place it beyond the reach of persons of limited
means at least in such quantities as the needs of their
families demand?[56]

The newspaper discovered the cause of excessive markups in the
rapacious rates charged by railroad companies to haul milk from
distant areas. It quoted testimony recently given before a State
Senate committee that the rates on milk coming into New York
were sixteen times higher than those on articles of similar weight
and value, and twice as high as those paid by other major cities
for the same service. "But for the greed of the railroad corporations, milk could be supplied in New York at little more than
half the price it now commands and still leave a fair profit to the
retailer. Every family man who pays eight or ten cents a quart
for milk has the satisfaction of knowing that a good portion of
that sum is unjustly extorted by the railroad companies, and that
to satisfy the avariciousness of those wealthy corporations his
pocket is emptied and children stinted in their natural and most
healthful food." The editorial sternly admonished the Railroad
Commission to look into the matter and to institute reform.

The second part of the campaign, demanding that the State's
health laws be enforced, received equal attention. In a lead news
article headlined OUR MAGGOTY MILK SUPPLY, the newspaper
pointed out that "the milk from along the line of the Harlem road
is, with few exceptions, so much rank poison for babes and little
children to drink. . . . The milk . . . passes the lactometer test and
therefore sells freely in New York. Its richness, however, is due
to the presence of diseased particles which, imbibed by the child,
produce cholera-morbus, diarrhoeal complaints and oft-times
death."[57] Walt McDougall contributed a Sunday cartoon contrasting the popular image of the dairy industry (milkmaids
watching over the cows as they grazed on vernal fields) with the
reality of filth and neglect and deceit.[58]

The Pig Market and its equivalents were not the only street
scenes to inspire protest. Overhead the sky gave way to a net-

[56] *World*, September 23, 1883, p. 4.
[57] *World*, August 31, 1883, p. 1; see also February 24, 1884, p. 12.
[58] *World*, February 22, 1885, p. 9.

work of ropes and lines, some stretching from building to building and adorned with tattered garments put out to dry; others—the telephone and telegraph lines—denoting progress for those who could afford them. "Glance down any of these [streets]," Walter G. Marshall challenged, "and . . . above, against the sky, you look upon a perfect maze of telephone and telegraph wires crossing and recrossing each other from the tops of houses. The sky, indeed, is blackened with them, and it is as if you were looking through the meshes of a net."[59]

The *World's* campaign to have the wires put underground took on added zeal because of the opportunity it offered to cross swords once more with a great corporate malefactor, in this case Cyrus Field and the telephone and telegraph companies under his control. Field had argued that to obey a statute requiring that the overhead wires be buried by November 1, 1885, would entail digging up the city streets during the hot summer months, the very time that New York was most vulnerable to epidemics of cholera. The newspaper derided his caution as a cruel device to save company funds. "To play upon the popular dread of cholera for the purpose of saving money for themselves is a most ingenious device on the part of the companies, but is none the less unjustifiable and cruel."[60] It satirized the singular logic which saw no health hazard in digging holes to install the poles for telephone and telegraph wires, but trembled for the consequences of holes to bury the wires. "Do not all these cavillers," asked the *World*, "know the difference between digging holes to put telegraph poles up and digging holes to take them down? Do they not know that while destroying the street to promote the interest of Brother Field's corporations may be a proper sanitary proceeding, disturbing the street against the wishes of these corporations may be a very dangerous and pestilence-breeding operation?"[61] A resolution by the Board of Health in April 1885 supporting Field's contentions aroused the newspaper to new fury. It charged that the Board was "distinguished for what it does not do to preserve the public health," but slavish in its concern for the con-

[59] Walter G. Marshall, *Through America, or Nine Months in the United States* (London, 1881), p. 7.
[60] *World*, March 13, 1885, p. 4.
[61] *World*, March 26, 1885, p. 4.

venience of the corporate masters of New York City.[62] So, too, did the *World* denounce a bill before the State Legislature to establish a commission which would oversee the task of bringing down the wires. "As the well-paid Commissioners are to receive their salaries, expenses and prerequisites from the Telegraph Companies, and as their offices will cease to exist when all the wires are buried, it can readily be seen that they will not be likely to oppose the wishes of the corporations or anxious to hasten the time of their own official dissolution. . . . We have proper authorities paid for enforcing the laws without creating a jobbing Commission to see every law carried out."[63]

The newspaper detected official neglect even in so rudimentary a matter as providing fire protection for lower class neighborhoods. It conceded that the insurance companies had a good idea when they petitioned the city to build cisterns in the downtown warehouse district which would provide water for fire-fighting during the ten or twelve minutes that it took to build up sufficient pressure from the aqueduct supply. But it heatedly questioned the system of values which agitated for cisterns to secure property, while tolerating the greater vulnerability of tenement dwellers. "If a fire should break out and spread in those [slum] districts millions of dollars of property would not be destroyed, and the profits of the insurance companies would not be seriously affected. But hundreds of human beings would be roasted alive, and misery and suffering would be entailed on thousands of others. Yet our insurance companies do not cry out against the danger the tenement-house residents are in, and we hear of no demand for 'cisterns' for their protection. Many people consider that the lives of these poor people are also worthy of consideration."[64] Nor were insurance firms the only agencies callous in their neglect. Even a cursory tour through the slums established that the Police and Fire Departments had not tried to enforce a long list of municipal ordinances requiring that fire escapes be constructed of noninflammable material, that they be accessible to women and children, and be kept clear of receptacles, household utensils, and other obstructions. "If the people do not take

[62] *World*, April 5, 1885, p. 4. [63] *World*, April 11, 1885, p. 4.
[64] *World*, September 10, 1883, p. 4.

seriously [sic] hold of this matter and demand reform," an editorial declared, "the tenement house population will continue to be hived in death-traps and subject nightly to the peril of a cruel death."[65]

The *World*'s recognition that many of the evils to be found in the slums would at least be alleviated if there were more parks raised a knotty problem, for it also believed that lower Manhattan was so built up that a meaningful park program could no longer be managed. In that case the only recourse remaining was to insure that the mistakes of the past would not be duplicated in the present. The newspaper did not arrive at the decision easily. "The lower part of the city is deplorably destitute of breathing places," it complained, "and the mistake of not providing them before the city was built up is every day made more apparent."[66] The clear implication, however, is that the original error of the 1807 Board of Commissioners in failing to set aside more green areas could no longer be redeemed, and that any reasonable amount spent annually on park construction in lower Manhattan would at best be a palliative.[67] There is a hopeless quality to the comment that "every sensible person regrets that Gouverneur Morris, Simeon De Witt and John Rutherford . . . did not [in 1807] provide lungs through which the city might now breathe freely instead of drawing in the tainted air of the crowded downtown tenement districts."[68] Despairing in this respect of helping those in need of help, the *World* asked that the present generation at least do better by its descendants. "New York's Manifest Destiny is unmistakable. We are making preparations for a city of four or five million inhabitants. Shall we commit the mistake our ancestors committed and fail to provide parks for the health, recreation and happiness of the coming generation?"[69] If not, the time had come to prepare for the city of the future, and to stand guard against the greed of those who would place parks for their own profit. "Common sense will point out where parks will be

[65] *World*, May 5, 1885, p. 4.   [66] *World*, December 3, 1883, p. 4.

[67] The commissioners reasoned that since the health-giving sea embraced Manhattan Island on all sides, they could pay first heed to the dictates of commerce in planning the city's growth. For a summary of their report, see Arthur Pound, *The Golden Earth* (New York, 1935), especially p. 125.

[68] *World*, March 16, 1885, p. 4.   [69] *Ibid.*

needed. . . . The parks ought to be placed where the population of the future is likely to be the most dense and at proper distances from each other. The great trouble is that jobs are likely to steal in when the question of location comes up, and this cannot be too carefully guarded against."[70]

Theodore Roosevelt, in 1885 a promising Assemblyman, held out for spending the money in relief of present need rather than in anticipation of future need. The bitterness of the *World*'s reply to what was, after all, a humane suggestion, and one it would ordinarily endorse, suggests that Pulitzer felt torn inwardly by his inability to agree with the legislator.[71] (Of course it did not help matters that Roosevelt and the *World* had disagreed on previous occasions, notably in 1884 when the Republican reformer decided to campaign for Blaine.) "Our highly esteemed contemporary, the *Evening Post*," a bad-tempered editorial began, "indorses the suggestion of the suckling reformer of the last Assembly, Mr. Theodore Roosevelt, that the money the new parks will cost might be better invested in the centre of the tenement-house districts, and calls the scheme for the parks 'essentially a rich man's idea.' " Repeating in huffy tones the arguments about needing to plan for future growth, the editorial went on to pose a question to Roosevelt and the *Evening Post* that could only have been rhetorical. "If the opponents of the new parks really believe that we ought to have 'breathing places' in the present crowded tenement districts if only 'two squares' in extent, why do they not propose to acquire the land and confer this boon on the poorer classes? That need not interfere with the new park policy."[72]

[70] *World*, December 3, 1884, p. 4; see also April 12, 1885, p. 4.

[71] The Legislature finally followed Roosevelt's advice, but to little avail. The Tenement House Committee of 1894 reported that an act passed eight years previously, during the administration of Mayor Abram S. Hewitt, which allocated $1,000,000 annually to carve out parks below 155th Street, had resulted in an expenditure to date of only $522,000. Funds allocated for two other parks—one of them in the Mulberry Bend district—had so far not been used because of delays in effecting slum clearance. As a result, the 707,520 people who in 1895 lived below 14th Street, in an area of 2,528 acres (or 3.95 square miles), had access to a total park area of only 64.6 acres. Precisely, 2.55 percent of lower Manhattan's real estate, the most densely populated in the world, was uncovered by asphalt, as opposed to a citywide average of 7.5 percent. See the "Report of the Tenement House Committee of 1894," pp. 42-43.

[72] *World*, March 25, 1885, p. 4.

The sincerity of the *World*'s commitment to the tenement poor is beyond question, as is the good work it did in focusing attention on how the poor lived. Publicity given to cases of great suffering or rascality had its own justification in a city where one-half of the population knew little or nothing about the condition of the other half. In providing such publicity, Joseph Pulitzer filled a function not unlike that which brought fame to muck-rakers like Upton Sinclair and Lincoln Steffens; indeed, in many ways he qualifies as the first of the breed.[73] He understood, as they did, that horror stories too often repeated soon lose their impact, and avoided that danger by using the publicity for a purpose, to win a reform or punish a wrongdoer. The *World*'s accounts bristled with demands that greedy landlords be curbed, that sanitary laws be observed, that negligent public officials be discovered and replaced. "Why is it," an editorial asked, "that in the most crowded part of the city, while we have a supposed Building Bureau and laws and ordinances made apparently for the protection of life, such death-traps are tolerated and allowed to be crowded with human beings?"[74] The answer appeared in almost every issue. "The greed of owners, the exactions for rent, the neglect of the authorities lie at the foundation of the evil, and for the public safety as well as in the cause of humanity a strong and sweeping remedy ought to be applied."[75] At this level the newspaper's crusade on behalf of the tenement poor did all that conscience or reason could require.

Unfortunately, its exhortations to virtue and integrity largely missed the point. Immigration of increasing proportions had created in New York City a social problem of first magnitude, one entailing far weightier risks than those posed by a handful of greedy landlords and incompetent housing inspectors. While the whole concept of industrial and urban development in America stood challenged, the *World* delivered homilies against petty villains who cheated obscure householders.

[73] Robert Park put it more strongly when he wrote that "it was Pulitzer who invented muckraking." Robert E. Park, "The Natural History of the Newspaper," reprinted in Robert E. Park, Ernest W. Burgess, and Roderick D. McKenzie, *The City* (Chicago, 1925), p. 95.

[74] *World*, July 1, 1884, p. 4.

[75] *World*, September 20, 1883, p. 4.

This is simply to say that Joseph Pulitzer, like other leading reformers of the time, suffered the disadvantage of using a nineteenth century liberal's arsenal against a twentieth century menace. It was all very well to demand that the tenement slums be torn down, but Pulitzer certainly did not conceive of government as the logical agency to do so. Side by side with editorials urging the broadest reforms were others urging that the city government reduce its expenditures. One such, in December 1884, noted approvingly that a constitutional amendment soon to become operative limited taxation to two percent of the total valuation on real and personal property in the city. Since New York's projected budget called for $3,000,000 more than the amendment would allow in taxation, the *World* drew the necessary conclusion. "There is only one proper way to meet the difficulty, and that is to decrease our expenditures. It ought not to cost us $30,000,000 a year to run our city government. There is ample room for economy."[76] A similar reaction on the national level followed Benjamin Butler's promise to workingmen that he would provide full employment and higher wages. The *World* seized on the slogan "He Will Feed Us All." and jibed: "This is carrying the paternal idea into politics with a vengeance."[77]

It is clear in retrospect that only a determined expansion of governmental activity would have made inroads against problems like overcrowding and urban decay. The *World*'s failure to understand as much determined that its suggestions for ultimate reform, when the problem demanded more than rhetoric, and when more than an isolated instance of malfeasance was at issue, would suffer from obscurity or lack of reality. No one could deny the newspaper's good intentions, but as regards the larger view, its helpfulness could very well be questioned.

In September 1883, for instance, the *World* ran a long article showing that houses built for speculative purposes, with the most flimsy materials and specifications allowed by law, were bound to become slums before they had fully settled on their foundations. Substandard housing increasingly defaced the city because "capitalists and contractors were bent on making

[76] *World*, December 6, 1884, p. 4.
[77] *World*, July 7, 1884, p. 4.

money."[78] The newspaper had isolated an important part of the problem, but it offered no suggestions as to what might be done. It proposed neither government owned housing, government financed housing, nor even a great expansion in government supervision of housing construction. Part of the reason is that almost any of the meaningful solutions would have entailed important additional responsibilities for local or state authorities, a course which did not agree with contemporary liberal thought. A more striking example of the *World*'s inability to meet the issues it raised in a meaningful way came in an editorial of December 1884, when after carefully considering the slum problem as it had developed over recent decades, the newspaper discovered two trends which promised even grimmer conditions for the future. First, an "over-production of genteel and uselessly ornamented flat houses, utterly unadapted to the wants of the poor, is making constant encroachments on the quarters where poverty, destitution and vice are herded. Instead of supplying the poor tenement population with cheap dwellings, these pretentious structures only force that population into other . . . neighborhoods." The second discovery followed from the first. "Improvements not always the most expedient have made it less and less possible every year for this [poor] population to spread out and lose its identity as a class in wide distribution." The editorial likened New York's depressed class to "the carbonic acid gas in our atmosphere. The very best safeguard is dissemination." Again the analysis stopped at the critical moment. Although the *World* "regretted . . . that local legislation and police surveillance, no less than local enterprise" did not counteract the forces that were segregating "the multitudinous poor . . . into the oldest and rankest localities," it failed to make clear what would meet the challenge. For as the same editorial pointed out, "capital is not disposed to be philanthropic while it is in the market."[79]

Of course the final irony is that the *World*'s failure was also part of its success. If reform-minded members of the middle class did not trust government to take an active role in instituting

[78] *World*, September 8, 1883, p. 5.
[79] *World*, December 29, 1884, p. 4.

CHAPTER TEN

CRUSADING FOR LABOR

A newspaper which saw in Grover Cleveland the intellect and convictions needed to lead reform, and which honored Samuel Tilden, a conservative corporation lawyer, as an earlier leader of the reform movement, was not likely to let its crusades against social and economic injustice become the basis for a broader attack on laissez-faire capitalism. It has been noted that the newspaper's sincere, and even impassioned, reports on the living conditions of the poor in New York City during the 1880s were followed by no demands for state or federal intervention. The *World* was perfectly consistent in this respect, for in the series of editorials which appeared during the first weeks of Pulitzer's proprietorship it had carefully distinguished between reform-mindedness and radicalism. "Democracy," the journal declared, "sometimes from ignorance, more frequently from malice, has been represented as radicalism and destructiveness. It is nothing of the kind. True Democracy, based on equal rights, recognizes the millionaire and the railroad magnate as just as good as any other man, and as fully entitled to protection for his property under the law."[1]

The *World*'s refusal to repudiate out of hand a philosophy inherited from Adam Smith and Herbert Spencer, as much as its willingness to agitate for reform when obvious need arose, determined its popularity among the people in New York City who had benefited least from the triumph of individualism and private initiative. This seeming paradox reflects the remarkable agreement between the social classes in rejecting state planning as a solution for social ills, and in relying on private good works to alleviate the worst symptoms of poverty. Of course the classes had separate goals, but laborers in general, as shown by the history of their trade unions, and immigrants in particular, as shown by the

[1] *New York World*, May 11, 1883, p. 4.

negative public philosophy of the wardheelers who won their trust, never really questioned the moderate conservatism of America's professional and white collar groups.

One issue did sorely agitate the community, however, and bring it as close as it would come to a division along class lines. Labor's rights in the newly emerging industrial society—whether to bargain collectively, to strike, to picket, to impose secondary boycotts—were contested by opposing ranks in blue collars and white with deep and implacable bitterness. While the employed class struggled to avoid exploitation by an impersonal economy, the employer class and its allies struggled just as determinedly against what it took to be the first symptoms of European radicalism.

In arguing labor's case, the *World* made a notable commitment to the democracy it espoused in hundreds of editorials. It was one thing to crusade for better housing conditions, something any respectable middle class organ could do, and quite another to take sides in what the newspaper came dangerously close at times to describing as a class war. The stand provided final evidence that when choice was necessary, the *World* would be an organ of the dispossessed elements in the city.

The willingness of trade unions to work within the framework of existing institutions enabled the newspaper to make the commitment without violating its own principles, or the principles of the society in which it functioned. "There is no enmity towards Capital on the part of Labor, . . ." it exulted after the Labor Day parade of 1884. "There is no natural antagonism between the Mechanic and the Millionaire."[2] Such statements, debatable at least, reflect its commitment to the dogma of a conservative age. But the relative innocuousness of supporting labor against capital when labor is not radical does not detract from the importance of the support, both as an evidence of the *World*'s crusading zeal, and of its determination to win the loyalty of the depressed groups which had not hitherto been notably newspaper readers.

Its attempt to establish a special relationship with workingmen got underway within the first week of Pulitzer's arrival. On

[2] *World*, September 2, 1884, p. 4.

— 288 —

May 13, 1883, in an editorial deploring the "codfish" aristocracy coming to prominence in New York City, the paper suggested a different group as deserving social primacy.

> Our aristocracy is the aristocracy of labor. The man who by honest, earnest toil supports his family in respectability, who works with a stout heart and a strong arm, who fights his way through life courageously, maintaining his good name through privations and temptations, and winning from his children respect as well as love, is the proudest aristocrat in the American Republic.[3]

It concluded with the assurance that "the new *World* is [the laboring man's] organ." An editorial mocking the pretension of a visiting French aristocrat repeated that "The *World* is a Democratic newspaper, and it cares more for the humblest toiler in the Hocking Valley, if he be an honest man, than for any individual whose claim to distinction rests upon a noble title."[4] The following year, when James Blaine and Benjamin Butler threatened between them to undercut the normal Democratic majority in New York City, a pro-Cleveland editorial reminded workingmen that the *World* had consistently taken their side. "We need not assure the workingmen of New York that the *World*, under its present management, is their staunch and steadfast friend. Our splendid success, unprecedented in the history of journalism, is the best proof that they know and appreciate that fact."[5]

These declarations of friendship were supported by scores of editorials pleading for labor on a wide variety of issues. The newspaper had ample opportunity to crusade, for workingmen in New York City at that time wrestled with problems that almost defied solution. Trade unions were still in their infancy, and the nagging aftereffects of the Panic of 1873, together with a new panic in 1884 and mounting immigration, meant that thousands of men searched in vain for jobs. Even the most skilled workers had difficulty maintaining their standard of living in the absence of greater bargaining power, and for the unskilled, which increasingly meant immigrant workers, the challenge literally reduced to one of subsistence.

[3] *World*, May 13, 1883, p. 4. [4] *World*, December 23, 1884, p. 4.
[5] *World*, October 28, 1884, p. 4.

The *World* tried to alert the city to the toll exacted of the men and women who made the wheels of industry go round. It assumed—a symptom of an optimistic age—that reform would necessarily follow if only the privileged part of the community could be made aware of the need in their midst, and denied the luxury of forgetting. Any particular victory the newspaper managed to achieve by its nagging was secondary to the greater function of serving as conscience to a people just starting to come to terms with the meaning of industrial capitalism. Never before or since have newspapermen so believed in the power of the press, and in this respect, as in so many others, Joseph Pulitzer showed the way.

An early series of articles focused on the padrone system, by which Italian immigrants indentured themselves to the men who purchased their steamship tickets to America. The padrone, who came from the old country himself, but who was wise in the ways of the new world, contracted with American employers to provide gangs of men at fixed rates to do various types of physical labor. He rounded up workers by sending tickets to his friends or acquaintances in Italy, on the understanding that the debt would be paid off when they reached the United States and joined his crew. The padrone negotiated jobs for the men, and distributed wages to them. In principle, both parties to the bargain benefited equally. The newcomer was shielded from the worst excesses of American employers, and had the opportunity to work among his own people in his own language. His patron enjoyed a labor supply at once cheap and compliant. Unfortunately, the American business ethic proved more formidable than European paternalism. Old loyalties died as the padrones discovered that their own fortunes lay in hiring labor cheaply and selling it dearly. That discovery dashed the dreams of the unfortunates who had traveled across the ocean to make a new start. They sweated over pick and shovel for a dollar a day, ignorant of their plight or helpless to improve it. It was all but impossible on the pittance they received to buy out of the contract which brought them to the United States in the first place.

The *World* forgot its otherwise unsympathetic treatment of Italians in reporting the case of two such padrones who forced their countrymen into virtual bondage. MODERN SLAVEHOLDERS a headline charged. HOW ITALIANS ARE IMPORTED AND HELD IN BONDAGE.[6] An appeal by several of the victims to the Italian Vice-Consul in New York City gave the story greater impact than the usual one of oppressed workers, a fact the *World* immediately exploited. It dispatched a reporter to interview Victor T. Revel, the Vice-Consul, and quoted him at length on how the system operated.

> The fare from Naples is $28 or $30, but when the emigrants are landed here they are forced to sign papers acknowledging that they owe $66. . . . When the emigrant has acknowledged his debt for passage he is compelled to pay $3, $5, and sometimes $15 to get a place. As he is in debt to the padroni they make him board at some place that they either own or are interested in. The laborers are not given work every day. . . . Their board goes on just the same, and at the end of the month they are in debt to the padroni, who makes contracts for their work and receives the wages. . . . Cases have been reported here where men have worked six months and have been in debt $20 and even more for board and their passage still to be paid for.[7]

The series continued a few days later with the call to a public meeting, under the sponsorship of Signor Revel, at which several plans were to be submitted for liberating Italian immigrants from their wage slavery.[8]

Many more articles exposed and condemned the workings of the sweatshop system. Partly because sweating posed a particular problem in New York City during the 1880s, partly perhaps because Pulitzer's own Jewish background conditioned him to regard the plight of fellow Jews with sympathy, the *World* published numerous accounts of the economic hardships endured by those engaged in the manufacture of clothing.[9] "You would

[6] *World*, December 16, 1884, p. 3.
[7] *World*, December 21, 1884, p. 6.
[8] *World*, December 26, 1884, p. 8.
[9] Most of the garment workers in the city spoke Yiddish, a fact which had the Jewish immigrant huddled over a sewing machine or hot iron almost before he debarked from his ship. "A friend of mine who manufactures cloth," Jacob Riis related, "once boasted to me that nowadays, on cheap clothing, New

— 291 —

like to know how we all live on such sums," a seamstress replied in an article describing piece rates. "It is a problem, but we do, after a fashion, as you see. I have a friend who rooms with me, and together we pay $6 a month for this room. Nearly all of us have to room with one or more other women. . . . We have to buy our food in the very smallest quantities. . . . The smaller you subdivide the articles the more they seem to cost."[10] One measure of the success of such stories in arousing public sympathy came in 1884, when the newspaper reported the struggle of a Mrs.

York 'beats the world.' 'To what,' I asked, 'do you attribute it?' 'To the cutter's long knife and the Polish Jew,' he said." Jacob A. Riis, *How the Other Half Lives*, p. 121.

The sweatshop system entailed four stages in the manufacture of clothing. Wholesale manufacturers cut and bunched garments, which they distributed in job lots to smaller contractors, each a specialist in his line. Coats, for example, went to one place for finishing, trousers to another, dresses to another, and so on. The manufacturer ceased to concern himself with the garment after it left his factory, caring neither how nor where it was finished. About half of the goods thus distributed were prepared for retailing in the contractors' own factories. They subdivided the other half to sweaters, whose shops usually occupied the largest of two or three rooms in a tenement flat. The sweater lived with his family in one room, and employed up to twenty sewers and pressers in the other rooms. He, in turn, might subcontract about half of the work to neighborhood families, delivering cut material to them and receiving finished garments. Hand labor at that level turned out approximately one-quarter of all clothing manufactured in New York City, and a larger proportion of children's clothing. Each step down the scale, from manufacturer to contractor to sweater to home workers, entailed a diminution of compensation and responsibility. As John DeWitt Warner put it in *Harper's Weekly*, "The profit of each (except the wretch at the bottom) is 'sweated' from the next below him." (John DeWitt Warner, "The 'Sweating System' in New York City," *Harper's Weekly*, xxxix [February 9, 1885], 135-36).

The system derived in the first place from a legislative oversight. New York State boasted a fairly liberal factory law for the time, providing for a ten-hour day, a forty-five-minute lunch break, strict curbs on child labor, and a mandatory closing time of 9 P.M. The very liberality of the law gave sweaters their competitive edge, since nothing in it applied to work carried on in private dwellings. By recruiting labor from immigrants just off the ship, and paying them piece-rate at a scale requiring fifteen to eighteen hours of daily labor for subsistence (wages still totaled one-third to one-fourth less than those in contractors' shops), the sweater so underbid machinery as to turn a profit for himself and the contractor who supplied him. Not surprisingly, the net swept in only the most desperate candidates: the poorest immigrants, widowed or abandoned women, children supplementing family income. For an authoritative report on the system, see U.S. House of Representatives, *Committee on Manufactures in the Sweating System*, Report 2,309, 52nd Congress, Second Session (Washington, D.C., 1893).

[10] *World*, February 3, 1884, p. 10.

Morgan to survive on 30 cents a day.[11] Although the article did
did not solicit contributions, they started to come in, and at a rate
soon embarrassing to the editors. "We have Mrs. Morgan's receipt for $59 collected by us in her behalf," the *World* reported
ten days after the publication of the original article. "Our understanding is that she is now quite comfortable and there is no
necessity for further contributions."[12]

The long hours put in by many workers raised a stickier
question, since in 1883 Governor Cleveland had vetoed a bill
setting a twelve-hour day for horse-car drivers. The *World*
offered an ingenuous defense of his action at the height of the
following year's campaign, arguing that since the bill provided
that drivers would still be paid by the trip rather than the day,
its result would be to bring their total wages below subsistence
levels. "The drivers and conductors ought to hold a mass-
meeting to thank Governor Cleveland for vetoing a bill so absurd
and so adverse to their interests," an editorial suggested.
"Demagogues may bluster and promise, but no legislative enact-
ment has ever yet been invented that will secure a man fifteen
hours' pay for eight hours' labor."[13] As to the obvious question,
why a bill could not provide for both minimum pay and maximum hours, the *World* argued that the matter was "regulated by
the law of supply and demand."[14]

Its statements before and after the campaign, when Cleveland's indiscretion did not have to be justified, were much more
in accord with prevailing labor sentiment. As early as May 1883,
the *World* took issue with the arguments raised against legislative control of working hours.

> It is not sufficient answer to this brutality of em-
> ployment that the persons subjected to it are free
> agents, and can accept or decline the work at their
> will. Their wants compel them to submit to the tyr-

[11] *World*, February 13, 1884, p. 2. The article on Mrs. Morgan appeared as
a sequel to the one on February 3rd, both of them headlined: GUSSET, SEAM
AND BAND.
[12] *World*, February 23, 1884, p. 4.
[13] *World*, July 15, 1884, p. 4.
[14] *World*, July 25, 1884, p. 4.

anny, and when they complain they are told that hundreds stand ready to take their places. . . .

Alarm and indignation are manifested whenever legislation is proposed limiting the hours of labor, and we are reminded of the outrage of interfering with the right of contract. But . . . to sodden the intellect of the working classes by oppressive and unnatural employment is a public danger.[15]

Theodore Roosevelt's objection in the State Assembly to a bill which would have reduced the car drivers' workday to twelve hours without a reduction in pay triggered an explosive response from the newspaper. Although the *World* itself would deride such proposals a few months later as contrary to the law of supply and demand, Roosevelt laid himself open to rebuttal when he labelled the bill as communistic. "If it be Communism, nice, dainty, cultured Mr. Roosevelt," the *World* sneered, "to say to these favored corporations, 'Twelve hours shall be a legal day's work,' pray what is it when the corporations say to their employees, 'You shall slave for sixteen hours a day or starve?' "[16]

The newspaper returned to the attack after the November elections had been safely weathered. Although it endorsed Cleveland's veto, at least by implication, by opposing in January 1885 a second bill to limit the working day of horse-car drivers without maintaining their pay, the post-election *World* saw no reason why the transit companies should not be coerced into paying fair wages for a twelve-hour day.[17] A threatened strike by the drivers to win that concession found the *World* urging restraint, but not without disputing the *New York Tribune*'s contention that a strike would be foolish since as unskilled workers they could easily be replaced. "Because they are not skilled is no reason why they should be killed, . . ." an editorial declared. It doubted the wisdom of a strike only because on this issue labor's interest was allied with the public interest, and the public could demand justice without the need for a work stoppage.

When sordid individuals obtain a valuable public franchise from the people, the people bind them to do

[15] *World*, May 20, 1883, p. 4.   [16] *World*, February 2, 1884, p. 4.
[17] The editorial opposing the bill which duplicated the one vetoed by Governor Cleveland appeared on January 23, 1885, p. 4.

certain things for the safety and convenience of the public and to charge a certain rate of fare. They have just as much right, as a condition of the gift of the franchise, to bind those who receive it to respect the rights of their employees and to pay them the fixed wages and adopt the fixed hours that prevail in the city departments in the employment of labor.[18]

Clearly, the *World* was willing to go far beyond its Presidential candidate in applying pressure on private companies for the common good.

The consequences of long hours of labor for insufficient wages included more than poverty and despair for thousands of workingmen in New York City. Unable to support a household by his own efforts, the worker increasingly called upon his wife, and even his children, to take jobs which would contribute to the family income. Their contribution had long since been assumed among such depressed groups as garment workers and cigarmakers, but the passage of years saw even the elite troops of labor joined by recruits dressed in knee pants and petticoats.[19] As a result, the number of women employed full time in New York City tripled in less than two decades, from 70,000 in 1867 to 200,000 in 1885.[20]

The hopes of working class families that they might earn enough for comfort and security by pooling the incomes of several members had already been dashed by the time the *World* undertook its great crusades. Women and children offered cheap

[18] *World*, February 27, 1885, p. 4.

[19] Edward and Eleanor Aveling, who visited this country in 1890, reported finding women "forced to work for wages because the husband's were insufficient for even bare subsistence," and "parents obliged to . . . send children to the mills to earn sufficient for the maintenance of their family." Edward B. and Eleanor Aveling, *The Working Class Movement in America* (2nd ed.; London, 1891), pp. 98-101.

[20] So many sub-factors are involved in such a comparison that it can provide no more than a rough approximation of the greater pressure on women to contribute to the family income. For example, many of the 70,000 women working in 1867 had been called out of the home by the Civil War, which suggests that the trend of twenty years was even more pronounced than the statistics reveal. But at the same time, many of the 200,000 working in 1885 represented women of the middle class enjoying a status revolution. It is difficult to say much more with certainty than that in each decade there was greater pressure on working class families to have wives join their husbands as wage earners.

labor, with disastrous consequences for wage scales generally. By the 1880s the real income of a whole family tended to approach what one had earned previously. Moreover, their presence almost undoubtedly impeded the progress of unionization. Since they worked for different reasons than men (supplementing family income rather than earning it), they were less inclined to wage industrial warfare for what seemed insignificant gains. Their unwillingness to strike made them effective scabs at a showdown.

Employers exacted a severe price of the women and children for the privilege of earning their keep. Marie Dressler's line, that "heaven will protect the poor working girl," applies to the 1880s only as a subtle reminder that nobody else would. A series of investigations conducted by the Working Women's Society established that women generally earned less than the minimum amount needed for subsistence.[21] On a citywide average, their pay totalled about half as much as men's, and although the differential varied from occupation to occupation, it struck hardest in the industries with a living wage for masculine labor. In the few cases without significant differential—among cigarmakers, hatters, printers, etc.—workers of both sexes received less than subsistence pay.

The large number of children in the working force were just as vulnerable, despite the best efforts of reformers to protect them. It had been hoped that their participation in the economy would be curbed by the passage of a compulsory education law, requiring that youngsters between the ages of ten and fourteen show proof of having attended school three months in the year before working in shops or factories, and, if under sixteen, of being able to read and write English. Experience soon taught that such legislation had little meaning in an era of unrestrained capitalism, certainly without an army of inspectors to enforce it. Prior to 1890, New York State delegated one full-time official to track down truants in Manhattan. In any case, the law only dabbed at symptoms of the social cancer it was expected to cure.

[21] For a discussion of how women workers were exploited by their employers, see Helen Stuart Campbell, *Women Wage-Earners: Their Past, Their Present and Their Future* (Boston, 1893), especially p. 213.

Desperation, not callousness, impelled parents to put their children in factories, and desperation kept them there. They learned the magic qualities of the number "16" before they could recite the alphabet because their bodies, more than their minds, needed nourishment. Even if the law had tried to stop them, the need would have remained, and so would the response to the need. Indeed, the most efficient factory law would have been inadequate, since for each child tending a machine, nine or ten polished shoes or peddled flowers—if anything smiled upon as budding Horatio Algers.[22]

Their participation suited the system for obvious reasons. The young ones worked for next to nothing; they often performed routine chores more efficiently than adults; they made poor candidates for unions or agitation. Most important, the employer armed with a notarized statement attesting to the child's age had nothing to fear from factory inspectors. The child could be sent to a reform school, and his parents prosecuted for perjury, but the man who profited from juvenile labor broke no law. Not that penalties were often invoked. Inspectors usually put underage children on the street with a warning, fully aware that they would return to their jobs in an hour or two.

A spate of magazine articles appeared during the 1880s deploring the use of underaged workers at all, and beyond that, the treatment to which they were subjected.[23] Like women, they had little bargaining power and were easily exploited in a system that honored profit as the highest good. The common law shielded employers from liability for accidents which their young and overtired charges might suffer, while the same social sickness which put children in factories in the first place determined that their conditions of employment would shock the conscience of whoever bothered to investigate.

[22] The New York Child Labor Committee estimated in 1901 that about 450,000 of the State's 1,500,000 children between the ages of five and eighteen did not attend classes at all. Ten percent of that number worked in factories, the rest as bootblacks, newsboys, peddlers, delivery boys, and other occupations outside the scope of the law. See Thomas Cochran and William Miller, *The Age of Enterprise* (New York, 1942), p. 278.

[23] See, for example, Helen Campbell *et al.*, "White Child Slavery. A Symposium," *The Arena*, I (April 1890); Emma E. Brown, "Children's Labor: A Problem," *Atlantic Monthly*, XLVI (December 1880); William F. Willoughby, "Child Labor," *Publications of the American Economic Association*, V (1890).

The *World* tried to help the women and children by telling their story, again on the assumption that in the glare of publicity injustice must perish. It wisely eschewed the techniques of sensationalism in dozens of articles which soberly and authoritatively recounted the plight of the weakest members of the working force. If the articles sometimes stirred outrage, it was because of what they reported rather than their tone. There was nothing sensational, for example, in the article that described how fur workers absorbed dangerous quantities of the arsenic used in preparing the pelts, and how they often suffered respiratory ailments because of the hairs they inhaled. "In my own case," a woman told the *World* reporter, "the absorption of arsenic into my system has, as you see, given me a very fair complexion, but I am slowly dying from the poisoning. The evil was too far advanced before I realized it."[24] The articles reported matter-of-factly the pay female workers earned, and how they tried to subsist on that pay.

> The general average [for shirt-makers] is from $5.50 to $6 per week, when work is steady and a girl is at her machine ten hours a day. Cloakmakers average a little higher—from $6 to $7 per week. Fur-sewers about the same. . . . Tailoresses, whose work is hardest and heaviest of all machine sewing, earn from $6 to $7 per week. . . .
>
> [In shops, the girls] usually begin as cash-girls at $2 a week. As salesladies their wages vary from $5 at which they begin, to $15 or $18, which an exceptionally good one, who is of value to the firm employing her, may receive. The average salary is from $6 to $7. . . .
>
> Sewing girls and salesladies constitute over one-half of the working women of New York. . . . Bindery girls average $6 to $7 per week. . . . Paperbox makers do not average more than $6. . . . Milliners earn higher wages than any of the other trades of this class, averaging from $12 to $18 per week. But it must be remembered that theirs is what is known as a 'season trade,' and their work is good only for three months each in the spring and fall.

[24] *World*, April 6, 1884, p. 10.

By these figures the average pay of working women is shown to be $7 per week. . . . The usual price of a clean hall bedroom in a respectable house, with reasonably good and sufficient food, is $5 per week. . . . Washing at the lowest estimate is 50 cents per week; fire, a necessity in winter, 50 cents more. If lunch is not furnished that will be sixty cents per week, at the very least. And if a girl is obliged to ride to and from her work, there is 60 cents more for carfare. . . . Is there a financier in this country skillful enough to inform the public how [the budget is to be managed?][25]

Finally, *World* reporters accompanied workingwomen to their homes and described what it meant to them in their daily domestic routine to have too little money.[26]

More than publicizing their problems, the newspaper tried through its editorial page to interest the public in supporting schemes to ease the drudgery such women accepted as their lot. One of the *World*'s favorite projects was the Working Girls' Vacation Society, which solicited funds to enable those who could not otherwise afford it to have some time away from their jobs. "A nobler and more beneficent work than this," the paper declared, "which outreaches the individual and touches the community and the race, has not been undertaken by local humanitarians."[27]

It applied a somewhat different strategy in urging help for the children of the slums. The *World* had more than once proved its willingness to endorse any reform on behalf of the weak and dispossessed, but only so long as it did not include government intervention on a significant scale. (Even the famous ten-point program postulated by Pulitzer a week after acquiring the newspaper, presumably a statement of radicalism, boils down to five points on taxing wealth, one on tariff reform, and four on honesty in government.[28]) The moderate tone was perfectly ac-

[25] *World*, April 19, 1885, p. 18. For other articles on the same theme, see February 3, 1884, p. 10; and March 6, 1885, p. 3.
[26] See, for example, the *World*, March 2, 1884, p. 12; and May 3, 1885, p. 19.
[27] *World*, August 17, 1884, p. 4.
[28] The ten points are listed in Chapter One, p. 14.

ceptable to labor, and accorded with a genuine reform mentality, when taken together with the newspaper's endorsement of unionism. It made sense in the 1880s to believe that collective bargaining would solve all of the problems of labor, male and female labor alike, and that government assistance posed more risks than opportunities. The logic broke down when applied to children, however, for they were not the best prospects to walk a picket line. Unless the federal or state governments accepted the responsibility of policing factories in a meaningful way, the children working in them would continue to suffer. Their potential role as scabs during periods of industrial conflict would also impede the development of strong unions.

The *World's* solution, an unrealistic one so long as tenement families needed the income of children as well as adults, was to encourage the poor to keep their offspring in school. There would be no need for extensive governmental regulation if the end could be achieved voluntarily. The newspaper repeatedly reminded its readers that the offspring of the lower classes were born with as much innate ability as those of the upper class, and that neglect more than heredity retarded their development. An occasion for one such sermon came in July 1883, with the death of the author of the famous monograph on the Jukes family, which contended that criminal traits were transmitted by heredity. "It is mere waste of words to argue that the habits of life [are] . . . inherited, . . ." the *World* insisted. "As it is, the poorest and plainest man takes his pride and consolation in observing that the loftiest triumphs of genius are achieved by the sons of the people."[29] The following year, a reporter sent to interview Lawrence D. Kiernan, Secretary of the Board of Education, returned with this exchange:

> "Do the children of the wealthy class display greater or less proficiency or aptitude than the children of poor parents?"
> "I have found that after all the question of proficiency or talent cannot be confined to any social class. In fact intellect cannot be divided into classes. . . . The grades of the schools in poor neighborhoods

[29] *World*, July 29, 1883, p. 4.

— 300 —

are quite as high as those located in the most wealthy parts of the city."[30]

It was idle to urge the poor to educate their children unless the city provided facilities for them. Significantly, although not a single statement appeared in the *World* demanding wider governmental control of child labor in factories, a host of editorials called upon the city to remake the school system. Some of them urged that funds be allocated to repair the buildings that had fallen into a dangerous state of decay;[31] others that the salaries of primary school teachers be raised in order to attract more and better people into the profession.[32] But the most constant theme was the need for new buildings to house a population desirous of education. THEY WANT MORE SCHOOLS, the headline on one of those articles proclaimed, setting the tone of the entire crusade.[33] On occasion the *World* at least implied that the struggle for schools was part of a larger struggle between the classes for survival.

> There is something wrong in the adaptation of our Public School system to the needs of the population when 553 children are refused admission in one month for want of school accommodations. It would be a curious calculation to ascertain how many of the school children receiving a free education have wealthy parents who are quite able to purchase the best instruction, and how many needy and worthy little ones are kept out in the cold by them.[34]

It could come no closer to including children in the crusade on behalf of the city's embattled proletariat.

To argue that the *World* preferred that laborers help themselves through trade unions, rather than rely on beneficent legislation, is only part of the story, for at the time the union concept appalled large numbers of Americans. Pulitzer's newspaper defied the bias of some of the most influential elements in the society when, consistent in its logic, it took the side of organized labor.

The most dramatic evidence of anti-union sentiment is seen

[30] *World*, July 10, 1884, p. 3.
[31] For example, the *World*, November 23, 1883, p. 4.
[32] *World*, December 3, 1883, p. 4.
[33] *World*, February 23, 1885, p. 2. See also December 28, 1884, p. 4.
[34] *World*, December 19, 1884, p. 4.

in the enthusiastic reception accorded *The Bread-winners*, a novel first published anonymously in 1882, and later credited to John Hay. It quickly climbed the list of best sellers, and ran as a serial from August 1883, to January 1884, in *Century Magazine*, becoming a conversation piece among middle class people who worried about the relationship between labor and capital. Hay offered a straightforward enough theme. The great majority of American workingmen, he believed, were decent and well motivated. Unfortunately, they listened to "unscrupulous leaders and politicians" who preached disrespect for property and authority. Trade unions were tolerable as long as they followed "sound economic principles," but they needed responsible leaders to show the way. If men of breeding and substance did not come forward to provide such leadership, the proletariat would squander itself attempting to reconstruct the industrial order.[35] One of the dramatic moments in the novel occurred when a demagogue approached Hay's "honest and contented workman":

> "What are we, anyhow?" continued the greasy apostle of labor. "We are slaves; we are Roosian scurfs. We work as many hours as our owners like;

[35] George F. Baer, President of the Philadelphia & Reading Railway Company, used much the same logic two decades later in assuring a correspondent that the company's vigorous suppression of a strike by the United Mine Workers was justified. "My dear Mr. Clark," he wrote: "I do not know who you are. I see that you are a religious man; but you are evidently biased in favor of the right of the working man to control a business in which he has no other interest than to secure fair wages for the work he does. I beg of you not to be discouraged. The rights and interests of the laboring man will be protected and cared for—not by the labor agitators, but by the Christian men to whom God in His infinite wisdom has given the control of the property interests of the country." (The letter, dated 17th July 1902, is reproduced in David A. Shannon, *Twentieth Century America, The United States Since the 1890's* [Chicago, 1963], following p. 90.) Edwin Lawrence Godkin, an earlier-day Walter Lippmann, sealed the verdict for most right-minded people with an article in *Atlantic Monthly*, decrying the notion that laborers were abused and needed to gird for self-defense. As editor of the *Nation* and the *New York Evening Post*, an ardent supporter of civil service reform, and a leading participant in the Mugwump revolt against James G. Blaine in 1884, he was almost literally the voice of the responsible middle class. There is "no more mischievous person," this spokesman for reform declared in 1896, "than the man who, in free America, seeks to spread . . . the idea that [the workers] are wronged and kept down by somebody; that somebody is to blame because they are not better lodged, better dressed, better educated, and have no easier access to balls, concerts, or dinner parties." Edwin L. Godkin, "Social Classes in the Republic," *Atlantic Monthly*, LXXVIII (December 1896), 725.

we take what pay they choose to give us; we ask their permission to live and breathe."

"Oh, that's a lie," Sleeny interrupted, with unbroken calmness. "Old Saul Matchin and me come to an agreement about time and pay, and both of us was suited. If he's got his heel onto me, I don't feel it."[36]

That exchange, with its obvious villain and hero, and its dated concept of how wage agreements were negotiated, described as well as any the attitude of middle and upper class New Yorkers when workingmen rose in protest.

The *World* demonstrated time and again that it did not share the prejudices of the Mugwump reformers. It courted trade unions with an almost self-conscious ardor, in its private dealings with them as much as in editorials for public consumption. Whether Pulitzer and his staff were motivated primarily by principle, or by the realization that many of their subscribers belonged to the laboring class, they made the *World* an outspoken champion of a movement still struggling for respectability.

The opportunity to prove good faith came early. On the evening of May 24th, 1883, Pulitzer and Cockerill returned to the World Building from the ceremonies dedicating the Brooklyn Bridge with plans to put out a special edition the next morning. They discovered to their horror that the printers had called a wildcat strike in protest against an economy move by Business Manager John McGuffin depriving them of soap and ice. Recognizing that Pulitzer could hardly afford to bargain at that juncture, John R. O'Donnell, Night Editor of the *New York Herald* and President of Typographical Union No. 6, quickly forced him to concede on the issue. Pulitzer made an even broader concession in agreeing that henceforth union-card holders would be permitted to work in what had hitherto been a nonunion shop. The typographers had hoped for some time to win this point as a first step toward turning the *World* plant into a closed shop. In return, O'Donnell temporarily accepted for the printers a nonunion wage scale of 40 cents per 1,000 ems of type set. On the basis of this bargain, hurriedly struck in Keenan's Cafe adjacent

[36] John Hay, *The Bread-winners* (New York, 1884), p. 78.

to the World Building, the printers returned to their jobs, and the newspaper appeared the next morning with its coveted Brooklyn Bridge story.

Pulitzer manifested in this instance not so much a pro-union sentiment as a businessman's awareness of when to compromise. He did more to win the goodwill of labor when the union's contract with the other newspapers in the city expired and a new one was signed, paying 46 cents per 1,000 ems. Although his agreement with O'Donnell was binding until November, Pulitzer voluntarily raised the *World* scale to 45 cents in order to maintain only a token differential between his own contract and that just signed. The extra cost to the newspaper did not amount to much—$1,797.80—but it proved the publisher's goodwill and his determination to bargain equitably with the men in his employ.[37]

Cynics answered that the gesture was an unsubtle sort of propaganda, and that Pulitzer's true stripes were revealed by the non-union status of the men working for him on the *St. Louis Post-Dispatch*. As might be expected, *The Journalist*, under Leander Richardson, leveled the sharpest accusations. It picked up an item that first appeared in the *New York Extra* reporting that Pulitzer's employees in St. Louis worked in an open shop, and on that basis branded the publisher a hypocrite. "The *Extra* proved very conclusively that Mr. Jewseph Pulitzer was insincere in his professions of interest in the workingman. He pays union prices in New York because he must. He pays non-union rates in St. Louis because he can. Mr. Jewseph Pulitzer is a humbug and a fraud in this respect as in many others. He does not mean what he professes."[38] While Richardson as usual hurt his own case by the

[37] The story of Pulitzer's dealings with the union is told in Don C. Seitz, *Joseph Pulitzer, His Life & Letters* (New York, 1924), pp. 142-43. The publisher's success in fostering good relations with his employees is further evidenced by a petition addressed to him the following November, when the *World* started to pay the citywide union wage scale. "We, the undersigned," it declared, "beg leave to express to you and Mr. McGuffin our heartfelt thanks for the manner in which you have treated our Committee from the Union, who waited upon you today, as well as granting the increase in the rate of composition, thereby carrying out the principles of the paper in advocating the cause of the workingman." The petition, dated November 15, was signed by fifty-one men. *Pulitzer Papers*, Columbia University Libraries.

[38] *The Journalist*, September 6, 1884, p. 1.

virulence of his tone, and the anti-Semitism which poisoned it, his arguments cannot be dismissed out of hand. The separate status of Pulitzer's employees in New York and St. Louis would certainly lend credence to the argument that the *World*'s pro-unionism was as much a matter of convenience as of principle. The newspaper had every economic reason for taking the stand that it did in New York City, and a case might be made that self-interest alone explains its liberalism.

The truth of the matter is that Pulitzer was probably neither an uncritical friend of labor nor a disguised enemy. Professor Julian S. Rammelkamp, an authority on the publisher's years in St. Louis, makes the case that his reactions were really those of a middle class, small businessman. He had little love for the great corporations that threatened the survival of men like himself, and naturally supported labor in its crusade against them. "But, . . . at least in St. Louis, when it came to unions 'coercing' businesses like his own, he was distinctly unhappy and often balked."[39]

The analysis makes a good deal of sense, particularly, as Professor Rammelkamp cautions, when applied to the St. Louis phase of Pulitzer's career. The *Post-Dispatch* found its audience primarily among the middle class of that city, and could be expected to reflect middle class views. But the same does not apply to the *New York World*. Pulitzer undertook when he went east to publish a sensational journal that would set new circulation records in the United States. He necessarily had to appeal to the group that was most numerous and most susceptible to persuasion, which in the case of New York City at least, meant the vast army of native and foreign-born workers. Of course people of many different backgrounds found features in the *World* to attract them, but the fifty percent or so of the population who lived in tenement houses comprised the nucleus of his following. It was on their behalf that he constantly enjoined his staff to keep the paper simple in language and format, and to see that it remain lively and brisk and sympathetic to the cause of the down-

[39] The statement is contained in a private letter to the author. Rammelkamp goes on to question whether much in the *World* that presumably reflected a lower class, immigrant orientation was not in fact directed to the middle class.

trodden. No New Yorker ever had reason to doubt where the paper's sympathies lay.

If a different question were put, not whether Pulitzer took the side of workingmen, but whether he did so unqualifiedly, the answer would be more complicated. It would certainly make sense, in that case, to examine some of the differences between the way he ran the *Post-Dispatch* and the *World*. Other points could also be raised. For example, Walt McDougall claimed credit for deciding the paper's policy at the time of the Homestead strike, and alleged that Pulitzer went along for less than noble reasons.

> I frequently practically dictated the policy of the paper by making a cartoon in advance of editorial comment, as, for instance, in the case of the Homestead strike, when my picture sided with the strikers instead of with Carnegie before Pulitzer had decided on his policy. Without showing any feeling, he remarked on the position in which I had placed the paper, and within a day or so was pleased to say that my point of view was the correct one. With me, of course, it was not policy, but simply sympathy with the laboring man, and I did not then know that the policy of a modern newspaper is usually nothing more than political or business expediency.[40]

The cartoonist made essentially the same point in an earlier article, when he complained that "the writings of some of his former employees are creating a demi-god out of a highly commercial gentleman who knew exactly what every cent in a dollar was worth and what sort of literature would most cheaply extract pennies from the lower classes."[41]

Against such statements, we have the abundance of evidence that Pulitzer really did care about the plight of the dispossessed classes in nineteenth century America. The editorials during the 1880s convey a sense of outrage that could not be simulated, and in later years, when Pulitzer's fortune was made, and when self-interest might have dictated a more moderate tone, the same outrage remained.

[40] Walt McDougall, "Pictures in the Papers," *The American Mercury*, VI (September 1925), 70.
[41] McDougall, "Old Days on *The World*," *ibid.*, IV (January 1925), 23.

In any event, the extent to which expediency rather than principle dictated the editorials is almost beside the point. The fact is that the *World* was liberal and did support workingmen at a time when they critically needed support. Even putting the worst light on Pulitzer's motives—something difficult to do considering his consistency in pleading for reform throughout the years—it is still true that the cause he fought for was more important than the route which brought him to the cause.

Almost two years after the negotiations with the Typographer's Union, in April of 1885, another opportunity came for Pulitzer to win the affection of organized labor. By that time, with a circulation exceeding 100,000 daily and almost 150,000 on Sundays, the *World* was starting to dominate New York journalism. Evidence of its success appeared not only in the certified circulation figures printed almost daily, but in the announcement early in 1885 that henceforth the newspaper would publish a special edition in Brooklyn. It took large ads in the other metropolitan journals (with the exception of the *Herald*, which refused to run the ad), to publicize the Brooklyn edition. Unfortunately, one of the papers in which the ad appeared, the *New York Tribune*, was currently under boycott by the Central Labor Union because of its extremely anti-labor editorial policies. Pulitzer received a letter from George K. Lloyd, Corresponding Secretary of the C.L.U., expressing dismay at this failure to honor a union boycott. "Believing or knowing that the *World* has become very popular with the Trade Unionists," Lloyd wrote, "I need not inform you that the Central Labor Union has passed resolutions to boycott the *Tribune* and all its advertising patrons." He asked that the *World* withdraw its ad and cooperate by refusing to engage in any further business transactions with the offending journal. Pulitzer printed the letter on the *World*'s editoral page, and with it an apology and promise that the error would not be repeated. "It must be admitted that the insertion of the advertisement of the *World* in the *Tribune* was an inadvertence," the publisher replied.

> An announcement of our new Brooklyn Edition was prepared and handed to our agent with instructions to insert it in all the morning newspapers of the city.

> No special thought was given to the subject. . . . If we had thought for one moment of the attitude of the *Tribune* toward the Labor Organizations of the country we certainly would not have permitted our advertisement to appear in the *Tribune*.[42]

The response can be explained away as one of panic (on the theory that a labor boycott would hurt the *World* far more than the *Tribune*), or as an attempt to curry favor with the group that constituted so vital a part of the newspaper's audience. A letter which appeared two days later from a newly converted subscriber supports the latter interpretation.

> A lifelong "Democrat" and reader of the *Sun*, I voted for Butler, trusting these twins had the welfare of the wage-workers at heart, contrary to the advice of the *World*. Now I read and strive to advance the the circulation of the *World*, believing it to be worth all other city papers put together and more, and your reply to the Central Labor Union of today makes my belief the more positive.[43]

But it makes as much sense to say the obvious: that the newspaper supported a boycott against one of its own, on an issue fundamental to the working of the press, in order to prove not only its commitment to labor, but its willingness to act on that commitment.

The *World*'s news and editorial content provided still clearer indications of its goodwill toward the men who worked in the city's factories and shops. No metropolitan journal covered labor affairs more exhaustively, particularly the monthly meetings of the Central Labor Union. The stories could not have been very interesting to nonwage-earners, indeed to nonmembers of the C.L.U., but they appeared faithfully, reporting such things as the plans for a reception in honor of Henry George, the tactics to be used in boycotting an antagonistic firm, and the lobbying priorities of delegates sent to Albany.[44] The same bias was evident in the paper's reports on subjects of broader interest. A

[42] *World*, April 23, 1885, p. 4.
[43] *World*, April 25, 1885, p. 4.
[44] The examples cited appeared in the issues of February 25, 1884, p. 8; March 24, 1884, p. 8; and April 21, 1884, p. 7.

strike called by employees of the Missouri Pacific Railroad, after they had been forced to take successive wage reductions of 10 and 5 percent so that the line could pay its regular dividends on watered stock, found the newspaper almost alone in taking the side of labor. "We believe it to be cruel and barbarous," an editorial declared, "for any corporation to demand their unskilled employees to subsist on the small pittance of $1 or $1.18 per day, as it is certainly a life of slavery to them, and ought not to be tolerated in any civilized community."[45] The fact that Jay Gould owned a large bloc of shares in the Missouri Pacific, and that he was currently enjoying a cruise on his luxury yacht, suggested a style of editorializing which the *World* immediately used to good effect.

> Mr. Jay Gould, in the enjoyment of the large wealth he has secured by his successful railroad ventures, goes on a grand pleasure tour to the Antilles on his magnificent steam yacht, the *Atlanta*. His daily expenses are as much as the wages of 200 workingmen in the employ of his grand system of railroads. One bottle of his choice wine costs more than a Missouri Pacific laborer can spend for food for his family in two weeks.
> While Jay Gould is sailing, the employees of the great Gould system of Pacific Railroads are starving and striking. . . .
> This is the case in a nutshell. Dividends paid on watered stock which has gone to add to the hoards of millionaires who are sailing in their floating palaces among the soft breezes of the Antilles. Wages cut down to a miserable pittance of $1 to $1.18 a day, out of which the workman on the Western roads, if a married man, must feed and clothe a family.[46]

These were strong words in a newspaper appreciative of the system that produced Jay Goulds, and asking only that its worst excesses be moderated. The *World* must have thought so also. It tried to restore a more moderate tone by adding that the working-men who were reduced to "a life of slavery" while their employers sailed in "floating palaces" still had no bitterness in their hearts.

[45] *World*, March 15, 1885, p. 4.
[46] *World*, March 14, 1885, p. 4.

As the same editorial concluded, "what wonder there are Gaspards[47] among them who are ready to dip their fingers in the dirt of the roads and scrawl on the walls, not the one word 'BLOOD'—for there is nothing revolutionary in their hearts—but the one word 'BREAD.' " Workingmen could accept that qualification as by and large justified, and their spirits soared at the front-page headline announcing the successful end of the strike—THE STRIKERS FAIRLY WIN. THE MISSOURI PACIFIC OFFICIALS APPARENTLY GLAD OF ANY EXCUSE TO YIELD—because it told of a victory achieved through right.[48]

The newspaper's editorial support for striking miners in the Hocking Valley of Ohio the previous year is even more noteworthy, for in that case the strike was bitter and protracted, and punctuated by periodic outbreaks of violence. The story first came to prominent attention in September 1884, when 3,000 rioting strikers set fire to the railroad depot at Columbus, and ran amok until Governor George Hoadly ordered out the State Militia.[49] The *World* did not countenance violence, but neither did it countenance, particularly at the height of a Presidential campaign, the sort of industrial serfdom that inspired men to desperate action. It saw the real culprits not in the workers who carried torches, but in the company directors who dictated wages of 50 cents per ton of coal dug out with pick and shovel.[50] If Blaine as a stockholder in the Hocking Mines could be included in their number, all the better.[51] Week after week the articles appeared, prominently displayed in the newspaper, describing the hardships the strikers endured to win their cause. They told of families being evicted from their homes because they could not pay the rent, and reminded New Yorkers that many of them had suffered the same oppression in the old country. "Irishmen who are familiar with the eviction process as practised in the land of their birth will think of the men and their wives and children who are being driven from their homes to make way for Blaine's serfs,

---

[47] Gaspard is the peasant in Charles Dickens' *A Tale of Two Cities*, who, when his child was killed by the speeding coach of the Marquis St. Evremonde, entered the nobleman's chateau and stabbed him to death in his sleep.
[48] *World*, March 16, 1885, p. 1.   [49] *World*, September 1, 1884, p. 1.
[50] *World*, October 9, 1884, p. 1.
[51] *World*, September 20, 1884, p. 2.

before they cast their votes for him."[52] The stories tried to convey the dumb misery of men standing idle for months, and watching their places taken by scab labor imported from Europe.

> Probably 10,000 men are idle and have been so for months. The owners are employing miners from elsewhere, Italians and others, willing to accept lower rates, and also are using machinery where practicable. Thus these men in idleness, with families dependent, see their places to-day filled by foreigners and the last hope of employment at any price cut off. The mine owners have to hire guards to protect the men from violence, and the "blacklegs" have been virtually imprisoned in the mines.[53]

What wonder, the newspaper suggested, if as the miners watched, bitterness consumed them?

In October violence erupted once more, as persons unknown set fire to the Hocking mines. But by now the *World* was thoroughly committed, and it detected in the arson "the last and vilest card" of mine owners who hoped to crush the strike by disgracing it.[54] DID THE MINERS CONSPIRE TO PROLONG THEIR OWN SUFFERING AND STARVATION? a headline asked rhetorically. " 'We are not fools,' " a striking miner replied to the *World* man who interviewed him, " 'and we certainly would have known that to fire these mines would be to make us odious and lose all the good will that is now on our side. We had absolutely nothing to gain by it and everything to lose, because this will probably make the lockout permanent.' "[55] The newspaper urged New Yorkers to rally behind the strikers and sustain them through the coming winter. It asked donations for a fund not too dissimilar from that to put a pedestal under the Statue of Liberty.

> The fierce blasts of winter are just coming on, and not only do the miners themselves stand shivering and starving at its approach, but their wives and little children as well. They must not be allowed to suffer in a land overflowing with plenty. They can and must be saved from a frightful fate by contributions which

[52] *World*, September 20, 1884, p. 2.
[53] *World*, September 2, 1884, p. 1.
[54] *World*, October 13, 1884, p. 1.
[55] *World*, October 14, 1884, p. 1.

need not be a burden to any individual giver. The *World* will receive money from ten cents up to any sum for the Hocking Valley miners and will see that it is properly applied. Let everybody give something.[56]

Taking the side of labor involved more than reports on strikes and meetings. It was a total commitment, apparent in such things as a special review of *The Bread-winners*, criticizing John Hay for portraying workingmen with "a good deal of contempt and seldom with sympathy."[57] It was apparent also in the special crusades the newspaper waged on subjects not immediately pertaining to unions, but close to their interests. Such was the long series early in 1885 on the issue of contracting convict labor out to private firms. No practice agitated unions more, because if the scab labor of prisoners did not have as serious an impact on wages as that of women and children, neither could it be justified by any criterion but greed. Moreover, several industries—notably iron grates, hats, and shoes—had already been profoundly affected, and thousands of jobs lost, because of arrangements worked out between prison officials and manufacturers. The issue first came to a head in 1883 when the electorate approved by 406,000 votes to 267,000 a referendum forbidding the use of convict labor in competition with free labor. To the dismay of workingmen, a bill was introduced in the State Legislature the following year which attempted to evade the injunction by providing that contractors could henceforth hire convicts at piece-rates, rather than by the day. The bill reopened the controversy, and stirred the *World* to action. A series of articles and editorials summarized the state's previous experience in the use of prison labor, particularly as it had under-cut firms which drew workers from the open market, thus depriving thousands of men of jobs.[58] The newspaper rebuked the legislators who wished to restore a system responsible for privation and bribery. "The Prison Labor Bill reported by the Republican Committee of the Assembly is an adroit attempt to evade the judgment of the people and to restore State Prison con-

[56] *World*, November 21, 1884, p. 4.
[57] *World*, March 8, 1885, p. 16.
[58] *World*, February 18, 1885, p. 4; and February 21, 1885, p. 5.

tract labor under a thin disguise, . . ." it declared. "The bill shows how eager the Republicans are to return to a system which was a mine for State Prison officials, go-betweens and favored contractors, to the injury of honest labor."[59] The *World*'s vigilance was rewarded in May 1885, by a vote finally killing the measure, an occasion for still another editorial to celebrate a cause justly won.[60]

Trade unions deplored the importation of contract labor for much the same reason that they feared convict labor, and again they discovered in the *World* an effective spokesman to represent them. A long article, appropriately run in the Christmas Day issue of 1883, castigated the system that allowed "poor wretches [to] . . . place themselves in a position which is nothing more or less than slavery." SLAVES FOR MONOPOLISTS, an angry headline charged. BOUND TO CORPORATIONS FOR YEARS UNDER WORTHLESS AGREEMENTS. . . . DREAMS WHICH ARE QUICKLY DISPELLED.[61] Information received at the height of the 1884 Presidential campaign, that the National Republican Chairman, Mr. B. F. Jones of the Jones & Laughlin Steel Company, had profited by importing contract labor provided a convenient rod to use against Blaine. "When the striking Sons of Vulcan in Jones's foundry saw the Belgian workmen coming," the *World* reported, "they submitted to the terms of their employers. They were simply subjugated by the threat to fill their places with specially imported millhands."[62] It would be too much to maintain that isolated statements like these played a major role in bringing the legislation that finally outlawed contract labor, but at the very least they sustained morale, and provided martial music for a campaign just underway.

[59] *World*, February 22, 1885, p. 4.
[60] *World*, May 4, 1885, p. 4. The issue also figured in the previous year's campaign against Blaine. *World* researchers discovered that as a member of the Maine Legislature he had supported a bill to hire out convict labor at 40 cents a day. The newspaper printed the report as final, damning evidence against his candidacy. BLAINE ON CONVICT LABOR, the headline blared. HIS BOLD ADVOCACY OF IT WHILE IN THE MAINE LEGISLATURE. A REPORT SIGNED BY HIS OWN HAND WHICH HE WILL NOT DENY—HE WOULD HIRE CONVICTS OUT AT 40 CENTS A DAY—HOW HE HAS PAUPERIZED HIS OWN STATE. See October 9, 1884, p. 5.
[61] *World*, December 25, 1883, p. 8.
[62] *World*, August 28, 1884, p. 4.

Although several *World* campaigns have earned more space in histories of journalism—that in 1884 on behalf of Grover Cleveland, for example, or the one in 1885 to put a pedestal under the Statue of Liberty—none of them surpassed in ardor the newspaper's continuing, and carefully researched, drive for tax reform. It was one of the principles enunciated in the famous ten-point program, a staple of reform ideology during the late nineteenth century, and not least, an article labor and the middle class could agree upon as a major step toward realizing the promise of American life. The newspaper's editorials urging a more equitable distribution of the tax burden never lost sight of the fact that they were something for men in both white collars and blue to smile upon.

The *World*'s proposal was straightforward enough. It asked for an income tax on those earning over $10,000 a year, since the present system of raising revenue mainly through property taxes tended to fall unequally on owners of small holdings and on tenants who paid the penalty in higher rents. Excessive property taxes not only brought hardship to lower income families, they had a dampening effect on the entire economy.

> If all the money enjoyed by those of our citizens who are puzzled how to spend their enormous incomes could be made to bear its due proportion of the taxes, in this city alone, the rate of taxation on real estate would be so insignificant as to amount practically to exemption. Rents would then be more reasonable, retail storekeepers would be able to charge less for their goods, building would be encouraged, more employment would be supplied for laborers and mechanics and all business would receive an impetus.[63]

The retrogressive features of the tax structure were compounded by levies on such items as tobacco, sugar, and clothing, a burden for families that spent the largest proportion of their incomes on staples. "The laborer pays the same tax as the millionaire on the tea, coffee, sugar and tobacco he consumes and the blankets and clothing he buys. Men of moderate means spend all their income in the expenses of living, and hence every dollar they earn pays

[63] *World*, November 16, 1883, p. 4.

its share of taxation."[64] The obvious solution was to ease the load on low and middle income groups by imposing instead an inheritance tax and a tax on incomes over $10,000 a year. "New York is a good place to make a beginning," the *World* declared, because there speculative wealth immune from assessment existed most notably side-by-side with poverty.[65] Its campaign for reform received a notable lift when the State Assessors adopted the proposal in their end-of-year reports to the Legislature in 1883 and 1884.[66] Nor did the campaign suffer from interviews with financiers who attacked the program as unnecessary and unwarranted.[67]

The *World*'s crusade was all the more effective because it played down rhetoric or appeals to the oppressed poor, and instead assigned batteries of reporters to pore over records in the Department of Taxes and Assessments to discover how the tax burden was distributed, and what prominent New Yorkers actually paid. The figures by themselves were persuasive. In 1883, for example, the city collected $29,200,000, of which $24,700,000 represented a levy on real estate and only $4,500,000 on personal property.[68] Part of the objection to having real estate taxes provide almost 90 percent of the city's receipts was that such taxes were based upon assessed valuations that varied according to the influence of the taxpayer. A small householder could expect to have his property assessed to the legal limit, but individuals or corporations with a voice at City Hall paid on only a small fraction of their property's worth. "The fact is notorious," an editorial charged, "that large properties owned by newspapers, politicians or money kings who are useful

[64] *World*, November 16, 1883, p. 4.

[65] The arguments for an income tax appeared in dozens of editorials and articles. Among them were: *New Work World*, May 21, 1883, p. 4; July 11, 1883, p. 4; January 17, 1884, p. 4; September 17, 1883, p. 4; January 4, 1884, p. 4; January 25, 1884, p. 4; January 30, 1884, p. 4.

[66] References to those annual reports appeared in the *World*, January 24, 1884, pp. 1, 4; and February 14, 1885, p. 4. The *World* received support of a different sort when Representative Turner of Kentucky introduced a bill in Congress for a federal income tax. (See April 15, 1884, p. 4.) It endorsed a proposal in the State Senate to tax inheritances, but only as a first step toward the more important income tax. April 2, 1884, p. 4.

[67] *World*, January 25, 1884, p. 8.

[68] *World*, February 21, 1884, p. 4.

to the political parties are grossly undervalued, while property owned by men of limited means and no political influence is fully assessed."[69] The *World* offered in evidence the special privileges enjoyed by several of the newspapers in New York City. It hired two real estate agents to estimate the current market value of four buildings on Park Row, and compared the estimates with those on record in the Department of Taxes and Assessments:[70]

Property	Assessed Value	Estimated Value
Herald Building	$450,000	$1,000,000
Times Building	375,000	850,000
Tribune Building	400,000	1,000,000
Sun Building	150,000	450,000

If assessments in each case below 50 percent of the buildings' market value were not evidence enough, the *World* revealed the suspicious circumstances surrounding the listing for the Tribune Building. It had originally been recorded as worth $500,000, but a line was later struck through that figure and $400,000 inserted in its place. The correction bore the marginal notation, "Corrected by Tax Commissioners Oct. 26, 1883," well after the legal date for amending the books.[71] "How did [Reid] manage to reduce the assessed valuation of the Tribune Building last year from $500,000 to $400,000 by a red-ink process?" The *World* asked. "That is the people's business."[72]

Pulitzer showed great courage in printing these articles, for he could be sure that henceforth the influential men he had discomfited—Bennett, Reid, Dana, Jones—would use all the considerable resources at their command to discover and spotlight instances when he accepted favors from municipal or state officials. The publisher undoubtedly realized that he was on the way

[69] *World*, February 9, 1884, p. 4. See also January 16, 1884, p. 4; and January 29, 1884, p. 4.

[70] The original report appeared on January 16, 1884, p. 5, although in subsequent issues some of the figures were revised. I have used the revised figures. The *World* had a valid case in pointing out that the assessed valuations on the buildings were only a small part of their true market value: 45 percent for the *Herald*, 44 percent for the *Times*, 40 percent for the *Tribune*, and 33 percent for the *Sun*. It loaded the argument, however, by neglecting to mention that, legally, buildings were only supposed to be assessed at 60 percent of their market value.

[71] *World*, January 18, 1884, p. 8.

[72] *World*, January 18, 1884, p. 4. See also January 19, 1884, p. 4.

to a princely fortune, and had every reason to begin the process of back-scratching which makes life more comfortable for the privileged few. By electing to forego the chance to be accommodating, by disregarding the canons of "professional courtesy," he proved in the most convincing way that the *World*'s crusades were not simply devices to raise circulation.

A related question concerned how personal property in the city managed to decline in value during the same period that real estate values multiplied. The newspaper showed that between 1870 and 1883, when the valuation of real estate for taxation increased by almost 50 percent, from $742,103,075 to $1,079,-130,669, the declared value on personal property fell by more than 35 percent, from $305,285,374 to $197,546,495. "It is evident that there is one explanation, and one only, of this enormous apparent decrease in personal property," the *World* maintained. "Wealth escapes taxation. The owners of personalty either cover up their taxable property or perjure themselves by falsely swearing it out of assessment."[73] An examination of the tax rolls corroborated the charge. The entire Vanderbilt clan, for example, William H. and his sons William K., Cornelius, and Frederick, paid a total sum of $70,475, while the Astors, with more property in real estate, paid over $500,000. (William H. Vanderbilt and Cyrus W. Field had escaped taxation altogether until recent years by filing affidavits with the Board of Assessments declaring that their debts were in excess of their incomes.) Henry Villard, who owned majority control of the Northern Pacific Railroad, was assessed only $3,500, and Sidney Dillon, President of the Union Pacific Railroad, only $1,500.[74]

[73] *World*, January 13, 1884, p. 4.

[74] The data appears in an article on November 11, 1883, p. 9. See also April 20, 1884, p. 12; and April 22, 1884, p. 4. The *World* discussed apparent favoritism toward the Vanderbilt family in an earlier article dealing with property valuations on Fifth Avenue, between 8th and 82nd Streets. "It will also be interesting," the account suggested, "to note the different amounts placed opposite each name. Mr. Amos R. Eno, whose property, consisting of five lots, is located in the vicinity of Madison Square, where stores are crowding in, is assessed for $1,400,000, while Mr. W. H. Vanderbilt is assessed for only $1,000,000 for an elegant mansion, with eight lots, in a more desirable locality. Mr. Vanderbilt's house is said to have cost nearly $3,000,000, and though the law provides that property must be assessed for 60 per cent of its real value, it is really taxed for only about one-third of its cost. When Mr. Vanderbilt deeded to his son Frederick the old home on Fifth Avenue and Fortieth Street

Probing *World* reporters discovered similar data in Brooklyn. Mayor Seth Low paid no taxes at all until shortly before his first term in office, when he voluntarily appeared at the office of the Board of Assessors and put his worth down as $10,000. Two of the moral guardians of that city, the Reverends Henry Ward Beecher and T. DeWitt Talmadge, did not appear at all on the tax rolls.[75]

Although it would be three decades before the *World* won its suit for an income tax, the investigations undertaken in the mid-1880s laid the early groundwork. More to the point, they accorded with labor's deepest interest, and from the wording of the editorials, were obviously addressed to workingmen. Such a series, no less than one urging justice for workers on the Jay Gould railroad system, helped to sustain trade unions in their struggle for a more just society.

Underlying the *World*'s concern for labor was an awareness of several broad truths. It realized, for example, that in the absence of strong unions and collective bargaining, a large percentage of the city's workingmen, far from sharing in the miraculous wealth produced by industrial capitalism, were being systematically reduced to poverty. The exact proportion of those in need or near-need is impossible to determine, largely because state and private fact-finding agencies lacked the funds to conduct exhaustive inquiries.[76] America was just on the verge of discovering its poor, and had not yet started to count them. Richard T. Ely described how his attempt to ascertain the exact number of paupers in the country floundered when he found that neither the federal nor state governments kept listings of those in institutions or on relief.[77] In 1892 Congress directed the Commis-

---

he claimed that the property was worth a quarter of a million, but is assessed only for $140,000. Mr. W. K. Vanderbilt's house, adjoining that of his father, is assessed for $500,000, although its first cost was in excess of a million." *World*, October 14, 1883, p. 2.

[75] See *World*, March 16, 1884, p. 14. See also March 2, 1884, p. 12.

[76] See G. W. W. Hanger, "Labor Bureaus," in William D. P. Bliss, ed., *The New Encyclopedia of Social Reform* (New York, 1908), pp. 675-76. See also Robert H. Bremner, *From the Depths, The Discovery of Poverty in the United States* (New York, 1956), pp. 72-73.

[77] Richard T. Ely, "Pauperism in the United States," *North American Review*, CLII (April 1891), 397.

sioner of Labor to conduct an investigation of slum conditions in every city with a population of over 200,000, sixteen in all, and appropriated for the project a paltry $20,000. The report that followed pointed out that the sum had barely covered expenses for a survey of the slums in four major cities.[78] Charles B. Spahr found himself relying on "the common observation of common people . . . [as] more trustworthy than the statistical investigations of the most unprejudiced experts" when he undertook to study the distribution of wealth in the United States.[79]

Despite the scarcity of data, abundant evidence established that poverty in New York City was a problem affecting more than the unfortunate few. The annual reports of the Association for Improving the Condition of the Poor during the 1880s described hundreds of able-bodied men unable to support their families on the wages of unprotected labor. Jacob Riis provided a much grimmer summary for the decade when he estimated conservatively, on the basis of Charity Organization Society records, that at least one-third of the city's population depended at one time or other on charity in order to survive.

> . . . in a population of a million and a half, very nearly, if not quite, half a million persons were driven, or chose, to beg for food, or to accept it in charity at some period of the eight years, if not during the whole of it. There is no mistake about these figures. They are drawn from the records of the Charity Organization Society, and represent the time during which it has been in existence. It is not even pretended that the record is complete. To be well within the limits, the Society's statisticians allow only three and a half to the family, instead of the four and a half that are accepted as the standard of calculations which deal with New York's population as a whole.[80]

His estimate was corroborated by the proportion of New Yorkers who ended their existence at Potter's Field. "The last the poor

[78] Carroll D. Wright, *Slums of Baltimore, Chicago, New York, and Philadelphia*, Seventh Special Report, Commissioner of Labor (Washington, D.C., 1894), pp. 11-12.

[79] Charles B. Spahr, *An Essay on the Present Distribution of Wealth in the United States* (New York, 1896), p. v.

[80] Riis, *How the Other Half Lives*, p. 243.

will let go however miserable their lot in life, is the hope of a decent burial. But for the five years ending with 1888 the average of burials in the Potter's Field has been 10.03 per cent of all."[81] Robert Hunter added further confirmation a few years later when he reckoned that at least 25 percent of all New Yorkers did not have enough money to purchase the daily necessities of life.[82]

The *World*'s refusal to dismiss such statistics as manifestations of a Spencerian inability to survive is noteworthy. While it would have been convenient to believe that poverty measured the inferiority of the new immigrant stock, the newspaper could not shut its eyes to evidence much more chilling in implication. "The character of those applying for assistance has materially changed," it pointed out. "They are now more intelligent and evidently of a better class. Many of them are American born, others of the better class of German. Heretofore neither of these sought relief. This unmistakably shows that the pinching has begun to be felt by those who never dreamed of such a thing as asking for alms."[83] How could such a situation come to pass? The newspaper offered an obvious answer by showing that during the past decade the wages of unorganized labor throughout the United States had plummeted at the same time that profits were soaring. According to the Census of 1870, the 2,053,996 members of the working force received an annual per capita wage of $377.50; ten years later 2,738,895 workingmen earned an average wage of $346.50 per year. The same period saw the value of manufactured goods produced in the country increase from $4,282,-325,442 to $5,369,579,191. "While Republican protection had added $1,137,253,749 to the value of manufactured products in ten years of Republican rule, it had reduced the earnings of labor $84,905,745."[84] The newspaper illustrated what impersonal figures in millions and billions of dollars meant for individual working class families by printing a letter from "Humanitas" on the challenges of budgeting household expenses on $10 to $12 a week.

[81] Riis, *How the Other Half Lives*, pp. 244-45.
[82] Robert Hunter, *Poverty* (New York, 1904), p. 27.
[83] *World*, February 16, 1885, p. 1.
[84] *World*, October 29, 1884, p. 4.

Has it ever occurred to you to figure upon the outlay of a man whose wages are $2 per day and who
cares for a family of five? Let us look merely at the
cost of food provided for the members. . . .

Let us say 5 cents is the cost per meal for each
member of the family, the actual cost of the food
provided.

This makes 25 cents for each meal, 75 cents per
day and $5.25 per week for bodily sustenance out of
the $12 which the man who is getting good wages re-
ceives. We will not be extravagant, so we allow $10
per month for rent.

Truly this family is well off, for they have left
$4.44 per week . . . for other expenses—fuel, cloth-
ing and other incidentals. . . . I call attention to the
fact that if members of the family are reckless and
determined to live riotously and gratify their appetite
to the extent of demanding food which will cost for
each member 7 cents per meal instead of 5 cents
there will then be no money for clothes.[85]

One other consequence of union weakness was 75,000
workers unemployed in New York City alone. "Humanitas" had
considered the problems of relatively fortunate working class
families; many others faced a grimmer reality. EVERY TRADE
AND INDUSTRY SUFFERING FOR THE ERA OF OVER-PRODUCTION, a
World headline pointed out. SCANT CLOTHING, FRUGAL MEANS
AND A SCARCITY OF THE COMMONEST NECESSITIES OF LIFE.
WHAT "THE WORLD" REPORTERS DISCOVERED IN A TOUR AMONG
THE ARMIES OF UNEMPLOYED MEN AND WOMEN. A PROBLEM
FOR PHILOSOPHERS AND STATESMEN TO SOLVE.[86] At its worst,
unemployment meant absolute reduction of the body and the
soul, as the newspaper illustrated by describing the plight of mill
workers in a New Jersey town close to the city when the only
factory there shut down:

Little feet that had not known a shoe for many a
day were bound up in rags to guard them against the
nipping frost. Squalid children of older growth had
pieces of horse blankets bound around their lower

[85] *World*, September 19, 1883, p. 4.
[86] *World*, February 16, 1885, p. 1. For other reports on unemployment, see
October 25, 1884, p. 5; November 1, 1884, p. 5; and February 16, 1885, p. 4.

> limbs, and boys and girls were dressed alike. . . . The coverings of the beds had, in some instances, been stripped off and had been improvised into garments. . . . One of the families had subsisted for nearly a week upon the carcass of a big Newfoundland dog. [The father] said that the children eagerly ate the flesh and cried for more, although they knew whence it came. It is said that cats have also been eaten. Other incidents of a more sickening nature are related.[87]

It was almost a reflex action for the *World* to blame the situation on two decades of uninterrupted Republican rule, and to urge workingmen in the city to protect themselves through the ballot. *The party of James G. Blaine and of the millionaires living in opulence on Fifth Avenue had systematically deprived them of their fair share of the national wealth. The injustice would only be righted when in their wrath they seized what had not been given. They could start by casting out Republican politicians from the seats of power.* The *World* posed the challenge in a declaration dangerously alive with class overtones.

> The *Tribune* is endeavoring to persuade the workingmen of New York that they are receiving liberal wages, enjoying happy homes, living on the fat of the land and laying by money for old age, and that all this is due to the blessings of Republican rule. This will be interesting news to the tens of thousands of willing and worthy men and women who are toiling for wages but little above starvation rate and to other thousands who are out of work, without food for to-day or hope for to-morrow. Such fables may sound well when read in Fifth Avenue brownstone mansions; but in crowded tenement-houses they are words of mockery and insult.[88]

More than recognizing that labor's weakness (and not the convenient survivability quotient cited by so many industrialists) had reduced tens of thousands of families in the city to a life of privation, the *World* noted a dangerous lack of concern

[87] *World*, January 11, 1885, p. 20.

[88] *World*, October 20, 1884, p. 4. For other comments contrasting the living conditions of workers and their employers, and blaming the discrepancy on Republican misgovernment, see July 20, 1884, p. 4; and October 27, 1884, p. 4.

on the part of the "haves" as to the condition of the "have-nots," or what was almost as bad, an assumption that prosperity purchased moral superiority as well as material things. The nabobs satisfied their wildest whims because they felt no guilt at enjoying extreme wealth in a city of poverty.[89] They were happily confident that the money came to them as a form of divine blessing, or, if we are to take them at their word, they did not realize that widespread poverty even existed. "It is constantly alleged in vague and declamatory terms," William Graham Sumner wrote on their behalf from his comfortable sanctuary at Yale University, "that artisans and unskilled labor are in distress and misery or under oppression. No facts to bear out these assertions are offered."[90] Andrew Carnegie brooked no nonsense on the subject. "I defy any man," he challenged in 1887, "to show that there is pauperism in the United States."[91] It was this professed ignorance which so frightened the men who feared that communism or anarchism would emerge from the slums unless the evils festering there were soon eliminated. Washington Gladden, for example, a Congregational minister who played a leading part in reforming the Protestant church, despaired at how "profound and universal" was the popular ignorance among one-half of the society about how the other half lived.[92]

Even when members of the middle class recognized the problem, and participated in movements to alleviate it, they did so with an appalling lack of sensitivity. Sometimes, as in the case of Lillian Wald of the Henry Street settlement, or Jane Addams of

[89] A description of just how wild those whims could be appears in Frederick Townsend Martin, *The Passing of the Idle Rich* (Garden City, New York, 1911), especially pp. 32-57.

[90] Quoted in Henry David, *History of the Haymarket Affair*, 2nd ed. (New York, 1958), p. 10.

[91] Quoted in *ibid.*, p. 10.

[92] Washington Gladden, "The Problem of Poverty," *The Century*, XLV (December 1892), 246. Gladden, whose parish was in Columbus, Ohio, played a leading role during the late nineteenth and early twentieth centuries in liberalizing Protestant thought and policy. In the debate between those who read the Bible as the literal and infallible word of God, and the school of "higher critics" who subjected it to rigid historical analysis, he stood eloquently with the latter. He was also a leader of the "social gospel" movement, which pioneered in using the church's resources and influence to help those in need. Gladden was among the few clerics, for example, who supported the workers during the Hocking Valley strike.

Chicago, the help was given with an appreciation for the dignity of the receiver. But too often the social workers turned out to be officious prudes who demeaned the unfortunates they were meant to serve. The great difficulty inhered in their assumption that poverty was somehow evidence of moral unfitness, and that before sustaining the body they must first redeem the soul. Gordon Atkins points out that the annual reports of the Charity Organization Society and of the Association for Improving the Condition of the Poor during the 1870s and 1880s were studded with such words as "morally depraved," "idiots," "degraded," "vicious," and "unworthy" to describe the recipients of charity, and that the tenement house commission reports "refer to certain of the slum districts as being inhabited by 'a squalid and criminal population.' "[93] Even Jacob Riis, in so many ways a paragon of enlightened thought, referred approvingly to the policy of the Children's Aid Society on Duane Street requiring that the orphans go out with shoeshine boxes to earn the money for their upkeep. The child "is as free as any guest at a hotel, and, like him, he is expected to pay for what he gets. How wisely the men planned who laid the foundation of this great rescue work and yet carry it on, is shown by no single feature better than this. No pauper was ever bred within these houses. Nothing would have been easier with such material."[94]

The social workers, however well meaning they might have been, managed by their attitude to embitter the very people they tried to help. Armed with the formidable weapon of their own benevolence, they mistakenly assumed that a finger-wagging lecture would accomplish as much for the hungry as a bowl of soup, with the result that in the dispensing of charity class lines became hardened.[95] An Irish-American poet named John Boyle O'Reilly wrote angrily of,

[93] Gordon Atkins, *Health, Housing, and Poverty in New York City 1865-1898* (Ann Arbor, Michigan, 1947), p. 127.

[94] Riis, *How the Other Half Lives*, pp. 202-203.

[95] W. D. P. Bliss derided the assumed moral superiority of those who dispensed charity in a scathing article a few years later. "If the wives of the unsuccessful grow discouraged and become slack before the ever-lasting problem of how the family can live, cook, sleep, marry, and take in boarders, all in two rooms, let the agents, or better still, the wives and aesthetic daughters of the successful go down and investigate and see if the family be worthy;

The organized charity scrimped and iced
In the name of a cautious, statistical Christ.[96]

and William T. Stead sadly of societies with methods as bad as their aims were good.[97]

What concerned the *World* in all this, the rationale finally for every editorial urging reform, was its fear that if inequities existed, and if the fortunate half of society either ignored them or responded tactlessly, what had hitherto been a sentiment for reform could easily develop into class warfare and radicalism. The newspaper was much too conservative to regard that prospect with equanimity. If its pleas that something be done often imparted a sense of urgency, the thought of what labor might become, as much as what it suffered, explains it.

The *World* most certainly did not encourage radicalism, and in its moments of optimism like to recall that communism and anarchism had found no reception in the American labor movement. "The intelligent workingman," it declared, "recognizes the fact that capital is as necessary as his own bodily strength and his

---

and if they are worthy, let them give—not money (let them never give money to the poor), but let them pour forth good advice, how to economize, how to save, how to make bone soup, how to make something out of nothing, how to save, save, save, till at last worn out by saving, they can go to a better world in a pine coffin." (W. D. P. Bliss, "Social Faith of the Holy Catholic Church," *Christian Socialist*, viii [November 9, 1911], p. 9.) The same point was made by a character in one of Harry Leon Wilson's novels. "Curious thing about reformers," he said, "they don't seem to get a lot of pleasure out of their labours unless the ones they reform resist and suffer, and show a proper sense of their degradation. I bet a lot of reformers would quit to-morrow if they knew their work wasn't going to bother people any." Harry L. Wilson, *Ma Pettingill* (Garden City, 1919), p. 177.

[96] John Boyle O'Reilly, "In Bohema" (1886). The poem is quoted in Robert Bremner, *From the Depths*, p. 53, who in turn quoted it from Jane Addams, *et al.*, *Philanthropy and Social Progress* (New York, 1893), p. 135.

[97] William T. Stead, *If Christ Came to Chicago* (London, 1894), p. 127. Pulitzer's newspaper ran an urgent editorial on the same theme. "It may be a reprehensible and communistic feature of starvation that it cannot wait contentedly and decorously for red tape and investigations, but such is the fact. When a starving creature prays for food, weak, fainting, dying, it seems very like mockery to refer his case to the Charity Organization Society to inquire whether he is or is not a deserving subject for relief. Death, who has very little respect for form, is apt to step in and cut such inquiries short. . . . What we really need in New York is an organization which will give immediate and unquestionable relief in every pressing case of distress, even though it may occasionally be cheated by an imposter." *World*, July 12, 1883, p. 4.

acquired skill to enable him to earn his bread."[98] Henry George's modest single tax proposals, which two years later would bring him close to the mayoralty of New York City, impressed the newspaper as an irrelevant, and dangerous, response to American conditions. "Mr. George's theories may be right in Europe, where the evils of land monopoly and aristocracy exist. But they are absurd in this country, where totally different conditions exist—where there is no landed aristocracy, no law of primogeniture and no difficulty to become [sic] the owners of land even by those who in Europe are regarded as poor."[99] It noted approvingly that although people attended George's lectures and read his books, "they laugh at his fallacies."

But the most repetitive statements of optimism did not alter the fact that the masses would reject radicalism only as long as they had hope, and that hope had been sorely tried in the tenement slums of New York and other major cities. Enough indications offered of rumblings from below, even in the days before the bomb at Haymarket Square and the great Pullman strike, to convince the *World* that time had almost run out. It must be reform today, or radicalism tomorrow. Cracks in the hardening class structure were already warning how the battle lines of the future would be drawn.

> Everywhere we hear of reduced wages and discharged hands, and the tenement-houses in New York are filled with unemployed but willing workmen whose families are pinched by want. . . . But turn the kaleidoscope of beneficent Republican policy, and what do we see? . . .
>
> Vanderbilt, the king of a grand Republican monopoly, driving his fast horses or picking his teeth on the hotel balcony at Saratoga. Gould, the beneficiary of Republican legislation, sailing sweetly in his magnificent steam yacht. Field . . . speeding in a palace car on a special trip to California. . . .
>
> Yet, despite these kaleidoscope views, the *Sun* tells us there are no "classes" in this country. . . .
>
> No "classes" in this country, forsooth! Would to God there were none! But twenty-four years of Re-

[98] *World*, September 2, 1884, p. 4.
[99] *World*, April 30, 1884, p. 4.

publican rule have successfully built up classes and each year the Republican power lasts the distinction between the "classes" will be more sharply defined.[100]

It is noteworthy that the newspaper reported with utter seriousness on its front page the shipside comments of a socialist from Germany, who predicted an imminent revolution in this country. AN AMERICAN REVOLUTION, the headline warned. HERR MOST PREDICTS THAT WE ARE APPROACHING A GREAT CRISIS. THE POWER OF WEALTH TO BE OPPOSED BY THE WORKINGMEN— WILL THE GREAT CHANGE TAKE PLACE IN AMERICA BEFORE IT OCCURS IN EUROPE?[101]

In 1884 the symbol of impending uprising, terrible and final in its consequences, was a riot in Cincinnati set off when a culprit convicted in the public mind of murder escaped paying the penalty by being found guilty only of manslaughter. For three days and three nights mobs terrorized the city, breaking into the state arsenal for weapons, dynamiting the courthouse and other public buildings, in general looting, pillaging, burning. Before the militia could quell the disturbance, twenty-eight lives had been lost, and almost one hundred men seriously wounded.[102] The *World* gave banner treatment to the story, printing extras on three successive days, and seeing in it not only material for sen-

[100] *World*, September 3, 1884, p. 4. For further statements on the developing contrast between rich and poor in American society, see September 15, 1883, p. 4; July 27, 1883, p. 4; July 20, 1884, p. 4; October 20, 1884, p. 4; and October 27, 1884, p. 4. "At both ends of the scale," the newspaper declared in the first of these editorials, "we have the un-republican spectacle of excessive riches and excessive poverty, of enormous fortunes gathered in the hands of the few, of abject poverty the lot of only too many." The matter was to become one of increasing concern to thoughtful observers. John R. Commons noted in 1894 that "class lines have become more rigid, and the individual, if his lot be in the unpropertied class, is destined, as a rule, to remain there. His economic resources determine, by relentless pressure, what shall be his social environment." (John R. Commons, *Social Reform and the Church* [New York, 1894], p. 34.) It seemed increasingly unlikely to William Dean Howells, the leading exponent of the new realism, that those who suffered poverty could ever hope to escape their condition. "Here and there one will release himself from it, and doubtless numbers are always doing this, as in the days of slavery there were always fugitives; but for the great mass captivity remains." William Dean Howells, *Impressions and Experiences* (New York, 1896), p. 149.

[101] *World*, March 24, 1884, p. 1.

[102] The major reports on the riot appeared on March 29, 1884, p. 1 (five days after the interview with Herr Most); March 30, 1884, entire page 1; March 31, 1884, entire front page; and April 1, 1884, entire front page.

sationalism, but evidence of an impending social crisis. It argued, not unreasonably, that "the destruction of property, the sacrifice of innocent life," could not be "be charged only to the escape of one boy who deserved hanging. . . . Robespierre, Marat and Danton were not accidents. They were the natural product of long-continued abuses and outrages."[103] Pulitzer had his staff cover the riot as, in part, a political event. The headline over the lead story of March 31st, for example, told of SOCIALISTS AND THE RIOT. THEY CLAIM THAT IT IS THE BEGINNING OF THE PEOPLE'S UPRISING.[104] Several subsequent articles developed the same theme.[105]

Here was material for the sharpest warnings on what must follow if the demands of the people were not soon met. "Surely this deplorable outbreak ought to enforce a lesson of caution to all prudent men. . . . We cannot ride roughshod over the liberties of the people by purchasing elections with the money of favored corporations and monopolies. The terrible reaction is sure to come, no matter how patient the people are. And the reaction is apt to be more terrible than the evil itself."[106] Lest even this blunt warning miss the mark, it offered for the edification of the wealthy a lesson from history.

> Does Fifth Avenue forget that it is flanked by the tenements of Eleventh Avenue and Avenue B, and outnumbered 1,000 to 1 in point of mere numbers? . . . Our bankers and brokers . . . cannot too speedily recognize the peril of teaching the people to despise all law, by showing them that its grip is only firm on the threat of the poor and humble and that the rich and powerful may slip easily through its fingers.
>
> Will they regard this warning as improper? If so, they are to be pitied for their ignorance. If the French rulers and nobles had profited by the teachings of the writers of the middle of the eighteenth century, who taught them what the world ought to be, the "demoiselle" would never have brought so many of the high heads of the nation to her feet.[107]

[103] *World*, April 1, 1884, p. 4.
[104] *World*, March 31, 1884, p. 1.
[105] See, for example, the *World*, April 2, 1884, p. 4; and April 3, 1884, p. 4.
[106] *World*, April 1, 1884, p. 4.
[107] *World*, May 27, 1884, p. 4. See also November 25, 1884, p. 4.

The Cincinnati riot remained large in the newspaper's memory early the next year when Chauncey M. Depew lectured before the Y.M.C.A. on socialism, communism, and anarchism as disturbers of our "splendid" society. "The people as a rule are patient and conservative," it assured Mr. Depew. "Labor is easily contented, obedient to authority and faithful to its employers. It must be starved, overtaxed with work, abused in every way, before it rises in rebellion." But since labor was underpaid and overworked, Mr. Depew would do well to worry less about the importation of foreign ideologies, and more about persuading his colleagues to repair the grievances which made labor receptive to those ideologies.

> Mr. Depew would have done much . . . if he had pointed out to the greedy corporations and monopolies of which he is so brilliant a representative that there is no Communism in this country and can be none except through the insane folly of corrupt wealth. It is a hateful and poisonous plant of foreign growth. If law prevails and is made to reach the rich as well as the poor, if capital uses its power justly and makes no attempt to oppress and outrage Labor, all the Communism in the United States will be confined to a few beer cellars and Sunday meetings. But if corporations . . . encroach on the people's rights . . . our soil may eventually be prepared for the seed of Communism and prove as congenial as the soil of Europe.[108]

The *World*'s crusade on behalf of labor accords with its larger philosophy of updated liberalism. It did not defy the middle class prejudice against unions because it wished to remake the society, but on the contrary, because without unions and a larger share in the national wealth for labor, the society would topple of its own weight. In a sense every *World* editorial was written with one eye on circulation; the knowledge that the way to get one in the hundreds of thousands consisted in wooing labor would hardly have discouraged a progressive tone. But more compelling must have been the desire to conserve a way of life on the whole worth conserving, by admitting all Americans to its privileges.

[108] *World*, January 28, 1885, p. 4.

CHAPTER ELEVEN

THE *WORLD'S* TRIUMPH

Whatever Pulitzer's rivals thought of him, they could not deny that his methods worked. The immigrant editor arrived unheralded in New York City in May of 1883 to take control of a daily that the profession had all but pronounced as dead. His announcement to colleagues like Dana, Bennett, and Reid that he intended soon to beat them in circulation, and to make the *World* the foremost spokesman for liberal causes, was easily dismissed as the brashness of a publicity-seeking Jew. If the established press lords worried about the challenge, there is no indication of it in their journals. A few minor notices buried on the back pages announced that a Joseph Pulitzer from St. Louis had acquired the *World*, but thereafter the metropolitan press ignored him. As late as August 1884, *The Journalist* noted complacently that "none of [his rivals] would have anything to do with him, no matter what he said or how he said it."[1]

Although the studied slights continued well into 1884, Dana and Bennett and the rest realized within weeks that the emaciated-looking newcomer posed considerable problems for them. The *World's* circulation did not explode over night, but it gained steadily, and more frightening, benefiting by mid-1884 from word-of-mouth advertising and from the *Sun's* abdication as spokesman for the Democratic candidate in New York City, at an increasing rate.[2] One year after Pulitzer acquired the newspaper its readership had grown by fourfold, and at the end of two years by tenfold. Nothing like it had ever been seen before. Journalists of the future—Hearst, McCormick, Patterson—would have to measure their achievement against a new standard.

---

[1] *The Journalist*, August 9, 1884, p. 4.

[2] Pulitzer in fact credited much of his success to Charles A. Dana. By supporting Benjamin Butler in 1884, the publisher of the *Sun* left the field to the *World* to speak for the Democratic Party in New York City. The *World's* gain in circulation during that summer was closely matched by the *Sun's* losses.

The *World* had been in decline for some time prior to the change in ownership, and seemingly it was about to give up the ghost for good. On May 6, 1883, the last Sunday edition under the old management, it sold only 15,770 copies. (Subtracting unsold copies, the average Sunday circulation for the four weeks preceding the change in ownership was 14,014.) Pulitzer waited several months before issuing notarized statements on the newspaper's daily circulation, but his sworn statements on Sunday readership provide a clue as to how effectively he arrested the decline. On Sunday, June 10th, for example, the *World* distributed 18,580 copies; on Sunday, July 8th, 22,510 copies; on Sunday, August 12th, 27,620 copies. The impressive thing about these statistics is not the rate of growth, but the fact of growth itself. Newton's law about the properties of falling bodies has a corollary in journalism. A newspaper which is losing in circulation or advertising is like a physical object in free fall; the longer the fall continues the greater the momentum which builds up, until at some point the process is almost impossible to reverse.[3] The critical time for Pulitzer came in the summer of 1883, when he forced the line on the *World*'s circulation graph to rise again, and by laboriously adding readers month after month, demonstrated that he had not just snared a few temporary novelty seekers.

Once he had established a new trend, it was relatively easy for a journalist of Pulitzer's mettle to introduce the features and attractions which would add momentum to the upswing. By early November, when the *World* issued its first notarized statements on daily circulation, an average issue sold about 45,000 copies. The Sunday edition of February 24, 1884, went over 50,000 for the first time, a weekend figure the newspaper never again fell below. During April of 1884, distribution on weekdays hovered about 50,000, and on Sundays between 60,000 and 65,000. That summer found the journal more adroit in the techniques of sensation and illustration, and deeply immersed in the exciting Cleveland–Blaine election. Sunday circulation

---

[3] The death of the *New York Daily Mirror* in recent years, or *Collier's* magazine, demonstrates that the point can come while circulation and advertising revenue are still superficially impressive.

reached 70,930 on June 1st; 84,300 on August 17th; 91,070 on September 7th; and 103,670 on September 28th. Pulitzer marked the latter occasion with special celebrations. He bestowed a tall silk hat on each of his employees, and had 100 cannons fire a salute in City Hall Park. BOOMING FOR THE WORLD, a triumphant headline proclaimed. THE 100,000 MARK CELEBRATED BY THE FIRING OF CANNON.[4] This was occasion also for the newspaper to congratulate itself in an editorial, and to predict still greater things for the future. The *World*'s boast that it intended to surpass all previous circulation records in the United States, repeated now with the flush of victory upon it, no longer seemed chimerical.

> Yesterday the circulation of *The World* passed the ever-to-be-remembered-mile-stone on which was carved One Hundred Thousand. . . .
>
> Naturally we feel like congratulating ourselves. To have achieved such a circulation in less than a year and a half, with a basis of 15,000 to start on, is something, we take it, to be proud of.
>
> It is certainly demonstrated that the Eastern public appreciates a style of journalism that is just a bit breezy while being at all times honest, earnest, and sincere, and a journalism that represents every day a laborious effort to meet the popular demand for news seasoned with just convictions. . . .
>
> This we hold to be our first 100,000. From this time we march on to new glory. At the end of the year that is before us we confidently hope to score our second 100,000. With all due respect to our esteemed contemporaries we may say that we mean to eclipse the record in the matter of newspaper circulation.[5]

If the tone was expansive, and even boastful, it promised no more than the journal would soon deliver.

Six weeks after passing one milestone, the *World* sighted another. Most metropolitan dailies enjoyed a surge in circulation

---

[4] *World*, September 30, 1884, p. 4.

[5] *World*, September 29, 1884, p. 4. See also the statement on September 6, 1884, p. 4: "The future of the *World* is to be one of greatness and glory. We are determined that it shall not only be the newspaper of the largest circulation in this happy land, but that it shall be equally eminent in character and ability."

during the last exciting days of the Presidential election, but Pulitzer and his staff reaped the biggest windfall. The climax came on Wednesday, November 5th, with the issue reporting Cleveland's victory. On that day, the *World* printed and distributed 223,680 copies, or almost fifteen times as many as a typical press run a year-and-a-half before. An editorial pointed out exuberantly that save for the penny journals, which had the added advantage of publishing in the evening, no newspaper in America sold as many copies as the new *World*.[6]

The following week, when circulations had returned to normal, but when the *World* still distributed about 115,000 copies daily, an editorial took note of the anniversary marking Pulitzer's eighteenth month in control. "A success has been achieved such as American journalism has not hitherto known," it declared. "We think we have shown to the satisfaction of the public— first, that the *World* has increased in circulation more rapidly during the past year than any other paper in the universe. Secondly, that our present circulation, as shown by the very claims of our foremost contemporaries and the test of the past ten days, exceeds that of any newspaper printed in New York City."[7] The claim was probably somewhat premature. Penny journals such as the *New York News* had immense circulations (if Pulitzer included them in the comparison), and it was still too early to say whether the circulation lost by the *Sun* during the Presidential campaign would now drift back. But at most, the newspaper had jumped the gun. Within six more months the *World* reached and passed a second milestone, when the Sunday edition of May 3rd, 1885, sold 150,054 copies.

This was a particularly satisfying moment, not only because it put the paper in front of the field in New York City and the nation, but because it demonstrated for the benefit of all skeptics that the growth was not dependent solely, or even primarily, upon an exciting political contest. Between January and May 1885, long after the Cleveland charges and Blaine counter-charges had passed from the front page, the *World*'s Sunday edition took on readers at the rate of 10,000 a month. "It is no

[6] *World*, November 7, 1884, p. 4.
[7] *World*, November 11, 1884, p. 4.

exaggeration to say," an editorial rejoiced, "that no other newspaper on the Western Hemisphere printed and sold so many copies
yesterday. . . . Last year the marked growth was attributed in
some quarters to the Presidential canvass and general political
success. Certainly there has been no political excitement since
the First of January to stimulate newspaper reading, and yet the
figures show that the popularity of the paper expands in steady
ratio."[8]

A few days later the *World* celebrated its second anniversary
under Pulitzer with a spread worthy of Cleveland's election to the
White House. The entire front page, and almost three full columns
on page two, were devoted to what the newspaper called in headline, A REMARKABLE STORY OF NEWSPAPER SUCCESS. Circulation
ten times what it had been, hundreds of columns of new advertising, a basement stocked with the latest presses and folders, all
contributed to THE MOST UNQUALIFIED AND UNPARALLELED
JOURNALISTIC TRIUMPH OF THE NINETEENTH CENTURY.[9] These
were jubilant words, but they told the truth, and even the newspaper's bitterest foes had to concede them.[10]

Of course, circulation is only one measure of a newspaper's
success. An adage of journalism teaches that the last thing a
publication loses, and also the last it gains, is advertising, without which circulation is a luxury it can hardly afford.[11] The

[8] *World*, May 4, 1885, p. 4.
[9] *World*, May 10, 1885, entire p. 1; p. 2.
[10] As mentioned in Chapter Two (p. 50, note 10), I have used the *World's*
own figures to document its growth in circulation. The newspaper printed
notarized statements on Sunday circulation almost daily on its editorial page,
and occasionally in the ears on page one. For special statements, see September 30, 1884, p. 4 (comparing the Sunday circulation under the old management
and the new during April 1883, August 1883, and August 1884); November
10, 1884, p. 4 (comparing the circulation of the *World*, *Sun*, and *Herald* for
the week following Cleveland's election); November 11, 1884, p. 4 (listing the
World's circulation through the first ten days of November); p. 4 (comparing those figures with equivalent figures for 1880 and 1883); November 18,
1884, p. 4 (carrying the same figures through November 16); May 10, 1885,
p. 1 (listing the Sunday circulation of every issue from May 6, 1883, to May
3, 1885; the circulation for every day in 1885; and, in comparison, for every
day in April 1883, and April 1884).
[11] The adage was tested in recent years when the Luce empire launched
Sports Illustrated. The magazine operated at a loss for the first two or three
years, since its newsstand sales far outstripped the circulation on which advertising rates were based.

World's achievement in attracting the accounts of manufacturers and retailers weighed at least as heavily as its appeal to readers in determining its success.

Advertising lineage did not grow at the same steady and spectacular rate as circulation, for two reasons. First, such lineage is always much more subject to seasonal fluctuations: a period of doldrums through June, July, and August, an upswing during the fall, and a peak month in December, when merchants compete for the attention of Christmas shoppers. Even though the *World* ran fewer ads in July 1884, for example, than it did in December 1883, experienced eyes recognized that the difference was slight enough to speak of a gain in advertising only a shade less impressive than the gain in circulation. The fact that the business office did not quite match the achievement of the circulation department is further explained by the *Herald's* dominance at that time as an advertising medium for the metropolitan area. A journal's reputation as a place for sellers to announce their wares is not necessarily determined by its circulation. Bennett dominated the field long after Dana and the *Sun* had passed the *Herald* in circulation, and he continued for a while to hold the lead against the *World's* challenge. It was one thing for Pulitzer to persuade an army of tenement-dwellers to purchase his newspaper, and quite another to persuade advertisers that the *World* audience had the means or inclination to buy.

Considered in light of the handicaps it labored under, the newspaper's achievement was remarkable. It printed a total of 4,876 columns of advertising during 1883 and the next year, with Pulitzer at the helm throughout, a total of 8,675 columns. Compared to the *Herald's* figures these are insignificant, but the important point is that while Pulitzer picked up advertisers his competitor was losing them, dropping from 13,140 columns in 1883 to 11,194 in 1884.[12] Moreover, Pulitzer began to pull ahead within eighteen months of arriving in the city. The *World* printed 986 columns of advertising in November 1884, to 914 for the *Herald*, and 1,042 columns in December 1884, to 757 for the *Herald*.

---

[12] See the *World*, January 4, 1885, p. 4, for a monthly breakdown of the total advertising lineage in the *World* and the *Herald* during 1883 and 1884.

The paper took note of its achievement on December 1, 1884, a day when 89 columns (or two more than in the *Herald*) graced its pages, to claim for itself the crown that had once been Bennett's. "The general public will understand this when we say that for the first time in its history—and the *Herald* is nearly fifty years old—it has been eclipsed in the matter of advertising. . . . It has remained for the vigorous new *World* to remove the diadem-studded crown of the *Herald* in less than two years."[13] Two weeks later came a second "red-letter day," when the *World* printed 109 columns of advertising in a twenty-four page issue. "Naturally," an editorial declared, "[we] feel like pluming [ourselves]."[14]

Another way to measure growth is to ignore total lineage, and instead add up the number of individual advertisements which appeared in equivalent issues during successive years. It was a technique favored by the *World* to glorify itself, because its large circulation and cheap rates tended to bring in classified notices more readily than profitable, full-page spreads from department stores and other merchandizing establishments. But even conceding that the newspaper had loaded the comparison to its own advantage, the gains it recorded were impressive. On Sunday, April 20, 1883, for example, the *World* under the old management printed 238 separate advertisements. One year later, on April 22, 1884, it printed 1,180 advertisements. Still another year later, on April 19, 1885, the total had risen to 4,375 advertisements. This represents an eighteenfold increase in two years.[15]

Of course the *World*'s triumph over the *Herald* as an advertising medium occurred neither quite so quickly, nor so thoroughly, as these figures suggest. Bennett relied upon his newspaper's prestige long after the competition began to charge some of the highest rates in the city, while at the other end of Park Row, Pulitzer pulled in advertisers by offering space at rock-bottom rates, particularly in relation to the *World*'s circulation. Even though the *World* ran more ads than the *Herald* during the last months of 1884, it probably took in considerably less revenue

[13] *World*, December 1, 1884, p. 4.
[14] *World*, December 14, 1884, p. 4.
[15] The figures appeared over the masthead of the *World* on April 26, 1885, p. 1.

from them. The respective fees for classified notices offers one example why this should be. The *Herald* charged up to six cents a word, or forty-five cents a line, for what in the *World* cost as little as five cents a line. Pulitzer adopted a sliding scale, ranging from five cents a line for situations wanted, to fifteen cents for help wanted, to twenty and twenty-five cents for other notices.[16] He would have to print a great many more ads at those rates to match Bennett in total revenue. *The Journalist* probably exaggerated when it claimed that "the *Herald*, containing no more than half the advertising matter printed in the *World*, will make considerably the most money," but its logic was essentially sound.[17] Richardson went on to charge in the same article that the *World* reprinted marriage, birth and death notices from the *Herald* in order to inflate its advertising lineage. He cited as evidence the fact that such notices often popped up in Pulitzer's newspaper twenty-four hours after they had appeared in the *Herald*. If the allegation is at all true, the *World*'s position vis-à-vis the *Herald* must be further diminished.

One thing is clear. Whatever the competitive position of the newspapers, Pulitzer was attracting enough advertising accounts to convert the *World* into a highly profitable property. The fact that he managed to pay off the note to Gould out of the paper's earnings is incontrovertible evidence to that effect. To be sure, rumors were rife on Park Row for a long while that the *World* had overextended itself and could not pay its bills.[18] Richardson circulated the story that Pulitzer had fallen behind by $400,000 in trying to meet his obligation to Gould, purchase new presses, and pay for paper, and that as a result he was ready to sell the

---

[16] For derogatory evaluations of the *World*'s position as an advertising medium in relation to the *Herald*'s, see *The Journalist*, August 2, 1884, p. 5, and September 13, 1884, p. 2. A chart comparing the two papers' advertising rates can be found in the *Pulitzer Papers*, Columbia University Libraries.

[17] *The Journalist*, September 13, 1884, p. 2.

[18] See, for example, *The Journalist*, June 20, 1885, p. 2. "The keenest journalistic observers are uncertain about the exact financial status of the *World*. Whether it is making or losing money, however, it is at least spending a great deal, and is crowding the other journals very hard." The comment came from the pen of W. G. MacLaughlin, who succeeded Richardson as publisher of the magazine in February 1885, and who was almost as much for Pulitzer as Richardson had been against him.

Post-Dispatch to raise more capital.[19] The truth proved to be quite different. Under its new management, *The Journalist* printed an extract from the *World*'s financial statement for 1884, which put the paper's capital value at $500,000 and reported a cash dividend for the year of $150,000.[20] "If it made and divided $150,000," the periodical asked, "who will say that the *World* does not move and prosper, or that it 'gets nothing for its advertising.' "[21] Pulitzer provided corroborative evidence two years later when he settled a bet for William C. Steigers, Advertising Manager of the *St. Louis Post-Dispatch*. "Dear Mr. Steigers," he wrote: "Please do not for the future make any bets with regard to the *World*'s earnings, especially with Captain Slattery, who is a good fellow. At the same time, as you have blundered into this thing, I am bound to say that the earnings of the *World* for 1886 were over five hundred thousand dollars. Yours truly, Joseph Pulitzer."[22] While it is possible that the publisher exaggerated in order to trumpet his success, the amount sounds right, compared to the *World*'s profits two years before and to Pulitzer's luxurious standard of living two or three years hence.

The profits that would one day allow him to buy his yacht, *Liberty*, and to indulge a sick man's fancies, did not all come from minor notices listing jobs available or rooms for rent. Such notices continued to appear in plenty, occupying several successive pages in an average issue after March 1884, but they were increasingly joined by other, more substantial ads.[23] The first full-column spread appeared on January 27, 1884, announcing a pre-inventory sale by Simpson, Crawford, and Simpson, a popular department store on 19th Street and Sixth Avenue. Pulitzer may have meant to emphasize to his competitors and to the city that he had secured the account, because on this one occasion he

[19] *The Journalist*, January 31, 1885, p. 5.
[20] Since Pulitzer purchased the paper for $346,000, itself an inflated price, this represents an accretion in capital value of almost 50 percent in a little over a year-and-a-half.
[21] *The Journalist*, March 21, 1885, p. 5.
[22] The letter, dated May 13, 1887, is quoted in Don C. Seitz, *Joseph Pulitzer, His Life & Letters* (New York, 1924), p. 163.
[23] The first occasion under Pulitzer when the *World* devoted several successive pages exclusively to advertising was on March 16, 1884, pp. 5-8. They included notices of amusements (the most prominent announced P. T. Barnum's circus at Madison Square Garden, featuring Jumbo the elephant), want ads, rooms to let, and millinery and dress goods sales.

banished news from the front page in order to herald the virtues of that establishment's dry goods.[24]

Full-page ads soon became a commonplace in the resurgent *World*. Brooklyn's Wechsler & Abraham (now Abraham & Straus) announced its move to new quarters on Fulton Street with a spread that included a woodcut of the building six columns wide and the equivalent of seven columns long.[25] Vogel Brothers, a clothing chain with several outlets in Manhattan, took a page in the *World* to publicize its twenty-fifth anniversary sale.[26] Duffy's Barley Malt Whiskey developed into a lucrative account, promising A SURE AND POSITIVE CURE FOR CONSUMPTION, as well as for DYSPEPSIA, INDIGESTION AND ALL WASTING DISEASES, in headlines that spanned the page.[27] (It says something about the advertising ethics of the time that a subsequent Duffy's ad consisted of a bogus Presidential proclamation, in Cleveland's handwriting, urging the merits of the whiskey.[28]) The Reverend Henry Ward Beecher, the Honorable Horatio Seymour, Peter Cooper, Abram Hewitt, and a host of other notables lent their testimonials to a full-page ad for Clysmic natural mineral spring water, which was not only "highly effervescent," but promised "in scarlet, typhoid and other fevers [to] keep the kidneys in free action."[29] The Civiale Remedial Agency delivered a more personal message on behalf of its Elastic Self-Adjusting and Glove-Fitting Cradle-Compressor. "Is your generative power declining?" the company asked. "If so you are no exception to the rule. Nine out of every ten men are thus affected." But the ninety percent afflicted had no longer need to despair. "Cast aside all false shame, and seek at once for such remedies as will quickly and permanently restore to the

24 *World*, January 27, 1884, entire p. 1.
25 *World*, February 15, 1885, entire p. 7.
26 *World*, March 5, 1885, entire p. 8.
27 *World*, January 18, 1885, entire p. 15.
28 *World*, March 5, 1885, entire p. 7.
29 *World*, July 27, 1884, entire p. 15. Testimonial ads were already a favored technique. Thus, a famous manufacturer of pads for corns and bunions built its advertising campaign around an admiring letter from Mrs. Henry Ward Beecher. "I have used Allcock's Plasters for some years for myself and family," the minister's wife wrote, "and as far as able, for the many sufferers who come to us for assistance, and have found them a genuine relief for most of the aches and pains which flesh is heir to." *World*, April 13, 1884, p. 5.

Generative Organs such Strength, Vigor and Potency as should belong to every healthy man."[30] If this was flirting with the limits of good taste, *The Journalist* (under Leander Richardson) complained that Pulitzer's paper grossly overstepped the limit in a patent medicine advertisement one month later promising a cure for venereal disease and gonorrhea.

> Last Sunday there appeared a full page advertisement of some remedies for various kinds of loathsome diseases. In the middle of this advertisement there was a picture, the filthy suggestiveness of which is seldom equalled in the cesspool pages of the *Police Gazette.* . . .
>
> One would think that such material as that to which we have referred would not be printed, even by an unscrupulous newspaper proprietor, excepting under the temptation of a very large sum of money by the way of pay. The facts of the case in regard to the *World* and this particular advertiser are, that the paper received just three hundred dollars for publishing this nauseating news.[31]

Richardson was justified in arguing that the *World's* high-powered campaign for ads left it too little concerned with the propriety of what it printed, and as will be seen, he used that weakness to mount one of his most telling assaults on the paper.

Writing many years later, by which time he had become a sage of journalism, Whitelaw Reid observed that "the great newspapers are those which look for news, not advertisements. With the news come circulation, and when circulation demands, the advertisements seek the paper, not the paper the advertisements."[32] The argument seems to make sense, but it had not worked out that way for Pulitzer. Just as he achieved a great circulation by being brighter and more controversial than his competitors (others printed at least as much news), he attracted advertising to the *World* by aggressively going out and seeking it. The pub-

---

[30] *World*, December 14, 1884, entire p. 19.

[31] *The Journalist*, January 17, 1885, p. 4.

[32] Whitelaw Reid, "Journalism as a Career," *American and English Studies* (New York, 1913), p. 11; quoted in Helen MacGill Hughes, *News and the Human Interest Story* (Chicago, 1940), p. 16.

lisher won the day because he displayed a huckster's skill to rival that of any of his clients.

The point is made by contrasting the *Herald*'s inflexible canons of advertising with the *World*'s willingness to experiment. Bennett's journal kept its rates so high as to discourage all but the most prosperous firms, and imposed upon those which did elect to patronize it a host of arbitrary regulations handed down from an earlier era of journalism. Except under special circumstances (or the payment of a penalty), the *Herald* would not relax its columnar rules for ads more than one column wide; it refused to use bold type in the ads, forcing merchants to do what they could with 5½-point agate type; it forbade them to support their commercial messages with illustrations. Pulitzer's willingness to abandon those conventions made the *World* attractive as a medium for more reasons than its high circulation and low rates. No lines dissected its full-page spreads for department stores and patent medicine companies, and when Wechsler & Abraham requested a huge woodcut of the new store on Fulton Street, the newspaper happily complied.

Not only did the *World* adjust to the needs of its clients, it actively solicited their accounts. Its strongest selling point was the rising circulation, and businessmen were invited to verify the claims by visiting the *World* office and examining the books. "We have heard of but two cases where advertisers attempted this," *The Journalist* huffed, "and they knew less when they came out of the confusion than when they went into it."[33] The newspaper also rigged special feature stories to publicize its effectiveness as a selling medium. Early in 1885, on the day after Ehrich Bros., a dry goods emporium, had inserted identical announcements of a shoe sale in the Sunday *World* and *Herald*, a reporter went down to interview the ladies to discover in which newspaper they had seen the ad. He claimed to have received over 1,100 answers, of which 664 cited the *World* and 446 the *Herald*.[34] According to *The Journalist*, the stunt grew out of a bet Pulitzer made with Ehrich in an uptown restaurant some days before. He offered to run the ad without charge if it failed to bring in

[33] *The Journalist*, May 2, 1885, p. 4.
[34] *World*, February 27, 1885, p. 8.

more customers than an equivalent ad in the *Herald,* but if it did, Ehrich was to pay double rates. The trade periodical charged Pulitzer with all sorts of skulduggery in making good on the boast. "Five hundred dollars would buy an awful lot of boots at Ehrich's," it pointed out, "and various dodges might be employed to increase the number of customers."[35] Moreover, *The Journalist* alleged, Pulitzer had loaded the competition to his own advantage. "Will you observe the cunning of the *World* people. They selected an advertisement of cheap shoes. Half the readers of the *World* haven't got any shoes, so they made a strong point. The *Herald*'s readers are well shod and wear rubbers in the bargain." The following week's edition, which saw "Ehrich put four columns of advertising into the *Herald* instead of the customary two," seemed to substantiate the charges.[36]

The Journalist's cries of foul, justified or not, were in the main irrelevant. By aggressive, alert salesmanship the *World* was attracting the advertising to go with its rising circulation. It hardly mattered if the newspaper boasted, or juggled figures, or sometimes even arranged rigged demonstrations to make a case increasingly clear on its own merits. The point is that Pulitzer posed the first serious challenge to Bennett's advertising supremacy, and that he represented a new generation of press lords who were about to replace the old. Under its new management *The Journalist* recognized what the rest of Park Row had noted months before. It devoted an entire front page to a cartoon by James A. Wales, entitled "He Wakes Up At Last." The illustration showed James Gordon Bennett, Jr. arousing from a deep sleep to see Pulitzer running off with bags filled with feathers from his mattress. The bags were labeled "N.Y. World Enterprise"; the feathers represented advertising accounts which the brash newcomer to metropolitan journalism had taken from its older, and more established, rival.[37] Bennett, of course, would never get the feathers back.

[35] *The Journalist*, February 28, 1885, pp. 1-2. The periodical might have pointed something else out. If the *World* report was true, it meant that Pulitzer's reporter interviewed the ladies at a rate better than one every thirty seconds, for eight consecutive hours. This surely qualifies as a record of sorts for poll-takers.

[36] *The Journalist*, March 7, 1885, p. 5.

[37] *The Journalist*, March 21, 1885, p. 1.

In only one area did Pulitzer's aggressive tactics bring him to grief, and appropriately, it was an area that also proved to be the undoing of the *New York Herald*. Prostitutes and other dealers in vice during the late nineteenth century often used the classified department of widely circulated New York dailies to announce their availability. (The practice became particularly widespread after the Reverend Charles H. Parkhurst's sensational testimony before the Lexow Committee in 1895 succeeded in forcing prostitution underground.) The ads were difficult to police under the best of circumstances. Most of the people involved had enough sense to couch their messages in vague and suggestive terms, so that however clear the meaning, they seemingly dealt with artists' models, massage parlors, Turkish baths, rooming houses "with female clientele," and so on. Moreover, in an age when all of journalism accepted the morality of caveat emptor, as seen in the extravagant claims of patent medicine ads, publishers were loath to surrender any more advertising revenue than absolutely necessary. James Gordon Bennett, for example, refused to clean up the personal columns of the *Herald* even after his aides pointed out to him that Park Row blithely referred to them as "The Whore's Daily Guide and Handy Compendium."[38]

The *World*'s large circulation, as well as the class of people who patronized it, made it an obvious depository for such messages. They appeared with some frequency after 1883, exposing Pulitzer to attacks not unlike those Hearst launched against Bennett twenty-two years later, which resulted in the owner of the *Herald* being found guilty of violating the postal regulations and fined $25,000. The assault upon Pulitzer came from several directions, but most notably from *The Journalist*, which in this case had sufficient ammunition for its purpose.

Leander Richardson needed only to reprint items from the *World*'s columns to establish that the paper had become a clearinghouse for pimps and prostitutes. The messages which lent spice to its Personal Columns were not difficult to decipher.

[38] See Richard O'Connor, *The Scandalous Mr. Bennett* (Garden City, New York, 1962), p. 272.

A STYLISH LITTLE PHILADELPHIA lady, age 21, desires the acquaintance of a thorough gentleman; one of means, resident or frequent visitor of her city; no triflers. Address "MABLE GREY," Phila. Post Office.

A FIRST CLASS OPPORTUNITY IS OFFERED TO A prepossessing and refined young lady to make the tour of Europe. Address, with personal description, CHARLES MONTAGUE, World, uptown, 1267 Broadway.[39]

A REFINED YOUNG LADY OF HIGHEST RESPECTABILITY, stranger in the city, temporarily distressed in finances, desires the acquaintance of a wealthy, honorable gentleman, who would prove a friend. Address Helena P. Hamilton, Brooklyn Post-Office.

"Could the advertiser have worded her want more plainly?" *The Journalist* asked of the latter ad. "Could she have made understood in clearer terms what it was she wished to exchange for the assistance of the 'wealthy, honorable gentleman' she was seeking? Was not this a plain enough request for bids upon the kind of merchandise in which this particular young woman deals?"[40] For those who did not seek a woman, but a place to meet one already acquired, another type of ad promised satisfaction.

A WIDOW LADY, LIVING IN HER OWN HOUSE, recently meeting with reverses, will let to refined parties handsomely furnished parlors and bedrooms attached for $2 per day; less per week; permanently or otherwise; meals served in rooms if desired. SAFT, BOX 250, World, uptown, 1267 Broadway.

A LADY HAVING OPENED A NEW PRIVATE HOUSE, east side, convenient to all trains, will rent rooms transiently to parties from the country; elegant reception parlors, private letter boxes. Parties desiring every comfort address, ARISTOCRATIC, World, uptown, 1267 Broadway.[41]

These messages of commercial love became the exhibits in a campaign of persecution that mounted in ferocity. "They are

[39] The first two ads are cited in *The Journalist*, June 28, 1884, pp. 1-2.
[40] *The Journalist*, July 5, 1884, pp. 1-2.
[41] The two ads are cited in *The Journalist*, June 28, 1884, pp. 1-2.

simply disgraceful," *The Journalist* declared. "No paper containing them ought to be admitted to any decent family."[42] Or again, "[Pulitzer] has made the *World* a sewer for the stream of vice and filth which courses through the great city under the surface of decent life. He has made it the channel of communication between the brothers and their patrons, the massage harlots and their victims, and the assignation house keepers and their licentious customers."[43]

Pulitzer was not as vulnerable to the attacks as Bennett would be twenty-two years later, in part because Hearst addressed a larger audience than Richardson, and took more time to build up his case, and in part also because Bennett's readers were more sensitive to the charges.[44] The owner of the *Herald* was not only indicted by a grand jury and fined, but his paper suffered heavily in loss of prestige and circulation. By contrast, Pulitzer went from triumph to triumph during the 1880s, emerging from the decade indisputably the foremost newspaper proprietor in the United States. The allegations nevertheless caused him considerable embarrassment, for he intended not only to build a prosperous journal, but one which would be the moral conscience of its time. He could hardly square revenue from pimps and prostitutes with the high goals he had set for himself, and on this one occasion at least, Richardson's sniping put him on the defensive. After months of silence he took note of the charges to offer a defense notable for its apologetic tone. "*The World* cannot well undertake to vouch for the honesty of its thousands of adver-

---

[42] *The Journalist*, May 24, 1884, p. 5.

[43] *The Journalist*, August 16, 1884, pp. 5-6.

[44] Hearst had a team of reporters, under the leadership of Victor Watson, working on the exposé for almost a year. They rented postal boxes under assumed names, and diligently patronized the *Herald*'s advertisers. Their findings ultimately ran as a long series in the *New York American* (the *Journal* had become an afternoon paper), while another Hearst employee, S. S. Carvalho, used it as the basis of his testimony before a federal grand jury. The government indicted Bennett on charges of sending obscene matter through the mails, a charge successfully prosecuted by Henry L. Stimson, later Secretary of State under Hoover and Franklin Roosevelt's Secretary of War. Bennett was fined $25,000, the newspaper itself $5,000, and his advertising manager $1,000. Much more serious was the loss in circulation and advertising which the *Herald* suffered and never regained. It makes an ironic footnote to the episode that Hearst printed similar advertisements in his *San Francisco Examiner*. Only in New York City did "the Chief" serve as guardian of the public morality.

tisers," an editorial declared. "Advertisements which appear fair and honorable upon their face are accepted. . . . It is certainly asking a good deal when it is proposed to make [the editor] answerable for the good conduct and fair dealings of advertisers. If swindlers occasionally get access to our columns, we have only to be informed of the fact to apply the remedy."[45] With that statement, the newspaper let the matter drop.

Circulation and advertising are the two criteria by which journalistic achievement is measured, but a triumph as startling as the *World*'s was bound to show in other ways as well. Its investment in modern equipment, and later a new plant, is a case in point. Just as the World Building which went up in 1890 at the north corner of Park Row signified that the newspaper had taken its place in the front rank of American journalism, so the acquisition of modern presses during 1883 and 1884 convinced even the skeptics that Pulitzer had come to stay.

The newspaper he acquired from Gould was equipped with six ancient Hoe presses. They could run off only eight-page issues, and were bare of the latest mechanical refinements, such as Luther C. Crowell's device for putting uncollated sheets into half-page folds at the speed of a press run. Pulitzer immediately installed a seventh press, but as the *World* grew in circulation and size, the strain became intolerable. The result was the most intensive program of modernization that the American press had yet witnessed. By 1883 the Hoe Company had perfected its original press into a monster machine capable of running off issues of up to sixteen pages, or when collated at half-capacity, up to thirty-two pages. Pulitzer ordered two immediately, with two more to be delivered at a later date. (Don Seitz points out that "soon there was always a press on the stocks in the Hoe factory designed for the *World* establishment."[46]) By March 1884 the first pair had been installed, and although they worked imperfectly and required the constant presence of Hoe mechanics to keep them going, they marked a first step toward the time when the *World* would be the best equipped paper on Park Row. An editorial that month apologized for the erratic format

[45] *World*, March 13, 1885, p. 4.
[46] Don C. Seitz, *Joseph Pulitzer, His Life & Letters*, p. 154.

of the Sunday edition, which saw the editorials appear on page twelve rather than their customary page four, but promised that in a short time all would be set right. "These annoyances of growth will soon be obviated. Two of our new Hoe presses are now in our building, and in short time the other two will be delivered. With these four new presses we will be able to handle our various editions with facility—at least for a season."[47] The other two presses were installed in May and the *World* came closer (despite continued mechanical failures) to enjoying the facilities to match its growth.[48]

But still the growth continued, and with it the demand for more equipment. By October 1884, the *World* had eliminated the bugs in the first four presses, and installed two more besides them. It could now print, fold, and deliver 1,200 copies per minute, which meant 72,000 eight-page or 150,000 four-page copies per hour. The newspaper could not have been more proud if it had taken on 10,000 new subscribers overnight. "These machines are the finest, best and fastest that the ingenuity of man in this inventive age can produce, . . ." an editorial exulted. "No newspaper establishment in the United States is

[47] *World*, March 16, 1884, p. 12. The newspaper's makeup was upset in the same way the following Sunday.

[48] *The Journalist* reported the *World*'s difficulties with the presses in some detail. "They will go along all right for a little while, carrying off the edition as fast as possible. Then something will go wrong, tapes will break, and the whole machinery will get into such a hopeless tangle that there is doubt for some time whether the work can be finished early enough to get the paper out at its proper hour. Consequently there is a constant strain upon the managers in the *World* office, who hardly dare to leave the place until the whole edition is printed." (*The Journalist*, April 26, 1884, p. 7.) Things had not improved much a month later. The press "would run right along at a clipping gait until six or seven thousand copies were struck off, and then it would suddenly stop. From that time out no human ingenuity could get it to work again." (May 24, 1884, p. 6.) The following week brought the suggestion that Pulitzer might have valid grounds to sue the Hoe Company. "Although there have been half a dozen of Hoe's most expert mechanics fairly living in the press-room of the *World* since this press was put in," it pointed out, "they have found it totally impossible to reduce the machine to anything like reliability. . . . The *World* people, we are inclined to think, would have an excellent suit for damages against the Hoes. Here is a press which is relied upon to do certain work which is urgently demanded by the increased applications for the *World*. The paper has grown very rapidly during the past few months, and the proprietor would doubtless reap an exceedingly large reward if he could supply the demand. But his new Hoe press every day breaks down altogether." May 31, 1884, pp. 2-3.

better equipped than the *World* to-day, and yet we shall further add a double Hoe Perfecting Press to our present array in a few months, making, in effect, eight in all. These presses cost a fortune, and they are not indulged in as luxuries. They mean business of the most active kind."[49] Five months later, with the installation of a new double Hoe Perfecting Press—the equivalent of two conventional presses—the newspaper justly boasted of enjoying the equipment to match its ambitions. "No newspaper office in the United States is so well equipped with machinery as the *World* to-day," an editorial declared. More remarkable, it had reached such eminence almost one year to the day from the time when its plant housed six ancient Hoe presses, not much more advanced than the outmoded Bullocks. The editorial termed it "a feat unparalleled in journalism."[50] The *World* now had the capacity to run off 80,000 eight-page copies per hour, or 160,000 copies per hour the size of the *Sun*. It was at last ready to welcome the readers who would make it the most widely circulated journal in the United States.

The rapidity with which the *World* acquired those presses, and the number it bought, testifies to the prosperity Pulitzer enjoyed with his new journalism. The trade periodical quoted Colonel Hoe as saying that the newspaper had been charged a reduced price of $25,000 per press because it bought in bulk.[51] If that figure is accurate, it means that the publisher undertook capital expenditures of $200,000 in a single year, over and above his normal outlay for salaries, paper, rent, and so on. He could not have done so without considerable cash income in 1884, and the prospect that the income would rise appreciably in future years.

The *World*'s progress is measured also in its changing relationship with the other members of New York's competitive press. Pulitzer entered the arena untested and almost unknown, a newcomer barely to be tolerated. Within a year he was taunting his competitors for their outmoded methods, and within a few more years, when blindness forced him to relinquish direct con-

[49] *World*, October 26, 1884, p. 4.
[50] *World*, March 29, 1885, p. 4.
[51] *The Journalist*, March 14, 1885, p. 5.

trol of the newspaper, he was hailed by them as a giant. Journalism, like other professions, aspires to be its own severest critic and harshest judge. The accolades finally bestowed upon Pulitzer by his colleagues represented his final triumph.

The publisher's relationship with other newspaper proprietors was not always a happy one. He arrived on Park Row, for example, frankly admiring Charles Dana, who had given him his first job on an English-language daily. Pulitzer contributed signed dispatches to the *Sun* during the Tilden–Hayes contest in 1876 and—a signal distinction—had also been invited to submit comment under his by-line to the editorial page. Although by purchasing the *World* he became a rival of Dana's, he clearly hoped that his aging mentor would respect what he had accomplished and allow the rivalry to be a friendly one. His hopes were dashed within a year, and a feud developed which mounted in bitterness.[52]

The earliest exchange between the two occurred only days

[52] There is an interesting, and ironic, parallel between Pulitzer's student-teacher relationship with Dana, one that finally culminated in estrangement between them, and the relationship just beginning in which Pulitzer played mentor to William Randolph Hearst. Writing from Harvard to his father in the winter of 1884, Hearst urged the Senator from California to model his *San Francisco Examiner* along the lines of the *New York World*. "It would be well, . . ." he suggested, "to imitate only some such leading journal as the *New York World* which is undoubtedly the best paper of that class to which the *Examiner* belongs—that class which appeals to the people and which depends for its success upon enterprise, energy and a certain startling originality and not upon the wisdom of its political opinions or the lofty style of its editorials. . . . Another detail . . . is that we actually or apparently establish some connection between ourselves and the *New York World*, and obtain a certain prestige in bearing some relation to that paper. . . . Whether the *World* would consent to such an arrangement for any reasonable sum is very doubtful, for its net profit is over one thousand dollars a day and no doubt it would consider the *Examiner* is beneath its notice. Just think, over one thousand dollars a day and four years ago it belonged to Jay Gould and was losing money rapidly." (Quoted in W. A. Swanberg, *Citizen Hearst* [New York, 1961], pp. 30-31.) The following year, when Hearst was expelled from Harvard for sending to each of his instructors a chamber pot with the recipient's name engraved on the inside bottom, he did not hesitate in deciding what to do. He made for New York City and secured a position working under his chosen teacher, Joseph Pulitzer. In the words of his biographer, Swanberg, "If a man can be in love with a newspaper, Hearst was downright passionate about the *World*." (*Ibid.*, p. 34.) Of course history would repeat itself within a decade. Just as Pulitzer's arrival in New York City spelled evil tidings for Charles Dana, the man who had taught him most about journalism, Hearst's purchase of the *New York Journal* in 1895 meant that the *World*, in turn, would soon surrender its circulation leadership.

after Pulitzer arrived in New York City. The *Sun* took note of his presence to wish him welcome, but also observed that Pulitzer's career to date had been marked by a deficiency in judgment and staying power, and questioned whether the old pattern was once again to be repeated. Coming from anybody else, or from Dana in later years, such a comment would have stirred the publisher of the *World* to angry retort, but on this occasion he elected to ignore it. An editorial thanked Dana for the welcome, and turned aside the criticism by declaring how much Pulitzer owed to his former employer.

> We are delighted to receive a cordial welcome from the successful and shining *Sun*. Our delight is somewhat dulled, it is true, by the melancholy statement that the editor of the *World* is deficient in judgment and in staying power. He has always stayed where he pleased to plant himself until ready to move, and he has never made any moves which were not clearly for the better. We believe we can say the same thing for the gifted editor of the *Sun*, who, by the way, was long ago accepted as our model, guide and preceptor in journalism. It may have been bad judgment on the part of Mr. Dana to employ the present editor of the *World* as a correspondent for his paper; but if the editor of the *World* has shown deficiency of judgment in journalism heretofore, it has been because he tried not only to imitate but even to excel the *Sun* in its truthfulness, fearlessness, independence and vigor.[53]

More noteworthy, he inserted another editorial in the same issue, disputing the contention of Colonel A. K. McClure, owner of the *Philadelphia Times*, that Dana (or any journalist) was not qualified to be President. "Mr. Dana is vigorous, earnest, daring and inflexible," he wrote. "The people would rally round him, whatever the politicians might do, and we shall be glad to see him nominated as we should be confident of his success." The same statement somewhat self-consciously disclaimed any personal ambition on Pulitzer's part. "We are justified in taking this position," he pointed out, "because, fortunately, a grave con-

[53] *World*, May 16, 1883, p. 4.

stitutional restriction removes all suspicion of personal aspirations on our part."[54]

The *World* tried for over a year to win Dana's goodwill. When the *Sun* mocked its prose style and grammar, it replied in the softest possible tones. "Our fastidious neighbor the *Sun* should not be severely critical when dealing with the *World*'s English," an editorial pleaded early in 1884. "It is plain, old-fashioned and Democratic."[55] Its half-hearted attempts to answer with equivalent lapses from Dana's newspaper seemed almost to be apologetic. "We recognize the *Sun* as a master of English," the *World* commented a few months later. "Hence we are shocked when we find it saying, in a beautiful essay on Sullivan, the Slugger, that 'He could lick any one when in his right mind.' In the realms of Fistiana 'lick' is doubtless a good idiom, but is it the kind of word that an exemplary newspaper, such as the *Sun*, should employ in discussing the gravest of the subjects now before the American people?"[56] Necessity demanded that it not hold still for the *Sun*'s jibes, but it took every opportunity to insist that the exchanges represented no more than good-natured bantering between friends. A correspondent who expressed concern at the falling-out between New York City's two foremost Democratic newspapers was thus reassured. "The *World*, in its cheerful humors, sometimes indulges in a bit of criticism at the expense of the *Sun*," Pulitzer wrote in reply to his letter; "but bless your soul, Mr. Sanborn, the feeling between the two journals is as cordial as that which once existed between David and Jonathan. . . . Mr. Sanborn must not mistake the little passages between the *World* and *Sun* for the outcroppings of a hostile sentiment. We have no hesitation in saying that the *Sun* is an excellent newspaper. We admire the *Sun* and in a general way revere Brother Dana."[57]

[54] *World*, May 16, 1883, p. 4.
[55] *World*, February 17, 1884, p. 4.
[56] *World*, July 3, 1884, p. 4.
[57] *World*, March 7, 1884, p. 4. Pulitzer was probably justified at the time in so reassuring the worried Mr. Sanborn. A few months before he had responded favorably to a request from Dana to have the *World* participate in a crusade to save some of the natural beauty spots near New York City, and the publisher of the *Sun* was duly grateful. "Believe me," Dana wrote in a short note to Pulitzer, "I am greatly indebted to you for your cordial interest in the

This determination not to admit that mutual respect had turned to bitterness is still more evident in the *World*'s political columns. During the summer of 1884, when every enemy of Cleveland's was tenfold an enemy of the *World*'s, Pulitzer went far in forgiving Dana his apostasy from the Democratic cause. "Mr. Dana is a man of force and his widely circulated newspaper has great influence, . . ." he declared in July. "In a very short while we expect to see the *Sun* standing shoulder to shoulder with the *World* in support of Cleveland and Reform."[58] Summer turned into fall, and still the *Sun* editorially attacked Cleveland in support of the Butler candidacy. The *World*'s tone grew sharper, but it was not yet ready to lump Dana with all the other scoundrels and scalawags it saw infesting the political arena in 1884. "We look upon the editor of the *Sun* as an Erring Brother, . . ." an editorial in September declared. "Let us hope that Brother Dana will soon see the error of his way and that he will quickly return to the fold without being urged thereto by the protests of his Democratic readers, who feel that they have been deceived, abused, and put upon, as it were."[59] This was great forbearance for the *World* at the height of a political campaign.

As it turned out, politics finally forced the break between the two men. It was becoming harder to paper over the widening chasm between them as they each staked their reputations, and personal fortunes, on rival Presidential candidates. Soft words turned into harsher ones, until at last the air grew heavy with charges and countercharges. One example of increasingly taut tempers occurred in August, when the *World* claimed that even the *Sun* had admitted that Blaine suppressed one of the Mulligan letters. "This is simply lying of a sort that requires no further notice, and will get none," came back the hot retort.[60] *The Journalist* reveled at the spectacle of the esteemed old man of American journalism taking his upstart competitor to task. "There has rarely been a more contemptuous dismissal of a little

---

business." Letter dated December 18, 1883. *Pulitzer Papers*, Columbia University Libraries.

[58] *World*, July 16, 1884, p. 4.

[59] *World*, September 24, 1884, p. 4.

[60] *New York Sun*, August 8, 1884, p. 2. See page 103, note 31, for a discussion of the "Mulligan Letters" incident.

annoyance than this dismissal of Mr. Jewseph Pulitzer by Mr. Dana," it reported happily. "It is done with a good deal the air of some big, hard-skinned animal which brushes off a gnat or some other little pest."[61] The periodical could not know that 1884 had changed their relationship, and that henceforth, whatever the proper metaphor, it would not be of a gnat disturbing a ponderous animal.

Perhaps, in retrospect, Dana had most reason for bitterness. Just as the 1884 campaign was the making of the *World*, it proved to be almost catastrophic for the *Sun*. And to make it more galling, the one consequence followed directly from the other. Dana's stubborn support of Butler that year drove thousands of *Sun* subscribers into the willing arm of Pulitzer, with the result that his newspaper suffered a permanent circulation loss estimated at between 40 and 50 percent.[62] He responded with personal, and ever more bitter attacks, against the former protégé who had so arranged his downfall. Pulitzer, meanwhile, had grown increasingly disenchanted with Dana for abandoning the party when victory was finally in view.[63] He would no longer suffer criticisms or attacks by turning the other cheek.

The eruption which had been threatening for months finally occurred in January 1885, set off by a seemingly trivial incident. Pulitzer offended Dana's sense of propriety by his behavior

[61] *The Journalist*, August 9, 1884, p. 4.

[62] According to Seitz, the *Sun's* circulation dropped from 137,000 to 85,000 during the course of the campaign. (Seitz, *Pulitzer, Life & Letters*, p. 148.) Charles J. Rosebault, in his standard biography of Dana, makes the drop even more extreme, from 158,000 to 78,000. Charles J. Rosebault, *When Dana Was The Sun* (New York, 1931), p. 228. The important point is that Dana gave Pulitzer a magnificent opportunity to fill the void, and he never recovered his lost readers.

[63] A good example of this disenchantment is the four-column cartoon by McDougall which the *World* ran on its front page on the eve of the election. It was inspired by Dana's statement in the *Sun* on June 29, 1884, that "sooner than join in making James G. Blaine President of the United States, we would quit work, burn up our pen, and leave to other and perhaps rasher heads the noble controversies of politics and the defense of popular self-government." The cartoon showed Dana dressed as a noble Roman, burning his quill pen on a flame fed by consistency, good sense, honor, and reputation. Blaine, also dressed as a Roman, watches in the background, and holds in his hand a scroll of Mulligan letters labeled BURN THESE NEXT. McDougall entitled the cartoon THE GREAT PEN-BURNING CEREMONY. MR. DANA ABDICATES IN FAVOR OF "RASHER HEADS." *World*, November 3, 1884, p. 1.

that month at a banquet tendered by the Lotus Club in honor of George Augustus Sala, a visiting English journalist. Whitelaw Reid rose to welcome the guest, and in the course of his remarks made jocular reference to the recent election, pointing to the outcome as re-establishing southerners in the government. Pulitzer promptly answered him from the floor. Their exchange of words as reported in *The Journalist* did not amount to much.

> Reid: We've not only forgiven our countrymen, whom our guest used to sympathize with, but we've put—and are getting ready to put—the most of them into office.
>
> Pulitzer: A good deal better for the country.
>
> Reid: We are now considering how much they are going to forgive us.
>
> Pulitzer: We have a good deal to forgive.
>
> Reid: Seriously, gentlemen, we are very glad to see Mr. Sala here again, etc.[64]

Dana seized upon it, however, to write a long editorial in the *Sun* condemning Pulitzer for his boorishness and lack of manners. The publisher of the *World* had been elected to Congress from the Ninth District of New York, a Democratic stronghold, in the same election that put Cleveland in the White House. Dana's editorial accused Pulitzer of twisting elbows to get the nomination, and adjudged it a reasonable endeavor for a man so exposed in all his vulgarity at the Lotus Club.[65] It went on to charge

---

[64] *The Journalist*, January 24, 1885, p. 4.

[65] The actual circumstances behind Pulitzer's nomination appear to have been that the two factions in New York City's Democratic Party, the County Democracy and Tammany Hall, temporarily united by high hopes for Cleveland's election, prevailed upon Pulitzer to lend his prestige to the ticket by accepting a nomination from the solid Ninth District. The publisher agreed on the understanding that his election was a foregone conclusion, and that he would not be expected to campaign. He defeated his Republican opponent, Herman Thum, by 7,021 votes, and the following December took his seat in the Forty-Ninth Congress.

Pulitzer soon regretted that he had allowed himself to be persuaded to stand as a candidate. He much preferred the newspaper business to practical politics, and was constantly making the long trip to New York to help guide the *World* to new heights of circulation and prestige. Even while in Washington, he spent more time at the *World* bureau than in the halls of Congress.

A variety of considerations finally persuaded him to retire. The attempt to

that Pulitzer's first employment in St. Louis had been as a coachman for Captain James B. Eads, the noted engineer, in which position he had presumably acquired his uncultivated habits. The editor of the *Sun* wielded a pen which was like a rapier to Leander Richardson's scimitar, but his intention was the same: to cut down, and hopefully destroy, a man whose presence on Park Row threatened to engulf them both. Pulitzer would oblige one no more than the other. He replied with words as bitter as Dana's, and a feud commenced which both men carried to their graves. "Though it is not a matter of much consequence," he wrote, "we will tell the able and aged bully and blackguard of the *Sun* that nearly every line of the above extract contains a lie . . ."

> that the Editor of the *World* neither fifteen years ago nor at any other time held the interesting position described in the *Sun* or any other under James B. Eads, and that, instead of "devoting considerable zeal" to the "cultivation" of "working politicians" in the "downtown wards," the nomination referred to came to him totally unsought, unexpected and undesired.
>
> But we wish it distinctly understood that we would a thousand times rather be an honest coachman enjoying the esteem of honest people than the present editor of the *Sun*.[66]

combine public office with journalistic independence was proving increasingly difficult. Tammany Hall understandably regarded him as its own property, which the publisher just as understandably could not tolerate. And his record of absenteeism was providing impressive material for editorials in the *New York Sun*. He finally resigned the office on April 10, 1886, and thenceforth confined his participation in politics to editorial comments in the pages of the *New York World*.

[66] *World*, January 19, 1885, p. 4. Eads was in New York City on the day the editorial appeared, and he immediately dispatched a letter to Pulitzer confirming its accuracy. "I read with surprise in the *World* this morning," he wrote, "that your enemies, evidently jealous of your exceptional success as a journalist, have started the ridiculous lie that you were once employed by me as a coachman some fifteen years ago in St. Louis. For the information of your detractors, and others who may unwittingly accept their statements, I will be glad if you will permit me to state the fact to the 115,000 subscribers of the *World* that when I first became acquainted with you, fifteen years ago, you were one of the owners of the *Westliche Post*, a German paper of great influence in St. Louis." Although the letter went on to speak glowingly of the publisher's personal qualities, and his contributions to the community during the years in

Henceforth the *World* would be as diligent as the *Sun* in adding coals to a fire that hardly needed feeding. Dana came in for heavy and sustained abuse. "To what race of human beings does Charles Anderson Dana belong?" the newspaper asked editorially the following month. "The Danas, although a New England family of considerable Puritan and literary pretensions, have unquestionably a Greek derivation. . . . The modern Greek is a treacherous, drunken creature. . . . Mr. Charles Ananias Dana may be descended from a Greek corsair. If so, his career of treachery, hypocrisy, deceit and lying could be easily accounted for."[67] Nor was it enough to compile words of insult when the editor of the *Sun* could be personally embarrassed. The *World* somehow got hold of a letter from Dana to Andrew Johnson written seventeen years before, unsuccessfully petitioning for a federal appointment.[68] Pulitzer maliciously reproduced it on the editorial page, and under it added a statement mocking the supplicant.

> This letter is not modest, but it is self-reliant, bold and beseeching. It is couched in beautiful language. We doubt whether the Anglo-Saxon tongue was ever more adroitly employed in the art of office-begging. The Fact that this letter produced no results—that it was a case to the winds, as it were—should not discourage ambitious gentlemen who long to serve the public. The style and diction are what we commend.
>
> With an honest, decent man's name at the bottom this style of letter ought to "fetch" a small post-office or a gaugership every time.[69]

St. Louis, Pulitzer evidently did not consider the matter important enough to warrant a second statement. The letter was never published. Letter from James B. Eads to Joseph Pulitzer, dated January 19, 1885. *Pulitzer Papers*, Columbia University Libraries.

[67] *World*, February 15, 1885, p. 4.

[68] One wonders whether the letter was made available to Pulitzer as a first reward for services rendered during the recent campaign.

[69] *World*, February 18, 1885, p. 4. If these assaults seem unnecessarily small-minded on Pulitzer's part, it is worth remembering that he tended to be a hostage to his own rash temper. Almost anything could trigger the explosion. Walt McDougall, who remembered the publisher fondly as the most profane man he had ever encountered, described him in a typical moment of creation. "When J. P. was dictating an editorial upon some pet topic, such as Collis P. Huntington's ill-gotten wealth, Jay Gould's infamous railroad wrecking or

The same progression from recognizing a mentor to berating a rival is seen in the newspaper's later attitude toward the *Sun*'s literary style. (It is tempting to postulate that Pulitzer suffered a sense of insecurity from dealing with words in a language not his own. He was always particularly sensitive to criticisms of his own prose, or the prose that appeared in the *World*, and he regarded the literary pretensions of the *Sun* as a subject for special attention.) Dozens of editorials appeared after January 1885, denying what had once been admitted, that the *Sun*'s language set a standard for others to emulate as best they could. The new game was to find lapses in its grammar, and to use them to prove the hollowness of the claims. "Of course the *Sun* is not as amenable to criticism as if it had set up a very high standard of purity in writing the English language," the *World* declared after one such discovery, "but we submit that it is better to have some standard and is always more effective to write good English than to write about it."[70] No longer would Pulitzer concede any superiority to "that absurd pretender as a professed purist . . . which for years has tried to bully New York newspapers and the public generally into the use of its own peculiar and uncertain English. . . . The mere fact that the *Sun* pronounces anything proper or improper by no means makes it so."[71] The immigrant publisher detected a tendency in the *Sun* to "ignore its own [grammar rules] with unabashed steadiness,"[72] and even began "to suspect that the affected pedagogism of the *Sun* is a sort of opera-bouffe and not a serious performance."[73]

Cyrus Field's income, his speech was so interlarded with sulphurous and searing phrases that the whole staff shuddered. He was the first man I ever heard who split a word to insert an oath. He did it often, and his favorite was 'indegoddamnpendent.' " Such a man, hot-tempered by nature, and not noted for the saving grace of humor, was almost bound to over-respond to the thrusts of a wily old adversary like Charles Dana. McDougall suggested as much when in a different context he wrote that Pulitzer "was almost absolutely devoid of any sense of humor, save of a certain banal sort, and the stings of that human wasp, Dana of the *Sun*, drove him frantic." (The quotations are from Walt McDougall, "Old Days on *The World*," *The American Mercury*, IV [January 1925], 22, 23.) This does not excuse the publisher for his meanness, but does at least help to explain it.

[70] *World*, January 21, 1885, p. 4.   [71] *World*, January 22, 1885, p. 4.
[72] *World*, February 1, 1885, p. 4.
[73] *World*, February 3, 1885, p. 4. The *World* harped relentlessly on this theme. For editorials in a similar vein, see January 14, 1885, p. 4; February 2,

The long and pointless feud between two great editors demonstrates more than the continued importance of personal journalism in the 1880s. From Pulitzer's point of view, however unhappy the circumstances, it represented a sort of recognition from within the profession. No longer was he the upstart, easily ignored, and if noticed, dismissed with a wave of the hand. The fact that he traded invective with Dana, of all men, signified that he had ceased to be apprentice to any master. He did not necessarily seek combat, but if it was thrust upon him he would fight.

Fortunately, he did not have to become involved in bitter wrangles in order to win recognition from the other metropolitan dailies. The *Times* and the *Herald* conceded his presence in the most flattering way in September 1883, by cutting their price to two cents to compete with the *World* for newsstand sales. "The *World* when it passed under its present management promised in a modest way to revolutionize journalism in this neighborhood," an editorial chortled on the day after the *Times* came down from four cents a copy. "We rather think we have succeeded quite well. We have caused a ponderous four-cent newspaper to fly up and roost on a two-cent limb."[74] A second editorial suggested how George Jones' paper might further enhance its image, now that it had joined the ranks of the popular press.

> If our neighbor will only imitate us in style and tone, now, it may hope to amount to something. If, for instance, it should drop its ponderous magazine essays and its elongated editorial humor and fall in with the brief, breezy and briggity fashion of the *World* it would be able to flank the *Tribune* in a very short time. We have a patent on the pithy, paragraphic style of editorial writing so popular with the public, but our prosperity enables us to be liberal and we will waive all rights if our neighbor is really anxious to please and be powerful.[75]

But it did not really entertain much hope that the advice would be heeded, and as a last resort suggested a different remedy. "The

---

1885, p. 4; February 4, 1885, p. 4; February 6, 1885, p. 4; February 7, 1885, p. 4; and February 12, 1885, p. 4.
    [74] *World*, September 19, 1883, p. 4.   [75] *World*, September 19, 1883, p. 4.

Tribune has a Fresh Air Fund. It should divide it with its neighbor, the *Times*, which seems to be gasping for the lack of ozone, or something of that kind."[76]

This strutting and smug sense of well-being was reflected in dozens of editorials mocking the staid birds roosted on Park Row. Pulitzer's journal chastened the *Tribune* for devoting excessive attention to foreign affairs,[77] and commiserated that its dwindling circulation was found in the "aristocratic sections of the city," where the "pure in heart are found, and where the breath of the campaign slander is never wafted."[78] It airily dismissed Godkin's complaints about the "wickedness and triviality" of two-cent newspapers by questioning what value his opinion had for any journal but his own. "Strange to say," an editorial remarked, "none of the cheap newspapers have time to criticize the business and editorial management of the ponderous *Evening Post*. It is assumed that all the goody-goody people in New York who love a pure and lofty journal patronize the *Evening Post*. It has them all. This being the case, what encouragement is there for anybody to imitate its style of journalism?"[79] And when the *Daily Graphic* also bowed to the *World*'s presence in January 1885, by reducing its price to three cents, Pulitzer regarded the maneuver with something much akin to complacency. "This is a good move no doubt," he wrote, "but the *World*, price two cents, comes very near supplying the demand for illustrated daily journalism in this part of the country. Still, we welcome the *Graphic* as a noble competitor."[80]

Pulitzer had stirred up his contemporaries, but the rivalry which must have satisfied him most was with the august *New York Herald*. Bennett, father and son, had dominated the arena for decades, and to force their paper to give way, to make it concede the effectiveness of the new journalism, was a triumph of the first order. The initial concession came in September 1883, when one week after the *Times*, and presumably in response to

[76] *World*, September 20, 1883, p. 4.   [77] *World*, May 1, 1884, p. 4.
[78] *World*, December 17, 1884, p. 4.
[79] *World*, February 9, 1884, p. 4.
[80] *World*, January 8, 1885, p. 4. The *Daily Graphic* borrowed a leaf from Bennett's book by taking a full-page ad in the *World* to announce the reduction in price. See *World*, January 8, 1885, p. 3.

the strategy of the *Times*, the *Herald* reduced its price from three cents to two cents. "Another victim, another victory for the *World!*" an editorial rejoiced. "The *Herald*, too, has reduced its price to two cents, and the *World* is still booming. Brother Bennett, like Brother Jones, now believes in Western journalism."[81] To make the occasion even more notable, Bennett took full-page ads in the *World* for seven consecutive days to announce the reduction.[82] (HERALD AT TWO CENTS, the message proclaimed. CHEAPEST NEWSPAPER IN AMERICA.) This was too good an opportunity for a huckster like Pulitzer to ignore. He pointed out to his readers that the *Herald* had thereby conceded not only the *World's* increase in circulation, but its effectiveness as an advertising organ. "So far as the *World* is concerned," he wrote, "it has none of that prejudice against gratuitous mention of contemporaries which Brother Dana says afflicts the metropolitan press. We alone mentioned the *Herald's* reduction yesterday and charged nothing for it. To-day we surrender our fifth page to Brother Bennett, who, though far away across the ocean, understands the value of advertising in a newspaper with a large and growing circulation."[83]

It was easy thereafter to treat the *Herald* as cavalierly as the rest of the metropolitan press. When Bennett's paper experimented with illustration by running a few woodcuts of a Paris salon, the *World* responded with a typical offering of advice. "There is no flattery so sincere as imitation," an editorial declared, "and the *World* feels a sense of pride in noting the care with which the *Herald* follows in its wake. . . . But until the *Herald* equips it-

[81] *World*, September 26, 1883, p. 4.

[82] The ad appeared on page five in every issue of the *World* between September 27 and October 3. The location is worthy of note. The *World* gave special billing to the advertisement by placing it right opposite the editorial page, not usually a place for display ads of any size. An undated memorandum written by Pulitzer in the next decade, probably 1890-1895, cautioned his editors about using that spot. "Try to keep advts. off the 5th page as much as possible, . . ." he wrote. "The fifth page, being opposite to the editorial page, is entitled to some special consideration." *Pulitzer Papers*, Library of Congress. Bennett had to pay special rates to hire the space: $700 a day against the usual fee for a full page ad of $500 a day. Of course if he benefited thereby, so did Pulitzer, for the *World's* readers were put on notice that its major rival had chosen it as a medium to announce the reduction in price.

[83] *World*, September 27, 1883, p. 4.

self with sound principles, a few bright ideas and a collection of fresh brains, we shall not regard it as a formidable journalistic adversary."[84] It also gladly accepted the challenge when the *Herald* questioned its circulation claims. For ten consecutive days in December 1884, a statement appeared just below the masthead on page four guaranteeing to refund the money of advertisers if they could show that the *Herald*'s Sunday circulation was larger than the *World*'s, and further offering $1,000 to any advertiser who managed to persuade the *Herald* to open its books so the matter could be put to the test.[85] Pulitzer knew that in such a dispute he held the trump cards, and relentlessly pointed out as much to his readers and to his rivals down the street. "The *Herald* makes a mistake when it provokes a discussion of business matters with the *World*," an editorial warned, "and we are confident that Brother Bennett will take this same intelligent view when the facts are duly cabled to him in Paris. He will probably instruct his indiscreet representatives on this side of the ocean to maintain a peaceful and dignified silence concerning the affairs of their prosperous neighbors."[86] The prediction proved to be sound.

These publicly fought rivalries reveal the new stature Pulitzer had achieved for the paper he acquired from Jay Gould. It was an age of personal journalism, when newspapers conducted their bantering in public, and when those which excelled in circulation and advertising earned the right to speak boldly to the others. The dialogue indicates how quickly the *World* became an equal among equals, and then something more.

Pulitzer had as many bricks thrown at him as he threw himself, but that was part of the game. The remarkable thing is that within two years journalists began to appreciate the importance of his contributions, and to accord him new respect. He became a solon whose pronouncements on the press, and related matters, received the deepest attention. The first major statement in recognition of his newspaper genius appeared, appropriately enough,

[84] *World*, May 2, 1884, p. 4.
[85] An identically worded statement to that effect appeared below the masthead in every issue from December 5, 1884, to December 14, 1884.
[86] *World*, December 7, 1884, p. 4.

in the publication which had previously devoted itself to destroying him. In July 1885, having passed under the control of W. G. MacLaughlin, and edited now by C. J. Smith and Allan Forman, *The Journalist* took stock of Pulitzer's achievement in twenty-six months on Park Row. "The *World*, as it stands today," it declared, "is the best epitome of Joseph Pulitzer's character and achievements. His boldness, vigor and enterprise have deservedly placed that journal at the head of the American press by right of a circulation and influence won by real work, sound newspaper knowledge, honest devotion to principle and an unflagging devotion to the rights and interests of the people. The success of the *World* since it came under Mr. Pulitzer's control, little more than two years ago, is admittedly unexampled in the history of journalism." The article went on to consider the low ebb the newspaper had reached in May 1883, and how thereafter it went from plateau to plateau in achieving new heights of circulation. "It is not necessary to point out to newspaper men what these figures mean. Those who have watched the rise of the *World*'s circulation with close interest have not failed to notice the corresponding decline in public favor of the *World*'s great rivals in the metropolis." The newspaper had tested its appeal by single-handedly undertaking to save the nation from the disgrace of failing to provide a pedestal for the Statue of Liberty, and it had triumphed.[87] "As a popular subscription, carried on solely by one journal, in addition to all the calls upon the direction incident to printing a great newspaper, it certainly stands unparalleled." Meanwhile, its army of readers continued to grow, and at an increasing rate. "What position the *World* must attain in the near future it is not difficult to guess," the article concluded in peroration. "It has already passed the highest regular circulation ever attained by an American newspaper. At its present rate of increase, it would not be surprising if its circulation in five years should reach the amazing figures of

[87] At the time the article appeared, the *World* had received $98,000 (of its $100,000 goal) from 116,000 people. It proudly announced going over the top in the issue of August 11, 1885. Pulitzer's part in putting a pedestal under the Statue of Liberty was always an item of special pride for him. He shortly altered the page one vignette of the *World* to include the figure of Liberty, and still later christened his famous yacht by the same name.

the *London Daily Telegraph,* and, marching steadily on, fling its banner to the breeze at the head of the world's press, with the legend, 'Five hundred thousand a day—Excelsior.' "[88]

Pulitzer must have been gratified by those words, for they represented, what is no small thing, the ultimate praise of fellow professionals. He would have still more reason to feel proud five years later, at the bitter moment when blindness forced him to relinquish control of his newspaper. "Yielding to the advice of his physicians," a *World* editorial soberly announced on October 16, 1890, "Mr. Joseph Pulitzer has withdrawn entirely from the editorship of the *World.* . . . Those to whom the management of the *World* is intrusted will miss the inspiring direction, his sure intuitions of what is right and best, and his constant enforcement of a high and still higher ideal of excellence. But they will endeavor to prove their loyalty to him and to fulfill their obligation to the public by keeping the *World*'s course true to the chart which he has so plainly marked out in his splendidly successful direction of its progress in the past."[89] The announcement stirred an immediate reaction, as throughout the nation the press paid homage to the master journalist now abdicating his crown. But of all the voices, one was heard above the rest, both for its own prestige, and for the part it had once played in resisting the encroachment of the new journalism. The *New York Herald* spoke for all newspapers when it "drooped its colors" to a departed, but triumphant, adversary.

> Mr. Joseph Pulitzer the other day resigned his direct control of the *New York World.* It is needless to say that if this is really the case a great vacuum is made in the present actuality of American journalism.
>
> What the Greeleys and the Raymonds and the Bennetts did for journalism thirty years ago, Pulitzer has done to-day. It is true that his methods have been queer and peculiar, but after all they have suited the present American public.
>
> As for us of the *Herald,* we droop our colors to him. He has made success upon success against our

[88] *The Journalist,* July 25, 1885, p. 4.
[89] *World,* October 16, 1890, p. 4.

prejudices; has succeeded all along the line; has roused a spirit of enterprise and personality which, up to this time, has not been known. This man, however, who has given us a new line of thought and action now becomes a part of the past.

We have not always agreed with the spirit which has made his ideas a journalistic success, and we cannot refrain from regretting that he did not encourage us in the new departure which he made, instead of merely astonishing us, frightening us, and, we may add—now that it is past—perhaps a little bit disgusting us.

But, *le Roi est mort, vive le Roi!* The *New York World* is dead, long live the *World!* *Pacet!*[90]

Pulitzer could not have asked for a more generous or moving send-off, nor one which better expressed the enormity of what he had accomplished.

[90] *New York Herald*, October 17, 1890, p. 4.

AFTERWORD

I t is clear that several factors are essential in explaining the *World*'s rise to eminence during the last years of the nineteenth century. They all derived from Joseph Pulitzer's genius in the arts of his profession, and they all had to do with creating a newspaper suited to the temper of an America that had come of age as an industrial nation.

The most obvious thing should be mentioned first. Pulitzer was a uniquely skilled journalist, which is to say that he combined a "nose for news" with a mastery of the techniques required to present the news. Added to his mechanical skills was a creative bent. While it is notable how little the publisher contributed that in the strict sense was original, his accomplishment in adapting old tools to contemporary uses was immense. Between 1883 and 1885, the only feature to appear in the *World* that no newspaper before had ever tried was the use of ears on the masthead of the front page. It is so minor an advance as to be almost not worth mentioning. But when it comes to listing Pulitzer's achievement in taking ideas in the public domain, recognizing for the first time their full potential, and using them in the *World* as weapons in a war for circulation, a very different picture emerges. He was responsible for the first extensive use of illustration and the development of the sports page, and he played a role equal to that of any other publisher in making women part of the newspaper-reading public. In each of these areas Pulitzer established his credentials as a master journalist by responding quickly and adroitly to the drift of social change.

The publisher's regard for the dignity and responsibilities of his profession was also pivotal. It influenced him in many ways, notably in making him a leader among those who agitated for social reform. The very size of the *World*'s audience, and the presence in that audience of many who were dispossessed and helpless, lent a tone of personal involvement to the editorials that other papers did not share. It took the side of immigrants against a largely hostile native America; it agitated for housing reform in the slum districts of lower Manhattan; it argued labor's right to higher wages and better working conditions. There was a grittiness in those statements not to be found in highminded and conventional calls to public virtue. Whether or not its demands were always relevant to the needs that inspired them, the paper did play a leading role in focusing attention on the real issues of nineteenth century America.

The final factor behind Pulitzer's success was the remarkable extent to which he shared the attitudes and aspirations of the people he addressed. The publisher benefited throughout his career from a mentality that either reflected the popular mentality, or was at least readily susceptible to its influence. He is seen as a man of the time in his attitude toward the captains of American industry, admiring them for their material success and resenting how they achieved that success. His susceptibility to popular prejudice is demonstrated by the ease with which the *World* paid lip service to such emotions as jingoism and anti-intellectualism.

This common touch was extremely important, for from it followed his sure sense of what should and should not appear in a mass circulation daily. Sensationalism, for instance, entailed more than finding stories of sex and violence, although that was challenge enough. Equally important was the constant effort to ensure that the material which titillated a mass audience did not offend its moral sensibilities. Using illustration as part of the newsgathering process was not simply a technical feat, but a matter of knowing what sort of pictures would have wide appeal. The *World*'s success in attracting female readers—still a largely untapped group—involved recognizing the fact of woman's changing status while honoring the social conservatism of the lower and middle class families from which they came.

The same applies even to the newspaper's role as reformer. For all its crusading spirit, it rarely contradicted the assumptions of the men and women it represented. The dominant immigrant groups were prejudiced against newer immigrants, and the *World* shared that prejudice. The people hit hardest by the rapid development of industrial capitalism in nineteenth century America were by and large proponents of only the mildest reforms, and the *World* proved to be no more radical. It became a voice of the people as much by what it rejected as what it demanded.

The qualities that have been mentioned were personal to Pulitzer, and passed away with him. But the publisher also left a legacy. He taught his contemporaries, and those who came after, that in the new nation dominated by machines and cities, there was place and need for a new journalism. By his success, he forced the profession to listen. His monument, finally, is the modern America newspaper, which existed in the first instance in his imagination.

BIBLIOGRAPHY

NEWSPAPERS AND TRADE PUBLICATIONS

New York World.
New York Herald.
New York Sun.
New York Times.
The Journalist.
N. W. Ayer & Son's, American Newspaper Annual.
Special Supplement Commemorating the 100th Anniversary
  of Joseph Pulitzer, *St. Louis Post-Dispatch*, April 6, 1946.

DOCUMENTS

Joseph Pulitzer Papers. Columbia University Libraries.
Joseph Pulitzer Papers. Library of Congress.

REPORTS

DeForest, Robert W. and Lawrence Veiller (eds.). *The Tenement
  House Problem*, Including the Report of the New York State
  Tenement House Commission of 1900. 2 vols. New York: 1903.
Gould, Elgin R. L. *The Housing of the Working People*. Eighth
  Special Report of the Commissioner of Labor, prepared under
  the direction of Carroll D. Wright, Commissioner of Labor.
  Washington, D.C.: 1895.
New York Association for Improving the Condition of the Poor.
  Annual Reports. New York: 1880-1885.
New York State Legislature. *Report of the Tenement House
  Committee of 1894*. Assembly Documents, 118th Session,
  Vol. IX, No. 37. Albany: 1895.
New York State Legislature. *Report of the Tenement House
  Commission of 1884*. Senate Documents, 108th Session, Vol. V,
  No 36. Albany: 1885.
North, S. N. D. *History and Present Condition of the Newspaper and
  Periodical Press of the United States, With a Catalogue of the
  Publications of the Census Year*. Published as part of the United
  States House of Representatives Miscellaneous Documents, No.
  42, Part 8, 47th Congress, 2nd Session. Washington, D.C.: 1884.
Seligman, Edwin R. A. (ed.). *The Social Evil, With Special
  References to Conditions Existing in the City of New York*.
  Prepared under the Direction of the Committee of Fifteen, 1902.
  2nd ed. revised. New York: 1912.

U.S. Bureau of the Census. *Historical Statistics of the United States, Colonial Times to 1957.* Washington, D.C.: 1960.

U.S. Bureau of the Census. Special Reports. *Marriage and Divorce, 1867–1906.* 2 vols. Washington, D.C.: 1908-1909.

U.S. Bureau of Labor. Fourth Annual Report, 1888. *Working Women in Large Cities.* Washington, D.C.: 1889.

U.S. Commissioner of Labor. Eleventh Annual Report, 1895-1896. *Work and Wages of Men, Women, and Children.* Washington, D.C.: 1897.

U.S. House of Representatives. *Committee on Manufactures in the Sweating System.* Report 2309, 52nd Congress, Second Session. Washington, D.C.: 1893.

U.S. Senate. *Report of the Committee of the Senate upon the Relations Between Labor and Capital.* 5 vols. (5th vol. not issued). Report 1262, 48th Congress, Second Session. Washington, D.C.: 1885.

Wines, Frederick H. *Report on Crime, Pauperism and Benevolence in the United States at the Eleventh Census.* 2 vols. Washington, D.C.: 1895-1896.

The *World. Two Anniversaries: The World, 1883–1903; The St. Louis Post-Dispatch, 1878–1903.* New York, 1906.

Wright, Carroll D. *Marriage and Divorce in the United States: 1867–1886.* First Special Report. Commissioner of Labor. Washington, D.C.: 1889.

————. *The Slums of Baltimore, Chicago, New York, and Philadelphia.* Seventh Special Report. Commissioner of Labor. Washington, D.C.: 1894.

BOOKS

Aaron, Daniel. *Men of Good Hope. A Story of American Progressives.* New York: Oxford University Press, 1951.

Abbell, Aaron I. *The Urban Impact on American Protestantism, 1865–1900.* Cambridge: Harvard University Press, 1943.

Abbott, Edith. *Women in Industry.* New York: D. Appleton & Co., 1910.

Adams, Charles Francis. *Autobiography.* Boston: Houghton Mifflin Co., 1916.

Adams, Henry. *The Education of Henry Adams.* Boston: Houghton Mifflin Co., 1918.

Addams, Jane. *Twenty Years at Hull House.* New York: Macmillan Co., 1910.

Addams, Jane et al. *Philanthropy and Social Progress.* New York: Thomas Y. Crowell & Co., 1893.

Andrews, Wayne. *The Vanderbilt Legend. The Story of the Vanderbilt Family 1794–1940*. New York: Harcourt, Brace & Co., 1941.

Atkins, Gordon. *Health, Housing, and Poverty in New York City, 1865–1898*. Published Doctoral Dissertation from Columbia University. Ann Arbor, Mich.: Edwards Bros., Inc., 1947.

Aveling, Edward and Eleanor. *The Working Class Movement in America*. 2nd ed. enl. London: Swan Sonnenschein & Co., 1891.

Baehr, Harry W., Jr. *The New York Tribune Since the Civil War*. New York: Dodd, Mead & Co., 1936.

Barrett, James Wyman. *Joseph Pulitzer and His World*. New York: The Vanguard Press, 1941.

Beard, Charles A. and Mary R. *The Rise of American Civilization*. 2 vols. New York: Macmillan Co., 1927.

Beer, Thomas. *The Mauve Decade*. New York: Knopf, 1926.

Bent, Silas. *Ballyhoo: The Voice of the Press*. New York: Boni & Liveright, 1927.

——. *Newspaper Crusaders; A Neglected Story*. New York: McGraw-Hill Book Co., Inc., 1939.

Berger, Meyer. *The Story of the New York Times*. New York: Simon & Schuster, 1951.

Bleyer, Willard Grosvenor. *Main Currents in the History of American Journalism*. New York: Houghton Mifflin Co., 1927.

Bliss, William D. P. (ed.). *The New Encyclopedia of Social Reform*. New York: Funk & Wagnalls Co., 1908.

Bok, Edward William. *The Americanization of Edward Bok; The Autobiography of a Dutch Boy Fifty Years After*. New York: C. Scribner's Sons, 1920.

Boorstin, Daniel. *The Americans; The Colonial Experience*. New York: Random House, 1958.

Bowers, David Frederick (ed.). *Foreign Influences in American Life*. Princeton: Princeton University Press, 1944.

Brace, Charles Loring. *The Dangerous Classes of New York and Twenty Years Work Among Them*. New York: Wynkoop & Hallenbeck, 1872.

Bremner, Robert H. *From the Depths, The Discovery of Poverty in the United States*. New York: New York University Press, 1956.

Bryce, James. *The American Commonwealth*. 2 vols. Revised ed.; New York: Macmillan Co., 1891.

Calhoun, Arthur W. *A Social History of the American Family from Colonial Times to the Present*. 3 vols. Cleveland: Arthur H. Clark Co., 1917-1919.

Campbell, Helen Stuart. *Women Wage-Earners: Their Past, Their Present and Their Future.* Boston: Roberts Bros., 1893.

―――. *Prisoners of Poverty: Women Wage-Earners, Their Trades and Their Lives.* Boston: Roberts Bros., 1887.

Carlson, Oliver and Ernest Sutherland Bates. *Hearst, Lord of San Simeon.* New York: Viking Press, 1936.

Churchill, Allen. *Park Row.* New York: Rinehart & Co., Inc., 1958.

Cochran, Thomas and William Miller. *The Age of Enterprise.* New York: Macmillan Co., 1942.

Commager, Henry Steele. *The American Mind, An Interpretation of American Thought and Character Since the 1880's.* New Haven: Yale University Press, 1950.

Commons, John R. *Social Reform and The Church.* New York: Thomas Y. Crowell & Co., 1894.

Conwell, Russell H. *Acres of Diamonds.* New York: Harper & Bros., 1915.

Curti, Merle. *The Growth of American Thought.* New York: Harper & Bros., 1943.

David, Henry. *History of the Haymarket Affair; A Study in the American Social Revolutionary and Labor Movements.* 2nd ed. New York: Farrar & Rinehart, Inc., 1958.

Depew, Chauncey M. (ed.). *One Hundred Years of American Commerce.* 2 vols. New York: D. O. Haynes & Co., 1895.

Dreiser, Theodore. *A Book About Myself.* New York: Boni & Liveright, 1922.

Dulles, Foster Rhea. *America Learns to Play: A History of Popular Recreation, 1607–1940.* New York: D. Appleton-Century Co., Inc., 1940.

―――. *Labor in America, A History.* New York: Thomas Y. Crowell & Co., 1949.

Eaton, Dorman B. *The Government of Municipalities.* New York: Published for the Columbia University Press by the Macmillan Co., 1899.

Ely, Richard T. *Social Aspects of Christianity, and Other Essays.* New York: Thomas Y. Crowell & Co., 1889.

Emery, Edwin and Henry Ladd Smith. *The Press and America.* New York: Prentice-Hall, 1954.

Fadiman, Clifton (ed.). *The American Treasury, 1455–1955.* New York: Harper, 1955.

Fairchild, Henry Pratt. *The Melting Pot Mistake.* Boston: Little, Brown & Co., 1926.

Faithfull, Emily. *Three Visits to America.* New York: Fowler & Wells, Co., 1884.

Flint, Leon Nelson. *The Editorial: A Study in Effectiveness of Writing.* New York: D. Appleton & Co., 1920.

Flower, Benjamin Orange. *Civilization's Inferno; or, Studies in the Social Cellar*. Boston: Arena Publishing Co., 1893.

Ford, James. *Slums and Housing With Special Reference to New York City History Conditions Policy*. 2 vols. Cambridge, Mass.: Harvard University Press, 1936.

Gage, Matilda J. *Woman, Church and State*. Chicago: C. H. Kerr & Co., 1893.

Ghent, William James. *Our Benevolent Feudalism*. New York: Macmillan Co., 1902.

Goldman, Eric F. *The Crucial Decade: America, 1945–1955*. New York: Knopf, 1956.

———. *Rendezous With Destiny*. New York: Knopf, 1952.

Handlin, Oscar (ed.). *Immigration as a Factor in American History*. Englewood Cliffs, N.J.: Prentice-Hall, 1959.

Handlin, Oscar. *The Uprooted, The Epic Story of the Great Migrations That Made the American People*. Boston: Little, Brown, 1951.

Hay, John. *The Bread-winners*. New York: Harper & Bros., 1884.

Heaton, John L. *The Story of a Page, Thirty Years of Public Service and Public Discussion in the Editorial Columns of the New York World*. New York: Harper & Bros., 1913.

Hibben, Paxton. *Henry Ward Beecher, An American Portrait*. New York: George H. Doran Co., 1927.

Higham, John. *Strangers in the Land, Patterns of American Nativism 1860–1925*. New Brunswick, N.J.: Rutgers University Press, 1955.

Hofstadter, Richard. *The Age of Reform: From Bryan to F.D.R.* New York: Knopf, 1955.

Howells, William Dean. *A Hazard of New Fortunes*. New York: Boni and Liveright, Inc., 1889.

———. *Impressions and Experiences*. New York: Harper & Bros., 1896.

Hower, Ralph Merle. *The History of An Advertising Agency: N. W. Ayer & Son at Work, 1869–1939*. Cambridge, Mass.: Harvard University Press, 1939.

———. *History of Macy's of New York, 1858–1919, Chapters in the Evolution of the Department Store*. Cambridge, Mass.: Harvard University Press, 1943.

Hoyt, Edwin P. *The Vanderbilts and Their Fortunes*. Garden City, N.Y.: Doubleday & Co., Inc., 1962.

Hudson, Frederic. *Journalism in the United States, From 1690 to 1872*. New York: Harper & Bros., 1873.

Hughes, Helen MacGill. *News and the Human Interest Story*. Chicago: University of Chicago Press, 1940.

Hunter, Robert. *Poverty*. New York: Macmillan Co., 1904.

Ireland, Alleyne. *Joseph Pulitzer, Reminiscences of a Secretary*. New York: Mitchell Kennerley, 1914.

Jackson, Mason. *The Pictorial Press*: *Its Origin and Progress*. London: Hurst & Blackett, 1885.

Jones, Robert W. *Journalism in the United States*. New York: E. P. Dutton & Co., Inc., 1947.

Josephson, Matthew. *The Politicos, 1865–1896*. New York: Harcourt, Brace & Co., 1938.

————. *The Robber Barons, The Great American Capitalists, 1861–1901*. New York: Harcourt, Brace & Co., 1934.

Klein, Alexander (ed.). *The Empire City*; *A Treasury of New York*. New York: Rinehart & Co., Inc., 1955.

Kouwenhoven, John Atlee. *The Columbia Historical Portrait of New York, An Essay in Graphic History in Honor of the Tricentennial of New York City and the Bicentennial of Columbia University*. Garden City, N.Y.: Doubleday & Co., Inc., 1953.

Learsi, Rufus (pseud. for Israel Goldberg). *The Jews in America, A History*. Cleveland: World Publishing Co., 1954.

Lee, Alfred McClung. *The Daily Newspaper in America*; *The Evolution of a Social Instrument*. New York: Macmillan Co., 1937.

Lee, James Melvin. *History of American Journalism*. New York: Houghton Mifflin Co., 1917.

Loomis, Samuel Lane. *Modern Cities and Their Religious Problems*. New York: Baker & Taylor Co., 1887.

Lynes, Russell. *The Tastemakers*. New York: Harper, 1949.

Madison, Charles A. *Critics and Crusaders, A Century of American Protest*. New York: H. Holt & Co., 1947.

Mahin, Helen Ogden. *The Development and Significance of the Newspaper Headline*. Published doctoral dissertation from the University of Michigan. Ann Arbor, Mich.: G. Wahr, 1924.

Marshall, Walter G. *Through America, or Nine Months in the United States*. London: S. Low, Marston, Searle & Rivington, 1881.

Martin, Frederick Townsend. *The Passing of the Idle Rich*. Garden City, N.Y.: Doubleday & Co., Inc., 1911.

Meyer, Annie (Nathan) (ed.). *Woman's Work in America*. New York: H. Holt & Co., 1891.

Miller, John Anderson. *Fares, Please! From Horse-Cars to Streamliners*. New York: D. Appleton-Century Co., 1941.

More, Louise Bolard. *Wage-Earners' Budgets*: *A Study of Standards and Costs of Living in New York City*. New York: H. Holt & Co., 1907.

Morris, Lloyd. *Incredible New York, High Life and Low Life of the Last Hundred Years*. New York: Random House, 1951.

Morris, Richard (ed.). *The Encyclopedia of American History*. New York: Harper, 1953.

Mott, Frank Luther. *American Journalism, A History of Newspapers in the United States through 250 Years, 1690 to 1940*. New York: Macmillan Co., 1941.

————. *A History of American Magazines*. Cambridge, Mass.: Harvard University Press, 1938.

Myers, Gustavus. *History of Bigotry in the United States*. New York: Random House, 1943.

————. *The History of Tammany Hall*. 2nd ed., rev. and enl.; New York: Boni & Liveright, 1917.

Nevins, Allan. *The Emergence of Modern America, 1865–1878*. New York: Macmillan Co., 1927.

————. *The Evening Post, A Century of Journalism*. New York: Boni & Liveright, 1922.

Nevins, Allan and Frank Weitenkampf. *A Century of Political Cartoons, Caricature in the United States, 1800–1900*. New York: C. Scribner's Sons, 1944.

O'Brien, Frank M. *The Story of the Sun, 1833–1918*. New York: George H. Doran Co., 1918.

O'Connor, Richard. *The Scandalous Mr. Bennett*. Garden City, N.Y.: Doubleday & Co., Inc., 1962.

Orth, Samuel P. *The Boss and the Machine*: *A Chronicle of the Politicians and Party Organizations*. New Haven: Yale University Press, 1920.

Palmer, Archie E. *The New York Public School*: *Being a History of Free Education in the City of New York*. New York: Macmillan Co., 1905.

Park, Robert E. *The Immigrant Press and Its Control*. New York: Harper & Bros., 1922.

Park, Robert E., Ernest W. Burgess, and Roderick D. McKenzie. *The City*. Chicago: University of Chicago Press, 1925.

Parrington, Vernon Louis. *Main Currents in American Thought*. 3 vols. New York: Harcourt, Brace & Co., 1927–1930.

Patton, Clifford W. *The Battle for Municipal Reform*; *Mobilization and Attack, 1875–1900*. Washington, D.C.: American Council on Public Affairs, 1940.

Pollard, James E. *The Presidents and the Press*. New York: Macmillan Co., 1947.

Pound, Arthur. *The Golden Earth*: *The Story of Manhattan's Landed Wealth*. New York: Macmillan Co., 1935.

Powderly, Terence V. *Thirty Years of Labor, 1859–1889*. Columbus, Ohio: Excelsior Publishing House, 1889.

Presbrey, Frank S. *The History and Development of Advertising.* Garden City, N.Y.: Doubleday, Doran & Co., Inc., 1929.

Pringle, Henry F. *Theodore Roosevelt, A Biography.* New York: Harcourt, Brace & Co., 1931.

Ravenel, Mazyck P. (ed.). *A Half Century of Public Health.* New York: American Public Health Association, 1921.

Reynolds, Marcus T. *The Housing of the Poor in American Cities.* Baltimore: American Economic Association, 1893.

Riis, Jacob A. *How the Other Half Lives, Studies Among the Tenements of New York.* New York: C. Scribner's Sons, 1890.

—————. *The Making of An American.* New York: Macmillan Co., 1901.

—————. *The Battle with the Slum, Sequel to How the Other Half Lives, Relating All that Still Applied of the Old Volume with Much New Matter.* New York: Macmillan Co., 1902.

—————. *Children of the Tenements.* New York: Macmillan Co., 1903.

Rosebault, Charles J. *When Dana Was The Sun, A Story of Personal Journalism.* New York: Robert M. McBride & Co., 1931.

Saarinen, Aline B. *The Proud Possessors.* New York: Random House, 1958.

Salmon, Lucy Maynard. *The Newspaper and the Historian.* New York: Oxford University Press, 1923.

Schlesinger, Arthur Meier. *Learning How to Behave, A Historical Study of American Etiquette Books.* New York: Macmillan Co., 1946.

—————. *Paths to the Present.* New York: Macmillan Co., 1949.

—————. *The Rise of the City, 1878-1898.* New York: Macmillan Co., 1933.

Seitz, Don Carlos. *The James Gordon Bennetts: Father and Son, Proprietors of the New York Herald.* Indianapolis: Bobbs-Merrill Co., 1928.

—————. *Joseph Pulitzer, His Life & Letters.* New York: Simon & Schuster, Inc., 1924.

Shannon, David A. *Twentieth Century America, The United States Since the 1890's.* Chicago: Rand McNally & Co., 1963.

Sinclair, Upton. *The Brass Check, A Study of American Journalism.* Pasadena, Calif.: The Author, 1920.

Spahr, Charles B. *An Essay on the Present Distribution of Wealth in the United States.* New York: Thomas Y. Crowell & Co., 1896.

Stead, William T. *If Christ Came to Chicago, A Plea for the Union of All Who Love in the Service of All Who Suffer.* Chicago: Laird & Lee, 1894.

Steffens, Lincoln. *The Autobiography of Lincoln Steffens*. New York: Harcourt, Brace & Co., 1931.

———. *The Shame of the Cities*. New York: Sagamore Press, 1904.

Still, Bayrd. *Mirror for Gotham New York, as Seen by Contemporaries from Dutch Days to Present*. New York: New York University Press, 1956.

Stone, Candace. *Dana and the Sun*. New York: Dodd Mead & Co., 1938.

Strong, Josiah. *The New Era or The Coming Kingdom*. New York: Baker & Taylor Co., 1893.

Sumner, William Graham. *Essays of William Graham Sumner*. 2 vols. New Haven: Yale University Press, 1934.

Swanberg, W. A. *Citizen Hearst*. New York: Scribner, 1961.

Swinton, John. *Striking for Life, Labor's Side to the Labor Question. The Right of the Workingman to a Fair Living*. Philadelphia: A. R. Keller Co., 1894.

Tolman, William Howe. *Municipal Reform Movements in the United States*. New York: F. H. Ravell, 1895.

Townsend, Edward W. *A Daughter of the Slums*. New York: Lovell, Coryell & Co., 1895.

Tunnard, Christopher and Henry Hope Reed. *American Skyline: The Growth and Form of Our Cities and Towns*. Boston: Houghton Mifflin, 1955.

Turner, Ernest S. *The Shocking History of Advertising*. New York: Dutton, 1953.

Walker, James Blaine. *Fifty Years of Rapid Transit, 1864–1917*. New York: Law Printing Co., 1918.

Webb, Beatrice (Potter). *My Apprenticeship*. New York: Longmans, Green & Co., 1926.

Wecter, Dixon. *The Saga of American Society; A Record of Social Aspiration, 1607–1937*. New York: C. Scribner's Sons, 1937.

Weld, Ralph Foster. *Brooklyn Is America*. New York: Columbia University Press, 1950.

Werner, M. R. *Tammany Hall*. Garden City, N.Y.: Doubleday, Doran & Co., 1931.

Wilson, Harry Leon. *Ma Pettingill*. Garden City, N.Y.: Doubleday, Doran & Co., 1919.

Winkler, John K. *William Randolph Hearst: An American Phenomenon*. New York: Simon & Schuster, Inc., 1928.

Wirth, Louis. *The Ghetto*. Chicago: University of Chicago Press, 1928.

Wish, Harvey. *Society and Thought in Modern America*. New York: Longmans, Green & Co., 1952.

Woods, Robert A. *et al. The Poor in Great Cities, Their Problems and What Is Going to Solve Them*. New York: C. Scribner's Sons, 1895.

Young, Clarence Edward. *The Downtown Church*. Lancaster, Pa.: Intelligencer Printing Co., 1912.

ARTICLES

Anon. "Not Without Honor, Save in His Own Country," *Critic*, III (March 28, 1885).

Anon. "Tenement Life in New York," *Harper's Weekly*, XXIII (March 29, 1879).

Anon. "Things Talked Of," *Harper's Weekly*, XXXVII (April 22, 1893).

Anon. "Bookishness," *Life Magazine*, V (March 12, 1885).

Anon. "News and Notes," *Literary World*, XVI (March 21, 1885).

Anon. "Power of Irish in Cities," *Littell's Living Age*, LVI (November 6, 1886).

Anon. "Tenement House Commission," *Sanitary Engineer*, X (June 19, 1884).

Adams, Oscar Fay. "The Aristocratic Drift of Protestantism," *North American Review*, CXLII (February 1886).

Billings, John S. "The Diminishing Birth Rate in the United States," *Forum*, XV (June 1893).

Bliss, W.D.P. "Social Faith of the Holy Catholic Church," *Christian Socialist*, VIII (November 9, 1911).

Bocock, John Paul. "The Irish Conquest of Our Cities," *Forum*, XVII (April 1894).

Bok, Edward W. "At Home with the Editor," *Ladies' Home Journal*, IX (August 1892).

————. "The Young Man in Business," *Cosmopolitan*, XVI (January 1894).

Boyesen, H. H. "Dangers of Unrestricted Immigration," *Forum,* III (July 1887).

Brown, Emma E. "Children's Labor: A Problem," *Atlantic Monthly*, XLVI (December 1880).

Campbell, Helen *et al.* "White Child Slavery. A Symposium," *The Arena*, I (April 1890).

Clark, General Emmons. "Sanitary Improvement in New York During the Last Quarter of a Century," *Popular Science Monthly,* XXIX (July 1891).

Creelman, James. "Joseph Pulitzer—Master Journalist," *Pearson's Magazine*, XXI (March 1909).

Dio, Lewis *et al.* "The Health of American Women," *North American Review*, CXXXV (December 1882).

Ely, Richard T., "Pauperism in the United States," *North American Review*, CLII (April 1891).

Flower, Benjamin Orange, "Editorial Notes," *The Arena*, IV (August 1891).

Forman, Allan, "Some Adopted Americans," *American Magazine*, XV (November 1888).

Gallup, George. "Evaluation of Reader Interest," *Proceedings of the American Society of Newspaper Editors*, VIII (New York, 1930).

Gibbons, James Cardinal. "Wealth and Its Obligations," *North American Review*, CLII (April 1891).

Gladden, Washington. "The Problem of Poverty," *The Century*, XLV (December 1892).

Godkin, Edwin L. "Social Classes in the Republic," *Atlantic Monthly*, LXXVIII (December 1896).

Graham, Charles, III. "A Summer Resort on the Roof," *Harper's Weekly*, XXIX (August 1, 1885).

Inglis, William. "An Intimate View of Joseph Pulitzer," *Harper's Weekly*, LV (November 11, 1911).

Lawrence, William. "The Relation of Wealth to Morals," *World's Work*, I (January 1901).

McDougall, Walt. "Old Days on *The World*," *The American Mercury*, IV (January 1925).

———. "Pictures in the Papers," *The American Mercury*, VI (September 1925).

Merwin, Henry Childs. "The Irish in American Life," *Atlantic Monthly*, LXXVII (March 1896).

Parkman, Francis. "The Woman Question," *North American Review*, CXXIX (October 1879).

Robinson, Charles Mulford. "Improvement in City Life," *Atlantic Monthly*, LXXXIII (April, May, June 1899).

Rogers, William A., ill. "Tenement Life in New York—Sketches in 'Bottle Alley,' " *Harper's Weekly*, XXIII (March 22, 1879).

Russell, Charles Edward. "The Tenements of Trinity Church," *Everybody's*, XIX (July 1908).

Seitz, Don C. "The Portrait of an Editor," *Atlantic Monthly*, CXXXIV (September 1924).

Shearman, Thomas G. "The Owners of the United States," *Forum*, VIII (November 1889).

Sullivan, Robert B. "An Unidentified Man," *Esquire*, V (April 1936).

Thomas, W. I. "The Psychology of Yellow Journalism," *American Magazine*, LXVI (March 1908).

Warner, John DeWitt. "The 'Sweating System' in New York City," *Harper's Weekly*, XXXIX (February 9, 1885).

Wells, Kate. "The Transitional American Woman," *Atlantic Monthly*, XLVI (December 1880).

Willoughby, William F. "Child Labor," *Publications of the American Economic Association*, V (1890).

INDEX